# Paidology

The science of the child.

The historical child

Oscar Chrisman

Alpha Editions

This edition published in 2020

ISBN : 9789354005534

Design and Setting By
**Alpha Editions**
email - alphaedis@gmail.com

As per information held with us this book is in Public Domain.
This book is a reproduction of an important historical work. Alpha Editions uses the best technology to reproduce historical work in the same manner it was first published to preserve its original nature. Any marks or number seen are left intentionally to preserve its true form.

*Paidology*
*The Science of the Child*

# THE
# HISTORICAL CHILD

BY

OSCAR CHRISMAN, A.M., Ph.D.
*Professor of Paidology and Psychology in the Ohio University*

BOSTON
RICHARD G. BADGER
THE GORHAM PRESS

TO MY WIFE

# PREFACE

In the *Pedagogical Seminary* for December, 1893, in an article on "The Hearing of Children," the last paragraph, page 438, occurred for the first time in print the word *paidology*.[1] In *The Forum* for February, 1894, page 728, the first article explanatory of paidology appeared. A more complete outlining of the subject was as a doctor's dissertation at the University of Jena, Germany, 1896. In the first edition of the Standard Dictionary was included the word paidology, wherein it was defined as "The scientific study of the child." Paidology originated in my mind at a very unexpected moment one day in April, 1893.

This book is the first of a series that it is my purpose to write upon child life. The others will follow from time to time upon the different phases of child being. This book and the others it is hoped may appear are the outcome of several years of study and of teaching the subject to young men and women, which has proved to me that people are eager to know about children in the past as well as in the present. He who wishes to acquaint himself with children and child nature must have a knowledge of child life as it existed among the various nations of the world. The child as found in Ancient Mexico and Ancient Peru is given place here because the life and doings of these peoples have always been attractive reading to me, and also it is well to consider child life in these nations who reached such a high stage of existence among the lower forms of human society and so far removed from the civilizations of Asia and Europe. It is hoped there is value in this work to the student of child nature and that young people may find it interesting and profitable.

It will be noted that there are topics of a general nature given in this work, which purports to be a study of child life. When it is considered that the affairs of a nation affect every class and age of the persons constituting it and espe-

[1] The *ai* in paidology is pronounced as in *aisle*, as *i* in pine.

cially react upon women, the mothers, then it may be understood how vital these matters become in a study of child life among a people and how necessary they are for a better comprehension of what is directly connected with children. Too the term "child" is used here in a general sense, to include all ages up to full manhood.

It seems to me that everything done and studied in my whole life touches this science of the child and that every one with whom I have come in contact has aided me. It is wished here to express in a general way my thanks to these friends for their help. I must, though, mention by name a few who have more directly made this book possible. First of all is President G. Stanley Hall of Clark University, the great leader and pioneer in the study of children, with whom I spent two years and from whom I first obtained the right ideas of studying child life. Another is Professor Wilhelm Rein of the University of Jena, who kindly permitted me to use paidology as the subject for my doctor's thesis and extended the time for working on it, thus giving me opportunity for use of material at Berlin and when completed he endorsed the thesis, "Paidologie, Entwurf zu einer Wissenschaft des Kindes," to the Senate of his University. A third one to whom I am greatly indebted is Professor Rudolph Eucken of the University of Jena, whose lectures listened to for a year gave me a broader view of life and the sympathy he expressed for myself and work were of the utmost encouragement and too at a time when well needed. I owe much to Prof. Dr. W. Preyer of the University of Berlin, now deceased, who wrote me encouragingly of my work before my going to Germany and while there he talked over matters with me and went over the thesis when completed and had faith in the idea I was promulgating, new at that time, that the study of the child is a science in and of itself and for which I had originated the term paidology, and he advised and encouraged me to make it my life study.

I must take this opportunity to express gratitude to my wife who so willingly gave up the many things which are so dear to a woman and a mother that there might be acquired by myself the very best education the world could give and so make possible the coming forth of paidology and all it may contain.

O. C.

*The Ohio University.*

# CONTENTS

| CHAPTER | | PAGE |
|---|---|---|
| | PREFACE . . . . . . . . . . . | 7 |
| I. | THE CHILD IN MEXICO . . . . . . . . | 15–38 |
| | The people . . . . . . . . . . . | 15 |
| | Women and marriage . . . . . . . . | 16 |
| | Birth . . . . . . . . . . . . | 18 |
| | Casting the nativity of the infant . . . . | 19 |
| | Baptizing and naming child . . . . . . | 19 |
| | Care and treatment of children . . . . . | 19 |
| | Dress . . . . . . . . . . . . | 24 |
| | Food and drink . . . . . . . . . | 25 |
| | Lore . . . . . . . . . . . . | 27 |
| | Human sacrifice . . . . . . . . . | 28 |
| | Slavery . . . . . . . . . . . | 30 |
| | Industries . . . . . . . . . . | 30 |
| | Couriers . . . . . . . . . . . | 33 |
| | Amusements . . . . . . . . . . | 33 |
| | Education . . . . . . . . . . | 36 |
| II. | THE CHILD IN PERU . . . . . . . . | 39–51 |
| | The people . . . . . . . . . . | 39 |
| | Buildings . . . . . . . . . . | 41 |
| | Dress . . . . . . . . . . . . | 41 |
| | Food, drink, narcotics . . . . . . . | 42 |
| | Marriage . . . . . . . . . . . | 43 |
| | Care and treatment of children . . . . . | 44 |
| | The Virgins of the Sun . . . . . . . | 44 |
| | Human sacrifice . . . . . . . . . | 45 |
| | Industries . . . . . . . . . . | 45 |
| | Training of the Inca and the Order of the Huaracu . . . | 49 |
| | Education . . . . . . . . . . | 50 |
| III. | THE CHILD IN EGYPT . . . . . . . . | 52–84 |
| | The country . . . . . . . . . . | 52 |
| | The people . . . . . . . . . . | 53 |
| | Slavery . . . . . . . . . . . | 54 |
| | The home . . . . . . . . . . | 55 |
| | Women and marriage . . . . . . . . | 57 |
| | Child and parent . . . . . . . . . | 58 |
| | Dress . . . . . . . . . . . . | 59 |
| | Food and drink . . . . . . . . . | 62 |
| | Food and clothing of children . . . . . | 64 |
| | Industries . . . . . . . . . . | 65 |
| | Sickness and death . . . . . . . . | 74 |
| | Child and religion . . . . . . . . | 76 |
| | Amusements . . . . . . . . . . | 76 |

| CHAPTER | | PAGE |
|---|---|---|
| | Games, plays, and toys | 81 |
| | Education | 82 |
| IV. | THE CHILD IN INDIA | 85–103 |
| | Caste | 85 |
| | Women and marriage | 85 |
| | Boys and girls | 96 |
| | Infanticide | 97 |
| | Dress | 98 |
| | Amusements | 98 |
| | Rites | 99 |
| | Adoption | 99 |
| | Inheritance | 100 |
| | Education | 100 |
| V. | THE CHILD IN CHINA | 104–129 |
| | Women and marriage | 104 |
| | Infancy | 112 |
| | Boys and girls | 115 |
| | Child and parent | 116 |
| | Deformation of the feet | 117 |
| | Amusements | 118 |
| | Dress | 121 |
| | Religion | 122 |
| | Education | 123 |
| VI. | THE CHILD IN JAPAN | 130–160 |
| | Women | 130 |
| | Marriage | 134 |
| | The mother's memorial | 138 |
| | Dress | 140 |
| | Regulations | 140 |
| | The care of children | 143 |
| | Naming children | 145 |
| | Carrying children | 145 |
| | Adoption and inheritance | 145 |
| | Power and duty of father | 146 |
| | Amusements | 146 |
| | Lore | 152 |
| | Religion | 155 |
| | Suicide | 155 |
| | Work | 156 |
| | Education | 157 |
| VII. | THE CHILD IN PERSIA | 161–166 |
| | Characteristics | 161 |
| | Women and marriage | 161 |
| | Dress | 163 |
| | Child and parent | 163 |
| | Inheritance | 163 |
| | Amusements | 164 |
| | Education | 164 |
| VIII. | THE CHILD IN JUDEA | 167–176 |
| | Historical | 167 |
| | Women and marriage | 167 |

## Contents

| CHAPTER | | PAGE |
|---|---|---|
| | Care and treatment of children | 170 |
| | Duties of children | 171 |
| | Dress | 171 |
| | Amusements | 173 |
| | Education | 173 |
| IX. | THE CHILD IN GREECE | 177–211 |
| | Physical characteristics | 177 |
| | The people | 177 |
| | The home | 178 |
| | Girls and women | 178 |
| | Marriage | 182 |
| | Dress | 186 |
| | Food | 190 |
| | Child and parent | 191 |
| | Care of children | 191 |
| | Infanticide | 193 |
| | Duties of children | 194 |
| | Adoption and inheritance | 194 |
| | Toys and playthings | 194 |
| | Games and plays | 195 |
| | Sports and festivals | 197 |
| | Other amusements | 199 |
| | Sickness and death | 201 |
| | Religion | 202 |
| | Education | 203 |
| X. | THE CHILD IN ROME | 212–263 |
| | Characteristics | 212 |
| | The people | 213 |
| | Slavery | 214 |
| | The home | 215 |
| | Women | 218 |
| | Marriage | 224 |
| | Dress | 231 |
| | Food | 237 |
| | Child and parent | 238 |
| | Names | 239 |
| | Care and treatment of children | 239 |
| | Citizenship | 240 |
| | Inheritance | 241 |
| | Adoption | 242 |
| | Sickness and death | 243 |
| | Industries | 246 |
| | The spectacles | 249 |
| | Other amusements | 253 |
| | The bath | 254 |
| | Games and plays | 254 |
| | Religion | 255 |
| | Vestal Virgins | 255 |
| | Education | 257 |
| XI. | THE CHILD IN EARLIER AND MEDIEVAL EUROPE | 264–312 |
| | Historical and critical | 264 |
| | Feudalism | 265 |
| | The feudal castle and its life | 267 |

| CHAPTER | | PAGE |
|---|---|---|
| | Chivalry | 268 |
| | The peasantry | 271 |
| | The town people | 273 |
| | The aristocracy | 275 |
| | The home | 276 |
| | Women | 277 |
| | Marriage | 279 |
| | Dress | 282 |
| | Food | 285 |
| | Children of the ancient Britons | 287 |
| | Children among the early Christians | 289 |
| | Child and parent | 289 |
| | Care and treatment of children | 290 |
| | Apprenticeship | 290 |
| | Military training for the young | 291 |
| | Amusements | 292 |
| | Education | 296 |
| | The children's crusade | 302 |
| | Other child-pilgrimages | 310 |
| XII. | THE CHILD IN EARLIER UNITED STATES | 313–455 |
| | Customs relating to land | 313 |
| | The people | 314 |
| | Slavery | 316 |
| | Servants | 318 |
| | The home | 322 |
| | Women | 334 |
| | Marriage | 336 |
| | Dress | 348 |
| | Infants' clothing | 359 |
| | Boys' clothing | 360 |
| | Girls' clothing | 361 |
| | Food | 364 |
| | Drink | 369 |
| | Food and drink of children | 374 |
| | Infancy | 376 |
| | Number and names of children | 379 |
| | Child welfare | 380 |
| | Manners and courtesy of children | 382 |
| | Diary of a Boston school girl of 1771 | 384 |
| | Inheritance | 388 |
| | Sickness and death | 389 |
| | The illness of children | 396 |
| | Amusements | 398 |
| | Games and sports of children and young people | 407 |
| | Children's toys and story books | 412 |
| | Holidays and festivals | 413 |
| | Public punishments | 416 |
| | Manufactures | 421 |
| | Boys' work and manufactures | 422 |
| | Girls' and women's work | 423 |
| | Religion | 428 |
| | The child and religion | 438 |
| | Education | 442 |
| INDEX | | 457 |

# THE HISTORICAL CHILD

# THE HISTORICAL CHILD

## CHAPTER I

### THE CHILD IN MEXICO

**The People.** When the Spaniards entered Mexico, in the sixteenth century, and conquered it, they found the ruling people to be the Aztecs and whose capital city, Tenochtitlan (Mexico City), was on an island in the lake of Tezcoco. The Aztecs were not the first inhabitants of Mexico as they had entered the country some five hundred years before the Spanish conquest and through alliances and conquests had become the ruling power about a century before the appearance of the Spaniards. The people whom the Aztecs found when they entered Mexico told them of a great people who had lived before their time and the ruins of whose great buildings remained and still exist to the present day and who were designated the Toltecs. It has been claimed for the Toltecs a very high state of civilization, much in advance of the Aztecs, and some even holding that it really equaled the civilization of the present time.

Mexico at the time of the conquest by the Spaniards was a monarchy, in which the king stood supreme as he was a priest of their great god, commander-in-chief of the military forces, and supreme judge. The throne, however, was not hereditary, as upon a vacancy a ruler was selected by four officers appointed for that purpose by the nobles and principal officials of the kingdom. The king was usually taken from the ruling family and might have been a brother of the late ruler or a nephew belonging to an elder branch. The office-holders were usually appointed for life and at their death the vacancies were filled by appointment by the king. The people were divided into classes. The highest class was a landed aristocracy, who paid no definite taxes but owed service to the king; a second class, who ranked with the landed aristocracy, was a military nobility who held land at the king's goodwill; the next class embraced the freemen, who held land in common and paid taxes in common; below these were a class of freemen who rented the lands of the lord and made payment to him for the same; and the lowest of all were the serfs, who were bound to the soil. They maintained a military system and made war upon neighboring tribes: at the time of the coming of the Spaniards this seemed to have been carried on mostly for the purpose of securing captives for the human sacrifices demanded by their religion. They had an elaborate and efficient judicial system and the laws seem to have been justly administered to all alike, whether the ones before the courts were of higher rank or of the common people.

**Women and Marriage.** The women were described by the Spaniards as being pretty, with long black hair, and with a serious and rather melancholy cast of countenance. It would appear that they were treated with much consideration by the men who permitted them to engage in festivities and entertainments equally with themselves.

Marriage was an important institution with the Mexicans and it was held in such high esteem that there was a tribunal appointed for the sole purpose of attending to matters relating to it. The customary age with men for marriage was about twenty, women marrying at a younger age. When a young man reached this age it became his duty to marry and sometimes the high priest commanded it of him. The selection of the bride was made by the parents and if a young man refused to abide by his parents' decision and made his own choice, he was looked upon as being quite ungrateful to his parents. Should he refuse to marry, it was his duty to remain continent through his life and devote himself to the service of the gods. Should he afterward decide to marry, he was despised by his friends and publicly denounced for not keeping his vow to the gods and no respectable woman would marry him.

When the parents had decided it was time for their son to marry, all the relatives were called together and a feast given at which the father announced to them that the son was of proper age to be married. The son was then informed that his parents were about to select a bride for him, to which the young man gave consent. Then they called in the priests under whom the young man had received his education and their permission was obtained and one of the priests addressed the young man with advice for the occasion. The next step was to ascertain the day and sign of the young man's birth and also the birthday and sign of the young woman, which was obtained through astrologers or soothsayers. If the horoscopes of both were favorable and showed that the union would have good fortune all was well; if not, another girl had to be selected. If the augurs were favorable to the union, two discreet and virtuous elderly women were called in as go-betweens. These women were given their directions and they called upon the parents of the bride and after a second visit preliminaries were arranged.

The parents of the girl then called in the relatives and friends and informed them of the affair and the girl was given much advice by them. Then their decision was sent to the parents of the young man. A favorable day for the marriage was found by the augurs and both families made preparations for the day of marriage and sent out invitations to relatives and friends. On the day set for the marriage the relatives and friends of the bride went to her home as did also some of the bridegroom's relatives and friends and in procession escorted her to his home, where the best room in the house had been fitted up for the occasion and the house festooned with green branches and garlands of flowers. The bridegroom met the bride at the entrance to his home and took her by the hand and led her into the room for the ceremony. They were then seated upon a special mat, the woman at the left of the man. The mother of the bridegroom gave presents to the bride and the mother of the bride gave presents to the bridegroom. Then the priest made a long talk to the couple, defining their duties to one another and toward the married state. The couple then arose and the priest tied the end of the man's mantle to the dress of the woman. A feast was then partaken of but in which the couple did not participate as they were required to spend four days in fasting and prayer in the room, closely guarded by old women. Upon the fourth night two priests prepared a couch of two mats and the young people were left to themselves. The next day they underwent a baptismal ceremony and they were adorned with new apparel and some more advice was given them by the mothers-in-law or nearest relatives, another feast was given of which they partook, and the marriage ceremony was then fully completed.

Cousins were allowed to marry but not nearer relatives. As a rule a widow was not permitted to remarry except a brother of her deceased husband and in case she had children by the first marriage, then it was the duty of the brother-in-law to marry her that the children might not be without the care and protection of a father. Divorce was allowed but only after a careful hearing by the tribunal on marriage, and when a divorce was granted the couple could not under any circumstances be reunited. Concubinage was practiced and it might occur even with young people under marriageable age upon the consent of the parents. In this there was no contract or ceremony, the two simply living together. In case a child was born to them a marriage was performed or else the woman returned to her parents' house, taking the child with her which was then considered as belonging to her parents. This was not considered dishonorable on the part of the girl nor were her chances for marriage in any degree lessened by her having thus lived in a state of concubinage. Polygamy was permitted but perhaps it was not greatly indulged in and it was chiefly among the wealthiest people. The necessity for monogamy seemed to be understood, as a record is given of a father counselling his son that for the proper perpetuation of the race but one man is ordained but for one woman.

**Birth.** As soon as a woman was found to be pregnant the relatives and friends were informed of it and a feast was prepared, to which all were invited who had been present at the wedding. Speeches of congratulations and of admonition were made to the future parents. During the period before the birth of the child, the mother was careful and she observed many rules. "Thus, sleeping in the daytime would contort the child's face; approaching too near the fire or standing in the hot sun would parch the fœtus; hard and continued work, lifting weights, running, mental excitement, such as grief, anger, or alarm, were particularly avoided; in case of an earthquake all the pots in the house were covered up or broken to stop the shaking; eating *tzictli*, or *chicle*, was thought to harden the palate of the unborn child, and to make its gums thick so that it would be unable to suck, and also to communicate to it a disease called *netentzzoponiztli;* neither must the edible earth, of which, as we shall see in a future chapter, the Mexicans were very fond, be eaten by the mother, lest the child should prove weak and sickly; but everything else the woman fancied was to be given her, because any interference with her caprices might be hurtful to her offspring."[1] When the time of confinement drew near another feast was given and speeches and suggestions were made. Among the higher classes a midwife was procured and careful preparation was made for the confinement. A woman dying in childbirth was honored by a burial with great ceremony. When the child was born, there was rejoicing with praises to the mother and congratulations to parents and grandparents, and even the child itself was spoken to in welcoming words by the midwife as it was being dressed.

**Casting the Nativity of the Infant.** Astrology was held in high esteem by the Mexicans and it was used to decide the fortune of the infant. On the birth of a child the astrologer was summoned and upon being told the time of the event he cast the horoscope of the infant. If the augury was favorable he told of the great fortune coming to the child and of the honors and happiness to fall upon him. Should the augury prove unfavorable, it was made less severe by the horoscopist who found accompanying signs that helped allay the evil coming from the bad omens.

**Baptizing and Naming the Child.** The rite of baptism was early performed upon the child, at which time it was given a name. The house was decorated with branches and flowers, a feast was prepared, and relatives and friends invited. Miniature weapons were used, if a boy, to show that he was born a warrior, and, if a girl, small weaving utensils as symbols of her future calling of housewife. The child, if a boy, was usually named from the sign of the day or a bird or animal, and, if a girl, was named from a flower. Sometimes a child took its name from some important event which occurred at the time of its birth. A solemn invocation to the gods was made, after which the head and lips of the infant were touched with water, the name was given to it, and then it was lifted up to heaven and a prayer of blessing said over it.

**Care and Treatment of Children.** Upon the arrival of a child into a family, friends and neighbors congratulated them

---

[1] Bancroft, Native races of Pacific states, II, 267.

upon such, for it was deemed quite a blessing. Although children were welcomed, yet the discipline of younger children was rather severe and children were taught to reverence and obey their parents and superiors. Both boys and girls were carefully reared by the best parents.

The following admonitions of a father to his son show how greatly these ancient Mexicans would have their children observe a right living:—

"My son, who art come into this light from the womb of thy mother, like the chicken from the egg, and like it, art preparing to fly through the world, we know not how long heaven will grant to us the enjoyment of that precious gem which we possess in thee; but, however short is the period, endeavor to live exactly, praying God continually to assist thee. He created thee; thou art His property. He is thy Father, and loves thee still more than I do; repose in Him thy thoughts, and day and night direct thy sighs to Him. Reverence and salute thy elders, and hold no one in contempt. To the poor and the distressed be not dumb, but rather use words of comfort. Honor all persons, particularly thy parents, to whom thou owest obedience, respect, service. Guard against imitating the example of those wicked sons who, like brutes, that are deprived of reason, neither reverence their parents, listen to their instruction, nor submit to their correction; because, whoever follows their steps will have an unhappy end, will die in a desperate or sudden manner, or will be killed and devoured by wild beasts. . . .

"When any one discourses with thee, hear him attentively, and hold thyself in an easy attitude, neither playing with thy feet, nor putting thy mantle to thy mouth, nor spitting too often, nor looking about you here and there, nor rising up frequently if thou art sitting; for such actions are indications of levity and low breeding.

"When thou art at table do not eat voraciously, nor show thy displeasure if anything displeases thee. If any one comes unexpectedly to dinner with thee, share with him what thou hast; and when any person is entertained by thee, do not fix thy looks upon him.

"In walking, look where thou goest, that thou mayest not push against any one. If thou seest another coming thy way, go a little aside to give him room to pass. Never step before thy elders, unless it be necessary, or that they order thee to do so. When thou sittest at table with them, do not eat or drink before them, but attend to them in a becoming manner, that thou mayest merit their favor.

"When they give thee anything, accept it with tokens of gratitude; if the present is great, do not become vain or fond of it. If the gift is small, do not despise it, nor be provoked, nor occasion displeasure to them who favor thee. If thou becomest rich, do not grow insolent nor scorn the poor; for those very gods who deny riches to others in order to give them to thee, offended by thy pride, will take them from thee again to give to others.

"Support thyself by thy own labors; for then thy food will be sweeter. I, my son, have supported thee hitherto with my sweat, and have omitted no duty of a father; I have provided thee with everything necessary, without taking it from others. Do thou so likewise. . . .

"Stay no longer than is necessary in the market-place; for in such places there is the greatest danger of contracting vices.

"When thou art offered an employment, imagine that the proposal is made to try thee; then accept it not hastily, although thou knowest thyself more fit than others to exercise it; but excuse thyself until thou art obliged to accept it; thus thou wilt be more esteemed.

"Be not dissolute; because thou wilt thereby incense the gods, and they will cover thee with infamy. Restrain thyself, my son, as thou are yet young, and wait until the girl whom the gods destine for thy wife arrives at a suitable age; leave that to their care, as they know how to order these things properly. When the time for thy marriage is come, dare not to make it without the consent of thy parents, otherwise it will have an unhappy issue.

"Steal not nor give thyself up to gaming; otherwise, thou wilt be a disgrace to thy parents, whom thou ought rather to honor for the education they have given to thee. If thou wilt be virtuous, thy example will put the wicked to shame. No more, my son, enough hath been said in discharge of the duties of a father. With these counsels I wish to fortify thy mind. Refuse them not, nor act in contradiction to them; for on them thy life and thy happiness depend."[2]

The girl was not degraded among the Mexicans, and she

[2] Barnes, *Studies in education*, I, 75. ("The History of Mexico. By Francesco S. Clavigero. Translated by Chas. Cullen, London, 1787, vol. I., pp. 335 *et seq.*")

was treated with tenderness and love. How well cared for was the girl is attested by the following advice of an Aztec mother to her daughter:—

"My daughter, born of my substance, brought forth with my pains, and nourished with my milk, I have endeavored to bring thee up with the greatest possible care, and thy father has wrought and polished thee like an emerald, that thou mayest appear in the eyes of men a jewel of virtue. Strive always to be good; for otherwise who will have thee for a wife? Thou wilt be rejected by every one. Life is a thorny, laborious path, and it is necessary to exert all our powers to obtain the goods which the gods are willing to yield to us; we must not therefore be lazy or negligent, but diligent in everything. Be orderly and take pains to manage the economy of thy house. Give water to thy husband for his hands, and make bread for thy family. Wherever thou goest, go with modesty and composure, without hurrying thy steps, or laughing with those whom thou meetest, neither fixing thy looks upon them nor casting thy eyes thoughtlessly, first to one side and then to another, that thy reputation may not be sullied; but give a courteous answer to those who salute and put any question to thee.

"Employ thyself diligently in spinning and weaving, in sewing and embroidering; for by these arts thou wilt gain esteem, and all the necessaries of food and clothing. Do not give thyself too much to sleep, nor seek the shade, but go in the open air and there repose thyself, for effeminancy brings along with it idleness and other vices.

"In whatever thou doest encourage not evil thoughts but attend solely to the service of the gods, and the giving comfort to thy parents. If thy father or thy mother calls thee, do not stay to be called twice; but go instantly to know their pleasure, that thou mayest not disoblige them by slowness. Return no insolent answers, nor show any want of compliance; but if thou canst not do what they command, make a modest excuse. If another is called and does not come quickly, come thou, hear what is ordered, and do it well. Never offer thyself to do that which thou canst not do. Deceive no person; for the gods see all thy actions. Live in peace with everybody, and love everyone sincerely and honestly, that thou mayest be loved by them in return.

"Be not greedy of the goods which thou hast. If thou seest anything presented to another, give way to no mean suspicions; for the gods, to whom every good belongs, distribute everything as they please. If thou wouldst avoid the displeasure of others, let none meet with it from thee.

"Guard against improper familiarities with men; nor yield to the guilty wishes of thy heart; or thou wilt be the reproach of thy family, and wilt pollute thy mind as mud does water. Keep not company with dissolute, lying, or idle women; otherwise they will infallibly infect thee by their example. Attend upon thy family, and do not go on slight occasions out of thy house, nor be seen wandering through the streets, or in the market-place; for in such places thou wilt meet thy ruin. Remember that vice, like a poisonous herb, brings death to those who taste it; and when it once harbors in the mind it is difficult to dispel it. If in passing through the streets thou meetest with a froward youth who appears agreeable to thee, give him no correspondence, but dissemble and pass on. If he says anything to thee, take no heed of him nor his words; and if he follows thee, turn not your face about to look at him, lest that might inflame his passion more. If thou behavest so, he will soon turn and let thee proceed in peace.

"Enter not without some urgent motive into another's house, that nothing may be either said or thought injurious to thy honor, but if thou enterest into the house of thy relations, salute them with respect and do not remain idle, but immediately take up a spindle to spin or do any other thing that occurs.

"When thou art married, respect thy husband, obey him, and diligently do what he commands thee. Avoid incurring his displeasure, nor show thyself passionate or ill-natured; but receive him fondly to thy arms, even if he is poor and lives at thy expense. If thy husband occasions thee any disgust, let him not know thy displeasure when he commands thee to do anything; but dissemble it at that time, and afterwards tell him with great gentleness what vexed thee, that he may be won by thy mildness and offend thee no farther. Dishonor him not before others; for thou also wouldst be dishonored. If any one comes to visit thy husband, accept the visit kindly, and show all the civility thou canst. If thy husband is foolish, be thou discreet. If he fails in the management of wealth admonish him of his failings; but if he is totally incapable of taking care of his estate, take that charge upon thyself, attend carefully to his possessions and never omit to pay the workmen punctually. Take care not to lose anything through negligence.

"Embrace, my daughter, the counsel which I give thee. I am already advanced in life, and have had sufficient dealings with the world. I am thy mother. I wish that thou mayest live well. Fix my precepts in thy heart and bowels, for then thou wilt live happy. If by not listening to me, or by neglecting my instructions, any misfortunes befall thee, the fault will be thine and the evil also. Enough, my child. May the gods prosper thee."[3]

**Dress.** The men wore a long broad girdle or sash with the ends hanging down before and behind, which sash often was figured and the ends fringed or tasseled. They also wore a cloak or mantle, which was thrown over the shoulders and tied around the neck. The women wore a short tunic, usually without sleeves, and with it a short skirt under which they would wear another skirt of longer length, these skirts often being embroidered and ornamented. Over tunic and skirt they would wear a long loose robe, which might have at its upper part a hood attached, for wearing over the head. The material first used for clothing was of skins and later of maguey and cotton. Mantles of fur and of feather-work were also worn in cooler weather by both men and women. They wore sandals made of deer and other skins and also of nequen and cotton.

The ordinary way of wearing the hair was to cut it short on the forehead and temples and let it grow at the back. Unmarried girls wore their hair loose, while the virgins who served in the temple had their hair cut short. In some parts the heads of the children were shaved, with a tuft left behind. Women after marriage on becoming mothers would sometimes let their hair grow on all parts and arrange it on the head; one way was to plait it and cross it on the forehead, another way was to braid it and ornament it with flowers. Also, sometimes the women would use a dye made of herbs on their hair, which gave it a violet shade.

The women used paint on their faces, one fashion was to paint the face yellow and with a pottery stamp impress a pattern of red upon the cheeks. They painted the teeth with cochineal and also they painted the hands, neck, and breast. Among some peoples the women had their arms and breasts tattooed, incisions being made with a sharp instrument and

[3] Barnes, Studies in education I, 76-78.

a blue color inserted. Ornaments were worn by the men, women, and children, and by all classes of people. The higher classes used gold and gems, while people of the lower classes used shell and obsidian. There were a great variety of ornaments made for the arms and neck and attached to garments. Rings were worn on the fingers and rings and plugs in the ears. There also were rings and plugs for the nose and plugs for the lips, although it would appear that these were not so much in use as were the other ornaments. "There existed very stringent laws regarding the class of ornaments which the different classes of people were allowed to wear, and it was prohibited, on pain of death, for a subject to use the same dress or ornaments as the king."[4]

**Food and Drink.** There was quite a variety of foodstuffs in Mexico. Maize was the principal product but also there was great use made of other grain, yams, and beans, and there were fruits, as the banana and plantain. Their supply of meat was obtained very greatly from the game animals, among which were deer, wild hogs, rabbits, quails, pigeons, ducks, turkeys, and geese. Turkeys, ducks, and geese were domesticated, having been raised for their feathers as well as for food. Fish was another important article of food and both salt water and fresh water varieties were procured in abundance.

"Miscellaneous articles of food, not already spoken of, were *axayacatl*, flies of the Mexican lakes, dried, ground, boiled, and eaten in the form of cakes; *ahuauhtli*, the eggs of the same fly, a kind of native caviar; many kinds of insects, ants, maguey-worms, and even lice; *tecuitlatl*, 'excrement of stone,' a slime that was gathered on the surface of the lakes, and dried till it resembled cheese; eggs of turkeys, iguanas, and turtles, roasted, boiled, and in omelettes; various reptiles, frogs, and frog-spawn; shrimps, sardines, and crabs; corn-silk, wild-amaranth seeds, cherry-stones, tule-roots, and very many other articles inexpressible; yucca flour, potoyucca, tunas; honey from maize, from bees, and from the maguey; and roasted portions of the maguey stalks and leaves."[5]

There were three meals a day, morning, noon, and night, and among the higher class, at least, banquets and feasts were quite numerous. The food was cooked and eaten from pots, bowls, and dishes of pottery. Maize, when green, was boiled

[4] Bancroft, Native races of Pacific states, II, 372.
[5] *Ibid.*, II, 356.

and eaten, as roasting-ears with us now, and when dry it was sometimes parched or roasted. It was usually ground into meal and prepared in the form of cakes. To prepare the meal, the grain was thrown into boiling water, in which lime had been placed, and then the hull was removed. It was then washed and ground on grinding-stones, called *metlatl*, and then kneaded and rolled into cakes and baked, there having been many kinds of cakes. The meal was also boiled and made into porridge or gruel. Beans were boiled when green and also when dry. Meats were stewed, boiled, and roasted. Pepper was quite freely used, as was also salt. Fruits were eaten raw, although some, as the plantain and banana, were roasted and stewed.

There were two national drinks, *octli* and *chocolatl*, now known as pulque and chocolate, the first an intoxicant made from the maguey and the second from the cacao. There were other fermented drinks prepared from grain, and a kind of mushroom was used to put into drinks to make them more intoxicating. Intoxication was excusable in older people but the young people were severely punished for it and even in case of intemperance death was the punishment paid to the young while with the older persons only loss of rank and property was the punishment.

Tobacco was used by the Mexicans, having been smoked in pipes or in the form of cigars, and also it was made into snuff and used. "A kind of chewing-gum was prepared from resin or bitumen, though its use, at any rate in public, was confined by custom to unmarried girls." [6]

Human flesh also was eaten. This was not used as a common food but as a religious rite. The sacrifice was made on an elevated place and after the victim's heart was taken out as an offering to the gods, and if a warrior his head was taken off to be preserved as a trophy, the body was then cast down the steps and taken by minor priests and prepared for the table as other animals. A thigh was sent to the king's palace and the remainder was taken to the home of the warrior who captured the victim or if a slave to the house of the owner, who had the human flesh prepared with other dishes and served up in an entertainment to his friends. "This was not the coarse repast of famished cannibals, but a banquet teeming with delicious beverages and delicate viands, prepared with art, and attended by both sexes, who, as we shall see

[6] Joyce, Mexican archæology, 156.

hereafter, conducted themselves with all the decorum of civilized life."[7]

Although the eating of human flesh by the ancient Mexicans was not merely to satisfy the appetite for such food but in obedience to religion, yet there must have been quite a good deal of partaking of it as the number of human sacrifices each year was very great. Too, must be kept in view, the sacrifices included men and women, quite often young people, and likewise children, even infants. One peculiar custom was that the giver of the feast where the body of a human sacrifice was served did not partake of the flesh of his own captive, having been disbarred from this because he was supposed to stand to the victim in the relation of father to son.

**Lore.** "Various portents were drawn from the animal world; the cries of beasts of prey at night were supposed to forbode disaster to those who heard them, and the voices of certain birds were believed equally unlucky. The owl, so closely associated with Mictlantecutli, was especially regarded as the harbinger of ill-fortune and death, and if one of these birds perched upon the house of a sick man his demise was considered certain. It was held unlucky to encounter a skunk or a weasel, and the entry into the house of a rabbit or a troop of ants foreboded bad luck. If a certain kind of spider was found in the house, the owner traced a cross upon the ground, at the center of which he placed the insect. If it went towards the north, the direction of the underworld, it was regarded as a sign of death for the observer, any other direction foretelling misfortune of minor importance.

"Besides these superstitions there were a whole host of popular beliefs, of which only a few can be given here. Many of these were connected with food; it was customary to blow upon maize before putting it in the cooking-pot, to 'give it courage,' and it was believed that if a person neglected to pick up maize-grains lying on the ground they called out to heaven to punish the omission. If two brothers were drinking, and the younger drank first, it was thought that the elder would cease to grow; and it was also believed that the growth of a child was stopped by stepping over it when seated or lying down, but that the effect could be averted by stepping back again. Young girls were not allowed to eat standing,

[7] Prescott, Conquest of Mexico, I, 81.

for it was believed they would fail to get husbands, and children were prevented from licking the grindstone for fear they would lose their teeth. When a child lost one of its first teeth, the father or mother placed the tooth in a mousehole, a proceeding which was supposed to ensure the growth of the second tooth; and all nail-parings were thrown into the water in the hope that the auitzotl, a mythical water-animal which was believed to eat them, would make the nails grow. Sneezing was thought to be a sign that evil was being spoken of the sneezer, and there was a peculiar belief that the perfume of the flowers which were carried at banquets and in ceremonial dances might only be inhaled from the edges of the bouquet, since the center belonged to the god Tezcatlipoca."[8]

**Human Sacrifice.** The sad and degrading side of the Aztec civilization was that of human sacrifice. The number of sacrifices was very great, estimated from twenty to fifty thousand annually, and on one occasion alone, the dedication of a great temple, no less than seventy thousand human beings were sacrificed to the gods. The great object of war, along with the desire for the extension of the kingdom, was to obtain victims for the sacrifices and hence an enemy was never slain in battle if there was a chance of taking him alive. Mostly the victims were prisoners of war but slaves also were used as sacrifices. Sometimes they offered up children, generally infants, who were obtained by the priests, purchased from poverty-stricken parents, who, perhaps, gave their children as much from a sense of religious duty as for money. These children were dressed in beautiful garments, and adorned with flowers. They were then carried in procession of chanting priests through the city to the place of sacrifice. The cries they uttered were not heard because of the chants of the priests, and the tears they shed were favorable omens.

These sacrifices were so conducted as to exhibit something of prominence relating to the deity being worshipped. The following illustrates this:—

"One of their most important festivals was that in honor of their god Tezcatlipoca, whose rank was inferior only to that of the Supreme Being. He was called 'the soul of the world,' and supposed to have been its creator. He was depicted as a handsome man, endowed with perpetual youth. A year before the intended sacrifice, a captive, distinguished for

[8] Joyce, Mexican archæology, 98.

his personal beauty, and without a blemish on his body, was selected to represent this deity. Certain tutors took charge of him, and instructed him how to perform his new part with becoming grace and dignity. He was arrayed in a splendid dress, regaled with incense and with a profusion of sweet-scented flowers, of which the ancient Mexicans were as fond as their descendants of the present day. When he went abroad, he was attended by a train of royal pages, and, as he halted in the streets to play some favorite melody, the crowd prostrated themselves before him, and did him homage as the representative of their good deity. In this way he led an easy, luxurious life, till within a month of his sacrifice. Four beautiful girls, bearing the names of the principal goddesses, were then selected to share the honors of his bed; and with them he continued to live in idle dalliance, feasted at the banquets of the principal nobles, who paid him all the honors of a divinity.

"At length the fatal day of sacrifice arrived. The term of his short-lived glories was at an end. He was stripped of his gaudy apparel, and bade adieu to the fair partners of his revelries. One of the royal barges transported him across the lake to a temple which rose on its margin, about a league from the city. Hither the inhabitants of the capital flocked, to witness the consummation of the ceremony. As the sad procession wound up the sides of the pyramid, the unhappy victim threw away his gay chaplets of flowers, and broke in pieces the musical instruments with which he had solaced the hours of captivity. On the summit he was received by six priests, whose long and matted locks flowed disorderly over their sable robes, covered with hieroglyphic scrolls of mystic import. They led him to the sacrificial stone, a huge block of jasper, with its upper surface somewhat convex. On this the prisoner was stretched. Five priests secured his head and his limbs; while the sixth, clad in a scarlet mantle, emblematic of his bloody office, dexterously opened the breast of the wretched victim with a sharp razor of *itztli*—a volcanic substance, hard as flint,—and, inserting his hand into the wound, tore out the palpitating heart. The minister of death, first holding this up toward the sun, an object of worship throughout Anahuac, cast it at the feet of the deity to whom the temple was devoted, while the multitudes below prostrated themselves in humble adoration. The tragic story of this prisoner was expounded by the priests as the type of human destiny, which, brilliant in its commencement, too often closes in sorrow and disaster."[9]

**Slavery.** Slavery existed, the slaves having been criminals, prisoners of war, public debtors, persons who sold themselves into slavery, and children. Slavery was never the birthright of any child born in ancient Mexico. Children born to a slave were free. Yet children could be sold into slavery and were often sold by their parents, mostly on account of poverty. There was one peculiar thing in slavery here. With the consent of the master the parents could substitute a younger child as it grew up for an older one sold into slavery, which substitution could go on down to the youngest child. Slavery must have been rather mild, as in the presence of four witnesses the precise services were prescribed when a child was sold, and a slave could have a family and even hold other slaves, and, as was stated, all his children were born free, the worst feature having been that slaves were liable to be sacrificed.

**Industries.** Agriculture was in quite an advanced stage in ancient Mexico. Unlike in other parts of North America, the men engaged in the work, performed such labor as preparing the fields, planting, and reaping, while the women helped in scattering the grain, weeding, and winnowing. They had no useful domesticated animals, so that the people carried on all the kinds of farm work and the implements were simple, as, the hoe, spade, and basket. They fertilized the soil, let it recover from exhaustion by lying fallow, irrigated by means of canals, surrounded the fields by adobe walls and aloe hedges, and built granaries in which to store the harvests.

They mined silver, lead, tin, and copper. Gold was obtained in the form of nuggets on the surface of the ground or from the sand in the beds of rivers. They also got quicksilver, sulphur, alum, ocher, and other minerals which were used in making colors and for other purposes. Although there was an abundance of iron, it was not mined or used. They made tools of copper, hardened with tin. Most of the instruments, however, were of stone, such as axes and hammers. From obsidian, a kind of volcanic glass, by means of pressure they detached long flakes having a razor-like edge, which they used for making knives, razors, lancets, swords, arrow-heads, and spear-heads. They quarried stone from the hills and

[9] Prescott, Conquest of Mexico, I, 78-79.

mountains and often transported large blocks for long distances and erected great buildings.

The caste-system did not exist in Mexico but it was a custom, usually observed, for the son to learn the trade of his father. Trades were highly esteemed among them, being learned even by the nobles. A particular part of the city was given over to a particular trade, which had its own distinctive mark, something like a guild, having its own god, festivals, and the like. The high standing of the trades is shown by this advice given by an aged chief to his son: "Apply thyself, my son, to agriculture, or to feather-work, or some other honorable calling. Thus did your ancestors before you. Else how would they have provided for themselves and their families? Never was it heard that nobility alone was able to maintain its possessor." [10]

Among the manufactures were cloths made of cotton, maguey fiber, rabbit hair, fiber of palm-leaves, and also the cotton was mixed with the rabbit hair and with feathers in making a very fine kind of cloth. The cloths were dyed in different colors as they obtained a number of dyes from both vegetable and mineral substances, probably even excelling the Europeans in the art of dyeing. They tanned the skins of animals both with and without the hair. The making of mats and baskets was an important industry. Paper was made from maguey fiber, sometimes this was mixed with fiber from some other plants. Wood was used in making household furniture and farming implements and they also made cups and vases of lacquered wood. In the working of gold and silver they had reached a high degree of perfection. making most beautiful ornaments, which, in many instances, were superior to the work done in Europe. They were quite skillful in the use of feathers. Feathers were mixed with cotton and with other fiber for the making of clothing, tapestry, carpets, and bed-coverings. Feathers were used as ornaments and decorations, sometimes having been tipped with gold and set in precious stones, most beautiful fans were made in this way. The work with feathers they most excelled in was what has been called feather-mosaic, in which beautiful designs were worked out and colors harmoniously blended by the skillfully pasting of feathers on to cloth. For temporary use, as for decorations on the occasions of special festivals, they made designs with leaves and flowers similar to the feather-work. They were

[10] Prescott, Conquest of Mexico, I, 149.

quite skillful in working precious stones, making most beautiful ornaments from the stones found in the country, emeralds, amethysts, and turquoises being the most abundant. Pearls and bright colored shells were used with the stones in the formation of necklaces, bracelets, earrings, and other ornaments. "Mirrors of rock crystal, obsidian, and other stones, brightly polished and encased in rich frames, were said to reflect the human face as clearly as the best of European manufacture." [11]

The making of pottery was one of the leading industries, which products ran from coarse undecorated vessels to quite fine ware of various colors and highly ornamented. "The quality of the potting varies considerably according to locality, but the finer examples, such as the ware from Cholula and the Totonac district exhibit a very high standard of paste, form and technique, though the potters of this region of America cannot boast such consummate mastery over their material as the early inhabitants of the Peruvian coast." [12]

The agricultural and industrial products were not only used where produced but also carried to the different provinces and even to other countries by traders, which occupation was highly respected in Mexico. They took with them the products of their own country and brought back the products of other countries. These traders not only engaged in trade but also acted as spies for the king and brought to him much information concerning the places visited by them. The products of the country and those brought in from outside by the traders were displayed for sale in the great market-places of the principal cities. "The great market in Tlaltelolco moved the wonder of the conquerors; it is described as being three times as large as that of Salamanca, and one estimate places the daily attendance at twenty or twenty-five thousand persons. One of the conquerors gives the following picture of it. 'On one side are the people who sell gold; near them are they who trade in jewels mounted in gold in the forms of birds and animals. On another side beads and mirros are sold, on another, feathers and plumes of all colors for working designs on garments, and to wear in war or at festivals. Further on stone is worked to make razors and swords, a remarkable thing which passes our understanding; of it they manufacture swords and roundels. In other places

[11] Bancroft, Native races of Pacific states, II, 482.
[12] Joyce, Mexican archæology, 184.

they sell cloth and men's dresses of different designs; beyond, dresses for women, and in another part footgear. A section is reserved for the sale of prepared hides of deer and other animals; elsewhere are baskets made of hair, such as all Indian women use. Cotton, grain which forms their food, bread of all kinds, pastry, fowls, and eggs are sold in different sections; and hard by they sell hares, rabbits, deer, quails, geese and ducks. Elsewhere wines of all sorts are for sale, vegetables, pepper, roots, medicinal plants, which are very numerous in this country, fruits of all kinds, wood for building, lime and stone. In fact, each object has its appointed place. Beside this great market-place there are in other quarters other markets also where provisions may be bought.' Special magistrates held courts in the market-places to settle disputes on the spot, and there were market officials similar to our inspectors of weights and measures. Falsification of the latter was visited with severe punishment.''[13]

**Couriers.** The means of communication between different parts of the country was by couriers, who were trained for this purpose from childhood. One courier would carry his messages from one post-house to another, where another courier would take them and carry them to the next post-house, and so on. These couriers were so well trained from childhood that they traveled with remarkable speed, so that as much as two hundred miles a day would be covered by the chain of carriers.

**Amusements.** Feasts were of common occurrence and were given by people of all ranks of society. Each man vied with the other in giving banquets and it often happened that the host ruined himself financially by his hospitality, as it was the custom to distribute costly presents among the guests, and some went so far as to have sold themselves into slavery to raise funds to give at least one big feast that would make a name for them and thus be kept in the memory of their fellow-men. One form of entertainment at these feasts was the use of jesters, similar to the court-fools of European medieval times, who made jokes at the expense of the guests, imitated people of different nations in dress and manners, mimicked old women and well-known eccentric individuals, and the like.

"At the royal feasts given when the great vassals came to the capital to render homage to their sovereign, the people

[13] Joyce, Mexican archæology, 129.

flocked in from the provinces in great numbers to see the sights, which consisted of theatrical representations, gladiatorial combats, fights between wild beasts, athletic sports, musical performances, and poetical recitations in honor of kings, gods, and heroes. The nobles, in addition to this, partook daily of banquets at the palace, and were presented by the monarch with costly gifts."[14]

There were people who gave gymnastic performances and who performed acrobatic feats such as of the present day and with equal or even greater skill. There were running races, swimming matches, wrestling matches, contests in shooting with bow and arrow and in throwing the dart, and soldiers fought with wild beasts in enclosed places. Gambling greatly prevailed, property of all kinds was put up as stakes and even a man might jeopardize his own personal liberty on a game of chance. Dice was the most general gambling game.

Dancing was one of the leading amusements of the ancient Mexicans. It formed an important part in their religious ceremonies and much time was given by the priests in instructing the youth in this art. Drums and other musical instruments were used in the dancing and they were accompanied by chants and other music of the dancers. In some of the dances each sex danced apart, while in others they danced together. Sometimes they danced in threes, two men and a woman, or two women and a man, while again they danced in pairs, with their arms round one another's waist or neck. There was one dance which somewhat resembled the old English May-pole dance, in which ribbons were wound and unwound about a pole. In some of their great public dances thousands participated. These occurred in an open place, the musicians being placed in the center, about them was formed a circle of the nobles and elderly people, next came a circle of middle-aged persons, and then the young people formed a great circle around them all. Each person was to keep his own place on the circle while all circled about the musicians. The inner circle moved with slow and sedate steps, the middle circle moved more rapidly, and the outer circle of young people twirled rapidly about with many fantastic figures. With drums beating and other musical instruments going and all the dancers chanting, with arms, feet, heads, and bodies all moving in perfect accord, leaders directing, this dancing must have made a great spectacle to the onlookers.

[14] Bancroft, Native races of Pacific states, II, 286.

There were not a great variety of musical instruments. They had drums, rattles, gongs, trumpets, and whistles. There were bands of musicians and choirs, each temple having had a choir composed of singers of different ages, among whom were boys of four to eight years of age. There were contests in music and prizes were given to the successful competitors. There were a large number of popular songs or ballads, which were well known to all classes of the people. The drama existed among them. The plays were given on a terrace in the market-place or on a porch of a temple. The players usually wore wooden masks or were disguised as animals. The play generally was given in the form of a burlesque and ended with the animal players giving exhibits of the actions of the animals they represented.

"The national game of the Nahuas was the *tlachtli*, which strongly resembled in many points our game of football, and was quite as lively and full of scuffle. It was common among all the nations whose cult was similar to the Toltec, and was under special divine protection, though what original religious significance it had is not clear. Indeed, for that matter, nearly every game enjoyed divine patronage, and *Ometochtli*, 'two rabbits,' the god of games, according to Duran, was generally invoked by athletes as well as by gamblers, in conjunction with some special god. Instruments of play, and natural objects were also conjured to grant good luck to the applicant. As an instance of the popularity of the game of tlachtli, it may be mentioned that a certain number of towns contributed annually sixteen thousand balls in taxes, that each town of any size had a special playground devoted to the game, and that kings kept professionals to play before them, occasionally challenging each other to a game besides. The ground in which it was played, called the *tlachco*, was an alley, one hundred feet long and half as wide, except at each end where there were rectangular nooks, which doubtless served as resting places for the players. The whole was enclosed by smooth whitewashed walls, from nine to twelve feet high on the sides, and somewhat lower at the ends, with battlements and turrets, and decreasing in thickness toward the top. At midnight, previous to the day fixed for the game, which was always fixed favorably by the augurs, the priests with much ceremony placed two idols—one representing the god of play, the other the god of the tlachtli—upon the side walls, blessed the edifice, and consecrated the game by throwing the ball four times round the ground, muttering the while a formula. The owner of the tlachco, usually the lord of the place, also performed certain ceremonies and presented offerings, before opening the game. The balls, called *ullamaloni,* were of solid India-rubber, three to four inches in diameter. The players were simply attired in the maxtli, or breech-clout, and sometimes wore a skin to protect the parts coming in contact with the ball, and gloves; they played in parties, usually two or three on each side. The rule was to hit the ball only with knee, elbow, shoulder, or buttock, as agreed upon, the latter was however the favorite way, and to touch the wall of the opposite side with the ball, or to send it over, either of which counted a point. He who struck the ball with his hand or foot, or with any part of his body not previously agreed upon, lost a point; to settle such matters without dispute a priest acted as referee. On each side-wall, equidistant from the ends, was a large stone, carved with images of idols, pierced through the center with a hole large enough to just admit the passage of the ball; the player who by chance or skill drove the ball through one of these openings not only won the game for his side, but was entitled to the cloaks of all present, and the haste with which the spectators scrambled off in order to save their garments is said to have been the most amusing part of the entertainment. A feat so difficult was, of course, rarely accomplished, save by chance, and the successful player was made as much of as a prize-winner at the Olympic games, nor did he omit to present thank-offerings to the god of the game for the good fortune vouchsafed him." [15]

**Education.** Annexed to the temples were buildings devoted to the purpose of education for boys, youths, and young women. The education of the males was in the hands of the priests and of the females in the care of the priestesses. Thus the priesthood were enabled to mould the young in their own way. They brought the young so well under their sway that they were never able in after life to free themselves from such nor did they seem so to desire to do.

The sexes were not educated together nor was any intercourse allowed between them, and if such occurred the transgression was severely punished. The morals of both sexes were very closely looked after. Offences were severely pun-

---

[15] Bancroft, Native races of Pacific states, II, 297-299.

ished, sometimes by death. Love did not lead the Aztec youth in education, but terror.

The children of the common people and those of the higher classes did not attend in the same buildings. Both classes were taught such things in religion, music, painting, and the like, as belonged to their stations in life. The boys of the common people did the heavier and more menial work about the temples, such as the attending to the getting of fuel for the sacred fires and preparing the material for the repair of the sacred edifices. The young nobles attended to the higher duties, such as caring for the fires of the sanctuaries, keeping the upper parts of the temples clean, and decorating the shrines of the gods with flowers. The children of the common classes were obliged to sleep in the school buildings but they took their meals at home while the young nobility remained in the buildings for meals as well as for sleeping.

For the most part the girls who attended the schools belonged to the nobility. They attended to the lower part of the temples, prepared the offerings of meats to the idols, and wove and embroidered the fine cloths for the altars. They were strictly guarded so that no intercourse could take place between them and the youths. When they went out they were accompanied by their teachers and they were not permitted to pay any attention to any one, and if they did so they were severely punished. They were instructed in religion, household arts, spinning, the weaving of mantles, the making of feather-work, and the like.

In the higher schools, the noble boys were taught much that was given to the other boys and also in many of the arts and sciences, such as the study of heroic songs and sacred hymns, history, religion, philosophy, law, astronomy, astrology, and the writing and interpreting of hieroglyphics. Those destined to be priests were further educated in the priestly duties, while those who were to enter upon a military life were exercised in gymnastics, and trained to the use of weapons, to shoot with the bow, to manage the shield, and to cast darts at a mark.

When the young reached the age when marriage was permissible or when business cares should be entered upon, they were sent from the schools with the commendations of the officers and teachers, which were of great aid to many in securing positions in life.

## LITERATURE

1. Bancroft, Hubert Howe, The native races of the Pacific states of North America.
2. Barnes, Earl and Mary S., Education among the Aztecs. *Studies in Education*, I, 73-80.
3. Joyce, Thomas A., Mexican archæology.
4. Mason, Otis Tufton, Woman's share in primitive culture.
5. Nadaillac, Marquis de, Prehistoric America.
6. Prescott, William H., History of the Conquest of Mexico.

## CHAPTER II

#### THE CHILD IN PERU

**The People.** The origin of the people found in Peru at the time of the Spanish conquest is unknown. The people themselves held to a tradition that the empire began with a settlement in the Cuzco valley, the central region of Peru. By the time of the coming of the Spaniards in the first part of the sixteenth century, through military expeditions this Inca power had been extended to include the country from the river Ancasmayu, just north of the city of Quito, Ecuador, to the river Maule, just south of the city of Santiago, Chile, or from about the second degree of north latitude to the thirty-seventh degree of south latitude, territory embraced at the present time by Ecuador, Peru, Bolivia, part of Chile, and north-west Argentina. Before these Inca people there seemed to have existed a race of well advanced people who left imposing architectural remains that the Inca people were unable to account for. To hold together the parts of the empire, great roads were built leading from Cuzco, the capital, to the extremities of the country. One of these great roads ran over the grand plateau north to Quito and south to Chile, and a second one ran each way, north and south, along the lowlands on the border of the ocean, and these two were connected by cross-roads. "The road over the plateau was conducted over pathless sierras buried in snow; galleries were cut for leagues through the living rock; rivers were crossed by means of bridges that swung suspended in the air; precipices were scaled by stairways hewn out of the native bed; ravines of hideous depths were filled up with solid masonry; in short, all the difficulties that beset a wild and mountainous region, and which might appal the most courageous engineer in modern times, were encountered and successfully overcome. The length of the road, of which scattered fragments only remain, is variously estimated at from fifteen hundred to two thousands miles; and stone pillars, in the manner of European mile-stones, were erected at stated intervals of somewhat more than a league, all along the route. Its breadth scarcely exceeded twenty feet. It was built of heavy flags of freestone, and, in some parts at least, covered with a bituminous cement, which time has made harder than the stone itself."[1] Along these roads were a series of posthouses for couriers, selected for their swiftness of foot, who carried messages back and forth between the capital and the different parts of the empire. The statement is made that these couriers covered the distance from Quito to Cuzco, over a thousand miles, in eight days. Along the routes were also placed storehouses with provisions for troops or for those who travelled on state affairs, who really were the only travellers.

At the time of the Spanish invasion, Peru was a huge bureaucracy, which had evolved from a primitive communism as the territory was extended by conquest. The empire was divided into provinces and placed under rulers, below whom was a hierarchy of officials, running down to an inspector of ten heads of families. A careful census was kept of the people and resources of each province, which censuses were sent regularly to Cuzco. From these returns was estimated the tribute each person was to give to the state, which was not paid in money but in labor or products. No one but the sick was permitted to remain idle and there was constant supervision over all. No man was exempt except by special regulation from agricultural work and military service. "From the cradle to the grave the life of the individual was marked out for him; as he was born so would he die, and he lived his allotted span under the ceaseless supervision of officials. His dress was fixed according to his district; he might not leave his village except at the bidding of the state, and then only for state purposes, he might not even seek a wife outside his own community."[2] Yet every one was cared for, widows, orphans, aged, and sick, in fact no one was allowed to suffer. The state stored in buildings provisions for times of scarcity of crops, so as to prevent famine. At the head of the empire was the sovereign and who bore the title of Sapa Inca, Only Inca, the divine ruler; next to the sovereign came the nobility of royal blood, the Inca nobility, and who held the principal offices of the state; then came a lower nobility, the Curaçaa, who were of the original rulers of conquered states; and last were the common people.

[1] Prescott, Conquest of Peru, I, 65.
[2] Joyce, South American archæology, 104.

**Buildings.** The buildings of the highlands were of stone, while on the coast stone was used for foundations and brick made of clay mixed with reeds or tough grass was used for the walls. With stone mortar was sometimes used and sometimes not. In the great buildings where large stones were placed in the walls no mortar was used, and it is stated that in some of the remains of such buildings the stones are fitted so closely that not even a knife-blade can be inserted in the joints. The exterior walls were often of great thickness and the interior of the building was arranged around a court, with windows and doors from the rooms opening on to the court. Some of the buildings were of immense sizes, in particular those built as fortifications and for religious purposes. The doors were narrowed at the top, and with a stone across the top, the arch with the keystone not showing in Peruvian architecture. The roofs were thatched and in the large buildings the ceilings sometimes were vaulted by having the upper courses of masonry overlap and the whole topped by a single slab, thus forming a kind of arch. On this lower part a second story was built, which did not open on to the first floor, but was approached from the hill against which the building was built. Inside the building the walls were niched for the purpose of decoration and also gold plates and jewels were placed on the walls as ornaments.

**Dress.** The two principal garments of the ancient Peruvians were the tunic and the robe. In the simplest form the tunic consisted of an oblong piece of cloth, folded crosswise in the middle and a piece cut out of the fold for the head to go through, and the edges on each side sewed together except a place left for the arms. Sometimes the tunic was made with short sleeves. Often a belt was worn about the tunic at the waist. In the coast country the material used for clothing was cotton while wool was used in the highlands in the interior. The quality of the clothing differed with the rank of the wearer, the coarsest clothes were used by the common people while the finest were reserved for the nobility and the very finest for the sovereign. The cloths were colored and designs woven in them and sometimes they were fringed and embroidered and sometimes even they were further decorated with feathers and small plates of silver and gold.

On the head were worn conical or flat-topped caps, some having flaps to cover the ears and the back part of the head, while others enclosed the entire head, coming down under the chin, leaving only the face exposed to view. Women wore their hair long while with men the length of the hair proclaimed the rank, as the higher the rank the shorter the hair was worn, the sovereign alone having a closely cropped head. The ruling class wore a fringed cord of vicuña wool wound round the head three or four times, the color designating the rank of the wearer, that of the sovereign being crimson, of the heir to the throne yellow, and the higher officials wore other colors. Hair was not allowed to grow on the face and it was kept pulled out by means of small silver and copper tweezers. They wore sandals made of the hide of the llama or of vegetable fiber and they were fastened to the feet with cords.

Another mark of rank, along with their colored fringed cord, was the wearing of studs in the lobe of the ear, the largest size having been permitted to the sovereign only, and the sizes diminished according to rank. These ear-ornaments were so heavy as to pull the lobes of the ears down, making them quite large, the sovereign's ears being distended nearly to his shoulders. Sometimes the nose and the lower lip were pierced and ornaments worn in them. They wore necklaces made of beads of colored shell and turquoise, finger-rings, anklets, and bracelets of silver and gold, and pins for fastening the cloaks. Tattooing was practiced, designs having been worked into the skin with a blue pigment.

**Food, Drink, Narcotics.** Because of the country's lying for the most part in the tropics and also being of a mountainous nature, thus allowing different climatic conditions, there was a plant life as found in both tropical and temperate zones such as to offer a variety of food. In the uplands maize was one of the staple foods, which was usually eaten whole, roasted or boiled, maybe not used by them as bread except at festivals, and the leaves were eaten as a vegetable. Quinoa was another grain used by them, a kind of buckwheat. Another staple was the potato, most commonly used in the form of *chuno*, in which the potatoes were exposed to the frost for some time, then pounded and dried in the sun, which made quite nourishing food and could be stowed away and kept for some time. Beans and tomatoes were also used by them. On the lowlands along the coast were found bananas, cocoa-nuts, the guava, and the manioc. Birds were abundant, as were also fish, both from the lakes and the ocean. The llama and the deer and the wild sheep of the mountains were used as food, as was the flesh of some other animals. This flesh was often cut into strips and dried, which was called *charqui,* probably from which came the term "jerked" beef.

Syrup and a kind of vinegar were made from the juice of the maguey and also syrup was made from the juice extracted from the stalk of the maize. They made from the grain of the maize *chica,* which was the national drink of Peru, and chica also was made from the grain of the quinoa. But more desired than food or drink was the narcotic effect of the coca, whose leaves were gathered and dried, mixed with lime or bone-ash, and thus made into a preparation for chewing. Tobacco was used by the Peruvians but they "differed from every other Indian nation to whom it was known, by using it only for medicinal purposes, in the form of snuff."[3]

**Marriage.** By law in ancient Peru, every person, both male and female, was to marry at a marriageable age, which should be not less than twenty-four in males and eighteen or twenty in females, it being recognized that not until that age were people prepared to care for a family. The nobility were allowed more than one wife but the common people were limited to one.

According to law, each person was to marry within his own kindred. This was not a very great restriction since all of his community, including the town and often the whole province, were counted his kin.

The queen of the ruler was selected from among his sisters. No other person in the realm was allowed to marry his own sister. This was commanded of the ruler so that only the purest blood—the blood of the heaven-born children of the sun—would thus flow in their offspring, thereby preventing anything earthly from being a part of their great rulers.

No marriage was considered legal unless the consent of the parents had been given; nor was any contract performed without the contracting parties so desiring it.

The ceremony was very simple and yet quite peculiar. On a certain day of each year, designated by law, all persons of marriageable age came together in the open squares of their native places. The ruler of the district would take the hands of the different couples in his and place them in each other's and pronounce them man and wife. Among the kindred of

[3] Prescott, Conquest of Peru, I, 142.

the Inca this ceremony was performed by the Inca in person.

After all the marriage vows were performed, there was a general good time had by the newly married pair and their friends, which was carried on for several days. It can be seen that these festivities must have been very general over the whole empire, as all weddings occurred on the same day, and as in every circle there must have been one wedding, so there must have been among the participants in the afterfeasts nearly all, if not all, the people of the country.

The newly married pair were not left to find a home for themselves. Each district furnished a house for each married couple within its boundaries and gave a certain portion of land to them, and as children came additional allotments were made for the support of each child. For a son twice as much land was assigned to the parents as for a daughter. This allotment of land occurred each year and amounts were given in accordance with the size of the family.

**Care and Treatment of Children.** Infants were placed in cradles, somewhat like Indian cradles, and fastened in them and kept in this manner, not even having been taken out and into the mother's arms when fed. When they were weaned an important ceremony occurred. In the first place the hair was cut. The first lock of hair was cut from the head by an elder relative with a stone knife and the rest of the hair was cut by the relatives in the order of closeness of kin. The child was then given a name, presents were given to it, and a feast closed the proceedings. When the heir to the throne underwent this ceremony, the High-priest of the Sun cut the first lock of hair, and the child received many fine presents, among them being presents from the rulers of the various provinces of the empire. A very careful record of births and deaths was kept.

**The Virgins of the Sun.** The Peruvians worshipped the sun and they trained for this worship young women who were called Virgins of the Sun. They were taken from their homes at an early age and placed in convents solely consecrated to their instruction and training. One of these institutions, located at Cuzco, was for the girls of royal blood. In the other provinces they were for the girls of the higher and inferior nobles, and occasionally a girl of remarkable beauty from among the common people was placed among the inmates.

These girls were put in charge of old, reliable women, who

had spent many years in the convents. They taught the girls how to spin and to weave the hangings for the temples. They prepared the apparel for the ruler and his people. They were instructed in their religious duties, one of these being the watching over the sacred fires.

When the girls entered the convents they were shut entirely away from the world, not even being permitted to see or to hear from their friends and relatives. Morality was carefully inculcated. If one of the young women should be caught in an intrigue, she was buried alive, her lover was strangled, and his native town razed to the ground.

No one was allowed to enter these convents except the king and his lawful queen. The institutions were inspected each year by persons sent for that purpose, who made a report of what they noted on their visits.

The buildings themselves were as finely furnished as were the palaces of the Incas and the temples, as they were for the accommodation of the Daughters of the Sun and so were in especial charge of the state.

When these young women reached a marriageable age, the most beautiful among them were chosen to become brides of the ruler, others were given by him as wives to the higher nobles, while others remained in the service of religion, vowing perpetual virginity, and who were held in the very highest respect.

**Human Sacrifice.** Human sacrifice was of rare event in Peru. This only occurred to mark some great public affair. The victims usually were children and beautiful maidens. They were selected from the various parts of the empire and they travelled in regular convoys, the children too young to walk being carried by their mothers. As they journey they received the adoration of all the people on the way. In offering them up as sacrifices, the priests strangled them or broke their necks with a stone implement, while with some the throat was cut and blood from the wound sprinkled on their faces. In some cases the hearts of the victims were plucked out and offered to the divinity. These sacrifices were never served up at feasts, as in Mexico, but all were buried in special cemeteries. Human sacrifice never came to be a great part of the religion of Peru under the Incas, as was the case in Mexico, and where it did occur there was never any cannibalism with it.

**Industries.** Agriculture was the main occupation of the

ancient Peruvians. Every one was required to put in some time in agricultural pursuits unless excused by special permit by the authorities. The land was divided into three parts, one portion was reserved for the Sun, to be used to produce revenue to care for the temples and the priests and others connected with the religion, a second part was reserved for the state, and the third part was given over to the people for their own use, each head of a family receiving a plot and additional plots for each unmarried child. There were no animals for use in the fields, so the people had all the work to do. The men used a digging-stick, which was a long stake with a sharpened point, sometimes having the point covered with copper, and with a cross stick about a foot up from the pointed end for a foot-rest for digging with the foot. The men would turn up the soil with their digging-sticks and the women would follow and break up the clods with a rake and pull out the weeds. The men unable to dig and the boys acted as scare-crows or used blow-guns and slings to keep the birds away. Every bit of ground was cultivated and to add to this terraces were formed on the hillsides by means of parallel walls of rough stones, one above the other. To add further to the area of tillable land, where the soil was rocky and dry they would make excavations, sometimes as much as an acre in extent and sunk to the depth of fifteen or twenty feet, and would line these with walls of adobe, sun-dried bricks. The bottom of the pits probably reached down to where there was some moisture and they were prepared for cultivation as the other fields.

As is well known, much of the coast region of the country which was occupied by the empire of the ancient Peruvians is arid, as the prevailing winds are from the east and the moisture is taken from them by the high Andes mountains, and thus the rivers are few and with but little water in them, often dry for a long time, and there is but little rainfall, if at all. In order to overcome this lack of moisture and to add to the fertile area of the country, the Peruvians built reservoirs and aqueducts. These aqueducts were sometimes above ground and sometimes underground and some were quite long, one at least having been between four and five hundred miles in length and twelve feet deep and wide. As they did not use the arch they could not well cross depressions or streams and had to make long detours, and sometimes they tunneled in the mountains for the passages. They had sluices by means of which the water could be turned on to the land and they were very careful in allowing the right amount of water to be used on the fields. The construction of these aqueducts, and other great buildings, is all the more remarkable when it is considered that these people had no iron tools of any kind whatever.

They were acquainted with the principle of fertilizing the crop. A small sardine-like fish was abundant along the coast, which they caught and often placed with the grains of maize in the holes in planting. Guano, the deposit of sea-fowls on the islands along the coast, was used in great quantity by them, and much care was given to its proper distribution to the different districts. No one was allowed on the islands during the breeding season and such trespass and killing the birds at any time were punished by death. "Inland other forms of manure were used."[4]

As most of the country of the Peruvian empire lay in the torrid zone and consisted of low coast land, elevated land, and mountainous regions, it would have all ranges of climate, according to elevation, and without any great changes of temperature in any one part. Thus all kinds of agricultural products could be cultivated, such as would be found in tropical and temperate regions. In the warm coast region cotton was grown in great abundance and the banana and the cassava; in the more elevated regions the great staple produced was maize and also manioc, guava, groundnuts, tobacco, beans, gourds, and tomatoes; and in the higher and colder parts were found the potato, quinoa, coca, and maguey.

Fishing was an important industry and on the coast regions it ranked next to agriculture. They had a kind of raft, *balsa*, made of bundles of reeds or poles fastened together and they used nets, harpoons made of copper or tipped with copper, and hooks of bone or copper. Fowling was carried on by means of nets and quite largely engaged in especially along the coast where there were great numbers of birds. Game was plentiful in the mountainous regions and often great drives were made, sometimes as many as fifty or sixty thousand people took part in one and in which thirty thousand head of game might have been taken. They used dogs in hunting, having had at least two varieties of hunting dogs. Beasts of prey, such as pumas, bears, foxes, and wild-cats were killed. The real purpose of the hunt, though, was to

[4] Joyce, South American archæology, 121.

capture the huanaco and vicuña, from which the wool was cut and then the greater part of them, the females and best males, were turned loose to let the wool grow for another year, some being kept for food. Besides these wild animals, they kept great flocks of llamas and alpacas, the alpaca having been raised for its wool and the llama for a beast of burden, for its wool, and also for its flesh for eating.

The Peruvians excelled in the art of weaving. They made cloth, tapestry, gauze, and embroidery. They used cotton and wool for the most part, although there was a thread made from the fiber of the maguey. One of the principal occupations of the women was the preparation of the thread for weaving. In the early times it would seem that the loom was unknown but at the time of the entrance of the Spaniards into the country the work was done by true weaving on the loom. There were a number of designs used, variations showing from one period to another. Various colors were used. The patterns were woven in the material or placed on the cloth in the form of embroidery or painted on the cloth, and sometimes the cloth was ornamented with feathers placed on it in the form of patterns. They also wove a double-faced cloth in which the colors were different on the two sides. Delicate gauzes were made in which designs were embroidered on fine net background.

Pottery was another important industry. There were very many designs and all kinds of utensils and the workmanship was good. Gold was obtained from deposits in streams and silver was mined. These metals were cast, hammered, soldered, and inlaid, as the people were very skillful in working with these metals and did especially fine work. They made vases, bracelets, mirrors, necklaces, and all kinds of delicate ornaments. Copper was greatly used, tin having been mixed with it. They made from this various kinds of implements and tools and weapons. They were quite skillful in wood-carving and inlaying was widely practiced, not only on wood but also on bone and shell and stone. They displayed skill in stone-carving, being able to cut the hardest stones, as emeralds and other precious stones. Their implements were of copper or stone, as iron was not at all in use.

Money was not in use among the Peruvians and so there was required an exchange of products. As the products of the country varied it became necessary that ways should be provided whereby people could have opportunity to exchange what they had for things greatly needed from other people of a different calling. This was done by means of fairs held throughout the empire. In the more populous places they took place three times a month. "These fairs afforded so many holidays for the relaxation of the industrious laborers."[5]

**Training of the Inca and the Order of the Huaracu.** "In his early years, the royal offspring was intrusted to the care of the *amautas*, or 'wise men,' as the teachers of Peruvian science were called, who instructed him in such elements of knowledge as they possessed, and especially in the cumbrous ceremonial of their religion, in which he was to take a prominent part. Great care was also bestowed on his military education, of the last importance in a state which, with its professions of peace and good will, was ever at war for the acquisition of empire.

"In this military school he was educated with such of the Inca nobles as were nearly of his own age; for the sacred name of Inca—a fruitful source of obscurity in their annals—was applied indifferently to all who descended by the male line from the founder of the monarchy. At the age of sixteen the pupils underwent a public examination, previous to their admission to what may be called the order of chivalry. This examination was conducted by some of the oldest and most illustrious Incas. The candidates were required to show their prowess in the athletic exercises of the warrior; in wrestling and boxing, in running such long courses as fully tried their agility and strength, in severe fast of several days' duration, and in mimic combats, which, although the weapons were blunted, were always attended with wounds, and sometimes with death. During this trial, which lasted thirty days, the royal neophyte fared no better than his comrades, sleeping on the bare ground, going unshod, and wearing a mean attire—a mode of life, it was supposed, which might tend to inspire him with more sympathy with the destitute. With all this show of impartiality, however, it will probably be doing no injustice to the judges to suppose that a politic discretion may have somewhat quickened their perceptions of the real merits of the heir-apparent.

"At the end of the appointed time, the candidates selected as worthy of the honors of their barbaric chivalry were presented to the sovereign, who condescended to take a principal

[5] Prescott, Conquest of Peru, I, 140.

part in the ceremony of the inauguration. He began with a brief discourse, in which, after congratulating the young aspirants on the proficiency they had shown in martial exercises, he reminded them of the responsibilities attached to their birth and station, and, addressing them affectionately as 'children of the Sun,' he exhorted them to imitate their great progenitor in his glorious career of beneficence to mankind. The novices then drew near, and, kneeling one by one before the Inca, he pierced their ears with a golden bodkin; and this was suffered to remain there till an opening had been made large enough for the enormous pendants which were peculiar to their order, and which gave them, with the Spaniards, the name of *orejones*. This ornament was so massy in the ears of the sovereign that the cartilage was distended by it nearly to the shoulder, producing what seemed a monstrous deformity in the eyes of the Europeans, though, under the magical influence of fashion, it was regarded as a beauty by the natives.

"When this operation was performed, one of the most venerable of the nobles dressed the feet of the candidates in the sandals worn by the order, which may remind us of the ceremony of buckling on the spurs of the Christian knight. They were then allowed to assume the girdle or sash around the loins, corresponding with the *toga virilis* of the Romans, and intimating that they had reached the season of manhood. Their heads were adorned with garlands of flowers, which, by their various colors, were emblematic of the clemency and goodness that should grace the character of every true warrior; and the leaves of an evergreen plant were mingled with the flowers, to show that these virtues should endure without end. The prince's head was further ornamented by a fillet, or tasselled fringe, of a yellow color, made of the fine threads of the vicuña wool, which encircled the forehead as the peculiar insignia of the heir-apparent. The great body of the Inca nobility next made their appearance, and, beginning with those nearest of kin, knelt down before the prince and did him homage as successor to the crown. The whole assembly then moved to the great square of the capital, where songs and dances and other public festivities closed the important ceremonial of the *huaracu*."[6]

**Education.** Education in ancient Peru was wholly reserved for the nobility. The common people were treated

[6] Prescott, Conquest of Peru, I, 22-25.

very kindly by the ruling class, but it was the theory of their government that the masses were only children and must be treated as such. The following from one of their leading sovereigns portrays this idea: "Science was not intended for the people; but for those of generous blood. Persons of low degree are only puffed up by it, and rendered vain and arrogant. Neither should such meddle with the affairs of government; for this would bring high offices into disrepute, and cause detriment to the state."[7]

The youth of the nobility were placed under "wise men," who were the only ones having sufficient learning to do such work. The youth were trained for the especial kind of duties they were to perform in after life. They were taught the laws of their country, the principles of government, and were well grounded in the use of their mother tongue. Those who were to enter into a religious life were carefully instructed in regard to the rites and ceremonies of the religion of the country. All were made familiar with the use of the quipus.

The quipus were used for counting and computing numbers. The quipu was a cord near two feet long, made of threads of different colors twisted together and having smaller threads hanging from them like fringe. These threads were of different colors with knots in them which served instead of ciphers in computing. Sometimes the threads represented abstract ideas, as, white stood for peace, red for war, and, again they represented concrete objects, as, white was for silver, yellow for gold.

## LITERATURE

1. . . . Ancient Peru—Its people and its monuments. *Harper's Magazine*, VII. (1853), 7-38.
2. Joyce, Thomas A., South American archæology.
3. Nadaillac, Marquis de, Prehistoric America.
4. Prescott, William H., History of the conquest of Peru.
5. Winsor, Justin, Narrative and critical history of America.

[7] Prescott, Conquest of Peru, I, 120.

## CHAPTER III

### THE CHILD IN EGYPT

**The Country.** The desert stretching across Africa from the Atlantic Ocean on the west extends into Western Asia and in its whole extent it is broken only in one place and that is the long, narrow valley made by the Nile river. In this valley snow and frost are unknown and the chief characteristic of the climate is its combined warmth and dryness. There is but little rainfall throughout this region and yet there is abundance of moisture, which comes from the annual overflow of the Nile, and which overflow also greatly enriches the soil. The deserts surrounding Egypt and the cataracts of the Nile at its southern border isolated this country so that it was not readily disturbed by outside peoples. This isolation, with the warm climate and the productive soil, gave just the conditions necessary for the development of mankind in its early times and thus arose a people in this region which developed into a great nation, extending from about 5,000 years before Christ down to its overthrow by the Persians in 525 B. C. The country was divided into Upper Egypt, the principal city of which was Thebes, Middle Egypt, with Memphis as the principal city, and Lower Egypt, which included the Delta, its chief city being Heliopolis.

From the cataracts on the South to the Mediterranean Sea the Nile pursues its course for over five hundred miles, till within sixty miles of its mouth it divides into branches and forms the part called the Delta. The cultivable land, depending upon the extent of the inundation, averages about five and a half miles in width, varying from two miles in its narrowest part to ten and three-quarters in its widest part, including the river. On the west of the valley is a range of hills, which protects it from the sand of the desert, and on the east, between the Nile and the Red Sea, is also another range of hills. Lying at the foot of the hills is a strip of sand, sometimes as great as two and a half miles in breadth, which is not reached by the inundation and consequently remains a waste. The demarcation between this waste and the fertile soil is very marked, so as to be readily noted. The rock in these hills varies, at the southern extremity being found the granite, from which were cut out their monoliths and made into obelisks and collossi; further north is found sandstone of various colors, and from which were built the palaces and temples of that region; and following this district is a part wherein there is a limestone formation, in which region are found the pyramids, mostly composed of this stone.

**The People.** The ancient Egyptians, although in Africa, were not from African races but were of Asiatic descent, as the formation of their skulls, their features, their hair, and their language, show that they were of a Caucasian race. "The Egyptians appear to have been among the darkest races with which the Greeks of the early times came into direct contact. . . . The hair was usually black and straight. In no case was it 'woolly,' though sometimes it grew in short, crisp curls. . . . The forehead was straight, but somewhat low; the nose generally long and straight, but sometimes slightly aquiline. The lips were over-full; but the upper lip was short, and the mouth was seldom too wide. The chin was good, being well-rounded, and neither retreating nor projecting too far. The most marked and peculiar feature was the eye, which was a long, narrow slit, like that of the Chinese, but placed horizontally and not obliquely. An eyebrow, also long and thin, but very distinctly pencilled, shaded it. The coloring was always dark, the hair, eyebrows, eyelashes, and beard (if any) being black, or nearly so, and the eyes black or dark brown.

"In form the Egyptian resembled the modern Arab. He was tall; his limbs were long and supple; his head was well placed upon his shoulders; his movements were graceful; his carriage dignified. In general, however, his frame was too spare; and his hands and feet were unduly large. The women were as thin as the men, and had forms nearly similar. Children, however, appear to have been sufficiently plump; but they are not often represented."[1]

The people were divided into classes and although the separation of the classes was very marked and distinct, yet there was really no rigid caste system, as the boundaries were crossed by people ascending from a lower class into a higher.

[1] Rawlinson, History of ancient Egypt, I, 103.

Of course, as with all people, it was quite customary for the son to take up the work of his father, but, at least, in some cases this was not compulsory. In one instance it is shown where the occupation of architect had descended from father to son for twenty-one generations. There is difficulty in knowing just what were the divisions of society but at any rate there were at least three distinct classes, which were the priestly class, the military class, and the rest of the people. The first two classes, from whom came the king, were exempt from taxation. The rest of the people had to bear the burden of the taxes, to construct the public works, to perform the agricultural tasks, and to carry on all mechanical and other pursuits. They had a hard time and yet the laws regarding them seem to have been justly administered and it would appear as if they were contented with their condition.

"The occupations of the common people in Egypt were carefully watched by the magistrate, and no one was allowed to live an idle life, useless to himself and to the community. It was thought right that the industrious citizen should be encouraged, and distinguished from the lazy or the profligate; and in order to protect the good and detect the wicked, it was enacted that every one should at certain times present himself before the magistrates, or provincial governors, and give in his name, his place of abode, his profession or employment, and the mode in which he gained his livelihood, the particulars being duly registered in the official report. The time of attendance was fixed, and those from the same parish proceeded in bodies to the appointed office, accompanied by their respective banners, and each individual being introduced singly to the registering clerks, gave in his statement and answered the necessary questions."[2]

**Slavery.** Slavery has a very early date, as it is found at the very beginning of history, which is true in Egypt as elsewhere. The origin of slavery cannot be traced but in the early history of Egypt it appears that the slaves came from outside countries, gained through wars and raids and by purchase from dealers. Many of the captives who became slaves were placed in the service of the king and used on public works, as the building of temples, cutting canals, raising dykes and embankments, and the like. They were used in private, both black and white, to do the work in the fields and in the homes and elsewhere. They attended on guests

[2] Wilkinson, Popular account of ancient Egyptians, II, 199.

at banquets and also were used to amuse them by singing and dancing and in other ways.

The master had full power over his slaves, could sell them, remove them from place to place, if they escaped could pursue and recapture them, and do with them as he pleased, and yet he could not wilfully murder one of them or, if so, he himself was put to death. "The very kind treatment of Joseph, the mode of his liberation, and his subsequent marriage with the daughter of a freeborn Egyptian, a high functionary of the sacerdotal order, are striking proofs of the humanity of the Egyptians and of their indulgent conduct toward manumitted slaves."[3] At the same time, as with slaves everywhere and at all times, no doubt they were often cruelly treated, as is given concerning the Israelites, when "there arose up a new king over Egypt, which knew not Joseph."[4]

**The Home.** The houses in the towns varied in size, many of one story and maybe some of four or five stories, but for the great part not above two stories. The streets of the towns were narrow. The poorer classes lived much in the open air and so did not use their houses greatly. The wealthier classes built their houses so as to be cool throughout the summer. To keep their houses cool "a line of trees ran parallel with the front of the house; and to prevent injuries from cattle or from any accident, the stems were surrounded by a low wall, pierced with square holes to admit the air."[5] The material used in constructing the houses was crude brick, baked in the sun, a material peculiarly suited to the climate. Wood was used for beams and doors, sometimes for floors, and the finer imported woods for decorative purposes.

The houses were of different sizes and arrangement. Some of the houses were small, having an open court in front, with three or four small rooms adjoining for storing grain and other things, and a single chamber on a second floor above these rooms, stairs leading to it from the court. Such houses as these small single ones probably were found only in the country. In the towns the smaller houses were usually built in a solid row along a street, with a courtyard, common to several dwellings. The wealthier people had separate houses,

---

[3] Wilkinson, Manners and customs of the ancient Egyptians, I, 459.
[4] Exodus I, 8.
[5] Wilkinson, *op. cit.*, I, 346.

which sometimes were quite large, covering a good deal of ground.

Before the front door was a portico or porch, about twelve or fifteen feet high and supported on columns of stone, or if of wood they were stained to represent stone. There was a large front entrance and on either side a small door, probably for servants and ordinary use. Sometimes on the lintels or imposts of the entrance the owner's name was written and over the door was placed a phrase, as, "The Good House." Inside next to the entrance was a small open court with a receiving door for visitors, on the opposite side of which was a door through which the master of the house came to receive the callers. From this small court doors led to a larger court, which was shaded by trees. The rooms of the house were arranged on the right and left of the large court, opening into it. The rooms on the ground floor were used chiefly as store-rooms for furniture, goods of various kinds, wines, oil, etc. Over the rooms on the ground floor were placed the chambers of the upper story, with stairs leading to them.

The ceilings of the rooms were formed with rafters of the date tree with transverse layers of palm branches or planks and sometimes they were vaulted and made of brick and in the houses of the rulers they might have been arched with stone. The floors were of stone or a composition made of lime and other materials. The doors opened inward, both of the rooms and the outside entrance. The doors were made of wood, often stained to imitate foreign and rare wood. They were made of one or two valves and they turned on pins of bronze, which were fastened to the wood with nails of the same metal, and they were secured within by means of a bar or bolt or with a wooden lock. The openings for the windows were small as the cloudless sky of Egypt gave out brilliant light and small openings let in less heat. The windows had wooden shutters of one or two valves, opening on pins and secured by bars and bolts, as the doors. The walls and ceilings were stuccoed and ornamented with various devices painted on them, being tastefully done in form and arrangement of colors. A terrace was placed on top of the house and covered with a roof and supported by columns, which during the summer provided a refuge from the heat of the day and a sleeping-place at night.

Beside these town places there were villas, which sometimes were quite great in extent with a large mansion and beautiful gardens, watered by canals from the Nile, and all surrounded by a wall.

The poorer classes of people sat cross-legged, crouched on the ground, knelt on one or both knees, or sat on the heels. Sometimes as a token of respect to superiors, the people of the higher classes knelt or sat on the heels, but usually they used chairs or stools or couches.

The chairs were of various kinds, some of them of elegant form and made of ebony and other fine woods, inlaid with ivory, and covered with rich stuffs. Beside the single chair, they had a double chair for two persons, which often was reserved for the master and mistress of the house, and occasionally offered to guests. Most of the chairs had backs, some had a raised piece at the back, while others were made in the form of camp-stools. They were usually about as high as they are now, but some of the chairs were quite low, the seat sometimes being as low as eight inches from the floor. The legs were usually made in imitation of those of an animal, as, of the lighter chairs like the legs of an antelope, of the heavier like those of a lion. In the finer chairs bars were not used to unite the legs. The seats were made of wood or leather and sometimes of interlaced string or leather thongs, over which a cushion was placed.

The finer stools were very much as the chairs, of fine workmanship and of rare woods inlaid with ivory. Some of the cheaper ones had solid sides while others had three legs. They had footstools with open or closed sides, covered with leather or interlaced string, as with the chairs. They used couches, some of which were most beautiful in form and workmanship. They used mats and carpets and rugs.

The tables of the Egyptians were round, square, or oblong. They were generally made of wood, although some were of stone or metal. The smaller tables often had but one support, in the center, while the larger ones had three or four legs or were made with solid sides. In sleeping, for the head they used a low half cylinder, usually of wood, sometimes of pottery or stone, some of the wooden ones being made of rare woods and ornamented. The poorer people slept on mats on the floor but probably the wealthier people had bedsteads made in wicker form of palm branches and some, perhaps, were of wood and bronze.

**Women and Marriage.** We find the women having considerable power in ancient Egypt. They had full control of the home, as it appears that the husband entered the house of his wives, rather than the wives to have entered his. Royal authority and supreme direction of affairs were intrusted without reserve to women. The women went often into public, at some of the public festivals they were even expected to attend with their husbands. Even greater privileges were accorded to the women of the middle and lower classes as they often went and came as they liked.

Plurality of wives was allowed, except in the case of priests, who by law were permitted but one wife. Yet the Egyptians generally restricted themselves to one wife. Marriage of brother and sister was permitted and seemingly encouraged from a religious point of view.

Although in most cases they might not have had but one wife, yet they had concubines. These appear to have been obtained mostly in war or bought as slaves from foreign dealers, not for most part being native Egyptian women. These concubines were both white and black, but the black were used as domestics in the family. Sometimes the white concubine took a prominent part in the family, ranking next to the wives and children.

All the children born to a father were considered legitimate whether the offspring of a wife or of some other woman, but those who were born of a brother and sister in legitimate marriage took precedence of those whose mother was of inferior rank or a slave.

The people of old Egypt held strong opinions on the behavior of their women and so punished adultery very severely. A woman detected in adultery had her nose cut off, as it was thought this would be a severe blow to her charms and so make her less attractive. The man was condemned to receive a bastinado of one thousand blows. If a man used force toward a free woman he was very cruelly punished.

**Child and Parent.** The Egyptians were very fond of their children. Even the most consequential pontiff did not affect indifference toward them. They cared for the children and did not permit the father to have any right over the life of his offspring. The punishment for child-murder was very severe. They did not take the life of the offender, but gave to him a punishment which would well portray to him the heinousness of the crime. In the case of the killing of a child, it was ordered that the corpse of the child be fastened to the neck of the parent offending, and for three entire days and nights was the embrace of the dead child to continue, under the watchful eyes of a public guard. The murder of a parent was considered the most wicked of all crimes. In this case the criminal was sentenced to be lacerated with sharpened reeds and after being thrown on thorns he was burnt to death. In case a pregnant woman was sentenced to death, the punishment did not take place till after the birth of the child, both because they thought it wrong to take the life of an innocent being and also they did not wish to deprive the father of the child, which might become his support in later life.

Children were taught to pay great respect to old age. The children's greatest duty was respect for and care of parents. This was just as binding among the upper classes as with the lower. This was carried up even to the very highest, as the sons of the king acted as fan-bearers to him, and they also walked on foot behind his chariot in triumphal processions.

**Dress.** The lower orders of the Egyptian people dressed in a very simple manner. The men wore a sort of apron, or kilt, held at the waist by a girdle or sash, or else short drawers, extending half way to the knees. Sometimes the apron was simply bound round the loins and lapped over in front. When at heavy labor the men would even wear less clothing, as they would use the girdle about the body at the waist and fasten to it in front a roll of linen and pass this between the legs and fasten it to the girdle at the back. The men of the higher orders used the apron also and wore over it a dress which extended to the ankles and had large sleeves. Sometimes this dress was fringed on the border around the legs. Over this for cool weather they wore a woolen cloak. Sometimes they wore over the apron a skirt with short sleeves and over this a loose robe with the right arm left exposed. As a distinguishing mark, the princes wore a peculiar badge at the side of the head, which descended to the shoulders and was frequently adorned and terminated with a gold fringe.

The women of the lower classes usually wore a loose robe or shirt, with tight or full sleeves, fastened at the neck with a string, and over this they wore a sort of petticoat with a girdle about it at the waist, and, often while at hard work, this costume was further simplified by their wearing merely the loose shirt or robe and going barefooted. The women of the higher orders wore a petticoat, or gown, held by a colored sash at the waist or by straps over the shoulders, and over this they wore a large loose robe, with full sleeves and tied in front below the breast. Slaves and servants were not allowed to dress as their mistresses. They wore a long tight gown, tied at the neck, with short sleeves, reaching nearly to the elbows. When entertaining guests by dancing or otherwise at banquets and the like, these women wore over their dress a long loose robe and strings of beads around their hips.

The material used for the clothing was sometimes cotton but linen was preferred. Wool was used for cloaks for colder weather. Some of the material was of very fine texture, this being particularly true of the linen. There was a great variety of patterns in brilliant colors. In some of the striped patterns, the stripes were of gold threads, alternating with red lines as a border. The most elegant stuff and beautiful patterns were reserved for the robes of the deities and the dresses of queens.

The men of ancient Egypt shaved the head and face, never letting the hair grow except when they were in mourning. Women, on the contrary, never had their hair cut off, even in mourning or after death. They wore their hair long and plaited, generally in a triple plait, the ends being left loose; but more usually two or three plaits were fastened together at the ends by a woolen string of the same color as the hair, and falling around the head to the shoulders. An ornamental fillet was bound around the head and fastened with a lotus bud, which fell over the forehead. The plaits of hair at the side were held in place by a comb or band and sometimes a round stud or pin was thrust into them at the front. The male slaves had their heads and faces shaved as their masters. The female slaves generally bound their hair at the back of the head into a sort of loop; sometimes they arranged it in long plaits at the back and at the sides of the neck and face.

The men wore wigs both within the house and without. Sometimes the whole wig was of plaited hair, sometimes the upper portion was of curled hair and the lower part of plaited hair, and again the whole wig was of short locks of equal length. Too, cheap wigs were made in woolen and other stuffs in imitation of hair. "The wig was worn by every gentleman; and though it might appear ill-suited to a hot climate, the interlaced texture of the ground to which the hair was fastened, and the protection of this last against the sun, rendered it a most effective, and at the same time the coolest, kind of covering for the head."⁶

"The most singular custom of the Egyptians was that of tying a false beard under the chin, which was made of plaited hair, and of a peculiar form, according to the person by whom it was worn. Private individuals had a small beard, scarcely two inches long; that of a king was of considerable length, square at the bottom; and the figures of gods were distinguished by its turning up at the end. No man ventured to assume, or affix to his image, the beard of a deity; but after their death it was permitted to substitute this divine emblem on the statues of kings, and all other persons who were judged worthy of admittance to the Elysium of futurity, in consequence of their having assumed the character of Osiris, to whom the souls of the pure returned on quitting their earthly abode."⁷

Both men and women wore sandals, which often were carefully and beautifully made. They were made of leather, and lined with cloth, or of palm leaves, papyrus stalks, or other similar materials in a sort of woven or interlaced work. Some were pointed and turned up in front, some had a sharp flat point, while still others were nearly round.

The Egyptians liked ornaments very much. They used gold and silver and precious stones, and also cheaper materials were used in imitation of these. Women wore earrings, some quite large. The women seem to have been exceedingly fond of rings, sometimes wearing two or three on the same finger, often wearing them on every finger of the left hand and at the same time on a finger or two of the right hand, and they even wore a ring on the thumb. They wore anklets. Both men and women wore armlets, bracelets, and necklaces.

The men carried walking-sticks. These were of various lengths, running from three to six feet. Some had a knob at the top while others had a peg projecting from the side. On entering a house the sticks were left at the door or in the hall. Where a party was being given, sometimes a poor man was employed by the master of the house to hold the sticks of the guests. Quite often the name of the owner was written in hieroglyphics on the stick.

For improving their appearance, the ladies of ancient Egypt used paints and cosmetics. They applied kohl to the

⁶ Wilkinson, The Egyptians in the time of the Pharaohs, 40.
⁷ Wilkinson, Manners and customs of the ancient Egyptians, II, 333.

eyes, they used ointment on the body, the ointment having been scented in various ways, they stained the fingers with red *henneh* and the eyelids with a moistened powder of a black color. They kept the paints and ointments in bottles and boxes and vases of various forms and materials, some being ornamented. They had pins and needles. Some of the needles were of bronze and from three to three and a half inches in length. Some of the pins were seven or eight inches in length, with or without heads, used for arranging the plaits or curls of the hair. They had combs, usually of wood, about four inches long and six wide, some being double with small teeth on one side and large teeth on the other side. They had mirrors of mixed metal, chiefly copper, carefully made and highly polished, nearly round in form, and with handles of wood, stone, or metal.

These people were of cleanly habits, both men and women. As was given before, the men kept the head and face wholly shaved. They used warm and cold baths. "The priests were remarkable for their love of cleanliness, which was carried so far that they shaved the whole body every three days, and performed frequent daily ablutions, bathing twice a day and twice during the night."[8]

**Food and Drink.** Beef and goose constituted the principal part of the animal food throughout Egypt, yet the cow was held sacred and forbidden to be eaten.[9] Among the animals used for food were the ox, kid, wild goat, and gazelle. Of fowls there were the goose and duck, the widgeon and quail and other wild birds. There were fish in plenty. They had a variety and abundance of vegetables, among them being onions, garlic, lentils, beans, cucumbers, and melons. The lotus, papyrus, and other plants that grew abundantly along the Nile furnished the greatest food for the poorer people. Among the grains they had wheat, barley, and durra. Of the fruits were dates, figs, pomegranates, olives, almonds, peaches, and grapes.

For grinding the grain they had a mill of two circular stones, the lower one fixed and the upper one arranged to turn on a pivot. The grinding was done by a woman turning the upper stone by a handle, the grain being poured through an opening in the center of the upper stone so as to get between the stones to be crushed and ground. The same kind

[8] Wilkinson, Manners and customs of ancient Egyptians, II, 331.
[9] *Ibid.*, II, 22.

of a mill was made on a larger scale and turned by animals. The better classes used bread made from wheat while the poorer people used cakes of barley or durra flour.

Dinner probably came at midday and supper in the evening. It would seem that they washed before the meal as well as after partaking of it. A napkin was presented to each person for wiping the mouth after drinking. It was their custom to sit together about a table at their meals, as we do now. Men and women sat together, although sometimes the sexes were entertained separately in a different part of the room, on which occasion the master and the mistress of the house sat close together on two chairs or on a double chair at the upper end of the room. Water, cooled in porous bottles, or wine was served to the guests. Knives were used for the carving of a large joint and spoons were provided the guests, for soups and other liquids, but they did not have knives or forks, so they ate with their fingers, each one dipping his bread into a dish placed in their midst, one after another according to rank as guests.

"The Egyptians, a scrupulously religious people, were never remiss in expressing their gratitude for the blessings they enjoyed, and in returning thanks to the gods for that peculiar protection they were thought to extend to them and to their country, above all nations of the earth. They therefore never sat down to meals without saying grace; and Josephus says that when the seventy-two elders were invited by Ptolemy Philadelphus to sup at the palace, Nicanor requested Eleazer to say grace for his countrymen, instead of those Egyptians, to whom that duty was committed on other occasions." [10]

"It was a custom of the Egyptians, during (or according to Herodotus after) their repasts, to introduce a wooden image of Osiris, from one foot and a half to three feet in height, in the form of a human mummy, standing erect, as Plutarch informs us, in a case, or lying on a bier, and to show it to each of the guests, warning him of his mortality, and of the transitory nature of human pleasures. He was reminded that some day he would be like that figure; that men ought 'to love one another, and avoid those evils which tend to make them consider life too long, when in reality it is too short'; and while enjoying the blessings of this world, to bear in mind that their existence was precarious, and that

[10] Wilkinson, Popular account of ancient Egyptians, I, 186.

death, which all ought to be prepared to meet, must eventually close their earthly career."[11]

Wine was their favorite beverage and they had several different kinds of it. They indulged in it very freely and there were no restrictions on its use by individuals. It was used by all classes of the people, by the priests, furnished to soldiers, offered to the gods, and prescribed as medicine. Women, both young and old, were permitted to have wine, and it would appear as if there were no restrictions as to their use of it.

The Egyptians also had beer, which was made from barley, and as they did not grow hops they used lupins, skirret, and an Assyrian root for flavoring it.[12] "Besides beer, the Egyptians had what Pliny calls factitious, or artificial, wine, extracted from various fruits, as figs, *myxas*, pomegranates, as well as herbs, some of which were selected for their medicinal properties."[13]

There were excesses in drinking committed by people of all classes, both men and women. At the banquets of the rich stimulants were sometimes used to excite to further drinking, the cabbage having been one of the vegetables used for such purpose.

**Food and Clothing of Children.** Swaddling clothes do not seem to have been used by the Egyptians as they were among the Jews and some other nations. If the child could not walk, he was carried by the nurse or mother before her or at her side, in a shawl thrown around her back over a shoulder. It was the custom, no matter whether the child had little or no clothing on, to have a string of beads about the neck, having occasionally a charm suspended in the center, a symbol of truth and justice. These were for the purpose of keeping ill luck from the child, and to make him wise and virtuous.

"The dresses of children of the lower classes were very simple; and, as Diodorus informs us, the expenses incurred in feeding and clothing them amounted to a mere trifle. 'They feed them,' he says, 'very lightly, and at an incredibly small cost; giving them a little meal of the coarsest and cheapest kind, the pith of the papyrus, baked under the ashes, with

---

[11] Wilkinson, Manners and customs of ancient Egyptians, II, 50.
[12] Wilkinson, Egyptians in time of Pharaoh, 14.
[13] Wilkinson, Popular account of ancient Egyptians I, 54.

the roots and stalks of some marsh weeds, either raw, boiled, or roasted; and since most of them are brought up, on account of the mildness of the climate, without shoes, and indeed without any other clothing, the whole expense incurred by the parents does not exceed 20 drachmæ (about 13 shillings) each; and this frugality is the true reason of the populousness of Egypt.' But the children of the higher orders were often dressed like grown persons, with a loose robe reaching to the ankles, and sandals."[14]

**Industries.** The ancient Egyptians engaged in many industries and reached a high stage in the development of their country and their own powers. The country was immensely rich, as was shown from the objects of luxury found among them, and they loved pomp and splendor. Their accomplishments come to us from the accounts of ancient writers and are depicted through sculptures and paintings found upon the walls of temples, palaces, and tombs, and remains of their work still exist sufficient to show the great things they did.

The life of ancient Egypt depended upon the annual rise of the Nile, caused by the rains and melting of snow on the mountains in the interior of Africa. This rise begins in June, reaches the highest point in September, remains stationary a few days, then recedes, and by December the flood is past. This inundation, spreading over the whole country, left the land covered with a rich dressing so that no further fertilizing was necessary and made ancient Egypt probably the most fertile tract of country in the world. This rising of the Nile produced a line of industries, such as the building of canals and dykes and irrigation works as well as the greatest industry of all, that of agriculture.

Because of the favorable conditions in Egypt, as mentioned above, and the dense population, agriculture was the principal industry. So efficient did the people become in this and the agricultural laborers were so frugal in their mode of living that there was a great surplus of products each year, which gave Egypt advantages which no other country possessed, giving them the balance of trade with other nations. The principal grains were wheat, barley, and durra. Beside these grains they grew beans, peas, and lentils, clovers, lupins, and vetches, flax and cotton, various medicinal herbs, and of vegetables, garlic, leeks, onions,

[14] Wilkinson, Manners and customs of the ancient Egyptians, II, 334.

endive, radishes, melons, cucumbers, and lettuce, in fact, a very large number and a great variety of plants.

As soon as the water began to subside and land to appear, they began preparing to sow the grain. On the highlands right along the river this would generally be in October and the other parts following. The wheat and the barley were sown about November, the barley ordinarily ripening in about four months and the wheat in five. The durra was usually sown about April, as an after-crop when the wheat and the barley had been cut and taken off the ground. The ground was prepared by means of a very rude plow, but more often by the hoe. The seed was sown broadcast over the surface of the land. It would appear as if neither harrow nor rake was used to cover in the grain, but it was left as it fell on the ground to germinate. As was stated before, the water of the overflow of the Nile was carried by means of canals throughout Egypt and retained for irrigating the land. When the land was elevated, as along the banks of the Nile, they used the *shadoof*, a contrivance somewhat like the old well-sweep and bucket, to lift up the water from the river or wells to be poured over the soil. When crops were raised late in the year or on soil not covered by the Nile, they sometimes used fertilizing substances, as nitrous earth and some other kinds of dressing. In harvesting the wheat was cut a little ways below the grain with a toothed sickle and placed in baskets and carried to the threshing-floor, on which it was deposited and cattle driven over it to tread out the grain. It was then winnowed with wooden shovels and put in sacks and taken to the granary.

Of the domestic animals were cattle, sheep, goats, hogs, horses, asses, camels, cats, and dogs. The cat was a favorite animal among the ancient Egyptians. They never allowed a cat to be killed purposely, cared for them when ill, and embalmed them when dead. Dogs also were well considered by them and they had several breeds of them. They had learned the artificial process of hatching eggs and built ovens expressly for that purpose. There were great flocks of sheep and they were well taken care of, great attention having been given to their proper food in the various seasons and they were carefully treated when ill. The skill of the Egyptians in curing animals had reached a high stage.

Hunting was an industry as well as an amusement. There were quite a number of different animals that they hunted.

They used the bow and arrow and other weapons and also the net, which in hunting large animals was placed across ravines and the like to keep them from escaping. They hunted with dogs and they even had cats trained to hunt with. The Egyptians were expert fowlers, using for the most part nets and traps for catching the birds. The Nile was celebrated for its fish and fishing was an important industry. The net was greatly used in fishing and the rod and line and spear were also used. Salted as well as fresh fish were used as food.

There were a great number of people engaged in manufactures and many different trades were found among the ancient Egyptians. Whether each one was compelled by law to follow the trade of his father, it is probable that most of them did, so that often they were able to trace back the occupation in the family for many generations. It is probable that each craft had its own particular part of the city set aside for it wherein its members dwelt and carried on their particular work and which was called after it, as, the quarter of the goldsmiths, and so on. The workmen became very proficient in their work and a number of inventions were made which are the same as we have now, among some of the implements invented being the forceps, bellows, blow-pipe, and siphon.

They were celebrated for their manufacture of cloths, having made such of cotton, wool, and linen. They were woven on hand looms, some of which were vertical and others horizontal and must have been of considerable size, as they wove cloth five feet wide and at least sixty feet in length. The spinning and weaving was the work of women, although men did sometimes engage in this work. They colored the cloths, using dyes and paints, and varied the colors in them, making patterns and showing figures of animals and the like. Whether they understood the principle of the action of mordants, they used this agency to make the cloth take the color equally and also to change the hues.

Glass was known to the Egyptians and from it they made bottles, vases, and other utensils, beads and other ornaments, and they were quite skillful in the use of glass in counterfeiting the amethyst and other precious stones. They had glazed ware a long time before they used glass. There were quite a large number of people engaged in pottery work and they were quite skillful in the manufacture of this ware.

There were many varieties and forms of their work and it included rough unglazed ware up to fine glazed vases, highly decorated and colored. There were bottles not only of glass and earthenware but also of leather and of stone and there were glass bottles enclosed in wicker-work and others encased in leather. There were all kinds of vases, earthenware, stone, bronze, alabaster, glass, porcelain, ivory, bone, silver, and gold. Some of the vases were most beautiful in make and design, inlaid with precious stones and tastefully ornamented.

There was quite an industry in metal working among them. There was probably very little of any kinds of metals found in Egypt, having been brought in from other countries. Gold was early used for the making of ornaments. They soon found a way of hardening gold by alloying it with silver. They learned to work gold in various ways. They cast it into figures, molded it into beads by pressure, soldered it, drew it out into wire, used it in plaiting, beat it out into sheets for gilding, engraved it and inlaid it with precious stones. Silver came into use later than gold and in early times it was scarcer than gold. Copper was greatly in use among the ancient Egyptians and by alloying it with tin produced bronze. They made many utensils and implements of it and learned to make it so hard as to be used for wood-cutting tools and chisels for cutting limestone. Lead was used by them, as was also tin and antimony. Iron was perhaps used in the early times, but it would appear that it was not greatly in use till the time of the Greeks and the Romans in Egypt.

They were quite skillful in working in wood and there was a large class of wood-workers, divided into carpenters, cabinet-makers, wheelwrights, coopers, coffin-makers, and boat-builders. There was quite a good deal more wood in Egypt in ancient times than now and yet not a great variety. The principal trees were the date-palm, used for beams; the Theban palm, used for rafts, and other purposes connected with water, and for beams and rafters; the sycamore, used for large planks for boxes, tables, doors, and the like; the tamarisk, a hard and compact wood, used for the handles of tools and wooden implements; and the acacia, used for planks and masts of boats. For ornamental purposes and where fine woods were required, they were brought in from other countries, as, the cedar, cypress, cherry, walnut, and deal from Syria, and ebony and other rare woods from Ethiopia.

Wood was used for buildings and parts of buildings, for furniture, boxes, barrels, chariots, traveling cars, palanquins, coffins, statues, statuettes, and in boat-building. "Regarding the methods of woodworking, certainly the axe was the primitive tool, as shown by the royal architect being designated by the axe. In the scenes of the pyramid age we find the saw about three feet long worked with both hands, the mallet and chisel for cutting mortise-holes, and the adze in constant use for shaping and for smoothing wood. To this day the small adze is a favorite tool of the Egyptian carpenter and boat-builder. For smoothing down the caulking inside a boat, heavy pounders of stone were used, held by a handle worked out on each side of the block. Drills were also commonly used both on wood and stone, worked by a bow."[15]

As they had only the hand-saw, in making planks they usually placed the piece of timber upright and fastened it to stakes and then sawed downward through it. In joining two boards end to end, they would cut into their ends and join them and glue them and then insert a flat wooden pin through them from edge to edge and then pass a round wooden pin through the boards into the flat pin, thus effectually keeping the joints from opening and thereby showing the thoroughness of their work. They dovetailed and veneered and stained and painted and gilded and inlaid their woodwork, thus displaying a high degree of skill in working with wood.

One of the greatest industries with them was that of brickmaking, which was wholly under the control of the government and carried on solely by it. "The use of crude bricks baked in the sun was universal throughout the country for private and for many public buildings, and the dry climate of Egypt was peculiarly suited to those simple materials. They had the recommendation of cheapness, and even of durability; and those made 3,000 years ago, whether with or 'without straw,' are even now as firm and fit for use as when first put up in the reigns of the Amunophs and Thothmes, whose names they bear. When made of the Nile mud, or alluvial deposit, they required straw to prevent their cracking; but those formed of clay (now called *Háybeh*) taken from the torrent beds on the edge of the desert, held together without straw; and crude brick walls frequently had the addi-

---

[15] Petrie, Arts and crafts of ancient Egypt, 140.

tional security of a layer of reeds or sticks placed at intervals to act as binders."[16]

The tanning and preparation and use of leather was quite a leading industry of ancient Egypt, so much so that a section of the city of Thebes was set apart for the exclusive use of the workers in skins and leather. The demand for leather was so great Egypt itself could not supply the hides necessary and great quantities of hides were imported from foreign countries and also the skins of wild animals were brought in and used. They tanned the skins and dyed them and made some fine leather and also embossed the leather.

The tools used for working in leather were a semi-circular knife, a sort of chisel, an awl, a stone for polishing, cutting table, bending form, hone, and a few others. They made shoes, sandals, coverings and seats for chairs and sofas, bowcases, ornaments and harness for chariots, and adornments for harps. Skins were used to cover shields and other things and they were shaped into forms for carrying water, wine, and other liquids. They made thongs by twisting leather strips together, cutting the strips from circular pieces of leather as is done now.

The Egyptians were famed for their manufacture of paper, which was made from the papyrus plant. This grew almost altogether in Lower Egypt, on marshy land or in the ponds left after the inundation of the Nile. The right of growing and selling it belonged to the government and the particular species from which the paper was made was closely guarded and perhaps not allowed to grow anywhere else than in the restricted territory in the Delta. The paper was made by removing the outer covering of the stalk, cutting the interior lengthwise into thin pieces and laying these together side by side on a flat board and across them another layer, cementing the strips together with a kind of glue, then putting all under pressure, and after drying the paper was completed and ready for use.

The paper made from the papyrus differed in quality according to the growth of the plant and from which part of the stalk the pieces were taken, the stalk growing to about fifteen feet in height. The breadth of the paper differed, running from six inches under an early Dynasty to fourteen and a half inches under a later Dynasty. When a sheet of papyrus had been used for writing, it was rolled up, and if

[16] Wilkinson, Popular account of the ancient Egyptians, II, 194.

important and to be preserved for any length of time, tied round the middle and secured by clay stamps with a seal. The cost of the papyrus was so great that it was used only in funeral rituals, conveyances, deeds, and other public documents, and sometimes the old writing was erased and then the roll was written on again. For ordinary purposes of writing, pieces of broken pottery, stone, board, and leather were used.

The Nile traversing the entire length of Egypt formed a great avenue for trade, as it was an open and easy way for reaching all parts. Not only did the Nile give access to all parts about it, but also the canals going out from it and running parallel with it connected the various parts and gave ready ways on which domestic trade could go. The other nations bordering the Mediterranean Sea carried on important maritime trade with Egypt and, too, there was a great caravan trade with the interior of Africa and parts of Asia. From Ethiopia came gold, ivory, and slaves; from Arabia was obtained an incense necessary in the religious ceremonies; from India were received spices. "Syria took Egyptian chariots by hundreds; Tyre imported 'fine linen with broidered work'; Greece, large quantities of paper; India and Arabia, linen fabrics; Etruria, glass, porcelain, and alabaster; Assyria, perhaps, ivories. In the earlier times Egyptian manufactures must have been altogether unrivalled; and their glass, their pottery, their textile fabrics, their metalwork, must have circulated freely through the various countries bordering the Mediterranean and the Red Sea."[17]

Among the important industries of Egypt were the works in sculpture, painting, and architecture. The men engaged in these occupations ranked high, along with the scribes.

There were three kinds of sculpture in ancient Egypt. One kind was that of statuary, sculpture in the round, where the complete figure was shown; a second kind was relief, where the figure was raised from the flat surface by cutting away the stone about it; the third kind was intaglio, in which there was a cutting of the figure into the flat surface, sinking the figure below the surface, and in one form of this the cutting was done about the figure so as to leave it raised from the interior, almost up to the level of the surface of the stone.

The old Egyptians reached a stage of progress in which the

[17] Rawlinson, History of ancient Egypt, I, 496.

block of stone for the sculpture figure was cut away from the original rock and transported to the place where it was to stand. Yet the figure was rarely if ever cut entirely away from the stone and so did not stand forth separate, detached, a statute in and of itself. That which most kept Egyptians sculpture, perhaps, from reaching to the highest attainment was the conventionality in the displaying of figures. As the sculptures were used in the decoration of tombs and temples, religion, which is ever conservative, prescribed certain attitudes for the figures, so that there was not much left for the working out by the individual sculptor, and although there was an exactness of finish attained there was not that expression which comes through allowing freedom to the individual sculptor, and in consequence there is very much of a sameness in the products of the sculptors running through the twenty centuries of old Egypt.

As with sculpture so with painting, the conventional forms were demanded of the painter so that although mechanical skill became great, there was not that high artistic effect that is attained where individuality is permitted to display itself. The walls of buildings were not broken by windows, as the brilliancy of light was such that few openings were necessary and the openings let in heat. The walls on the interior were covered with a coating of stucco, which was white or whitish, and then decorated with paintings displaying scenes and events in the life of the people and the nation. The ceilings were also painted. The colors used were black and white, red, blue, and yellow, green and brown. Columns and other parts of buildings were also stuccoed and painted and even the same was done with statues and other products of the sculptors.

The early buildings in Egypt were made of brick or by the interweaving of palm-sticks. From these rude structures to the great temples and pyramids makes the architecture of that country a most marked feature of its progress. The architecture of Egypt in its rectangular form and massiveness fits well into the nature of the land, which frames plain and cliff about these buildings as a proper background. Yet size is not so much the essential characteristic of this architecture but rather strength and durability, which were the chief features of the structures, whether large or small. Although they were familiar with the arch and used it very much in brickwork, yet it would appear that it was not used in the great buildings of stone, or, if so, it was hid in the building and kept away from the external forms.[18]

The kinds of stone used in sculpture and architecture were limestone, sandstone, granite, basalt, alabaster, and diorite. The stone was cut out in blocks from the quarry, the surfaces were picked smooth with a short adze, the blocks were then sawn and cut with drills, and probably all prepared at the quarry ready for use at the building. Sand was used as the cutting material with the soft stones and emery with the harder ones. Whether the cutting material was used as powder or set as separate teeth on the copper saw blade cannot be determined, yet in some instances it would appear that the emery was set in the tool as teeth. The great problem to us is how these stones were transported from the quarries and set up in their places. One obelisk is estimated to have weighed 886 tons and it was taken over-land a distance of 138 miles. Some of the obelisks of seventy to eighty feet in length and weighing near 300 tons each were conveyed a distance of more than 800 miles.[19] Two great collossi, weighing 1,175 tons each, were carried upstream a distance of 450 miles.[20] It would appear that sometimes the stone were placed on sleds and drawn by oxen down to the river, where by an inclined plane they were placed on vessels, while again these blocks were hauled by large bodies of men over-land to their places of destination.

The greatest of all their buildings were the Great Temple at Karnak and the Great Pyramid at Ghizeh. The temple at Karnak was 1,200 feet long and 340 feet wide, with an entire area of 396,000 square feet, and with pylons, obelisks, and columns, and it is called "the greatest of man's architectural works." The Great Pyramid at Ghizeh has a square base the length of each side of which is 764 feet, covering an area of about twelve acres. Its original perpendicular height is estimated at about 485 feet. "The solid masonry which it contained is estimated at more than 89,000,000 cubic feet, and the weight of the mass at 6,848,000 tons. The basement stones are many of them thirty feet in length and nearly five feet high. Altogether the edifice is the largest and most massive building in the world, and not only so, but *by far* the largest and most massive—the building which

---

[18] Petrie, Arts and crafts of ancient Egypt, 6.
[19] Wilkinson, Manners and customs of ancient Egypt, II, 306.
[20] Petrie, *op. cit.*, 26.

approaches it the nearest being the Second Pyramid, which contains 17,000,000 cubic feet less, and is very much inferior in the method of its construction."[21]

**Sickness and Death.** It would appear that the study and practice of medicine began at a very early time in Egypt. Principles and remedies were given out from time to time till finally they were brought together in the form of medical works and all physicians were expected to study them and to use the prescribed remedies. The medical skill of the Egyptians became known to other parts of the world and they were consulted and called to foreign countries to give advice and treatment. They went so far as to divide the study and practice of medicine into specialties and so there were physicians attending to one kind of illness only, as, one for the diseases of the eyes, another for the diseases of the intestines, and so on, accoucheurs having been usually, if not always, women. The physicians were given salaries by the government and fixed by it and also they were permitted to receive fees for their advice and attendance upon patients, but when in military service they could not charge fees.

On account of the glaring light and the sandy plains and the overflow of the Nile, some of the prominent troubles were of the eyes and such as were connected with malaria. In treatment of illness, it was held that the patient had been attacked by some evil influence, hence to cure him was first necessary to find what was the nature of this evil spirit and to drive it out or to destroy it. This was the task of those skilled in sorcery, through incantations, amulets, and the like. Then the diseases that had been carried into the body by the evil influences were to be cured by medicine and medical treatment. Physicians were held responsible for their treatment of a disease and if contrary to the established system they were punished and the death of a patient under such circumstances was considered a capital offense. Yet if they had exhausted all the prescribed remedies without producing good effect, they could prescribe new remedies and hence an opportunity for advancement in the science of medicine. In their practice they strove to prevent illness by directing attention to regimen and diet; they purged the system by use of emetics or clysters; and they used drugs and medical herbs.

When a death occurred, all the women of the household

[21] Rawlinson, History of ancient Egypt, I, 204.

covered their faces with dust and mud and with bosoms exposed ran out through the streets, striking themselves and uttering loud cries of grief. Friends and relatives joined the procession and the demonstrations became the louder. If the deceased person had been of wide repute, many other people went into the line of mourners and hired mourners were employed to increase the lamentations and thereby enlarge the public display of respect to the dead. For seventy-two days the mourning was carried on in the house, lamentations were made, the funeral dirge was sung, all amusements and indulgences were abstained from, and the men allowed their hair and beard to grow. Thus they endeavored to show respect to the deceased and their great affliction by his departure.

One of the great arts of the ancient Egyptians was that of embalming. It constituted a distinct profession. The embalmers had wooden models of mummies, displaying the three different ways of embalming. The first way of embalming was very expensive and was used only by the wealthy class and people of high position; the second way was more simple and quite less expensive and used by the middle class of people; the third way was very simple and very cheap and employed by the lower classes. After embalming the body was returned to the family and put into a case and placed in a room upright against the wall, and sometimes they were retained by the family for quite a while before their burial.

When the time for burial came, the mummy was put into a coffin of wood or stone to be placed in a tomb, which may have been hewn in the rock or built up of brick or rock and usually on the western side of the Nile. Some of the tombs were of great extent and highly ornamented with paintings and sculptures and some were immense structures. The pyramids were built for tombs. The funeral of any important personage was a great occasion. There was much display and much noisy lamentations and it was very costly. Upon reaching the Nile the body was placed on the funeral barge and the procession went out on the river to the lake of the dead. Before the deceased could be taken across the lake for burial he had to meet the tribunal of death. Forty-two judges were at the bank of the lake and any one could bring accusation against the deceased. The judges considered the accusation and acted upon it and if the decision was acquittal then burial in the tomb took place, but if the accusation was sustained burial was denied. The judgment was carried out on the body of any person in the country, high or low, rich or poor, the meanest subject or a Pharaoh, and there are instances of deceased Pharaohs having been denied public burial.

"All the legitimate tendencies exerted by this singular institution were obviously for good. It sent forth from the very entrance of the tomb a most powerful persuasive to live a life of virtue. It appealed to some of the strongest of human motives, and enforced that appeal by the severest of all sanctions, the exclusion of the body from its sepulchre, and of the soul from the abodes of the blessed. It is not a little singular that a custom apparently so salutary, and so early introduced, should not afterwards have been adopted by other nations."[22]

**Child and Religion.** The child played a part in the religion of the ancient Egyptians. Even one of their gods, Harpocrates, was represented by an infant, having his finger to his mouth and that striking characteristic of a young child —a protruding abdomen. The birth of a child was a matter for thanksgiving offerings through the priests to the gods. Herodotus says: "When parents, living in town, perform vows for the recovery of their children's health, they offer prayers to the deity of whom the animal is sacred, and then shaving a portion, or half, or the whole of the child's head, they put the hair into one scale of the balance and money into the other until the latter outweighs the former; they then give it to the person who takes care of the animal to buy fish (or other food)."[23]

On some occasions when the sacred bull was led in procession through the town, the procession was led by children, and on such occasions it was thought that these children received the gift of foretelling future events. Wilkinson gives the following from Plutarch: "They even look upon children as gifted with a kind of faculty of divination, and they are ever anxious to observe the accidental prattle they talk during play, especially if it be in a sacred place, deducing from it presages of future events."[24]

**Amusements.** In the earlier times of ancient Egypt, as of all nations, when the struggle for living required the putting

[22] Dean, History of civilization, I, 381.
[23] Wilkinson, Manners and customs of ancient Egyptians, III, 243.
[24] Ibid., II, 455.

forth of the energies and but little leisure was allowed, there was not much time for recreation and the people were not much given to amusements. As wealth grew and there was leisure time, the desire for amusement and entertainment increased until there grew up in the Egyptian character a softness and inclination to luxurious living. Great banquets were given, where hosts vied with one another in entertaining lavishly and in furnishing amusement for the guests, till it would appear as if they devised every possible kind of amusement. Nor was the zest for amusement confined to the upper classes, for during the inundation of the Nile, when but little work could be done, the peasantry gave themselves up to pastime and sport. Many of the kinds of entertainment given at the banquets were performed on the streets and open places.

Dancing was an indispensable entertainment at an Egyptian party and music was required with the dance. They danced to the music of the harp, lyre, guitar, pipe, tambourine, and other instruments, and in the streets also to the drum. Dancing was not done by the guests, as it was held not to be proper for the upper classes to dance, although the lower classes indulged in this amusement and greatly enjoyed it. The dancing was carried on before the guests by slaves taught the steps for that purpose or by hired performers who made a profession of furnishing dancing and music for festive occasions. Graceful posings and movements and especial skill and grace in the use of the hands were the important features of the dance. Both men and women danced for hire, the women showing the superior grace and elegance and the men displaying the most spirit. The dress of the female dancers was usually a loose flowing robe, reaching to the ankles, fastened at the waist, and around the hips was a small narrow girdle of various colors and ornamented with beads. The material of the dress was of a very fine texture and thin, showing the form and movement of the limbs in dancing.

There were various ways of dancing. Sometimes one person danced alone, sometimes they danced in pairs, again there were several dancers together sometimes of both sexes and then of but one sex. Some danced to slow music, while others preferred lively tunes, men sometimes displaying great spirit, bounding from the ground. The aim of the dance was to display a succession of figures in which were exhibited a great variety of gestures. Twirling was much used in dancing and the pirouette was quite a favorite form with them. In one dance two parties would each dance on one leg toward one another and perform a series of evolutions and then retire from one another. In another step, standing on one foot the dancer would strike the ground with the heel, changing back and forth from one foot to the other. The dances of the lower classes were sometimes in the form of a pantomime, in which there was a preference shown for the ludicrous rather than the graceful.

Music was very popular with the Egyptians and they had both vocal and instrumental. They had numerous songs and for various occasions. They had quite a variety of musical instruments. Music was used in military movements, in religious exercises, in their social functions, and in the wailing for the dead. Music formed a part of the education of a member of the upper classes, but he did not display this at social functions, as that, like dancing, was given over to professionals. Both men and women of the priestly order, though, did render service with voice and instrument in religious ceremonies.

"It is sufficiently evident, from the sculptures of the ancient Egyptians, that their hired musicians were acquainted with the triple symphony; the harmony of instruments, of voices, and of voices and instruments. Their band was variously composed, consisting either of two harps, with the single pipe and flute; of the harp and double pipe, frequently with the addition of the guitar; of a fourteen-stringed harp, a guitar, lyre, double pipe, and tambourine; of two harps, sometimes of different sizes, one of seven, the other of four strings; of two harps of eight strings, and a seven-stringed lyre; of the guitar, and the square or oblong tambourine; of the lyre, harp, guitar, double pipe, and a sort of harp, with four strings, which was held upon the shoulder; of the harp, guitar, double pipe, lyre, and square tambourine; of the harp, two guitars, and the double pipe; of the harp, two flutes, and a guitar; of two harps and a flute; of a seventeen-stringed lyre, the double pipe, and a harp of fourteen strings; of the harp and two guitars; or of two seven-stringed harps and an instrument held in the hand, not unlike an Eastern fan, to which were probably attached small bells, or pieces of metal that emitted a jingling sound when shaken, like the crescent-crowned *bells* of our modern bands; besides many other combinations of these various instruments; and in the Bacchic festival of Ptolemy Philadelphus, described by Athenæus, more than 600 musicians were employed in the chorus, among whom were 300 performers on the *kithara*."[25]

As was stated before, dwarfs and deformed persons were attached to the households of the greater people as a means of entertainment as in Rome and Medieval Europe. These dwarfs and also others engaged in buffoonery for the entertainment of guests. There were various tricks performed by jugglers, and we find there the old cup or shell game, in which a little ball or pea is rolled about on a board from one inverted cup to another to guess under which it finally rested. There were many kinds of acrobatic feats, mostly performed by women, such as two performers swinging around in a reckless fashion while holding hands. This was varied by two men holding the hands of two women and whirling them around with feet braced together. There were tumbling exhibits of turning forward and backward on the hands, somersaulting off one another's shoulders, and even sometimes doing these feats while holding one foot with a hand. There were tests of strength wherein two men would sit back to back and each strive to rise first from the ground, and in another test they would try who could lift the heaviest weight or raise a bag of sand with a straight arm up over head. They would throw knives at a board, each contestant striving to strike his knife in the center of the board or on a mark.

The most common indoor games were odd and even, mora, and draughts, all of which it would appear were played in Egypt from very ancient times. In odd or even bones, beans, nuts, almonds, and coins were used and any indefinite number was held between the hands, the game being to guess whether odd or even. The game of mora was usually played by two persons, each at the same time quickly throwing out the fingers of one hand, then trying to guess the number of fingers shown by both. Draughts was a favorite game of all ranks. It was played by two people on a board similar to the present checker-board, but the pieces were not flat, being raised, more like the pieces in chess, and picked up like chessmen between thumb and finger. In another game hooked rods were used by which a small hoop was to be snatched from one another, the skill in this was for one per-

[25] Wilkinson, Manners and customs of ancient Egyptians, I, 438.

son to get his hoop loose from his opponent's rod and then snatch it away quickly before he had time to stop it. In one game a player knelt with face toward the ground between two others, who held over him in their closed hands shells or dice, the number of which he was to guess before being allowed to rise. They played with dice and probably played several other games of chance.

Wrestling was a favorite amusement among the lower classes. They fought with the single-stick and among the boatmen of the Nile were conflicts with long poles. Mock fights were common, especially with the military classes, sometimes quite a great affair wherein a temporary fort would be erected and attacked by a party with a battering-ram and other implements of war and vigorously defended by the party within the fort. There were bull fights, sometimes between the animals and again men would fight the bulls. The animals were carefully trained to fight and prizes were awarded to the owner of the victorious combatant. It is pretty certain that animals were taught to perform tricks and to dance.

All classes of the Egyptians delighted in hunting, fowling, and fishing. In hunting they used the bow, the spear, the lasso, and the net to place across enclosures. There were preserves on some of the estates in which animals were kept for hunting, but the greatest sport was hunting out on the desert. Dogs were used and different breeds reared, some for attacking, some for coursing, and the like. Sometimes there would be a great hunt arranged, with beaters for forcing the game into quarters where they could be enclosed with nets and then hunted within. In hunting for birds and water-fowl the real sportsman used only the throwing-stick, which was from a foot and a quarter to two feet in length, about one inch and a half in breadth, and slightly curved at the upper end. The hunter would usually go out in a boat into the places covered with tall reeds and lotuses and gliding swiftly in among the birds, or using a decoy bird to attract them toward him, he would cast the throwing-stick at them as they arose and thus fell them. Often a cat would accompany the hunter which was trained to get the birds as they fell and bring them to the boat. In the pleasure-grounds of villas were ponds well stocked with fish. The fish were caught from them by hook and line. But the real fisherman used the bident spear, which sometimes had feathers at one end, like an arrow, but more often without, and sometimes the spear had a string attached to it to bring it back when thrown. Running his boat over the surface of the water, as he would see a fish he would cast his spear at it. They prided themselves on their skill with the spear.

**Games, Plays, and Toys.** The children and young people among the ancient Egyptians engaged in many sports and they were encouraged in this by their elders, particularly in those activities of an outdoor nature, as they were considered to be conducive to good health through exercise of the body. The young people took part in the singing and other music and at least among the lower classes in the dancing. They went out with their parents and other relatives on fishing trips and bird hunting and the youth went with the men on hunting trips. The youth of both sexes practiced shooting at a target with the bow and arrow.

The game of ball was one of the great games of the Egyptians, participated in by children and adults of both sexes, but it appears to have been more indulged in by the women. Some of the balls were made of leather or skin, sewed with string, and stuffed with bran or husks of corn, some being about three inches in diameter. In one of the favorite games the ball was thrown and caught and the one failing had to carry the other woman who caught it on her back till this one failed to catch it, when she had to do the carrying. The women rode sidewise in short petticoats on the backs of the losers. In another game the ball was thrown as high as possible and the catcher would leap up and catch it before the feet would touch the ground. Again when the ball was thrown to them they would catch it with the hands behind the back and even while standing on one leg.

The playthings of the little child are often found buried with it. They had dolls of various kinds, being made of wood, stone, and enamelled pottery. They often were painted, the inferior ones being the most gaudily colored. Some were of rude construction with head and body and without arms and legs, while others were small models of the human figure. Some were jointed, the arms and legs moving on pins. Some had artificial hair, while others had beads in imitation of hair hanging from the head. Some grotesque figures were formed and by means of strings could be made to assume various postures. One such figure was that of a crocodile which could be made to amuse the child by its grimaces and by the opening and closing of its mouth. Some figures of persons could be made to go through the motions of washing and of kneading dough. One was the figure of a person with jointed arms and legs, which could be thrown about by the pulling of a string, and which still exists with us today in the jumping-jack. They also had pigs, ducks, pigeons on wheels, boats, balls, marbles, and miniature sets of household furniture.

**Education.** The ancient Egyptians were very much interested in the education of the young. It would appear that the parent was left entire freedom in the selecting what education and how much the child should have. In the matter of education there seemed to be no caste whatever, as the poor boy and son of one of the lower classes could take his place in school by the side of the rich boy or the son of the noble.

A clever boy in school had great opportunities, be he from whatever class of society. He was encouraged to go on to literary life, which meant, if successful, entering into the employ of the government and reaching the very highest places. Many a great nobleman so arose in Egypt and often was found on his monument after his death: "His ancestors were unknown people."

There were elementary schools, probably none provided by the state, and whether there were schools or not in a community, there were teachers to be had for the instruction of the young. With the temples were connected higher schools and in the capitals of the three districts of Egypt, Thebes, Memphis, Heliopolis, the temple schools were quite important centers of learning. The child started into the elementary school at near five years of age and continued till he left for work, or to enter a higher school, or else he might have gone into the office of a scribe or physician or architect to learn directly the work of his profession. The vast majority of the children received very little training beyond the rudiments of education and what instruction was given to them by their parents in teaching them their trades. Some of the young people continued with their schooling and entered the schools of the temples and there came in contact with the learned men of the state and received a higher education. A very few of these, who displayd special aptitude for learning, were permitted to enter into the deeper studies and to whom was thrown open all the knowledge possessed by the wisest men of their day. Little is known about the education of girls. As the women ranked high in Egypt and took part in the public festivities and religious ceremonies, they must have received such education as would prepare them for their duties in life.

The purpose of education in ancient Egypt was to prepare for some one of the callings of priest, scribe, architect, engineer, physician, soldier, musician, artisan. It was necessary to be educated to enter into office and to rise in position. Thus the education was of a utilitarian nature. The most important calling outside the priesthood was that of the scribe. The scribe learned about official documents and the management of business and to read and write the three forms of writing—hieroglyphic, hieratic, demotic—and also he studied ethics, philosophy, and law. The architect studied mathematics and science and the history that would give him a knowledge of art. The physician was taught such anatomy and physiology as was known, remedies and incantations, and other things pertaining to his calling. Whatever may be considered about this education, it did give Egypt a high place among the old nations of the world and caused its civilization to continue through many centuries.

In the home and in the school it was impressed on the children to be respectful to their elders. They were taught to be careful of looks and gestures, that such should be of a proper kind. It was not permitted to use any dance or ode at the feasts and sacrifices that had not been passed on by the proper authorities. The children were not permitted to hear or to learn any verses or songs than such as were of a virtuous giving character.

The discipline in school was quite severe. One teacher spoke thus: "The hawk is taught to fly and the pigeon to nest; I shall teach you your letters, you idle villain."[26] A pedagogical saying runs: "A young fellow has a back, he hears when we strike it."

"Plato says the Egyptians taught numbers to children in their play by distributing amongst them a certain number of fruits, or other things, the same number to be given to many or to few children, so that by dividing them amongst themselves they learnt lessons in arithmetic; and all sorts of numbers were given to them in their games and plays as arithmetical problems."[27]

[26] Laurie, Historical survey of pre-Christian education, 47.
[27] Wilkinson, Manners and customs of ancient Egyptians, II, 489.

For written work they had wooden blocks covered with red or white stucco. Copies were engraved on wooden or stone tablets and then the children copied them on their tablets. Work was also given by dictation. The older pupils wrote from dictation, or from copies, extracts from the best writers. This trained also in penmanship and spelling. Often the pupils copied an "instruction," which consisted of moral precepts of an ancient writer. Often the instruction consisted of letters between student and teacher.

## LITERATURE

1. Brugsch-Bey, Henry, A history of Egypt under the Pharaohs.
2. Dean, Amos, A history of civilization.
3. Graves, Frank Pierrepont, A history of education, Before the middle ages.
4. Laurie, S. S., Historical survey of pre-Christian education.
5. Maspero, G., Life in ancient Egypt and Assyria.
6. Maspero, G., The dawn of civilization.
7. Petrie, W. M. Flinders, Arts and crafts of ancient Egypt.
8. Rawlinson, George, History of ancient Egypt.
9. Wilkinson, Sir J. Gardner, A popular account of the ancient Egyptians.
10. Wilkinson, Sir J. Gardner, The Egyptians in the time of the Pharaohs.
11. Wilkinson, Sir J. Gardner, The manners and customs of the ancient Egyptians.

## CHAPTER IV

### THE CHILD IN INDIA

**Caste.** The caste system in India was the most fixed of any of the nations. In this way the natural divisions into which mankind placed itself in a free country was not allowed, but fixed and hereditary classes were formed. There were four principal classes: The Brahmans, the priests; the Kshatriyas, the warriors; the Vaisyas, the farmers and traders; the Sudras, the laborers. Below these was a class of the very lowest.

There was very little opportunity for a member of one caste going into a higher, so that an impulse for higher striving was of no avail, and if ever such came to a member of a lower caste it must have soon died away. This entailed especial disadvantages upon the children, for a boy's whole situation in life depended upon the class to which the father belonged and, consequently, his occupation and education. This rigid caste system might have brought contentment to the people, as there was no use of being discontented with one's lot, but such contentment could not bring great progress.

**Women and Marriage.** In the early times in India, women were not excluded as they were later, but they were honored and respected. They were considered as the intellectual companion of the husband, as helper in the daily life, and as partaker in the religious duties. They attended the courts and assemblies and public entertainments, being permitted to appear freely and openly on public occasions. The change took place when they were conquered by the Moslems, from whom the custom of the exclusion of women was learned by the Hindus or was thrust upon them.

The Code of Manu some three centuries before Christ set the status of woman thus, "During her childhood a woman depends on her father; during her youth, on her husband; her husband being dead, on her sons; if she has no sons, on the near relatives of her husband; or if in default of them, on those of her father; if she has no paternal relatives, on the sovereign. A woman ought never to have her own way." So it is no wonder that the wife was treated by the husband in the harshest manner and she to respond with the greatest humility. The following from a witness of a hundred or more years ago, portrays some of the relations which women bore to the opposite sex:

"The women, on the other hand, are so thoroughly accustomed to harsh and domineering treatment from their husbands that they would be quite annoyed if the husbands adopted a more familiar tone. I once knew a native lady who complained bitterly that her husband sometimes affected to be devoted to her in public and allowed himself such little familiarities as are looked upon by us as marks of affection. 'Such behavior,' said she, 'covers me with shame and confusion. I dare not show myself anywhere. Did anyone ever see such bad manners amongst people of our caste? Has he become a Feringhi (European), and does he take me for one of their vile women?'

"As a rule a husband addresses his wife in terms which show how little he thinks of her. *Servant, slave*, etc., and other equal flattering appellations, fall quite naturally from his lips.

"A woman, on the other hand, never addresses her husband except in terms of the greatest humility. She speaks to him as *my master, my lord,* and even sometimes *my god.* In her awe of him she does not venture to call him by his name; and should she forget herself in this way in a moment of anger, she would be thought a very low class of person, and would lay herself open to personal chastisement from her offended spouse. She must be just as particular in speaking of him to anyone else; indeed, the Hindus are very careful never to put a woman under the necessity of mentioning her husband by name. If by chance a European, who is unacquainted with this point of etiquette, obliges her to do so, he will see her blush and hide her face behind her *sari* and turn away without answering, smiling at the same time with contemptuous pity at such ignorance.

"But if women enjoy very little consideration in private life, they are in some degree compensated by the respect which is paid to them in public. They do not, it is true, receive those insipid compliments which we have agreed to consider polite; but then, on the other hand, they are safe from the risk of insult. A Hindu woman can go anywhere alone, even in the most crowded places, and she need never fear the impertinent looks and jokes of idle loungers. This appears to me to be really remarkable in a country where the moral depravity of the inhabitants is carried to such lengths. A house inhabited solely by women is a sanctuary which the most shameless libertine would not dream of violating. To touch a respectable woman even with the end of your finger would be considered highly indecorous, and a man who meets a female acquaintance in the street does not venture to stop and speak to her."[1]

Courtesans in India, as in Greece, if of great beauty and accomplishments, were accorded many more privileges than the other women. As these were used in the temples, they were permitted to learn to read and to sing and to dance, accomplishments which a respectable woman would have been ashamed to have acknowledged even if she should have learned them.

In the early times, during the Vedic period, it would seem that the girls had some choice in the selection of the husband, and yet the father must have exercised some control over the affair. But later the selection of both bride and groom was fast fixed in the hands of the parents, who arranged everything. With the young man's family the purity of the caste of the future wife was the greatest concern, beauty and personal attraction counting nothing, while the girl's parents thought more of the fortune of the bridegroom to be and of the character of his mother, because she was to become the absolute mistress of the young wife. Intermarriage between castes was not strictly forbidden, but a woman could not marry a man of lower caste without losing caste.

"To a Hindu marriage is the most important and most engrossing event of his life; it is a subject of endless conversation and of the most prolonged preparations. An unmarried man is looked upon as having no social status and as being an almost useless member of society. He is not consulted on any important subject, and no work of any consequence may be given to him. A Hindu who becomes a widower finds himself in almost the same position as a bachelor, and speedily remarries.

"Though marriage is considered the natural state for the generality of men, those who from pious motives remain unmarried are looked up to and treated with the utmost re-

[1] Dubois, Hindu manners, customs, and ceremonies, 339.

spect. But it is only those persons who have renounced the world, and have chosen to lead a life of contemplation, who can take vows of celibacy. In any other case marriage is the rule, and every one is under obligation of discharging *the great debt to his ancestors,* namely, that of begetting a son.

"But this privilege men possess of remaining single, and giving themselves up to a life of contemplation, is not shared by women. They at all events cannot, under any circumstances, take vows of celibacy. Subjected on all sides to the moral ascendancy of man, the very idea that they could possibly place themselves in a state of independence and out of men's power is not allowed to cross their minds. The opinion is firmly established throughout the whole of India, that women were only created for the propagation of the species, and to satisfy men's desires. All women therefore are obliged to marry, and marriages are carefully arranged before they arrive at a marriageable age." [2]

There were eight kinds of marriages described in the law, the Institutes of Manu: "Of which one half are honorable, and differ from one another only in some minute circumstances; in the fifth, the bridegroom bestows gifts upon the bride, her father, and paternal kinsman; the last three are rather species of unlawful connection, than forms of nuptial contract; one being voluntary and by mutual consent; the other forcible when a woman is seized, 'while she weeps and calls for assistance, after her kinsmen and friends have been slain in battle'; the last, 'when the damsel is sleeping, or flushed with strong liquor, or disordered in her intellect.'" [3]

The following verses from the Rig Veda, a very ancient Aryan collection of hymns, belonging to the Hindus, give the ceremony of marriage in those olden times:

"21. O Visvâvasu! (god of marriage), arise from this place, for the marriage of this girl is over. We extol Visvâvasu with hymns and prostrations. Go to some other maiden who is still in her father's house and has attained the signs of the age of marriage. She will be your share, know of her.

"22. O Visvâvasu! arise from this place. We worship thee, bending in adoration. Go to an unmarried maiden whose

---

[2] Dubois, Hindu manners, 205.
[3] Mills, British India, I, 308.

person is well developed; make her a wife and unite her to a husband.

"23. Let the paths by which our friends go in quest of a maiden for marriage be easy and free of thorns. May Aryaman and Bhaga lead us well. O gods! may the husband and wife be well united.

"24. O maiden! the graceful sun had fastened thee with ties (of maidenhood), we release thee now of those ties. We place thee with thy husband in a place which is the home of truth and the abode of righteous actions.

"25. We release this maiden from this place (her father's house), but not from the other place (her husband's house). We unite her well with the other place. O Indra! may she be fortunate and the mother of worthy sons.

"26. May Pûshan lead thee by the hand from this place. May the two Asvins lead thee in a chariot. Go to thy (husband's) house and be the mistress of the house. Be the mistress of all, and exercise thine authority over all in that house.

"27. Let children be born unto thee, and blessings attend thee here. Perform the duties of thy household with care. Unite thy person with the person of this thy husband; exercise thy authority in this thy house until old age.

"40. First Soma accepts thee; then Gandharva accepts thee; Agni is thy third lord; the son of man is the fourth to accept thee.

"41. Soma bestowed this maiden to Gandharva, Gandharva gave her to Agni, Agni has given her to me with wealth and progeny.

"42. O bridegroom and bride! do ye remain here together; do not be separated. Enjoy food of various kinds, remain in your own home, and enjoy happiness in company of your children and grandchildren.

"43. (The bride and bridegroom say), May Prajapati bestow on us children; may Aryaman keep us united till old age. (Address to the bride), O bride! Enter with auspicious signs the home of thy husband. Do good to our male servants and our female servants, and to our cattle.

"44. Be thine eyes free from anger; minister to the happiness of thy husband; do good to our cattle. May thy mind be cheerful; and may thy beauty be bright. Be the mother of heroic sons, and be devoted to the gods. Do good to our male servants and our female servants, and to our cattle.

"45. O Indra! make this woman fortunate and the mother of worthy sons. Let ten sons be born of her, so that there may be eleven men in the family with the husband.

"46. Address to the bride), May thou have influence over thy father-in-law, and over thy mother-in-law, and be as a queen over thy sister-in-law and brother-in-law.

"47. (The bridegroom and bride say), May all the gods unite our hearts; may Mâtarisvan and Dhâtri and the goddess of speech unite us together."[4]

Dubois goes quite fully into the ceremonies and functions of a Brahmin marriage of his time, from which is taken the following extract.[5]

There were four different ways of arranging the preliminaries of a marriage. In the first the father of the bride refused the sum of money to which he was entitled from the young man's parents and he bore all the expenses of the wedding. In the second way the parents of both parties agreed to share all the expenses. In the third way the youth's parents bore all the expenses of the wedding and also paid a sum of money to the father for his daughter. In the fourth method the girl's parents handed her over to the young man's parents to do with her what they would. It is needless to say that the first way was the most honored and respected and the last was most mortifying to the girl's parents and it was used by none but the very poorest.

As soon as the parents of a young man had discovered a suitable girl, when the auguries were favorable, they provided themselves with presents and went and formally asked for her. Then the parents of the girl, at a favorable moment, gave their consent and accepted the presents. Then the priest who presided at public and private ceremonies fixed on a lucky day and great preparations were made. The wedding garments were prepared, the stores for feasts and for presents were got together, and all the many other things needed. A canopy was erected and all the relatives and friends invited.

The marriage ceremony lasted for five days. The first day was the great day, as it was the day on which the most important and solemn ceremonies took place. The gods and the ancestors and other divinities were invited to be present. Then a number of rites and ceremonies were performed, in which the bride and bridegroom, the parents, and guests par-

[4] Dutt, Civilization in ancient India, I, 69.
[5] Dubois, Hindu manners, 214, *et seq.*

took. Near the close of these ceremonies the husband fastened round the neck of the young wife the *tali,* the little gold ornament which all married women wore round their necks, and which performed by the husband showed that henceforth the woman was to be his property. The day was ended with a specially magnificent feast.

Amongst the ceremonies of the second day was the placing of an ornament, covered with gold-leaf or gold paper and entwined with flowers, on the forehead of both husband and wife to avert the effects of the evil eye, the spell which is cast by the looks of jealous or ill-disposed people. On the third day the wife joined in the sacrifice offered by the husband, the only occasion on which a woman could take an active part in any of the sacrifices. The only remarkable ceremony on the fourth day was that the newly married couple rubbed each other's legs three times with powdered saffron, of which Dubois did not understand the meaning and fancied its only object was to kill time, just as Europeans under similar circumstances would spend their time in drinking. The fifth day was chiefly occupied in dismissing the gods and the ancestors and the other divinities that had been invited to the feast. Then followed the distribution of presents. The festivity ended with a solemn procession through the streets, which generally took place at night by torchlight in the midst of squibs and fireworks of all kinds.

A girl's lot after marriage must have been dreadful in many cases, as she became a servant to the mother of her husband, who too often tried in every way to make the young girl miserable. In her husband's home the young wife occupied the back of the house with the other women and she must take the humblest place in this apartment for women. The little girl was scolded quite a great deal and received no, or but little, praise. "I have several times seen young wives shamefully beaten by beastly young husbands who cherished no natural love for them. . . . A child of thirteen was cruelly beaten by her husband in my presence for telling the simple truth, that she did not like so well to be in his house as at her home."[6] Yet, there are here and there bright spots in this dark home life.

Polygamy was practiced in ancient India, and even down to later times, as was true among many other ancient nations, but as a rule it was confined to kings and wealthy lords. It

[6] Ramabai, The high-caste Hindu woman, 47.

was not looked upon with great favor. A person of inferior rank was not allowed to have more than one wife, except in case his wife was barren or had only borne female children, but before he could contract a second marriage he had to obtain the consent of the first wife.

"Women in India have ever been remarkable for their faithfulness and their duteous affection towards their husbands, and female unfaithfulness is comparatively rare."[7] Adultery was looked upon with the greatest detestation in India. Yet the heinousness of the crime was regulated by the caste of the offender, for a man of high caste committing adultery with a woman of low caste was by no means so severely punished as was a man of low caste with a woman of high caste. In case the man was a Sudra and the woman of one of the three higher castes he suffered capital punishment, but as on no account was a Brahmin to be punished with death, this offence could not bring it to him.

"Although no law has ever said so, the popular belief is that a woman can have no salvation unless she be formally married."[8] Perhaps for this belief parents became extremely anxious when their daughters were over eight or nine years of age and were unsought in marriage. This was so strong it frequently happened that poor parents feeling that their daughters must be married would marry girls of eight or nine to men of sixty or seventy. In the early times child marriages were unknown, but later boys among the Brahmins married at about sixteen years of age and girls generally at five or seven or, at the utmost, nine years of age. One author states that among the Brahmins, if any girl remained unmarried until she was eleven years old the family was suspended from caste.[9]

In early times in India, widows married and men belonging to one caste married widows of other castes. "A droll story is told of the daughter of a householder of Mâlava who married eleven husbands successively; and on the death of the eleventh husband the plucky widow would probably have welcomed a twelfth, but 'even the stones could not help laughing at her,' so she took to the life of an ascetic."[10] But Manu laid down that a widow should never even mention the name of

[7] Dutt, Civilization in ancient India, I, 172.
[8] Ramabai, High-caste Hindu woman, 34.
[9] Allen, India, 459.
[10] Dutt, *op. cit.*, II, 308.

another man after her husband had died, and that a second husband was nowhere prescribed for virtuous women. A widower, whatever his age might be, and to whatever caste he might belong, could marry again; but a woman of the Brahminical caste, whether she ever lived with her husband or not, was not allowed again to enter the married state. Sad was the state of these widows, for they were cast out of society, but however despised they might have been, if one remarried her lot became even worse, for she was shunned absolutely by every honest and respectable person. "I once witnessed amongst the *Gollavarus,* or shepherds, an instance of even greater severity. A marriage had been arranged, and, in the presence of the family concerned, certain ceremonies which were equivalent to betrothal amongst ourselves had taken place. Before the actual celebration of the marriage, which was fixed for a considerable time afterwards, the bridegroom died. The parents of the girl, who was very young and pretty, thereupon married her to another man. This was in direct violation of the custom of the caste, which condemns to perpetual widowhood girls thus betrothed, even when, as in this case, the future bridegroom dies before marriage has been consummated. The consequence was that all the persons who had taken part in the second ceremony were expelled from caste, and nobody would contract marriage or have any intercourse whatever with them. A long time afterwards I met several of them, well advanced in age, who had been for this reason alone unable to obtain husbands or wives, as the case might be."[11]

Suttee is the name given to the act of a woman immolating herself upon the funeral pile with the body of her deceased husband. This was not practiced in the early times of India, yet it was quite old as it was known from the time of Alexander, and even earlier. It continued down till the nineteenth century, when a noted Hindu, Raja Ram Mohun Roy, got up such an agitation against it that Lord William Bentinck, Governor-General of India, enacted a law in 1829, which prohibited suttee within British dominion and made all assistance, aid, or participation in any act of it to be murder and punishable with death. But it did not fully cease till near the middle of the century.

"Dr. Carey appears to have been the first who made efforts to ascertain the extent of this practice in Bengal, and he

[11] Dubois, Hindu manners, 39.

found that the number of widows who perished in this way, within 30 miles of Calcutta, in 1803, was 438. In 1817 the number of cases officially reported to the magistrate in Bengal was 706. In 1818 the number was 839, thus making 1,545 in two years. The number which took place in Bengal from 1815-1826, or for 12 years, as officially reported to the English magistrates, was 7,154. This number includes only those which took place in Bengal. There was no means of ascertaining the whole number of cases in the country. Mr. W. Ward estimated them at 3,000 annually."[12] The practice was chiefly among kings, princes, Brahmins, and the wealthy and this made it all the more horrid, because these were the men who practiced polygamy, and several of the wives were burned with the husband's dead body. Instances are recorded of 5, 10, 15, 25, and even more, who thus sacrificed themselves. Everything was done to get a woman to sacrifice herself and if after mature deliberation she decided to do so there was no turning back for her. For if she did not go on the funeral pyre of her own free will she would be dragged to it by force. This is well portrayed in the following:

"In 1794, in a village of the Tanjore district called Pudupettah, there died a man of some importance belonging to the *Komatty* (Vaisya) caste. His wife, aged about thirty years, announced her intention of accompanying her deceased husband to the funeral pyre. The news having rapidly spread abroad, a large concourse of people flocked together from all quarters to witness the spectacle. When everything was ready for the ceremony, and the widow had been richly clothed and adorned, the bearers stepped forward to remove the body of the deceased, which was placed in a sort of shrine, ornamented with costly stuffs, garlands of flowers, green foliage, etc., the corpse being seated in it with crossed legs, covered with jewels and clothed in the richest attire, and the mouth filled with betel. Immediately after the funeral car followed the widow, borne in a richly decorated palanquin. On the way to the burning-ground she was escorted by an immense crowd of eager sight-seers, lifting their hands towards her in token of admiration, and rending the air with cries of joy. She was looked upon as already translated to the paradise of Indra, and they seemed to envy her happy lot.

"While the funeral procession moved slowly along, the

[12] Allen, India, 417.

spectators, especially the women, tried to draw near to her to congratulate her on her good fortune, at the same time expecting that, in virtue of the gift of prescience which such a meritorious attachment must confer upon her, she would be pleased to predict the happy things that might befall them here below. With gracious and amiable mien she declared to one that she would long enjoy the favors of fortune; to another, that she would be the mother of numerous children who would prosper in the world; to a third, that she would live long and happily with a husband who would love and cherish her; to a fourth, that her family was destined to attain much honor and dignity; and so forth. She then distributed among them leaves of betel; and the extraordinary eagerness with which they were received clearly proved that great value was attached to them as relics. Beaming with joy, these women then withdrew, each in the full hope that the promised blessings of wealth and happiness would be showered on her and hers.

"During the whole procession, which was a very long one, the widow preserved a calm demeanor. Her looks were serene, even smiling; but when she reached the fatal place where she was to yield up her life in so ghastly a manner, it was observed that her firmness suddenly gave way. Plunged, as it were, in gloomy thought, she seemed to pay no attention whatever to what was passing around her. Her looks became wildly fixed upon the pile. Her face grew deadly pale. Her very limbs were in a convulsive tremor. Her drawn features and haggard face betrayed the fright that had seized her, while a sudden weakening of her senses betokened that she was ready to faint away.

"The Brahmins who conducted the ceremony, and also her near relatives, ran quickly to her, endeavoring to keep up her courage and to revive her drooping spirits. All was of no effect. The unfortunate woman, bewildered and distracted, turned a deaf ear to all their exhortations and preserved a deep silence.

"She was then made to leave the palanquin, and as she was scarcely able to walk, her people helped her to drag herself to a pond near the pyre. She plunged into the water with all her clothes and ornaments on, and was immediately afterwards led to the pyre, on which the body of her husband was already laid. The pyre was surrounded by Brahmins, each with a lighted torch in one hand and a bowl of ghee in the other. Her relatives and friends, several of whom were armed with muskets, swords, and other weapons, stood closely round in a double line, and seemed to await impatiently the end of this shocking tragedy. This armed force, they told me, was intended not only to intimidate the unhappy victim in case the terror of her approaching death might induce her to run away, but also to overawe any persons who might be moved by a natural feeling of compassion and sympathy, and so tempted to prevent the accomplishment of the homicidal sacrifice.

"At length, the *purohita* Brahmin gave the fatal signal. The poor widow was instantly divested of all her jewels, and dragged, more dead than alive, to the pyre. There she was obliged, according to custom, to walk three times round the pile, two of her nearest relatives supporting her by the arms. She accomplished the first round with tottering steps; during the second her strength wholly forsook her, and she fainted away in the arms of her conductors, who were obliged to complete the ceremony by dragging her through the third round. Then, at last, senseless and unconscious, she was cast upon the corpse of her husband. At that moment the air resounded with noisy acclamations. The Brahmins, emptying the contents of their vessels on the dry wood, applied their torches, and in the twinkling of an eye the whole pile was ablaze. Three times was the unfortunate woman called by her name. But, alas! she made no answer."[13]

**Boys and Girls.** "A son is the most coveted of all blessings that a Hindu craves, for it is by a son's birth in the family that the father is redeemed."[14] This accounted for the difference in the feeling for a boy and for a girl. So strong was the desire for a son that sonless mothers were filled with great care and anxiety lest the child should not be a boy. There is, perhaps, nothing which will so weaken mankind as the life of the mothers before the birth of the children, so what a great influence upon the Hindu race must have been this constant worry of women who were to become mothers. Well might the wives worry, for according to Manu, a wife who had all daughters and no sons could be replaced with another wife in the eleventh year of marriage.

This was also a burden to a girl born into the family. If a boy died soon after the birth of a girl, or if a girl was

[13] Dubois, Hindu manners, 361, *et seq.*
[14] Ramabai, High-caste Hindu woman, 12.

born soon after her brother's death, she was considered to be the cause of such death and was accordingly treated very cruelly. This also had a bad influence upon the boys, as they soon learned to know of their superior being and learned to despise and to mistreat their sisters and later all womankind. After several sons had come into a family a daughter might not be undesirable and in some cases really wished for. Such a daughter was kindly and even affectionately treated.

The following is a striking passage. "Young children will obey their father, because they fear punishment if they do not; but they will overwhelm their mother with abuse, and will insult her grossly, even going so far at times as to strike her. When they grow older they fail to respect even their father, and it often happens that he is obliged to give way to his sons, who have made themselves masters of the house. Strange to say, nowhere are parents fonder of their children than they are in India; but this fondness usually degenerates into weakness. If the children are good, they are extravagantly praised; if they are naughty, their parents show the utmost ingenuity in finding excuses for them. The mild punishments that their naughtiness or disobedience brings down upon them invariably err on the side of leniency. The parents do not dare to whip them or scold them sharply, or even inflict any punishment that they would be likely to feel. The father and mother content themselves with making feeble remonstrances about their bad behavior, and if these produce no effect, they leave them to grow up in their evil ways. The few sensible parents who show more firmness and severity with their children are met with a show of temper. Sons do not hesitate to resist the parental authority and threaten to escape it by running away and living elsewhere. This threat rarely fails to produce the desired effect; the parents' severity melts away and they become passive witnesses of the disorderly conduct of their sons, who, encouraged by this first victory, end by becoming absolute masters of the house. One must, however, do them the justice to say that, after having thus gained the mastery over their parents, they take great care of them, as a general rule, and see that they want for nothing in their old age. But I fancy that in acting thus they are moved less by filial affection than by considerations of what the world will say."[15]

**Infanticide.** It is not strange that under such beliefs and

[15] Dubois, Hindu manners, 307.

treatment as mentioned above that many female children should have been destroyed. Fathers were willing to destroy their girls because of so little value and mothers because of the saving to the girls the burdens which woman had to endure. Also the Hindus were very superstitious and a child born under an unlucky star was not only destined, according to common belief, to all sorts of troubles and accidents during his life, but he would also bring bad luck to his parents and relatives. Parents convinced that their child would bring bad luck, because of having been born on an unlucky day, would abandon the child at some place along the road, and even some would strangle and drown such babies.

**Dress.** All classes of women in India were very fond of ornaments. They wore jewels and rings in the ears and nose, rings on the fingers and toes, chains on the neck, and bracelets on the arms, wrists, and ankles. It was no uncommon sight to see a woman decked out in all her jewels, drawing water, grinding rice, cooking food, and attending to all the menial domestic occupations. But the greatest ornamenting was on the occasion of marriages, holidays, and other festive times.

The women not only profusely ornamented themselves, but they also took great pains and manifested much pride in ornamenting their children, both boys and girls. Often the small children would have but little clothing on but they would be wearing many ornaments, in some cases when all the clothing worn by the child would not exceed in value one dollar they would be wearing ornaments worth one hundred dollars. Children were frequently robbed and even murdered for these ornaments.

The dowry given with the girls at marriage consisted very greatly of the ornaments. What the girl received from her husband's people or from her home was clearly set forth in writing and they were considered her own personal property. If she became a widow she claimed all such things as her own.

**Amusements.** The amusements of the Hindus were for the most part of the sedentary and inactive kind. Yet dancing was one of the most prominent forms but they did not dance themselves but had hired performers, the dancers being young women supposed to be courtesans, and for the most part connected with the temples. There were feats of bodily agility and dexterity, as found with the tumbler and the juggler. They were fond of chess, cards, and other games of chance. Story-telling was a favorite diversion.

**Rites.** The Hindu performed a great many rites. We are concerned here only with the domestic ceremonies. The most important of the Domestic Ceremonies were Marriage, ceremonies performed during pregnancy of wife, birth of child, first feeding of child, tonsure, initiation, and return from school on the completion of education.

In marriage there were many parts to the ceremony, all of which had to be rigorously observed. During pregnancy there were rites to secure conception, a rite to cause a male child to be born, rites to insure protection to the child in the womb, and sometime between the fourth and eighth month was the ceremony of the husband affectionately parting the wife's hair.

On the birth of a child a rite was performed and a secret name given to the child, known only to the parents. The child was weaned at eight months, at which time he was given his first solid food, and an appropriate ceremony went with it. At one year another rite was performed, at which time the child's head was shaved, leaving such hair as might be desired for its arrangement as was the custom of the family.

The ceremony of initiation, or the giving over of the boy to his teacher for education, was a very important affair, participated in by the boy and by his teacher. After he had finished his education, the student returned home, which was the occasion for another important ceremony, which was followed by his marriage and the student was then changed into a householder. At the time of the initiation, the triple cord or sacred thread, which was worn by the three upper castes, was bestowed upon the boy. The age of the boy differed at this time according to which caste he belonged, the Brahmin boy being initiated between 8 and 16, the Kshatriya between 11 and 22, and the Vaisya between 12 and 24.

**Adoption.** When a Hindu had no sons, because of his wife's failure to bear them to him or because the sons borne to him had all died, two things were left to him to do, to take another wife or to adopt a son. If he adopted a child it was generally from among his own relatives or if a Brahmin, at any rate from his own caste. He might adopt a child or an adult, just as he should choose. Girls were adopted, but there were very few instances of such. The adoption was an event of importance and it was attended with solemn ceremonies.

"The adopted son renounces wholly and forever all his claims to the property and succession of his natural father, and acquires the sole right to the heritage of his father by adoption. The latter is bound to bring him up, to feed him, and to treat him as his own son; to have the ceremony of *upanayana*, or the triple cord, performed for him, and to see him married. The adopted son, in his turn, is obliged to take care of his adoptive father in his old age and in sickness, just as if he were his natural father, and to *preside at his obsequies*. On the death of his adoptive father he enters into full possession of his inheritance—assets as well as liabilities. Should there be any property left, he enjoys it; but if, on the other hand, there are debts, he is bound to pay them. He is, moreover, by his adoption admitted into the *gothram* or family stock of the adopter, and is considered to have left that in which he was born."[16]

**Inheritance.** It appears that the property was divided in earlier times equally among the sons upon the death of their father. Yet there was a joint system where all lived together and the eldest son supplied the place of the father, receiving all the property and then caring for all the others of the family. At one time it was the custom for a daughter to get one-fourth as much as a son, and at another time each son gave to the daughter one-fourth of his share. As was stated above, when a son was adopted, he renounced all claim to what his natural father might leave on his death, while he became the full heir of his adopted feather and upon his death got all that he might leave.

The right of inheritance and the duty of presiding at a man's obsequies belonged one with the other. When a man died without leaving direct descendants, if he was wealthy a crowd of relatives appeared and great disputes often arose as to whom belonged the honor of conducting the funeral rites. But if he was poor, and burdened with debts, then the survivors took every possible care to disprove near relationship.

**Education.** In the very early times in India, royal courts were the seats of learning, and the learned and wise of all nations were welcomed to them. Learned priests were retained in these courts not only to perform the religious duties

---

[16] Dubois, Hindu manners, 369.

but also for the purpose of imparting learning. On great occasions men of learning from all parts came to these places and discussions were held on ritualistic matters and likewise on such subjects as the human mind, the destination of the soul after death, the future world, and the like. Then later appeared Brahminic settlements called *Parishads*, answering to the Universities of Europe. These were at first, perhaps, conducted by three Brahmins who knew the Vedas, but the number was increased up to twenty-one. To these places men of the Brahmin caste who wished to become learned could go and receive instruction in the Vedas and such traditional law and astronomy and philosophy as was current. Besides these Parishads, there were private schools, established by individual teachers, who collected about them a body of students. Also learned Brahmins in their old age would sometimes retire to forests and gather students around them. Later great schools arose, such as noted by Houen Tsang, a Chinese traveler, who spent several years in India in the seventh century after Christ. ''Our traveler now came to the great NÂLANDA University, if we may call it by that name. The monks of this place, to the number of several thousands, were men of the highest ability, talent, and distinction. 'The countries of India respect them and follow them. The day is not sufficient for asking and answering profound questions. From morning till night they engage in discussion; the old and the young mutually help one another. Those who cannot discuss questions out of the *Tripitaka* are little esteemed, and are obliged to hide themselves for shame. Learned men from different cities, on this account, who desire to acquire quickly a renown in discussion, come here in multitudes to settle their doubts, and then the streams (of their wisdom) spread far and wide. For this reason some persons usurp the name (of Nâlanda students) and in going to and fro receive honor in consequence.' ''[17]

The Brahmins themselves received the highest education possible. This consisted in the memorizing of their sacred books and a study of the philosophy and science of their times. The second and third castes seem to have been accorded the right to study what the first caste did, yet the third caste must not have entered much into this but have received a somewhat meagre education. As boys followed the occupation of their parents, they would receive such ele-

[17] Dutt, Civilization in ancient India, II, 148.

mentary instruction as was needed in the trade or work to be performed. The fourth caste had no need for learning so they received none except in the duties which a servant was expected to perform.

In the olden times, when women were well respected and permitted to appear in public, girls were taught to read and to write and were given other education. But later they received no education further than the training for domestic duties. Education was not needed by women, as a woman must at all times depend upon some man for her knowledge of things. The dancing girls received some education, as it was considered that their religious duties would be better performed if they should receive some intellectual training.

The student was expected to be obedient and respectful to his teacher and to serve him in every way. The discipline of the school was very mild. Laurie quotes from Manu: "Good instruction must be given to pupils without unpleasant sensations, and the teacher who reverences virtue must use sweet and gentle words. If a scholar is guilty of a fault, his instructor may punish him with severe words, and threaten that on the next offence he will give him blows; and, if the fault is committed in cold weather, the teacher may dowse him with cold water."[18]

"To the Hindus we are indebted for our numerical notation, often wrongly attributed to the Arabs. During the fifth century after Christ they invented an algebra superior to that of the Greeks, although they were probably assisted by the work of the latter. They early learned how to calculate eclipses and find the location of planets by means of tables. They seem also to have had some knowledge of medicine. By 300 A. D. they possessed a treatise on rhetoric, and had worked out a logic two centuries before the time of Aristotle; while in the science of grammar, as early as the fourth century B. C., they were so far advanced that the Western world first learned what philogy was when the study of Sanskrit was opened to Europe a hundred or more years ago."[19]

[18] Laurie, Pre-Christian education, 176.
[19] Graves, A history of education, Before the Middle Ages, 86.

## LITERATURE

1. Allen, David O., India, Ancient and modern.
2. Dubois, Abbè J. A., Hindu manners, customs, and ceremonies.
3. Dutt, Romesh Chunder, A history of civilization in ancient India.
4. Graves, Frank Pierrepont, A history of education, Before the middle ages.
5. Laurie, S. S., Historical survey of pre-Christian education.
6. Letourneau, Ch., The evolution of marriage.
7. Mill, James, The history of British India.
8. Ragozin, Zénaïde A., Vedic India.
9. Ramabai, Pundita, The high-caste Hindu woman.
10. Rhys-Davids, T. W., Buddhist India.

## CHAPTER V

### THE CHILD IN CHINA

**Women and Marriage.** The Chinese have an old maxim that "a woman is thrice dependent; before marriage, on her father; after marriage, on her husband; when a widow, on her son." But this refers, no doubt, principally to support and subsistence, as the mother was greatly respected and had much authority for even "the emperor himself performs the ceremonies of the *ko-tow* before his own mother, who receives them seated on a throne."[1] This power of the mother was carried to the daughter-in-law, for after marriage the girl was no longer a daughter but a daughter-in-law and for a considerable part of her life she was under the absolute control of a mother-in-law. Cruel treatment was the rule rather than the exception and the only way out was through suicide, and suicide and attempts at suicide on the part of wives were so frequent as to cause but little comment. Christianity requires a man to leave his father and mother and cleave to his wife, but Confucianism requires a man to cleave to his father and mother and compels the wife to do the same. The sale of wives and children was not uncommon. "It is perfectly well known to those acquainted with the facts, that during several recent years in many districts stricken with famine, the sale of women and children was conducted as openly as that of mules and donkeys, the only essential difference being that the former were not driven to market."[2]

Modesty was deemed so essential in the female character that it was considered indecorous in women of birth and breeding to show even their hands, and the dresses were so made that the long sleeves usually covered the hands when touching or moving anything. Yet there was adultery, which was considered a most heinous offence, but instead of bringing the offender before a magistrate many cases were dealt with in private. The offender would be attacked by a band

[1] Davis, The Chinese, I, 264.
[2] Smith, Chinese characteristics, 205.

of men and sometimes his legs were broken, sometimes his arms, and again quicklime would be rubbed into his eyes, destroying the sight.

The laws of China did not sanction polygamy but they did permit concubinage. The man could have but one wife, who was distinguished by a proper title, while the concubines were inferior and their children belonged to the wife. If the wife had borne sons, it was considered somewhat discreditable for a man to take a concubine, and if he did and brought her into the same home with his wife there was usually great disturbance, which accorded with one of their proverbs, That nine women out of ten are jealous. These concubines were generally purchased with money and were from the lower classes, where poverty always prevailed, making occasion for the selling of the girls. In a few cases, concubinage in a family might have arisen through the wife's desire to have women and children to serve her, as they would come under her control.

There were seven grounds for divorce in China, being, barrenness, adultery, disobedience to the husband's parents, talkativeness, thievery, ill temper, and malignant disease. But divorce was not for the wife, for no offense, of whatever kind, on the part of the husband, gave a woman any right to claim a divorce from him. "Any of these, however, may be set aside by three circumstances: the wife having mourned for her husband's parents; the family having acquired wealth since the marriage; and the wife being without parents to receive her back."[3] The family of the woman was a great factor against divorce, not only on account of the unjustness or disgrace attached to it but also because when the woman married she gave up her home and no provision was made for her further support and especially so if her parents were dead as the property was divided among her brothers and she would be looked upon as an alien. Hence a husband would not be allowed to divorce his wife, except for a most valid cause.

It was considered disreputable for widows to remarry. But this was not true of a widower as he could marry whomever he should choose, nor did he have to wait for any length of time for the ceremony because of any period of mourning for his first wife. If the widow herself should be unwilling to marry, the law would protect her against those trying to

[3] Davis, The Chinese, I, 269.

make her do so. One of the strong motives against marrying again was that as long as she remained a widow she would be absolute mistress of herself and her children. The widow was occasionally sold as a concubine by her father-in-law, but this was rare, as it was considered a great degradation and especially as she would be separated from her children.

"A reverse view of matrimonial experiences is suggested by the practice of wives refusing to survive their husbands and, like the victims of suttee in India, putting a voluntary end to their existence rather than live to mourn their loss. Such devotion is regarded by the people with great approbation, and the deed of suicide is generally performed in public with great punctiliousness. The following account of one such suicide at Fuhchow is taken from the Hong Kong *Daily Press* of January 20, 1861:

"'A few days since,' says the writer, 'I met a Chinese procession passing through the foreign settlement, escorting a young person in scarlet and gold in a richly decorated chair; the object of which I found, was to invite the public to come and see her hang herself, a step she had resolved to take in consequence of the death of her husband, by which she had been left a childless widow. Both being orphans, this event had severed her dearest earthly ties, and she hoped by this sacrifice to secure herself eternal happiness, and a meeting with her husband in the next world. Availing myself of the general invitation, I repaired on the day appointed to the indicated spot. We had scarcely arrived, when the same procession was seen advancing from the Joss house of the woman's native village towards a scaffold or gallows erected in an adjacent field, and surrounded by hundreds of natives of both sexes; the female portion, attired in gayest holiday costume, was very numerous. A friend and I obtained a bench for a consideration, which, being placed within a few yards of the scaffold, gave us a good view of the performance. The procession having reached the foot of the scaffold, the lady was assisted to ascend by her male attendant, and, after having welcomed the crowd, partook with some female relatives of a repast prepared for her on a table on the scaffold, which she appeared to appreciate extremely. A child in arms was then placed upon the table, whom she caressed and adorned with a necklace which she herself had worn. She then took an ornamental basket containing rice, herbs, and flowers, and, whilst scattering them amongst the crowd, delivered a short address, thanking them for their attendance, and upholding the motives which urged her to the step she was about to take. This done, a salute of bombards announced the arrival of the time for the performance of the last act of her existence, when a delay was occasioned by the discovery of the absence of a reluctant brother, pending whose arrival let me describe the means of extermination. The gallows was formed by an upright timber on each side of the scaffold supporting a stout bamboo, from the center of which was suspended a loop of cord with a small wooden ring embracing both parts of it, which was covered by a red silk handkerchief, the whole being surrounded by an awning.

"'The missing brother having been induced to appear, the widow now proceeded to mount on a chair placed under the noose, and, to ascertain its fitness for her reception, deliberately placed her head in it; then, withdrawing her head, she waved a final adieu to the admiring spectators, and committed herself to its embrace for the last time, throwing the red handkerchief over her head. Her supports were now about to be withdrawn, when she was reminded by several voices in the crowd that she had omitted to drawn down the ring which should tighten the cord round her neck; smiling in acknowledgment of the reminder, she adjusted the ring, and, motioning away her supports, was left hanging in midair—a suicide. With extraordinary self-possession she now placed her hands before her, and continued to perform the manual chin-chin until the convulsions of strangulation separated them and she was dead. The body was left hanging about half an hour, and then taken down by her male attendants, one of whom immediately took possession of the halter, and was about to sever it for the purpose of appropriating a portion, when a struggle ensued, of which I took advantage to attach myself to the chair in which the body was now being removed to the Joss house, in order to obtain ocular proofs of her demise. Arrived at the Joss house the body was placed on a couch, and the handkerchief withdrawn from the face, disclosed unmistakable proofs of death. This is the third instance of suicide of this sort within as many weeks. The authorities are quite unable to prevent it, and a monument is invariably erected to the memory of the devoted widow.'"[4]

The most essential circumstance in a respectable family

[4] Douglass, History of China, 130, *et seq.*

alliance was, that there should be equality of rank on either side. A Chinese lover who should woo a young lady of good family would visit the house of her parents, where he was expected to display his accomplishments, especially in penmanship. There was romance and poetry in the wooing, as may be shown by this love song, which has been sung in Cathay for more than two and a half millenniums:

> "How rises the moon in radiant glory!
> And thou my lady, most charming and sweetest
> Oh, listen kindly to love's story!—
> Ah, poor my heart that vainly beatest!
>
> "How rises the moon in cloudless effulgence!
> And thou my lady, most winsome and purest
> Oh, grant thy lover more indulgence!—
> Ah, poor my heart what thou endurest!
>
> "How rises the moon in splendor most brightly!
> And thou my lady, loveliest, fairest
> Wilt never for my love requite me?—
> Ah, poor my heart what pain thou bearest!"[5]

"At the present day marriage is probably more universal in China than in any other civilized country in the world. It is regarded as something indispensable, and few men pass the age of twenty without taking a wife. Chinese legislators have at all times encouraged early marriages as having a pacifying effect upon the people. A man who has given hostages to fortune in the shape of wife and children has a greater inducement to follow the paths of steady industry, and is less likely to throw in his lot with brigands and rebels, than a man who has but himself to think of, and is without any immediate ties. Besides this the Chinese believe, in common with the ancient Greeks, that the shades of the unburied wander restlessly about without gaining admittance into Hades; so that non-burial came to be considered by them the most deplorable calamity that could befall one, and the discharge of the last service a most holy duty. To die, therefore, without leaving behind a son to perform the burial rites, and to offer up the fixed periodical sacrifices at the tomb, is one of the most direful fates that can overtake a Chinaman, and he seeks to avoid it by an early marriage."[6]

The two young people to a betrothal in China had very little to do with it. This was arranged by means of a go-

[5] Carus, Chinese life and customs, 81.
[6] Douglass, History of China, 115.

between, or match-maker. The negotiations generally originated with the family of the boy or young man. A card was made out containing data of the candidate, such as the ancestral name, the hour, day, month, and year of birth of the young candidate. At some time in the proceedings both parties had to make known to each other if there were any bodily or constitutional defect, what the true age of each was, whether born of a wife or a concubine, and whether real offspring or only adopted. Provided with the card, the go-between went to the other family and stated the object of the visit. The parents or guardians of the girl would then make inquiries about the other family, they would consult a fortune-teller to ascertain if it would be fitting and auspicious for the two young people to wed. If the offer was acceptable, then the go-between was furnished with a similar card about the girl to take to the other family. If within three days of the engagement an unlucky thing occurred, as the breaking of a china bowl or the losing of some article in the house, circumstances were considered to be sufficiently unlucky to warrant the instant termination of the negotiations. The betrothal was not binding till certain cards were interchanged between the families. The outside of the cards was covered with red paper, on which was pasted a paper dragon for the one and on the other a paper phœnix. Each card was adorned with two pieces of red silk. The card with the dragon was filled out with particulars relating to the family of the boy and retained by the girl's family, while the one with the phœnix had particulars of the girl's family and it was kept by the family of the boy. At the time of the exchange of cards presents were sent. For the girl was sent a pair of silver or gold wristlets and for her family articles of food, as pigs' feet, fruits, fowls, etc. For the boys' family were sent artificial flowers, bread, cakes, etc.

As usually in a family there was strict separation between the males and females, there was but little opportunity for the bride and groom to meet one another and often they would not have seen one another till the day of the wedding. The difficulty was increased after betrothal, for it was considered quite improper for the girl to be actually seen by the family of the future mother-in-law. The girl had to maintain the strictest seclusion. She must retire to the inner apartments when friends called upon her parents, and when going out she was to use a closed sedan chair. For this reason, most engagements were arranged between parties not living in the same place.

The time which might transpire between betrothal and marriage varied from a month or two to eighteen or twenty years, depending much on the age of the parties. "There are six ceremonies which constitute a regular marriage. 1. The father and elder brother of the young man send a go-between to the father and brother of the girl, to enquire her name and the moment of her birth, that the horoscope of the two may be examined, in order to ascertain whether the proposed alliance will be a happy one. 2. If so, the boy's friends send the go-between back to make an offer of marriage. 3. If that be accepted, the second party is again requested to put their assent in writing. 4. Presents are then sent to the girl's parents according to the means of the parties. 5. The go-between requests them to choose a lucky day for the wedding; and, 6, the preliminaries are concluded by the bridegroom going or sending a party of his friends with music to bring his bride to his own house." [7]

In the spring was considered the most appropriate time for marriage, and the month in which the peach-tree blossomed as the happiest time. The following poem translated from the "Book of Odes," illustrates this:

> "Sweet child of spring, the garden's queen,
> Yon peach-tree charms the roving sight;
> Its fragrant leaves how richly green,
> Its blossoms how divinely bright!
>
> "So softly shines the beauteous bride,
> By love and conscious virtue led,
> O'er her new mansion to preside,
> And placid joys around her spread." [8]

Some time previous to the day fixed, the bridegroom was invested ceremoniously with a dress cap or bonnet, and he took an additional name. About this same time the bride, whose hair had hung down in long tresses, had it done up in the style of married women of her class in society. Usually, the day before the wedding, the bride tried on the clothes she was to wear in the sedan going to the home of her husband, and what she was to wear the first day upon her arrival at his home. This was an occasion of great interest to her fam-

[7] Williams, The Middle kingdom, II, 54.
[8] Davis, The Chinese, I, 270.

ily, and the parents invited female relatives and friends to a feast that they might view the clothing and help to have things well prepared for the wedding-day.

On the wedding-day, the bridegroom or his best man and friends went with an ornamented sedan, accompanied with musicians, to the home of the bride. When evening came and the stars were just beginning to peep out, the bride, with a thick veil over her head and completely covering her features from view, entered the sedan and the procession, with music and lanterns, took its way to the home of the bridegroom. On reaching his residence, the bride was carried into the house in the arms of matrons and lifted over a pan of burning charcoal on the threshold. The bridegroom and bride seated themselves side by side, each trying to sit on a part of the dress of the other, as it was considered that the one who succeeded in so doing would rule the household. Then the bride returned to her chamber and her outer garments and veil were removed and she was dressed in her wedding finery and then with her husband she entered upon the wedding-dinner. Often this was the first time in the husband's life to behold the features of his wife. He could eat what he chose of the good things but she, according to established custom, must not take a particle, but must sit in silence, dignified and composed. The door of the room was left open and about it gathered the invited guests, the parents of the bridegroom and his relatives, all of whom scrutinized the bride and observed her deportment and expressed their opinions and criticisms. The cup of alliance was drunk together by the young couple and pledges were exchanged. On the next day they worshipped together the ancestral gods of the husband and paid their respects to his parents and relatives. This was the wife's last time to be in public with her husband, as husbands were never seen with their wives in public. On the third day after the wedding, the bride paid a customary visit to her own parents.

Whatever else might have been included in the marriage customs in China, the wedding-feast was the main feature of the occasion. This might occur upon the wedding-day or at some later time. Wedding and funeral feasts would be quite impossible were it not for the "share" system which they have worked out. Each guest, or each family, were not only expected but really required by a rigid code of social etiquette to contribute to the expense of the occasion. This was sometimes in food but usually in money and there was a scale according to which every one knew what his "share" should be.

"One of the most characteristic methods in which the Chinese lack of sympathy is manifested is in the treatment which brides receive on their wedding-day. They are often very young, are always timid, and are naturally terror-stricken at being suddenly thrust among strangers. Customs vary widely, but there seems to be a general indifference to the feelings of the poor child thus exposed to the public gaze. In some places it is allowable for any one who chooses to turn back the curtains of the chair and stare at her. In other regions, the unmarried girls find it a source of keen enjoyment to post themselves at a convenient position as the bride passes, to throw upon her handfuls of hay-seed or chaff, which will obstinately adhere to her carefully oiled hair for a long time. Upon her emerging from the chair at the house of her new parents, she is subjected to the same kind of criticism as a newly bought horse, with what feelings on her part it is not difficult to imagine."[9]

**Infancy.** "A Chinese baby is a round-faced little helpless human animal, whose eyes look like two black marbles over which the skin had been stretched, and a slit made on the bias. His nose is a little kopje in the center of his face, above a yawning chasm which requires constant filling to insure the preservation of law and order. On his shaved head are left small tufts of hair in various localities, which give him the appearance of the plain about Peking, on which the traveler sees, here and there, a small clump of trees around a country village, a home, or a cemetery; the remainder of the country being bare. These tufts are usually on the 'soft spot,' in the back of his neck, over his ears or in a braid or a ring on the side of his head."[10]

It was considered a deep disgrace if the children of a Chinese mother were not all born at the father's home, and in their efforts to have such occur women would do everything possible, even going to great inconvenience and hardship. If this should be the first baby and a boy, there would be great rejoicing in the whole household, but if a girl there would not only be no rejoicing but along with depression the young wife would be treated with coldness and often with harshness,

[9] Smith, Chinese characteristics, 198.
[10] Headland, Chinese boy and girl, 33.

and she might be beaten for her lack of discretion in not producing a son.

On the third day after birth, the child was washed for the first time. Friends and relatives were invited to take part and they brought presents to the child. Immediately after the washing, the ceremony of binding the wrists took place, which in some cases consisted of the tying of one or more ancient *cash* to each wrist by means of a red cotton cord while with others only a loose red string was put around each wrist. When the child was a month old, the mother and child left her room for the first time and the ceremony of naming the baby and shaving its head took place. All the relatives and friends were invited and they were expected to take dinner with the child, and, which was more important, to take presents.

"The presumption is that a Chinese child is born with the same general disposition as children in other countries. This may perhaps be the case; but either from the treatment it receives from parents or nurses, or because of the disposition it inherits, its nature soon becomes changed, and it develops certain characteristics peculiar to the Chinese child. It becomes *t'ao ch'i*. That almost means mischievous; it almost means troublesome—a little tartar—but it means exactly *t'ao ch'i*. In this respect almost every Chinese child is a little tyrant. Father, mother, uncles, aunts, and grandparents are all made to do his bidding. In case any of them seems to be recalcitrant, the little dear lies down on his baby back on the dusty ground and kicks and screams until the refractory parent or nurse has repented and succumbed, when he gets up and good-naturedly goes on with his play and allows them to go about their business. The child is *t'ao ch'i*." [11]

The baby in China has its toys to play with and it also has its Mother Goose rhymes and Headland states that he collected more than six hundred of such rhymes.[12] A few will be sufficient to give here to show their resemblance to our own. The following is as popular in China as "Jack and Jill" is here:

"He climbed up the candle-stick,
  The little mousey brown,
To steal and eat tallow,
  And he couldn't get down."

[11] Headland, Chinese boy and girl, 35.
[12] *Ibid.*, 9 et seq.

He called for his grandma,
But his grandma was in town,
So he doubled up into a wheel,
And rolled himself down.''

This next one easily calls up ''Lady bug, lady bug, fly away home:''

''Fire-fly, fire-fly,
Come from the hill,
Your father and mother
Are waiting here still.
They've brought you some sugar,
Some candy and meat,
Come quick or I'll give it
To baby to eat.''

The following is said over the baby's toes very much as ''This little pig went to market:''

''This little cow eats grass,
This little cow eats hay,
This little cow drinks water,
This little cow runs away,
This little cow does nothing,
Except lie down all day.
We'll whip her.''

The Chinese loved their children and yet infanticide existed with them, but mostly only that of girls. The greatest cause was poverty. Being too poor to care for their children parents thought best to kill them than to sell them into slavery. This perhaps was not large over the whole country and existed to a great extent only in certain parts, sometimes as high as eighty per cent. of all girl babies born. The following conditions as given as found some time before the year 1840, shows its prevalence in certain districts at that time, as this refers to a small village on the Amoy island. ''On a second visit, while addressing them, one man held up a child, and publicly acknowledged that he had killed five of the helpless beings, having preserved but two. I thought he was jesting, but as no surprise or dissent was expressed by his neighbors, and as there was an air of simplicity and regret in the individual, there was no reason to doubt its truth. After repeating his confession, he added with affecting simplicity, 'It was before I heard you speak on this subject, I did not know it was wrong; I would not do so now.' Wishing to obtain the testimony of the assembled villages, I put the question publicly,

'What number of female infants in this village are destroyed at birth?' The reply was, 'More than one-half.' As there was no discussion among them, which is not the case when they differ in opinion, and as we were fully convinced from our own observations of the numerical inequality of the sexes, the proportion of deaths they gave did not strike us as extravagant."[12]

It is difficult to judge this matter correctly when such contrary opinions are placed before us as in the following quotations, the first by an American who spent many years in China and the second by a Chinaman who spent many years in America. "Much has already been done by those who have had most opportunity to learn the facts, toward exhibiting the real practice of the Chinese in the matter of destroying female infants. Yet no more can be safely predicted than that this is a crime which to some extent everywhere prevails, and in some places to such a degree as seriously to affect the proportion of the sexes. It seems to be most common in the maritime provinces of the southern part of China, in some districts of which it is by the Chinese themselves regarded as a terrible and a threatening evil."[13] "I am indignant that there should be a popular belief in America that Chinese girls at birth are generally put to death by their parents because they are not wanted. Nothing can be further from the truth. In a country like China, where women do not appear in public life, it must follow that sons are more to be desired, for the very good reason that family honor and glory depend on them and ancestral worship necessitates either the birth or adoption of sons to perpetuate it. I venture to say that in proportion to population and distribution of wealth that infanticide is as rare in China as it is in this country."[14]

**Boys and Girls.** The relative estimation that was placed upon boys and girls in olden China is well expressed by a passage from one of their oldest classics, The Book of Odes. In describing the palace of an ancient king, the dreams of the king are treated and then comes the following:

"Sons shall be born to him; they will be put to sleep on couches;
They will be clothed in robes; they will have scepters to play with;
Their cry will be loud.
They will be (hereafter) resplendent with red knee-covers,

[12] Williams, The middle kingdom, II, 261.
[13] Smith, Village life in China, 259.
[14] Lee, When I was a boy in China, 43.

The (future) king, the princes of the land.
Daughters will be born to him. They will be put to sleep on the ground;
They will be clothed with wrappers; they will have tiles to play with.
It will be theirs neither to do wrong nor to do good.
Only about the spirits and the food will they have to think,
And to cause no sorrow to their parents."[15]

The baby boy was greatly welcomed upon his arrival into the family, while the baby girl might not only be unwelcomed but very greatly undesired. This was mostly because girls counted for so little as they would marry and then no longer belong to their family but entirely to the family of their husband. Boys would not only become the support of their family but they might have opportunity to acquire learning and thus add dignity and honor to their family. Too, there was great need of sons to carry on the ancestral worship and if not born into the family they must be procured through adoption or by means of concubines. Without a son a man would live without honor and would die unhappy. No matter how good or how beautiful a girl might become, she could never equal the very poorest and weakest boy.

**Child and Parent.** While his parents were alive, a son should continue to obey them, was the doctrine of the classics, the laws, and the customs of China. But a daughter, after she was married, was not subject to her own parents but to her husband's parents. Although instances were rare, parents had the right to bring their children before magistrates for aid in controlling and punishing them. With all this, it would seem that the children were not greatly disciplined nor did they give prompt obedience to their parents.

Public sentiment, especially in the older times of China, was strongly against the individual who would not accord to his parents due respect and obedience. No matter how old, how educated, or how wealthy he might become this respect and obedience was still due his parents. Confucius taught: "That parents when alive should be served according to propriety, that when dead they should be buried according to propriety, and that they should be sacrificed to according to propriety."[16]

"If a son should murder his parent, either father or mother, and be convicted of the crime, he would not only be beheaded, but his body would be mutilated by being cut into

---

[15] Smith, Village life in China, 237.
[16] Smith, Chinese characteristics, 175.

small pieces; his house would be razed to the ground, and the earth under it would be dug up for several feet deep; his neighbors living on the right and the left would be severely punished; his principal teacher would suffer capital punishment; the district magistrate of the place would be deprived of his office and disgraced; the prefect, the governor of the province, and the viceroy would all be degraded three degrees in rank. All this is done and suffered to mark the enormity of the crime of a parricide."[17]

**Deformation of the Feet.** The practice of footbinding among the Chinese females was carried on by all classes of society, so it was not a mark of rank. It was the fashion and all classes followed it, for in some places women sitting by the roadside begging had their feet bound, and in some places, where women worked in the fields, they would have to kneel to do their work because they could not stand upon their mutilated feet. But of course it prevailed most with the higher and wealthier and more fashionable people.

The practice of the compressing of the feet arose in China, it is thought, sometime during the ninth century of our era. It is only conjecture as to how and why this originated. Some accounts state that it arose from a desire to pattern after the club feet of a popular empress; another story is that it gradually came into use because of the admiration of small feet and the attempt to imitate them; and a third suggestion is that it developed through the men wishing to keep their wives from gadding. The Chinese women call their feet "golden lilies," which is accounted for from the popular idea that a certain empress was so beautiful that golden lilies sprang out of the ground wherever she stepped.

The age at which the binding began varied, being from six to eight years of age, but sometimes the bandages were put on as soon as the little girl was able to walk. The whole operation was performed, and the shape maintained by bandages, which were never permanently removed or covered by stockings. The bandages were of strong white cotton cloth, about two yards long and between two and three inches wide. The end of the strip was laid on the inside of the foot at the instep, then carried over the toes, leaving the great toe free, then under the foot and round the heel, and the bandage was so continued till all used up and then the end was sewed tightly

[17] Doolittle, Sketches of social life in China, Harper's Magazine, XXXI (1865), 442.

down. Each day the bandage was tightened and if the bones should spring back into place upon the removal of the bandage, sometimes they would be struck back into place with a blow from the heavy mallet used in beating clothes. These bandages would finally cause a bulge in the instep, a deep indentation in the sole, and the toes would grow down under and across the sole and come out on the opposite side, the great toe alone retaining its normal position, the foot becoming from four to six inches in length and sometimes even three or less.

The pain and suffering, as might be expected, was very severe and continued so for about three years. In some families the child would have to stay of nights in an outhouse or elsewhere away from the family so as not to disturb them through the night, while in others the mother or mother-in-law would have a big stick by the side of her bed, with which to get up and beat the little girl should she disturb the household by her wails. Toes would often drop off under binding and sometimes the entire foot. When grown up the women could walk alone with their maimed feet for short distances but usually they needed to be supported by some one or something. "Don't imagine, however, that Chinese ladies are unable to move. They can, most of them, walk short distances. But it is true that the spirit is taken out of them by this species of suffering, and that they are oppressed by a sense of physical helplessness and dependence." [18]

**Amusements.** "The active sports of Chinese boys are few. There are hardly any sports, so-called, that develop the muscles and render a lad graceful and agile. The Chinese boy at sixteen is as grave and staid as an American grandfather; and if he happens to be married soon after, he throws aside most games as being childish. At the best, he has nothing corresponding to baseball, football, cricket, bicycle-riding, skating, sliding, or tennis. Nor is he fond of exerting himself. He would rather sit for hours talking and joking than waste time in running and jumping. He thinks it work if his play entails much perspiration. His elders, too, frown upon boisterous games. They approve quiet, meditative lads who are given to study." [19]

"Active, manly plays are not popular in the south, and instead of engaging in a cricket-match or regatta, going to

[18] Lee, When I was a boy in China, 47.
[19] *Ibid.*, 34.

a bowling-alley or fives' court, to exhibit their strength and skill, they lift beams headed with heavy stones to prove their brawn, or kick up their heels in a game of shuttlecock. The outdoor amusements of gentlemen consist in flying kites, carrying birds on perches, sauntering hand in hand through the fields, or lazily boating on the water, while pitching coppers, fighting crickets or quails, kicking a shuttlecock, snapping sticks, chucking stones or guessing the number of seeds in an orange, are plays for lads.''[20]

"Children's games are always interesting. Chinese games are especially so because they are a mine hitherto unexplored. An eminent archdeacon once wrote: 'The Chinese are not much given to athletic exercises.' A well-known doctor of divinity states that, 'their sports do not require much physical exertion, nor do they often pair off, or choose sides and compete, in order to see who are the best players,' while a still more prominent writer tells us that, 'active, manly sports are not popular in the South.' Let us see whether these opinions are true.''[21] And this author goes on to give a large number of games, enough to bear out his statement in the preface to his book that, "to the careful observer of these different phases it becomes apparent that the Chinese child is well supplied with methods of exercise and amusement, also that he has much in common with children of other lands."

There were numerous holidays and festivals, giving abundance of entertainment for the children. The principal time of leisure and rejoicing was at the new year. On the night of the last day of the old year everybody would remain up and at midnight a great time was begun with an incessant firing of crackers and this was kept up for a number of days. Another great time was at the Feast of Lanterns, in which was a procession of men and boys with lanterns of all shapes and sizes, the procession ending with an immense and terrible dragon, forty feet or more in length, carried aloft on bamboo poles.

Kite-flying was a national recreation, indulged in by all ages and classes. It was not an unusual thing to see an old gray-haired man enjoying it in company of a young boy. All kinds of kites were used and of all sizes. The ninth day of the ninth month, which comes in October, was "Kites' Day." On that day the men and the boys would go out to

[20] Williams, The Middle kingdom, II, 89.
[21] Headland, Chinese boy and girl, 51.

the hills and have a great time. Rank and size and age made no difference, as all entered into the zeal of the sport just the same. The greatest sport consisted in the cutting of one another's kite strings while the kites were in the air, which was done by the sawing of one string on another.

There were plenty of little shows and juggling and gymnastic feats for the children and who might wish to see them. They had Punch and Judy, trained dogs and monkeys, the whirling of plates, the tossing of knives, juggling of various kinds, sword swallowing, and many other tricks and performances.

The Chinese children had plenty of toys, which, as in all countries, were suited to the wants of that country. The toys were not greatly complicated in structure. There were rattles for the baby, dolls for the little girl, and drums and knives and tops for the boys.

"There are not many games in which boys and girls play together. If they do play together it is only while they are children, under ten or twelve. Growing-up girls will have nothing whatever to do with boys, though Chinese boys and girls are very sociable, each with friends of their own sex." [22]

Girls have plenty of games they play among themselves—"Lots of them," which Headland says was the stereotyped answer that would come from any Chinaman to almost any question he might be asked about things Chinese. Several are given but one quoted here will be sufficient to show that their games are as full of life as among girls anywhere. "This small girl after some delay took control of the party and began arranging them for a game, which she called 'going to town,' similar to one which the boys called 'pounding rice.' Two of the girls stood back to back, hooked their arms, and as one bent forward she raised the other from the ground, and thus alternating, they sang:

> Up you go, down you see,
> Here's a turnip for you and me;
> Here's a pitcher, we'll go to town;
> Oh, what a pity, we've fallen down.

At which point they both sat down back to back, their arms still locked, and asked and answered the following questions:

> What do you see in the heavens bright?
> I see the moon and the stars at night.

[22] Lee, When I was a boy in China, 40.

> What do you see in the earth, pray tell?
> I see in the earth a deep, deep well.
> What do you see in the well, my dear?
> I see a frog and his voice I hear.
> What is he saying there on the rock?
> Get up, get up, ke'rh kua, ke'rh kua.

They then tried to get up, but, with their arms locked, they found it impossible to do so, and rolled over and got up with great hilarity." [23]

In the one city of Peking alone, Headland collected more than seventy-five different games. In his pictures and descriptions of games played by boys are such as would call out much vigorous exercise. One of their favorite games was "Skin the snake." In this game the boys all stood in line one behind the other. They would then bend forward and each put one hand between his legs and grasp a hand of the boy behind him. Then they all would back and the rear boy would lie down and the others would back over astride of him and each would lie down in turn, thus bringing the head between the legs of his neighbor. When all were down then the last boy that lay down would get up and each would get up in turn, raising each one after him, until all were up and standing straight, when they would let go hands and the game was finished.

Gambling was, perhaps, the greatest sport of the Chinese, and it was indulged in by both men and boys. "A boy with two cash prefers to risk their loss on the throw of a die, to simply buying a cake without trying the chance of getting it for nothing." [24] One of their means of gambling was through cricket-fighting. In the season, the crickets were hunted by men and boys, who would go out to the hills and waysides to get them. They were cared for and trained and some would become such great fighters as to command high prices.

**Dress.** The Chinese did not use wool in clothing. In the earlier times, before cotton was introduced, it is thought that they used for their garments some other vegetable fibers, such as rushes. When cotton was introduced into China, it became the chief material for clothing. They did not use underclothing but padded the outer garments for winter use and as the weather grew colder they would put on more wadded clothes till in full winter they would become about

---
[23] Headland, Chinese boys and girls, 80.
[24] Williams, Middle kingdom, II, 89.

double their usual size. Their shoes were made of cloth and so they were a poor protection from cold and moisture.

The young women enjoyed wearing colors, pink and green and blue being the ones most preferred. The ordinary dress was a large-sleeved robe of silk or cotton over a longer garment, under which were loose trousers fastened round the ankles just above the small feet and tight shoes. They wore their hair hanging down in long tresses, and the putting up of the hair was one of the ceremonies preparatory to marriage. The eyebrows were blackened with charred sticks and arched or narrowed to a fine curved line, to resemble a young willow leaflet or the moon when a day or two old. Cosmetics were used quite freely, on grand occasions the face being daubed with white paint and the lips and cheeks with red, so that all blushes were covered up. They wore bangles, bracelets, and ear-rings of glass, stone, and metal. "A belle is described as having cheeks like the almond flower, lips like a peach's bloom, waist as the willow leaf, eyes bright as dancing ripples in the sun, and footsteps like the lotus flower." [25]

In some parts of China, if not in all, the baby in summertime wore no clothing at all. In the winter it wore quilted trousers with feet attached. In some parts the trousers of the baby were partly filled with sand or earth, so that it was a common saying that a person who displayed small practical knowledge had not yet been taken out of his "earth-trousers." The older children wore the same pattern of clothing and cut out of the same kind of cloth as their parents and grandparents.

**Religion.** "In considering all systems of idolatry and superstition, one significant fact stands prominent, *the utter neglect of religious training of the young*. China's three great religions have nothing answering to the Christian Sunday School. Of course, boys and girls pick up some religious ideas in their intercourse with those about them. But nobody ever deliberately sits down to tell them of this god and that god, their origin, character and power. Only incidentally is such knowledge conveyed. There are many religious books; but from the difficulty of learning to read, they are necessarily sealed to the young mind. If the young are told to worship this idol and that idol, they never understand why and wherefore they should do this. In time they comprehend that they do it to obtain favor and to gain merit.

[25] Williams, Middle kingdom, II, 41.

"I well remember the first time I was led to a temple and there told to bend my knees to the idol decked out in a gorgeous robe, its face blackened by the smoke from the incense. On either side of the room stood four huge idols, with stern and forbidding faces. One of them was especially frightful. It was the God of Thunder represented by an image having the body of a man and the head of a highly caricatured rooster. This idol had a hammer in one hand and a large nail in the other, with which he is supposed to strike wicked persons. This god made such an impression on me that I had a horrible dream about it that very night. I saw him clad in fierceness; he moved his hands threateningly. Almost choked with fright though I was, I managed to cry out and that awoke me." [26]

**Education.** Education in China is of long standing. The Chinese from the earliest time, 2,000 B. C., or even earlier, held school education of high value. The competitive literary examinations of candidates for office was established about a thousand years later and about 700 A. D. the whole plan was gone over and arranged as found in the last century, previous to the changes of recent years. No other nation has so venerated scholars and scholarship.

Nevertheless of this high esteem for education, there were no public schools in the sense as with us as the government did not establish schools, except, perhaps, for the most advanced students. Yet there were a great number of schools, taken care of in a private way, and although every village did not have a school, yet they would have liked such, but mostly on account of poverty could not, for everywhere was the most profound reverence for education. There were three classes of undergraduate schools: "The primary, in which little is attended to beyond memoriter recitation and imitative chirography; the middle, in which the canonical books are expounded; and the classical, in which composition is the leading exercise." [27] Because of the great number of literary scholars who wanted to teach, the pay for the most part was quite meager.

School usually began about six in the morning, and it continued all day, with intervals for breakfast and lunch, sometimes running till dark. In some of the higher schools the scholars would return in the evening to their school work.

[26] Lee, When I was a boy in China, 70.
[27] Martin, The Chinese, 71.

School would continue throughout the entire week and the year, except one month during the New Year's festival and a vacation at wheat harvest and also at the autumnal harvest. If the teacher was preparing himself for a literary degree, there might be a vacation of about six weeks in the summer. The teacher was often not quite regular in his attendance at the school and the pupils were still more irregular than he, so that in a way made up for the lack of holidays.

There were scarcely any school-houses as such in China. The schools were held as a rule in the hall of a temple or in a private building, usually the ancestral temples were used for such purposes, and yet they might be held in a shed, which scarcely protected from the weather, or in the upper attic of a shop. In this room were placed a table, with an arm-chair, for the teacher. The writing-materials, which consisted of brushes, India ink, and ink-wells made of slate, were placed on this table. About the room were tables and stools for the pupils. In one corner of the room was placed a tablet or an inscription on the wall, dedicated to Confucius and the god of Letters.

Whatever may be said of education in older China, the teachers were educated men, the majority of them being unsuccessful candidates for literary degrees, but many of them were Bachelors and not a few were Doctors. For the work they had to do they were well prepared by a long course of study and they were usually competent. "In no country is the office of teacher more revered. Not only is the living instructor saluted with forms of the profoundest respect, but the very name of teacher, taken in the abstract, is an object of almost idolatrous homage."[28] Yet, "as a matter of fact, the Chinese teacher is often barely able to keep soul and body together, and is frequently obliged to borrow garments in which to appear before his patrons."[29]

The first day of school was a great and noted day in the life of a Chinese boy. He entered school in his seventh or eighth year. When he was to enter school, a lucky day was found for him, and with his good clothes on he started for school, feeling that this was the greatest event that was to happen in his life till he entered the Imperial Academy, which he was sure to do, so said all his friends. On entering the school-room he saluted, by prostrating himself, the

[28] Martin, The Chinese, 62.
[29] Smith, Village life in China, 73.

picture of Confucius and next, with almost as much reverence, saluted his teacher, for the teacher was held in very high respect.

The course of study for the schools of China was formulated a long time ago and rigidly held to in all the schools of the empire. It was divided into three grades of instruction. The Chinese language does not have an alphabet but there is a different symbol for each word. In the first period the pupil was to learn the most important symbols, learning also to write them, and to commit to memory the nine sacred books, known as the Four Books and the Five Classics. The Four Books are known as the Confucian Analects, the Great Learning, the Golden Medium, and the Sayings of Mencius; and the Five Classics are the Book of Changes, the Book of History, the Spring and Autumn Annals, the Book of Odes, and the Book of Rites. All this would take four or five years on the part of the pupil. As these books were written in the old Chinese language they would not be understood by the pupils and the second stage of learning consisted in the translation of these books and classics into the language of the pupils, and also there were lessons in composition. The commentaries on these works were taken up and their meaning explained. In the third stage of learning composition was entered upon and consisted in the writing of essays and poems, imitating the style and thought of the five classics and the better commentaries. A full comprehension of the four books and the five classics and the commentaries upon them and the use of this knowledge in the writing of essays and poems was the desired end aimed at by the Chinese scholar and which was all that was needed for the highest examination in the empire.

The methods of teaching with the Chinese were formal, being based upon methods handed down from the ages, so that all teachers taught in the one stereotyped way. In teaching reading the teacher would have the pupils come to his desk, stand in line, each holding his book open before him. The teacher would read aloud a line, the pupils would then read this in concert in a loud voice, and this would continue till the pupils could pronounce the line without the teacher's help. Then they would go to their seats and commit this line to memory, each shouting it out as loud as he could. "Every Chinese regards this shouting as an indispensable part of the child's education. If he is not shouting how can the teacher be sure that he is studying? and as studying and shouting are the same thing, when he is shouting there is nothing more to be desired."[30] When the pupil had learned the line, he would go to the teacher's desk, lay his book upon it, turn his back to the teacher, and shout out the line as rapidly as he possibly could do. This method gave to the Chinese the phrase "to back the book" as we have "to learn by heart." This method was continued till the whole book was committed to memory.

The only other subject taught in the elementary schools was writing. In teaching writing, the master would make a copy and the pupil would place it under transparent paper and trace it with a hair pencil and then copy it without the tracing till he could make it from memory. "In lieu of slates, they generally use boards painted white to save paper, washing out the writing when finished."[31] In China, writing takes the place that drawing and painting do here, so all strive to become fine penmen.

For most of the boys, three or four years was the extent of their schooling, but if higher education was desired they attended higher schools. Here they were given lectures explaining the meaning of classical authors, which lectures were greatly committed to memory. They were also taught prose and verse composition, in which they followed the thought, style, and meter of the sacred books or of great writers, memorizing these writings for the purpose.

The Chinese teacher was very severe. The more severe he was, the better teacher he was considered. Fear ruled in the Chinese school. That the boy might ever be reminded of the necessity of studying, the implements to help him were always kept in plain view, as, "a wooden ruler to be applied to the head of the offender and sometimes the hands, also a rattan stick for the body. Flogging with this stick is the heaviest punishment allowed; for slight offenses the ruler is used upon the palms, and for reciting poorly—upon the head."[32] Teachers carried their punishments to extreme lengths. The bad pupils were the stupid ones who did not get their lessons assigned in the given time. For such, severe beatings were administered, so severe that in one case "a pupil

---

[30] Smith, Village life in China, 80.
[31] Davis, The Chinese, I, 276.
[32] Lee, When I was a boy in China, 54.

was so much injured as to be thrown into fits, and such instances can scarcely be uncommon." [33]

Girls were not often educated in China, because the parents thought it of no use as they would marry and leave them, also there was no such incentive for girls as with boys, who might hold office, and besides popular opinion regarded reading and writing dangerous arts in female hands. Nevertheless here and there a woman came forth among the educated and celebrated instances were sometimes quoted of women who have been skilled in verse. When a woman did emerge with a good education, she was highly respected for her attainments. The girls of the better class were taught needlework, painting on silk, and music.

Education in China did not stop with the youth, as the manner of filling the offices through literary competitive examinations kept many studying even to old age. This system was very old, dating back to several centuries before Christ. In these examinations there were three grades of degrees conferred—"flowering talent," Bachelors; "promoted man," Master; "entered scholar," Doctor. Beyond this was yet another higher honor, as the very highest became members of the Imperial Academy, the "forest of pencils," at the court at Peking. The best and most finished scholar of all was so designated every three years by the Emperor, the very greatest honor. The only thing in history that seems to approach this honor is the winning of the foot-race at the Olympian Games.

Chinese education appears to fulfill the saying heard in this country in bygone days—Educate a boy and he won't work—for in China "the scholar, even the village scholar, not only does not plow and reap, but he does not in any way assist those who perform these necessary acts. He does not harness an animal, nor feed him, nor drive a cart, nor light a fire, nor bring water—in short, so far as physical exertion goes, he does as nearly as possible nothing all day. 'The scholar is not a utensil', (a Confucian saying), he seems to be thinking all day long, and every day of his life, until one wishes that at times he would be a utensil, that he might sometimes be of use. He will not even move a bench nor make any motion that looks like labor." [34]

[33] Smith, Village life in China, 79.
[34] Ibid., 93.

"There are among us who are enamored of state-systems which regulate education down to its minutest detail, and leave no room for the free play of mind: in China we have this indirectly accomplished and see in it all its necessary rigidity, uniformity, and pedantry. There are who advocate a secular system of education: in China we see this in full operation. There are who think that all success in the education of mind should be measured by external competitive tests: in China we have this elaborated into an iron system. There are who cling by the dogmatic and preceptive, and regard with suspicion the habituating of the mind of schoolboys to ideals esthetic and spiritual, including even the simple elements of humanity: in China they will find what they desire to see. There are who hold that teachers and school-inspectors are heaven-born, and are above the study of educational principles and methods (as the Emperor Sigismund was *supra Grammaticam*): so China thinks." [35]

Whatever may be said of Chinese education, it has lasted through the ages and it has sufficed for the needs of the nation. It may be that when this old nation gets a system of education based upon European and American ideas, and fills her offices with the most highly educated and only the most highly educated, then may China lead the world.

## LITERATURE

1. Barnes, Earl and Mary S., Historical ideas and methods of Chinese education. *Studies in education*, I (1896-97), 112-118.
2. Carus, Paul, Chinese life and customs.
3. Davis, John Francis, The Chinese.
4. Doolittle, Justus, Sketches of social life in China. *Harper's Magazine*, XXXI (1865), 429-442.
5. Douglass, Robert K., China.
6. Flower, William Henry, Fashion in deformity.
7. Graves, Frank Pierrepont, A history of education, Before the Middle Ages.
8. Headland, Isaac Taylor, Home life in China.
9. Headland, Isaac Taylor, The Chinese boy and girl.
10. Laurie, S. S., Historical survey of pre-Christian education.

[35] Laurie, Pre-Christian education, 150.

11. Lee, Yan Phou, When I was a boy in China.
12. Little, Mrs. Archibald, Intimate China.
13. Martin, W. A. P., The Chinese.
14. Martin, W. A. P., The lore of Cathay.
15. Smith, Arthur H., Chinese characteristics.
16. Smith, Arthur H., Village life in China.
17. Williams, S. Wells, The Middle Kingdom.

## CHAPTER VI

### THE CHILD IN JAPAN

**Women.** Although women have always stood higher in Japan than in any other oriental country, yet they were much more highly considered in the early times than in the later times. There was no seclusion, they had a station in society, they shared in the recreations of their fathers and husbands, they possessed intellectual and physical vigor, they filled offices of state and religion; in fact, they ranked alongside of men as among the best nations of the earth. Among the rulers of Japan there have been nine empresses, the most noted having been Jingu and who led a conquering expedition into Corea about 200 A. D., from whence came letters, religion, and civilization into Japan.

"Of one hundred and twenty-three Japanese sovereigns, nine have been women. The custodian of the divine regalia is a virgin priestess. The chief deity in their mythology is a woman. Japanese women, by their wit and genius, made their native tongue a literary language. In literature, art, poetry, song, the names of women are among the most brilliant of those on the long roll of fame and honor on whose brows the Japanese, at least, have placed the fadeless chaplet of renown. Their memory is still kept green by recitation, quotation, reading, and inscription on screen, roll, memorial-stone, wall, fan, cup, and those exquisite works of art that delight even alien admirers east and west of the Pacific.

"In the records of the Japanese glory, valor, fortitude in affliction, greatness in the hour of death, filial devotion, wifely affection, in all the straits of life when codes of honor, morals, and religion are tested in the person of their professors, the literature of history and romance, the every-day routine of fact, teem with instances of the Japanese woman's power and willingness to share whatever of pain or sorrow is appointed to man. In the annals of persecution, in the red roll of martyrs, no names are brighter, no faces gleam more peacefully amidst the flames, or on the cross of transfixing spears, or on the pyre of rice-straw, or on the precipice edge, or in the open grave about to be filled up, than the faces of the Christian Japanese women in the seventeenth century. Such is the position of woman in Japan in the past."[1]

In later times woman fell from her high estate and even lost power over herself, as she came under her father in the home, under her husband when married, and under her son when widowed. "The introduction of the Chinese civilization with the Confucian system of moral philosophy, and of Buddhism, and later on the establishment of Feudalism, were prejudicial to this high position of women. Chinese philosophers seem not to have had much respect for women; while Buddhism regards women as sinful creatures, a temptation and snare, an obstacle to peace and holiness. In our feudal system, in the code of Bushido, there was no reverence for women as in the Western Chivalry."[2] Buddhism entered into Japan in the sixth century of the Christian era and Confucianism came in some earlier, while Feudalism existed in Japan earlier than in Europe and continued later, from the fifteenth to the sixteenth centuries being the time during which the feudal system received its most perfect development and the *Bushido*, or "The Way of the Samurai," was fully elaborated.

The Japanese women had a love for beauty, order and neatness; they were patient and long-suffering; their hopes lay in their children and they tended and cared for them as, perhaps, no other nation of women ever did. They had plenty to keep them busy with their numerous household duties and the making of their own clothing and that of their children. Many of them were engaged in the care of silk-worms and in tea-picking. The country wife was busy in the rice-field, doing her work alongside her husband and sons, as well as performing the other duties that came into her country life. "Among the daily tasks of the housewife, one, and by no means the least of her duties, is to receive, duly acknowledge, and return in suitable manner, the presents received in the family. Presents are not confined to special seasons, although upon certain occasions etiquette is rigid in its requirements in this matter, but they may be given and re-

[1] Griffis, The Mikado's empire, II, 553.
[2] Kikuchi, Japanese education, 261.

ceived at all times, for the Japanese are pre-eminently a present-giving nation.''[3]

"As regards our standard of beauty. . . . A woman to be considered beautiful by us, need not be tall. Height may be divinely imposing, but not essential to human beauty. With us, about five feet would be considered the most desirable height, but if one must err, it is advisable to err by exceeding rather than by falling short of the mark. The figure should be slender without being bony, the waist long and the hips narrow. To secure grace, the body should be held slightly forward, not boldly erect. A very important feature is the neck, which should be long, white, slender, and gracefully curved. The hair should, of course, be abundant, long, and perfectly straight, and while no deviation from black is tolerated, it should not be just black, but should be so glossy that it seems blue-black. The face should be oval and long, with a straight nose, which should also be high and narrow. As for the eyes, opinions are divided, one school of connoisseurs demanding that they should be large with a double line of the lid, while another school prefers that the eyes should be long and narrow and slightly slanting upwards at the outer corner. The color of the eye should always be clear and deep brown; the lashes thick, long, and curved; the eyebrows black and distinct, their line long, and well arched; the mouth small; lips thin, curved, and red; teeth small, regular, and white. The ears must be evenly curved, with no angle, and in size not too small, for pinched lobes look poverty-stricken. Large ears, like those of the probable inhabitants of Mars, lately described by Professor Perrier, if not exactly beautiful, are believed to be lucky. As for the shape of the forehead, there are four types. By the one termed 'horned,' we mean that in which the hair grows to a point in the middle of the forehead and high at the sides after the fashion called by the Germans *Geheimraths-Ecke* or the 'Councillor's corners.' Then there are the square and the round types; but the forehead most admired is high and narrow at the top, and obliquely slanting at the sides, suggesting the outline of our sacred mountain, Fuji. As for the complexion, it should be fair, with a tint of the rose on the cheek, only, in our parlance, we would call it cherry-hued.''[4]

[3] Bacon, Japanese girls and women, 96.
[4] Nitobe, The Japanese nation, 96.

One of the phases of the life of women in Japan is that of the dancing-girls, the *geisha*. These are girls obtained when quite young from poor parents or as orphans and trained in establishments for entertaining at tea-houses or at private gatherings. They are taught the old Japanese dances, and other dances, to sing and to play on instruments, to serve wine, and in other ways to entertain. These are from ancient times. "The *geisha* are not necessarily 'bad women,' as you call them, not any worse professionally than the actresses and vaudeville artistes of America."[5] Whatever the geisha may be, there is no question about the *jōrō*, or courtesans, because licensed houses exist in every part of Japan. Yet this is claimed of rather recent origin, as in the older times such houses did not exist, and especially in the villages and towns of the interior, where there were even but few of such women. The saddest side of these houses is their filling through filial obedience, the one thing considered most important for Japanese women. "The Japanese maiden, as pure as the purest Christian virgin, will, at the command of her father, enter the brothel tomorrow, and prostitute herself for life. Not a murmur escapes her lips as she thus filially obeys. To a life she loathes, and to disease, premature old age, and an early grave, she goes joyfully. The staple of a thousand novels, plays, and pictures in Japan is written in the life of a girl of gentle manners and tender heart, who hates her life and would gladly destroy it, but refrains because her purchase-money has enabled her father to pay his debts, and she is bound not to injure herself. In the stews of the great cities of Japan are today, I doubt not, hundreds of girls who loathe their existence, but must live on in gilded misery because they are fulfilling all righteousness as summed up in filial piety."[6]

Old age was not a burden or a fear among the Japanese women, nor was it something to be ashamed of. Old age was really welcome, and especially in the last centuries when woman's freedom was taken away and obedience to the men introduced, for old age brought freedom, as then the mother became a person of much consideration, to be waited upon and cared for by children and grandchildren, the burdens of life being turned over to them. "As she bears all things, endures all things, suffers long, and is kind, as she serves her

[5] Nitobe, The Japanese nation, 165.
[6] Griffis, The Mikado's empire, II, 555.

mother-in-law, manages her husband's household, cares for her babies, the thought that cheers and encourages her in her busy and not too happy life is the thought of the sunny, calm old age, when she can lay her burdens and cares on younger shoulders, and bask in the warmth and sunshine which this Indian Summer of her life will bring to her."[7]

**Marriage.** A young woman in Japan was expected as a matter of course to marry. Any young woman was not forced to marry any young man, for there was a certain freedom of choice on her part. Young people were expected to marry within their rank. In the early times, marriage between a brother and sister of the same mother was not permitted, but if by the same father by a different mother they could marry, as they were not considered related as in the first instance. In these earlier times marriage was permitted at sixteen in man and thirteen in woman. Marriage was not a religious affair, and not even a contract between the parties. It was rather a giving away of the girl to the man who was to be her husband and to his family, so that the bride's person and property passed completely under the control of the husband and his family.

At one time, according to one authority, when a youth had fixed his affections upon a maiden of suitable condition, he disclosed his passion by attaching a branch of a certain shrub (the *Celastrus alatus*) to the house of the damsel's parents. If this emblem of his passion was neglected, it implied that his suit was rejected; if accepted, so was the lover; and should the young lady wish to express reciprocal tenderness, she forthwith blackened her teeth, though she must not pluck out her eyebrows until after the wedding.[8] In other times, the affair was arranged by a go-between. A young man would get a married friend to help him select a bride, to make his wants known to the girl and her family, and to arrange a meeting between the young people at the home of a mutual friend, where they could decide the matter. Again the matter may have been arranged by the families, it might be a long time in advance, so that the young people did not have much to do with it.

When the matter was decided on, then presents were exchanged, the young man usually sending a piece of handsome

[7] Bacon, Japanese girls and women, 121.
[8] ———, Manners and customs of the Japanese, 127.

silk, used for the *obi* or girdle, which corresponded to the engagement-ring of Europe and America, but sometimes the young man sent other presents, and because of which a handsome daughter was considered rather an addition to the fortune of a family. A formal betrothal was then entered into, and a lucky day found for the wedding.

Just before the wedding, generally on the morning of the wedding-day, the bride's trousseau and the household goods, which the bride was expected to take with her, were sent to the house of the bridegroom. These varied according with the rank and position and wealth of the bride's family. The trousseau would contain dresses for all seasons and sashes of all kinds, and since fashion unchanged a woman might enter her husband's home with a supply of clothing that could last her through a lifetime.

As in old times the wedding ceremony occurred in the afternoon, toward noon there was a bridal procession from the bride's home to the home of the bridegroom. The bride was seated in a palanquin, clothed and veiled in white, escorted by two bridesmaids, and accompanied by relatives, neighbors, and friends, the men all in their dress of ceremony and the women in their gayest robes. When the procession reached the bridegroom's home, the bride was escorted by the bridesmaids into the room of state, where sat the bridegroom in the post of honor, surrounded by parents and nearest relatives.

When the real ceremony was performed there were present the bridegroom and his parents, the bride and her parents, a few of the most intimate relatives or friends, and the cup-bearers, perhaps not over a dozen people in all. There was no religious ceremony, no words were spoken, no promises, no vows, no prayer. When all was ready, the wedding-cup, a two-spouted cup, was filled by a young girl with native wine (*saké*) and presented to the mouths of the bride and groom alternately, till all was drank by them, being a symbol as husband and wife of the equal sharing of their joys and sorrows of married life. Then the young couple arose and offered cups of *saké* to their parents, after which the bride removed her veil, and the ceremony was ended. Then the wedding-guests, who had been in other rooms during the ceremony, joined the wedding-party and all partook of a feast prepared for the occasion, with the mirth and joy that usually accompany weddings among all peoples and in all times.

On the third day after the wedding, the newly-married couple were expected to make a visit to the bride's family. The bride's family prepared a dinner for the occasion, with music and dancing by professional performers, and other entertainment. A large number of the relatives and friends were invited and the bride appeared as hostess with her mother. Within the course of two or three months, the newly married couple were expected to entertain either in their own home, the home of the bridegroom's parents, or at a tea-house.

"There are wedded couples who labor and save heroically for years, in order to pay the expenses of their marriage festival. There is one rather amusing custom, however, whereby this expense may be avoided. A couple of respectable people have a daughter, who is acquainted with a good young fellow who would be an excellent husband for her, except that he lacks the necessary means to give her the customary wedding-presents and keep a free table for a week, for the two families. The parents, coming home from the bath one fine evening, do not find their daughter at home. They inquire in the neighborhood; nobody has seen her, but all the neighbors offer their services in assisting to find her. The parents accept the offer, and the procession, constantly increasing in numbers, passes from street to street, until it reaches the dwelling of the lover. The latter, protected by his closed screens, in vain pretends to be deaf; he is at last obliged to yield to the demands of the crowd. He opens the door, and the lost daughter, in tears, throws herself at the feet of her parents, who threaten her with their malediction.

"Then, the tender-hearted neighbors, moved by the scene, intercede; the mother relents; the father, remains haughty and inexorable; the intercession of the neighbors increases in eloquence, and the young man promises to be the most faithful of sons-in-law. Finally, the resistance of the father is overcome; he pardons his daughter, pardons the lover, and calls the latter his son. All at once, as if by magic, cups of saké circulate among the crowd; everyone takes his or her place on the matting of the room; the two outlaws are seated in the midst of the circle, drink their bowl of saké together, the marriage is proclaimed in the presence of a sufficient number of witnesses, and the police officer enters it upon his list the next morning."[9]

There is another side of Japanese marriage, where the young man enters the home of the bride. If in a family there was no son to inherit the name and no son was adopted, upon the eldest daughter's coming of age, her family would seek some young man who would be willing to marry the daughter and give up his own name and take that of the family. The young men were usually attracted to such a marriage because thereby they could inherit wealth or rank or both, but sometimes such was entered upon solely on account of the attractiveness of the young lady.

It is a question whether polygamy in itself ever existed in Japan, but there is no question about concubinage, as it began at an early time, for the Emperor was allowed twelve supplementary wives and the nobles (samurai) two. It seems from the earliest there was one legal wife, and whatever the other women were they were subservient to her. But concubinage did not prevail very much among the middle and lower classes, and with the upper classes only with the wealthier members. These concubines were kept in the home unless the legal wife was strong enough to keep them out, when they were furnished separate dwellings. They were ever a discordant element in the life of the family. Since both Shintoism and Confucianism called for ancestral worship, where there were no offspring by the legal wife, this might call for concubinage to raise up children, and sometimes where there was no heir, the wife might for that cause urge the husband to take a handmaid to raise up sons to preserve the ancestral line. If the child of a concubine was adopted into the family, it was taken from the mother and she became no more to it than any other of the servants and had no more to do with it than they did.

During feudalism in Japan, the legal status of women was very low. They had no legal rights and their evidence was not admitted in a court of justice. The husband had unlimited power of divorce, but under no circumstances could a wife demand to be separated from her husband, but she had to abide his will. A great reason for a wife suffering much and not leaving her husband was that the children belonged to him and in case of a separation their disposal rested absolutely with him.

[9] Taylor, Japan in our day, 148.

"Seven causes for justifiable divorce are laid down in the classics of Confucius, which are the basis of legal morals in Japan as in China, or as those of Justinian are with us. The wife may be divorced:

1. If she be disobedient to her parents-in-law. (After marriage, in her husband's home, his parents become hers in a far more significant sense than among us.)
2. If she be barren. (If the husband loves his childless wife, he keeps and supports her.)
3. If she be lewd or licentious. (She must not be given to loose talk or wine. It is not proper for her even to write a letter to any other man.)
4. If she be jealous (of other women's clothes, or children, or especially of her husband).
5. If she have a loathsome or contagious disease. (If dearly beloved, she may be kept in a separate room and cared for.)
6. If she steal.
7. If she talk too much.

"It is needless to say that the seventh and last reason is the one frequently availed of, or pretended. The Japanese think it is a good rule that works but one way. The husband is not divorced from the wife for these equal reasons. Of course, woman in Japan, by her tact, tongue, graces, and charms, is able to rule her husband generally by means invisible to the outer world, but none the less potent. Though man holds the sword, the pen, and divorce, and glories in his power, yet woman, by her finer strength, in hut as in palace hall, rules her lord."[10]

**The Mother's Memorial.** "A sight not often met with in the cities, but in the suburbs and country places frequent as the cause of it requires, is the *nagaré kanjō* (flowing invocation). A piece of cotton cloth is suspended by its four corners to stakes set in the ground near a brook, rivulet, or, if in the city, at the side of the water-course which fronts the houses of the better classes. Behind it rises a higher, lath-like board, notched several times near the top, and inscribed with a brief legend. Resting on the cloth at the brookside, or, if in the city, in a pail of water, is a wooden dipper. Perhaps upon the four corners, in the upright bamboo, may be set bouquets of flowers. A careless stranger may not notice the odd thing, but a little study of its parts

[10] Griffis, The Mikado's empire, II, 557.

reveals the symbolism of death. The tall lath tablet is the same as that set behind graves and tombs. The ominous Sanskrit letters betoken death. Even the flowers in their bloom call to mind the tributes of affectionate remembrance which loving survivors set in the sockets of the monuments in the grave-yards. On the cloth is written a name such as is given to persons after death, and the prayer, '*Namu miō, hō ren ge kiō*' (Glory to the salvation-bringing Scriptures). Waiting long enough, perchance but a few minutes, there may be seen a passer-by who pauses, and, devoutly offering a prayer with the aid of his rosary, reverently dips a ladleful of water, pours it upon the cloth, and waits patiently until it has strained through, before moving on.

"All this, when the significance is understood, is very touching. It is the story of vicarious suffering, of sorrow from the brink of joy, of one dying that another may live. It tells of mother-love and mother-woe. It is a mute appeal to every passer-by, by the love of Heaven, to shorten the penalties of a soul in pain.

"The Japanese (Buddhists) believe that all calamity is the result of sin either in this or a previous state of existence. The mother who dies in childbed suffers, by such a death, for some awful transgression, it may be in a cycle of existence long since passed. For it she must leave her new-born infant, in the full raptures of mother-joy, and sink into the darkness of Hades, to wallow in a lake of blood. There must she groan and suffer until the 'flowing invocation' ceases, by the wearing-out of the symbolic cloth. When this is so utterly worn that the water no longer drains, but falls through at once, the freed spirit of the mother, purged of her sin, rises to resurrection among the exalted beings of a higher cycle of existence. Devout men, as they pass by, reverently pour a ladleful of water. Women, especially those who have felt mother-pains, and who rejoice in life and loving offspring, repeat the expiatory act with deeper feeling; but the depths of sympathy are fathomed only by those who, being mothers, are yet bereaved. Yet, as in the presence of nature's awful glories the reverent gazer is shocked by the noisy importunity of the beggar, so before this sad and touching memorial the proofs of sordid priestcraft chill the warm sympathy which the sight even from the heart of an alien might evoke.

"The cotton cloth inscribed with the prayer and the name

of the deceased, to be efficacious, can be purchased only at the temples. I have been told, and it is no secret, that rich people are able to secure a napkin which, when stretched but a few days, will rupture, and let the water pass through at once. The poor man can get only the stoutest and most closely woven fabric. The limit of purgatorial penance is thus fixed by warp and woof, and warp and woof are gauged by money. The rich man's napkin is scraped thin in the middle. Nevertheless, the poor mother secures a richer tribute of sympathy from her humble people; for in Japan, as in other lands, poverty has many children, while wealth mourns for heirs; and in the lowly walks of life are more pitiful women who have felt the woe and the joy of motherhood than in the mansions of the rich.''[11]

**Dress.** The ordinary dress of both sexes in Japan in the older times was quite similar but differed in color and texture. It consisted of a number of loose, wide gowns worn over each other, fastened at the waist with a girdle. The family arms were woven or worked into the back and breast of the outer garment. The sleeves of the garments were wide and long. Within doors the feet were bare or covered with socks and outdoors clogs of straw, matting, or wood were worn, kept on the feet by an upright pin or button held between the two large toes.

The men shaved the front and crown of the head, leaving a sort of tuft on top; the boys' head was shaved in different ways, but at fifteen the boy's hair was dressed exactly like a mature man, because then he attained his majority. Among the women the hair was worn long but arranged differently for a married woman than a young girl, and, too, the married women removed the hair of the eyebrows.

The infant was free from swathing; at three its clothes was bound at the waist with a girdle. At seven or later the boy of noble birth wore a short sword in his girdle which at fifteen, when he became a man, he would exchange for the two swords of the samurai.

**Regulations.** During the two hundred and fifty years— sixteenth-nineteenth centuries—when Japan was cut off from all outside people, the strictest economy was necessary for the nation to be able to care for itself. To this end regulations were laid down to which the different classes had to adhere closely. These were binding and must have proved

[11] Griffis, The Mikado's empire, I, 169.

irksome, yet they preserved the nation. It seems well to give some of the regulations her.

"The following are examples, first, of the rules applying to the *bungen* (station in life) of a farmer of seventy-five to one hundred *koku* ($375 to $500), and, second, to that of a common farm-laborer:

### I. For a Farmer of 100 *Koku*.

1. Such a farmer may build a house whose length is ten *ken* (about sixty feet), but there must be no parlor (*zashiki*), and the roof must not be tiled. If the householder wishes to tile the roof, to protect it against fires, he must first get permission.

2. On the occasion of a marriage of a son or daughter, the gifts of the householder must be limited to the following:

Two *nagamochi* (a chest used for bed-clothes).
One *tansu* (a chest of drawers).
One *tsuzura* (a vine used in basket making).
One *hasami-bako* (a case for scissors).
A *yuinō obi* (a present, usually the sash called *obi*, exchanged at the time of the wedding).
One *sensu* (a fan).
One *taru* (a vessel containing wine).
*Surume* (a kind of fish).
*Kobu* (a kind of seaweed).
*Tai* (a kind of fish, used on occasions of ceremony).

3. The viands on the wedding-day must be as follows:
(1) *Zōni-zuimono* (a kind of soup).
(2) The things placed on the *honzen* (a small table): (a) in the *hira* (one of the dishes), *namasu* (a kind of fish); (b) in the *choku* (the other dish), something roasted or broiled.
(3) *Hikimono* (viands taken home by each guest): (a) *suimono* (soup), two kinds; (b) *torimono* (a liquid), two kinds; (c) *hikigashi* (a kind of cake). These three kinds altogether must not make more than a small amount.

4. The family must never wear silk clothes. If a son or a daughter is to marry a person whose station allows the use of silk, the householder must request him not to use it on the occasion of the wedding.

5. No guests should be invited other than relations of the family, *ko-bun* (people who are under obligations to the householder for kindness received, and stand in the place of

children), and a few of the most intimate friends. But this rule refers only to the day of the wedding.

6. At a wedding or New Year's call, the use of *jū* (lacquer boxes, containing confectionery, given as presents) is forbidden.

7. When a member of the family makes a visit to a relation or elsewhere, he should not carry valuable presents. When he is visiting a sick friend, he may take anything which happens to be at hand.

8. When there is death (*fukō*), and people come to the house on visits of condolence, no wine should be offered.

9. At a funeral (*butsuji*) wine should not be offered to the persons who follow to the grave.

10. On such occasions, the viands should be of five kinds only; but there should be no wine. If wine is offered, it should be given in soup-cups, not in wine-cups, nor should *tori-zakana* (a dish served only with wine) be prepared.

11. On the occasion of the birth of a first child (*Uizan*), the presents from the grandparents should be as follows only:

A cotton garment.
One set (four boxes) of *jū*.
One *taru*.
Viands.

From the other relations only small money-presents, if any should be sent.

12. When the child is taken to the *mura* (village) temple (the occasion called *miya-mairi*), *jū* may be offered to the grandparents, but not to others.

13. At the time of *hatsu-bina* (girls' festival), and *hatsu-nobori* (boys' festival), grandparents and other relations should not present *hina* and *nobori* (dolls and flags), the whole family should present a single *kami-nobori* (paper-flag) and two *yari* (spears), and relatives may also make small money-presents.

## II. For the *Bungen* of a Farm-laborer.

1. The house may be five and a half *ken* (about thirty-two feet) in length, and the roof should be of straw or bamboo thatch.

2. The presents at a wedding may be:
One *tsu zura* (a vine used in basket making).
*Nagamochi* (chests) are forbidden.

3. At entertainments, one *hira* (dish) and one soup may be offered, but not in cups.

4. The collar and sleeve ends of the clothes may be ornamented with silk, and an *obi* (belt) of silk or silk crêpe may be worn, but not in public.

5. Hair ornaments should consist of *norihiki* and *motoi*, and nothing more.

6. Footwear should be *narazōri* (sandals made at Nara) not *setta* (sandals of iron and leather). Women are to wear bamboo-thonged sandals ordinarily, but at occasions of ceremony sandals with cotton thongs; men should wear only bamboo-thonged sandals on all occasions.

7. At the time of *Uizan* (birth of first child) the grandparents may send two *jū* (set of confectionery boxes), and money for rice and fish; other relations should send only money for fish.

8. At the time of *hatsu-nobori*, the grandparents may present a *yari* (spear), and at the time of *hatsu-bina* a *kami-bina* (paper doll), or *tsuchi-ningyo* (earthen doll).

"Accompanying these specific regulations, made with careful reference to each man's station in life, there were also general rules to meet unspecified contingencies. For example, only in case of absolute necessity could an umbrella be used by the ordinary laborer. He must usually content himself with the protection of a straw raincoat. Another provision related to costly articles which a family might happen to have. Special permission was necessary to make use of them, and no articles of luxury were to be used if on hand."[12]

**The Care of Children.** The birth of a child among the Japanese was a cause of rejoicing, a boy being somewhat more welcome than a girl. At the birth of a child, a special messenger was sent to notify relatives and intimate friends, who must soon visit the baby and take it presents, and especially so if it was the first in the family. Yet infanticide was not uncommon, for poverty sometimes decided against the infant, and this also might be true of a child born maimed or deformed. "In old days, when the new-born child was laid at the father's feet, the father could refuse to take it, and the child was then exposed to die in a bamboo-grove. The custom exists no longer; I doubt whether it ever prevailed to any very great extent, but it has left behind it a

[12] Knapp, Feudal and modern Japan, I, 109-115.

very picturesque reminder. If parents have lost a child by death, they often, not perhaps unnaturally, look upon their loss as the visitation of an angry Heaven, which must need be propitiated by the free-will offering up of the next born child. So when the next child is born it is taken to the bamboo-grove and left by its parents. The exposure is, however, nothing very serious; a friend of the family is waiting round the corner for the weeping parents to abandon their infant, and a few minutes afterwards he comes in, quite as if it were by accident, and tells the bereaved couple that he has just picked up a fine, handsome baby boy (or girl), which he hopes they will take and rear. Thus the anger of Heaven has been, figuratively at least, averted, and the baby is known in after life by the word *sute* ('abandoned') prefixed to his personal name. He is known as *sutejiro* or *sutesaburo*, as the case may be ('the abandoned second son' or 'the abandoned third')." [13]

The baby's dress was loose and easily put on, so it was soon dressed. The dresses were made like the *kimono* of the mother, being wide-sleeved and straight, silk, cotton, or flannel, as the season demanded, and long enough to cover the feet and hands. Red and yellow were the colors of the young baby's dress, and if a girl high colors prevailed later, but a boy's clothing became subdued in color. Near the one hundredth day of the child's life, long dresses were left off and also about the same time it was weaned. The baby's head was kept shaved bald until it was three years of age, when only a part of it was shaved; it might all be shaved but a tuft on top, or tufts at the side, or bare on top and encircling the head at the sides, just as the mother might wish. "There is no limit set to the whimsical mother's taste in this matter of tonsorial landscape gardening." [14]

Since the Japanese sat on the floor with their legs under them, the baby was placed on the floor with its knees bent under it, which trained it to the right way of sitting. The baby in learning to walk did not have chairs and the like to bump against and fall over and it had soft-matted floors to bump down upon without injury. It was quite noteworthy if the baby of his own accord should walk before its first birthday, and *mochi* (rice pastry) was made to celebrate the auspicious event. When the baby went outdoors,

[13] Lloyd, Every-day Japan, 324.
[14] Scherer, Young Japan, 48.

then its feet were hampered by sandals or clogs fastened to the feet by straps passing between the toes, but he soon learned to use them all right, so that babies of two or three could get around all right in these clogs. One good thing, these clogs did not bind the children's feet, but let them grow naturally. These clogs left the toes of the Japanese children free and thus they retained some of their prehensive powers so that in adult life the feet were still used somewhat for holding and grasping. It would seem that the baby learned to talk some earlier than in other countries, as the Japanese language is conducive for such since it abounds in expressions easy for children.

**Naming Children.** On the seventh day, some authors say the thirteenth, the child received its name, at which time very little ceremony took place; at seven years of age this name gave way to another name; which occurred again upon reaching his majority at fifteen. When he married he received another name; again he was given a new name if he took office; another new name came if promoted; and, finally, after death, he received his last name, which was engraved upon his tomb.

**Carrying Children.** The babies were carried upon the back of some member of the family, quite often an older brother or sister and sometimes these were not over five or six years of age. The baby was tied upon the back of the one carrying it, face front, head and feet out, and even in quite cold weather. The babies soon learned to hold on and thus they looked out for themselves so as not to be dropped by the one carrying them. "The mother bears the bairns, but the children carry them. Each preceding child, as it grows older, must lug the succeeding baby on its back till able to stand. The rearing of a Japanese poor family is a perpetual game of leap-frog." [15]

**Adoption and Inheritance.** There was a great desire, especially in feudal times, to have a male heir to keep up the ancestral line, which otherwise would be a disgrace to the family. There being no male heir, it might be that a son would be adopted in early life to grow up as the heir, or he might be adopted with the idea of his marrying one of the daughters later, or there might be no formal adoption but a young man would marry a daughter and give up his own name and take that of the family and thus become the

[15] Griffis, The Mikado's empire, II, 356.

heir. The childless wife, if not divorced, would often care for the adopted child as if her own, which care would be reciprocated by the adopted son in her old age. In feudal times, in case a man should die leaving no children, either natural or adopted, his death was concealed till the lord gave permission for him to adopt a son, and not till then was his death announced, for otherwise the lands escheated to the lord.

**Power and Duty of Father.** As in Rome, the family was the unit in feudal times in Japan, and the head of the family held complete power. He had the full control of the persons and property of his children and he could do with them as he chose, only being held back by that most binding of all laws—custom. Yet, as he had great power, so had he great responsibilities, as he was responsible to the state for the doings of his family.

**Amusements.** Old Japan was a realm of sports. It was a nation of players. There seemed not to have been any distinct line of demarcation between the amusements of the children and those of the adults. The grown-up people entered with zest into games which were in many cases the same and in many others similar to the games of the young people. There were numerous holidays and festivals, on which days the whole nation of people seemed to give themselves over to the toy-sellers and showmen and story-tellers and musicians and games and plays—to a time of general enjoyment. Perhaps there was never any other people or country in the entire world at any time that took as much interest in the pleasures of their children as did the old Japanese.

When the evenings were pleasant they were spent out-of-doors, and on pleasant moonlight evenings almost the entire population of a town would be on its streets. At other times the evenings would be spent in the home, the entire family being together, including the grandparents and even the servants. Sometimes the father would tell stories of Japanese history and of folk-lore, sometimes they would play chess and checkers, but the greatest time was spent with cards. One such game was known as "The poems of a hundred poets." On one card was written the half of one hundred famous Japanese poems and the other half on another card, half of these cards being distributed among the players and the other half being given to a reader. The reader would call off the half of one poem and the one having the other half would call back and this would continue till all the cards were matched. There was dancing of evenings, usually by the young women, sometimes by the men, but, perhaps, never by men and women together. In some places of moonlight nights the young people would dance all night in the streets or open places near the castle-gates.

"Among the ghostly games intended to test the courage of, or perhaps to frighten, children, are two plays called, respectively, 'Hiyaku Monogatari' and 'Kon-daméshi,' or the 'One Hundred Stories' and 'Soul-examination.' In the former play a company of boys and girls assemble round the hibachi, while they, or an adult, an aged person or a servant, usually relate ghost-stories, or tales calculated to straighten the hair and make the blood crawl. In a distant dark room, a lamp (the usual dish of oil), with a wick of one hundred strands or piths, is set. At the conclusion of each story, the children in turn must go to the dark room and remove a strand of the wick. As the lamp burns down low, the room becomes gloomy and dark, and the last boy, it is said, always sees a demon, a huge face, or something terrible. In the 'Kon-daméshi,' or 'Soul-examination,' a number of boys, during the day plant some flags in different parts of a graveyard, under a lonely tree, or by a haunted hillside. At night, they meet together, and tell stories about ghosts, goblins, devils, etc.; and at the conclusion of each tale, when the imagination is wrought up, the hair begins to rise and the marrow to curdle, the boys, one at a time, must go out in the dark and bring back the flags, until all are brought in."[16]

The children had plenty to see to keep them amused. There were visits to the theaters, sometimes the performances lasted all day, in which were displayed the doings of historical peoples and lore heroes. There were all kinds of gymnastic feats and juggling of various kinds. "At the fair at Asakusa, in addition to the performances of jugglers of all kinds, there are collections of animals which have been taught to perform tricks—bears of Yezo, spaniels which are valuable in proportion to their ugliness, educated monkeys and goats. Birds and fish are also displayed in great quantities. But the most astonishing patience is manifested by an old Corean boatman, who has trained a dozen tortoises, large and small, employing no other means to direct them than his songs and

[16] Griffis, The Mikado's empire, II, 460.

a small metal drum. They march in line, execute various evolutions, and conclude by climbing upon a low table, the larger ones forming, of their own accord, a bridge for the smaller, to whom the feat would otherwise be impossible. When they have all mounted, they dispose themselves in three or four piles like so many plates."[17]

Among the leading amusements were the Festivals. These were of frequent occurrence and of the greatest diversity, so that the young people had plenty to amuse them. There were five great annual Festivals, which were the Festival of the New Year, the Festival of the Dolls, the Festival of the Banners, the Feast of Lanterns, and the Feast of Chrysanthemums.

The New Year Festival occurred on the first day of the first month of the old Japanese year. At this time congratulations and presents were much given and taken. This was a time for pleasure and all the members of the family laid aside their work and their dignity and entered into the fun and the sport that characterized this festival.

The Festival of the Dolls occurred on the third day of the third month. This day was especially devoted to the girls, and to them it was the greatest day of the year. All the dolls belonging to the family were brought out and which had been accumulating in some families for hundreds of years. When a daughter was born in a home, two images of wood or enameled clay were bought for her, with which she played, and when she was married she took them to her new home and kept them for her children, as well as any other dolls she might have. "The Tokugawa collection, of which I have spoken, is remarkably full and costly, for it has been making for hundreds of years in one of the younger branches of a family which for two and a half centuries was possessed of almost imperial power, and lived in more than imperial luxury; but there are few households so poor that they do not from year to year accuumulate a little store of toys wherewith to celebrate the feast, and, whether the toys are many or few, the feast is the event of the year in the lives of the little girls of Japan."[18]

On the fifth day of the fifth month was celebrated the Festival of the Banners, which was celebrated in honor of the boys, and it was to them the greatest day in the year.

[17] Taylor, Japan in our day, 163.
[18] Bacon, Japanese girls and women, 31.

On this day all kinds of military toys were displayed, such as heroes, warriors, generals, soldiers, etc. Also there were flags, streamers, banners, etc. A set of these toys was bought for every son born in the family. So as with the display of dolls, in old Japanese families the display on the Feast of Banners was very great.. About the houses and on poles in the yards were hung long paper pennons of every color, banners with coats of arms, and also attached to a pole by a string was a paper fish, hollow so that as the wind filled it out it would flop its tail and fins in a most natural way. This paper fish was to show that a son had been born during the year or that there were sons in the family.

The Feast of Lanterns occurred on the seventh day of the seventh month. On this occasion the whole city or town was decorated with lanterns. In some places little girls would go in crowds through the streets and sing with all their might while swinging paper lanterns.

"The fifth festival takes place on the ninth day of the ninth month, and is called the Feast of Chrysanthemums. At all the family repasts during the day, the leaves of chrysanthemum flowers are scattered over the cups of tea and saké. It is believed that the libations prepared in this manner have the power of prolonging life. The citizen of Tokio would consider that he was wanting in his duty as a good husband and father, if he should partake sparingly of this specific." [19]

That children enjoyed themselves and that they were helped to enjoy themselves was well shown in the abundance of toys and toy-shops and many holidays on which to display them. The streets of the towns and cities were full of toy-shops, where every kind of toys imaginable could be found. Too, toys, and especially the religious varieties, were displayed for sale about the temples on feast days. There were images of the various gods and of implements and appliances used about the temples. There were on the streets toys of all kinds of animals, of wrestlers and acrobats, of soldiers, etc., etc. Dolls were one of the strongest features of toy-makers and toy-sellers. "Here let me tell you something you certainly never heard of before in relation to Japanese dolls,—not the tiny O-Hina-San I was just speaking about, but the beautiful life-sized dolls representing children of two or three years old; real toy-babes which, although

[19] Taylor, Japan in our day, 156.

far more cheaply and simply constructed than our finer kinds of Western dolls, become, under the handling of a Japanese girl, infinitely more interesting. Such dolls are well dressed, and look so life-like,—little slanting eyes, shaven pates, smiles, and all!—that as seen from a short distance the best eyes might be deceived by them. Therefore, in those stock photographs of Japanese life, of which so many thousands are sold in the open ports, the conventional baby on the mother's back is most successfully represented by a doll. Even the camera does not betray the substitution. And if you see such a doll, though held quite close to you, being made by a Japanese mother to reach out its hands, to move its little bare feet, and to turn its head, you would be almost afraid to venture a heavy wager that it was only a doll. Even after having closely examined the thing, you would still, I fancy, feel a little nervous at being left alone with it, so perfect the delusion of that expert handling.

"Now there is a belief that some dolls do actually become alive.

"Formerly the belief was less rare than it is now. Certain dolls were spoken of with reverence worthy of the Kami, and their owners were envied folk. Such a doll was treated like a real son or daughter: it was regularly served with food; it had a bed, and plenty of nice clothes, and a name. If in the semblance of a girl, it was O-Toku-San; if in that of a boy, Tokutarō-San. It was thought that the doll would become angry and cry if neglected, and that any ill-treatment of it would bring ill-fortune to the house. And, moreover, it was believed to possess superantural powers of a very high order.

"In the family of one Sengoku, a samurai of Matsue, there was a Tokutarō-San which had a local reputation scarcely inferior to that of Kishibojin,—she to whom Japanese wives pray for offspring. And childless couples used to borrow that doll, and keep it for a time,—ministering unto it,—and furnish it with new clothes before gratefully returning it to its owners. And all who did so, I am assured, became parents, according to their heart's desire. 'Sengoku's doll had a soul.' There is even a legend that once, when the house caught fire, the Tokutarō-San ran out safely into the garden of its own accord!

"The idea about such a doll seems to be this: The new doll is only a doll. But a doll which is preserved for a great many years in one family, and is loved and played with by generations of children, gradually acquires a soul."[20]

There was an abundance of outdoor sports among the Japanese children. Beginning with the New Year there came the great game with the girls of battledore and shuttlecock. The girls made a beautiful sight, of which, no doubt, they were aware. With their gayest dresses, hair arranged in a most pleasing way, faces powdered and lips painted, the graceful, rhythmic motion of their bodies, their bright eyes and laughing faces, all combined to make them and their sport a most attractive scene. Kite-flying was about as great an amusement in Japan as in China. All kinds and sizes of kites were used. Some represented birds, others men, and yet others monsters. Kite-fights were of frequent occurrence. A part of the kite-string was smeared with glue and then sprinkled with powdered glass, which prepared it for sawing another kite-string in two, thus causing it to fall and become the property of the one sawing the string. To make the fight the more realistic, at the top of the frame of the kite was set a piece of whalebone, which in vibrating in the wind made the most blood-curdling howls. Also contests in tops were held, in which it was the aim to damage one another's tops and stop the spinning. There was leaping and running and jumping and wrestling and slinging. They played blind-man's-buff, prisoner's base, and pussy wants a corner, but in these last two instead of the officer and Puss, the *oni,* or devil, was the chief performer. They had stilts and handled them so well as to play games on them and run races. Where there was snow and ice, the Japanese children coasted, built snow-forts, fought battles with snowballs, and the like. They made snow-men in the likeness of Daruma, a follower of Buddha, who lost his legs by paralysis and decay from long meditation and prayer in a squatting position.

The Japanese children in their plays imitated their elders, just as children everywhere do. Playing the doctor was one of the great imitative plays of the younger children, and there were dinners and tea-parties and weddings and funerals. One of the great amusements of the Japanese was wrestling-matches and the children imitated these with much precision, as they would stamp their feet, eat their salt, rinse their mouths, slap their knees, and then clinch and tug

[20] Hearn, Glimpses of unfamiliar Japan, I, 266.

till one or the other was victor. "Another game which was very popular was called the 'Genji and Heiké.' These are the names of the celebrated rival clans, or families, Minamoto and Taira. The boys of a town, district, or school ranged themselves into two parties, each with flags. Those of the Heiké were red, those of the Genji white. Sometimes every boy had a flag, and the object of the contest, which was begun at the tap of a drum, was to seize the flags of the enemy. The party securing the greatest number of flags won the victory. In other cases, the flags were fastened on the back of each contestant, who was armed with a bamboo for a sword, and who had fastened, on a pad over his head, a flat, round piece of earthenware, so that a party of them looked not unlike the faculty of a college. Often these parties of boys numbered several hundred, and were marshalled in squadrons, as in a battle. At the given signal, the battle commenced, the object being to break the earthen dish on the head of the enemy. The contest was usually very exciting. Whoever had his earthen disk demolished had to retire from the field. The party having the greatest number of broken disks, representative of cloven skulls, was declared the loser. This game has been forbidden by the Government as being too severe and cruel. Boys were often injured in it." [21]

**Lore.** The lore of Japan is as rich as that of other countries. Only a few of the things concerning children can be given.

"Japanese papas, who find, as other fathers do, how much it costs to raise a large family, will not let an infant, or even a young child, look in a mirror (and thus see a child exactly like itself, making apparent twins); for if he does, the anxious parent supposes the child, when grown up and married, will have twins.

"Children are told that if they tell a lie, an *oni*, or an imp, called the *tengu*, will pull out their tongues.

"If a boy rests a gun on top of his head, he will grow no taller. Children must not carry any kind of basket on their heads, nor must they ever measure their own height.

"Children are told if they strike anything with their chopsticks while at their meals, they will be struck dumb.

"When a maimed or deformed child is born, people say that its parents or ancestors committed some great sin.

"In Japan, as with us, each baby is the most remarkable

[21] Griffis, The Mikado's empire, II. 464.

child ever seen, and wondrous are the legends rehearsed concerning each one; but it is a great day in a Japanese home when the baby, of his own accord, walks before his first birthday, and mochi (rice pastry) must be made to celebrate the auspicious event.

"Young girls do not like to pour tea or hot water into a cup of *kawaméshi* (red rice), lest their wedding-night should be rainy.

"Little boys, tempted to devour too much candy, are frightened, not with prophecies of pain or threats of nauseous medicines, but by the fear of a hideous worm that will surely be produced by indulgence in sweets." [22]

A peculiar superstition was in connection with the sacred trees, which were found quite numerous in both city and country. The patron gods of these trees were thought to inflict great injury upon those who might desecrate the trees. Believing this, sometimes a young woman whose affections had been stirred and then set aside used these sacred trees as a means of avenging herself. Making a rude image of straw to represent her former lover, at the "hour of the ox," two o'clock in the morning, she carried this straw man to one of these trees. Having on her feet the high clogs, worn in Japan, her hair disheveled, dressed in a loose flowing white night-dress, carrying in her hand nails and hammer, she proceeded to the tree and crucified on it the straw image of her lover. Then she beseeched the gods to whom the tree was dedicated to bring down affliction and even death upon him who mutilated the tree. These visits were repeated and the same things gone over till her recreant lover sickened and died. It is not told whether this always occurred or not.

"The wonderful story of 'Raiko and the Oni' is one of the most famous in the collection of Japanese grandmothers. Its power to open the mouths and distend the oblique eyes of the youngsters long after bedtime, is unlimited. I have before me a little stitched book of seven leaves, which I bought among a lot of two dozen or more in one of the colored print and book shops in Tōkio. It is four inches long and three wide. On the gaudy cover, which is printed in seven colors, is a picture of Raiko, the hero, in helmet and armor, grasping in both hands the faithful sword with which he slays the ghoul whose frightful face glowers above him. The *hiragana* text and wood-cuts within the covers are greatly worn, show-

[22] Griffis, The Mikado's empire, II, 468.

ing that many thousand copies have been printed from the original and oft-retouched face of the cherry-wood blocks. The story, thus illustrated with fourteen engravings, is as follows:

"A long time ago, when the mikado's power had slipped away into the hands of his regents, the guard at Kiōto was neglected. There was a rumor in the city that *oni*, or demons, frequented the streets late at night, and carried off people bodily. The most dreaded place was at the Ra-jō gate, at the southwestern entrance to the palace. Hither Watanabé, by order of Raiko, the chief captain of the guard, started one night, well armed. Wearily waiting for some hours, he became drowsy, and finally fell asleep. Seizing his opportunity, the wary demon put out his arm from behind the gate-post, caught Watanabé by the neck, and began to drag him up in the air. Watanabé awoke, and in an instant seized the imp by the wrist, and, drawing his sword, lopped the oni's arm off, who then leaped onto the cloud, howling with pain. In the morning Watanabé returned and laid the trophy at his master's feet. It is said that an oni's limb will not unite again if kept apart from the stump for a week. Watanabé put the hairy arm in a strong stone box, wreathed with twisted rice straw, and watched it day and night, lest the oni should recover it. One night a feeble knock was heard at his door, and to his challenge his old aunt's voice replied. Of course, he let the old woman in. She praised her nephew's exploit, and begged him to let her see it. Being thus pressed, as he thought, by his old aunty, he slid the lid aside. 'This is my arm,' cried the old hag, as she flew westward into the sky, changing her form into a tusked and hairy demon. Tracing the oni's course, Raiko and four companions, disguised as *komusō* (wandering priests), reached the pathless mountain Oyé, in Tango, which they climbed. They found a beautiful young girl washing a bloody garment. From her they learned the path to the oni's cave, and that the demons eat the men, and save the pretty damsels alive. Approaching, they saw a demon cook carving a human body, to make soup of. Entering the cave, they saw *Shu ten dōji*, a hideous tusked monster, with long red hair, sitting on a pile of silken cushions, with about a hundred retainers around him, at a feast. Steaming dishes were brought in, full of human limbs, cooked in every style. The young damsels had to serve the demons, who quaffed saké out of human skulls. Raiko and his band pretended to join in the orgies, and amused the demons by a dance, after which they presented them with a bottle of saké which had been mixed with a narcotic. The chief drank a skullful and gave to his retainers. Soon all the demons were asleep, and a thunder-storm of snores succeeded. Then Raiko and his men threw off their disguise, drew sword, and cut off their heads, till the cave flowed blood like a river. The neck of the chief demon was wider than Raiko's sword, but the blade miraculously lengthened, and Raiko cut the monster's head off at one sweep. They then destroyed the treasure, released all the prisoners, and returned to Kiōto in triumph, exposing the huge head along the streets."[23]

**Religion.** Before the introduction of Christianity into Japan, there were but three religions: Shintoism, Confucianism, and Buddhism. The first is native to Japan and the other two are importations. Shintoism teaches nature and ancestor worship, cleanliness, and purity. As is the nature of the Japanese, so this native religion has some merrymaking in it. Confucianism teaches implicit obedience to those who are in power, as emperor, parent, and teacher. Buddhism is somewhat similar to Christianity in making its followers kind to those in lower life, as, the poor, and animals. "In a word, 'Shintoism furnishes the object of worship, Confucianism offers the rules of life, and Buddhism supplies the way of future salvation.' "[24]

There is no doubt that all three of these religions had much to do in moulding the character of the young in Japan, for in nearly every house of the reigning class were the books or emblems or symbols or idols of these three religions.

The school children had a god all to themselves, who was supposed to aid them in their study. This god was called "Ten-jin," or "Heavenly Man." As the boy desired to become a scholar, learned in the Chinese characters and an excellent penman, so he prayed to Ten-jin to help him in all these.

**Suicide.** The Japanese did not fear death nor dread the consequences of a future world, so that suicide was not looked upon as in Europe and America today. "As for the young lovers of whom I speak, they have a strange faith which effaces mysteries for them. They turn to the darkness with

---

[23] Griffis, The Mikado's empire, II, 491.
[24] Griffis, Japan in history, 75.

infinite trust. If they are too unhappy to endure existence, the fault is not another's, nor yet the world's; it is their own; it is *innen*, the result of errors in a previous life. If they can never hope to be united in this world, it is only because in some former birth they broke their promise to wed, or were otherwise cruel to each other. But they believe likewise that by dying together they will find themselves at once united in another world. Sometimes they make a little banquet for themselves, write very strange letters to parents and friends, mix something bitter with their rice-wine, and go to sleep forever. Sometimes they select a more ancient and more honored method: the lover first slays his beloved with a single sword stroke, and then pierces his own throat. Sometimes with the girl's long crape-silk under-girdle (*koshi-obi*) they bind themselves fast together, face to face, and so embracing leap into some deep lake or stream.'' [25]

"Bravery has always been the chief ideal of Japanese character. What beauty meant to the Greeks, and right to the Romans, and purity to the Hebrews of old, bravery has meant to Japan." [26] In older Japan one of the bravest deeds was that of taking one's own life when there was a need. Thus arose the practice of *seppuku* (belly-cutting) or *hara-kiri*, the more common term. This act was performed by cutting across through one's bowels. This brought into practice the wearing of two swords, a long one for enemies and a short one for the wearer's own body. The young men were taught how to perform this deed upon themselves and they were so impressed that when the time came for its performance they were able to meet death without a tremor and with perfect composure. The young women were taught the equivalent duty of *jigai*, which was the piercing of the throat with a dagger so that a single cut would sever the arteries.

**Work.** The children were taught to work. The girl was instructed in household duties and the care of children. She was taught how to receive and entertain guests, how to take care of the rooms and furniture, how to cook and prepare and serve the dishes, how to do the marketing, how to sew, and all such duties, so that when she should enter a home of her own she would know how to perform the duties of wife and mother.

The apprenticeship system was used in Japan. The boy

---

[25] Hearn, Glimpses of unfamiliar Japan, I, 286.
[26] Scherer, Young Japan, 149.

had to serve a long apprenticeship with no pay, or but little pay, although his needs of food, clothing, and lodging were attended to. Somewhat akin to this was the entering of boys into the homes of those of distinction and education. The young men performed the services required about the home and they were cared for by the ones having them in charge and given instruction in the things needed by them for the future.

**Education.** In the early times of Japan there seems to be nothing to prove that children received any education other than domestic training, and the higher classes had a training in the implements of warfare. Later, schools grew up and children of both sexes and of all ranks attended the lower schools and those of higher rank went on into schools of a higher grade. In the eighth century of the Christian era, a university was established at the capital and branch schools in the several provinces. In the university instruction was given in Chinese literature, history, law, music, medicine, mathematics, and astronomy and astrology. Students were sent to China along with the Japanese ambassadors to that country and some of these students remained for a number of years to complete their studies.

The art of writing was brought into Japan from Korea in A. D. 284. Previous to this it would appear that the Japanese had no way of recording events, as books and writing were unknown. Writing was at first with the Chinese characters, which were used to represent Japanese words. Later a system was devised whereby only parts of the Chinese characters were used for writing and a syllabry was formed.

In the university mentioned above, "the training of the students in medicine chiefly consisted in making them familiar with the methods which prevailed in China. The properties of medicinal plants, the variations of the pulse in health and disease and in the changing seasons, and the anatomy of the human body were the chief subjects of study. The human cadaver was never dissected, but a knowledge of anatomy was obtained from diagrams which were wholly hypothetical. In early times medical officers were appointed to experiment with medicines upon monkeys, and also to dissect the bodies of monkeys. From these dissections, as well as from the printed diagrams of Chinese books the imperfect knowledge which they had reached was derived.

It was not till 1771 that Sugita Genpaku and several other Japanese scholars had an opportunity to dissect the body of a criminal, and by personal observation found the utter falsity of the Chinese diagrams on which they had hitherto relied, and the correctness of the Dutch books, which they had, contrary to the laws of the country, learned to read."[27]

A large part of the education of the young samurai was of a military order. He was well trained to ride a horse, to shoot a bow, and to handle the spear and the sword. The *hara-kiri* was an especial part of this training. "They are instructed as to the proper mode of performing this act, the ceremonies that should accompany it, varying with the occasion, and according as it is done publicly or privately, and under what circumstances a well-bred man should feel himself obliged thus to destroy himself."[28]

The girls were taught needlework, music, the arranging of flowers, etc. They were instructed in household duties and the things needed by a wife and mother. Some girls received higher education, becoming able to understand the Chinese characters used by the Japanese, and they were especially well learned in the history of their country. "Plutarch tells us that the ambition of a Spartan woman was to be the wife of a great man and the mother of illustrious sons. *Bushido* set no lower ideal before our maidens; their whole bringing up was in accordance with this view. They were instructed in many martial practices for the sake of self-defense, that they might safeguard their person and their children; in the art of committing suicide, that in case no alternative opened to save them from disgrace, they might end their lives in due order and in comely fashion."[29] There were a number of books, which appeared from time to time, upon the education of the girl, till a library arose which were often bound in one volume.

"If the reader will imagine a volume composed of the Bible, 'Ladies' Letter-writer,' 'Guide to Etiquette,' 'The Young Ladies' Own Book,' Hannah More's works, Miss Strickland's 'Queens of England,' a work on household economy, and an almanac, he will obtain some idea of the contents of the *Bunko*, or 'Japanese Lady's Library.' With text and illustrations, the volume is very large; but if translated and

---

[27] Murray, Japan, 112.
[28] ———, Manners and customs of the Japanese, 126.
[29] Nitobé, The Japanese nation, 166.

printed in brevier with the cuts, it would not probably occupy more space than one of our largest monthly magazines. The books composing it, in their order of importance, are the *Ŏnna Dai Gakŭ* ('Women's Great Learning'—the moral duties of woman, founded on the Chinese classics); *Ŏnna Shŏ Gakŭ* ('Woman's Small Learning'—introduction to the above); *Ŏnna Niwa no Oshiyé* ('Woman's Household Instruction'—duties relating to furniture, dress, reception of guests, and all the minutiæ of indoor life, both daily and ceremonial); *Ŏnna Imagawa* ('Moral Lessons' in paragraphs); *Ŏnna Yŏ-bunshŏ* ('Lady's Letter-writer'); *Nijiu-shi Ko* ('Twenty-four Children'—stories about model children in China). Besides these works of importance, there are *Hiyaku Nin Isshiu*—a collection of one hundred poems from as many poets, written in the old Yamato dialect, and learned in every household, and perpetually repeated with passionate fondness by old and young; a collection of lives of model women; household lore; almanac learning; rules and examples to secure perfect agreement between man and wife; and a vast and detailed array of other knowledge of various sorts, both useful and ornamental to a Japanese maiden, wife, widow, or mother. This book is studied, not only by the higher classes, but by the daughters in almost every respectable family throughout the country. It is read and reread, and committed to memory, until it becomes to the Japanese woman what the Bible is to the inmate of those homes in the West in which the Bible is the first, and last, and often the only book.''[30]

## LITERATURE

1. ———, Manners and customs of the Japanese. *Family library*, No. 142 (1841).
2. Bacon, Alice Mabel, Japanese girls and women.
3. Griffis, William Elliott, Japan in history, folk lore, and art.
4. Griffis, William Elliott, The Mikado's empire.
5. Gulick, Sidney L., Evolution of the Japanese.
6. Hearn, Lafcadio, Glimpses of unfamiliar Japan.
7. Kikuchi, Baron Dairoku, Japanese education.
8. Knapp, Arthur May, Feudal and modern Japan.

[30] Griffis, The Mikado's empire, II, 558.

9. Lloyd, Arthur, Every-day Japan.
10. Lombard, Frank Alanson, Pre-Meiji education in Japan.
11. Mitford, A. B., Tales of Old Japan.
12. Murray, David, Japan.
13. Nitobé, Inazo, The Japanese nation.
14. Scherer, James A. B., Young Japan.
15. Taylor, Bayard, Japan in our day.

## CHAPTER VII

#### THE CHILD IN PERSIA

**Characteristics.** Persia proper was a table-land, lying between the Caspian Sea and the Persian Gulf, with deep valleys and rapid rivers. It was such a country, with such a climate, as required a constant struggle by mankind for existence. Thus was produced a vigorous race, a race of our own blood, Aryans, that had one great wave of emigration to the West, peopling Europe, and a later wave into India. The Persians were quick, keen-witted, lovers of art and poetry, filled with energy and courage, and having a very high regard for truth. "He was free and open in speech, bold in act, generous, warm-hearted, hospitable. His chief faults were an addiction to self-indulgence and luxury, a passionate *abandon* to the feeling of the hour, whatever that might happen to be; and a tameness and subservience in all his relations towards his prince, which seem to moderns almost incompatible with real self-respect and manliness."[1]

**Women and Marriage.** As in other oriental countries, the parties to a marriage were often betrothed in infancy, and they had never seen one another till on their wedding-day. Boys sometimes married at the age of fifteen and girls at twelve, but as a rule men were between the ages of twenty-five and thirty and women from fourteen to nineteen. Parents usually arranged for the marriage of their children, but sometimes the men would get a female friend to select a partner for them. When the consent of all had been obtained, then a formal betrothal took place and gifts were exchanged.

A day having been set for the wedding, on that day the women would gather at the home of the bride and the men at the bridegroom's house. As soon as it was dark, the bride was escorted to the home of the bridegroom, amidst the beating of drums, the playing of tambourines, and the flashing of lanterns. Arrived at his house, a man would grasp the bride about the waist to carry her within, which would

[1] Rawlinson, Seven great monarchies, II, 319.

cause a strife for if this was done by a friend of the bridegroom then he would in the future be able to maintain due authority over his wife, but if it was by a friend of the bride then she "would keep her own side of the house." When the bride had passed into the reception-room, the bridegroom made his appearance and he would hold a looking-glass before her that he might get a good look at her face, and he was aided in his decision of her looks by the ladies present who would strive to get a look also at her face. "After this, the bridegroom takes a bit of sugar-candy, and, biting it in two halves, eats one himself, and presents the other to his bride. He then takes her stockings, throws one over his left shoulder, places the other under his right foot, and orders all the spectators to withdraw. They retire accordingly, and the happy couple are left alone."[2]

There was a form of marriage peculiar to Persia, and which must have originated in a very early time, in which the contract was only temporary. In this form a woman would enter into an agreement to live as a wife with a certain man for a limited period on consideration of receiving a specified sum. The time might be for a part of a day or for a long number of years. If the man should leave the woman before the time had expired, she received the sum of money just the same. But she had no other claim upon him nor had she the right to inherit property from him. At the end of the time the woman could not marry again for a month and if then found to be with child a longer time had to elapse before her marriage again and the child, as well as other children born to the union, was acknowledged and supported by the man with whom she had been living.

It is quite well known that incest existed among the ancient Persians. They even went further in this than did the Egyptians or Peruvians, as not only were brothers and sisters permitted to marry but even a mother and son or father and daughter. As with the ancient Peruvians so with the ancient Persians, these unions were sometimes required for their religion called for the offspring of such unions for the sacrifices.

Since the number of sons a Persian had was a source of pride to him, this made polygamy a desired and necessary thing. Hence in ancient Persia a man was allowed to have

[2] Fraser, History of Persia, 289.

several wives and besides an additional number of concubines, in order that many sons might be born to him.

Divorce was permitted almost at will to the husband, custom holding him in check. Another thing that checked divorce was that the husband had to restore the dowry with the returning of the woman to her home. The most usual causes of separation were bad temper, extravagance, or some complaint of that kind against the wife.

**Dress.** The boy was dressed somewhat as his father. Of the poorer classes, the males wore a tunic and trousers of leather, with a strap or belt around the waist, and high shoes tied in front with a string. The richer classes wore long robes with loose hanging sleeves, sleeved tunics reaching to the knees, fine shoes, drawers under the tunics, gloves on the hands, and socks or stockings under the shoes. These were all of rich material and handsomely made. The principal attire of the women was a wrapper with trousers beneath, over these was worn a jacket with a shawl, cloak, or furs, according to the state of the weather, round the head was wound a silk handkerchief in form similar to a turban, and on the feet were stockings and slippers. Under Mohammedan rule, when going out the women put on a long, loose wrap that enveloped them from head to foot and left only a small opening for the face, which might be covered with open lacework or a veil. The girls were dressed similar to their mothers.

**Child and Parent.** The boy remained with the women till his fifth year, his father never seeing him till then, which was said to have been done to prevent the father from being afflicted by the loss if the child should die young. "Children had to yield absolute obedience to their parents; but so convinced were they of the sacredness of the family tie as founded on love and reverence that they maintained 'that never yet did any one kill his father or his mother, but in all such cases they are sure that, if matters were sifted to the bottom, it would be found that the child was either a changeling or else the fruit of adultery, for it is not likely, they say, that the real father should perish by the hands of the child.' (Herod.)"[3]

**Inheritance.** The Persian was considered to have reached manhood when he was fifteen years of age. "The offspring

[3] Laurie, Pre-Christian education, 183.

of the temporary unions, or of any sort of union, are all equal before the Persian law, which merely subjects them to the right of primogeniture. At the death of the father, the eldest son, though born of a slave mother, takes two-thirds of the succession. The remaining third of the property is divided amongst the other children, but in such a way that the share of the boys is half as large again as that of the girls."[4]

**Amusements.** The chief amusements of the Persians were hunting and playing at dice. The boys no doubt followed their elders and had imitation hunts. The boys also played games similar to blindman's buff and tag. They flew kites and played ball. Boys and girls did not play together. The girls preferred to sit about and listen to fairy stories, or at least such was the case in later days. Both boys and girls were fond of singing.

**Education.** Among the ancient Persians, education does not seem to have been given other than to the higher classes, except that general training that comes through religion and custom and institutions that would be shared in by every citizen. Education was not meant to be literary or scholastic but principally of such a kind as would produce warriors.

There were five periods in the life of the Persian. The first ended at the fifth year, or, as some claim, at the seventh year; the second period ended with the fifteenth year; the third ended at twenty-five; the fourth ended at fifty, and the fifth period was the time after fifty years of age.

During the first period the child was under the care of the mother and the other women of the family. "'Up to the fifth year,' Herodotus tells us, 'they are not allowed to come into the sight of their father, but pass their lives with the women. This is done that if the child die young, the father would not be afflicted with the loss.'"[5] The child was not supposed to be capable of distinguishing between right and wrong, and so he was taught simply to obey the directions given him. A child was not to be whipped before his seventh year, and he was to receive only kind treatment.

At the close of this first period, at the end of the fifth year, the boy left his mother and went into the care of the state. This second period was a time of physical training. The boy was given exercises in running, stone slinging, bow shoot-

[4] Letourneau, Evolution of marriage, 332.
[5] Laurie, Pre-Christian education, 190.

ing, and javelin throwing. He was taught to ride, and, later, to hunt. He was trained to endure heat and cold and hunger and fatigue. Through the national traditions, the boys learned of the doings of the heroes and the meaning of noble deeds. They were taught to speak the truth and learned to be just and pure and courageous and to gain self-control. They were instructed in the myths of the gods and other religious matters, and about the fifteenth year the boys were invested with the holy girdle.

At fifteen the boy entered the youth period. During this period military training was the great exercise. The youth received careful training in the use of military implements, in the knowledge of military terms and usages, and given the strict discipline of military life. "The Magi required a higher education. This must have consisted in the study and explanation of the sacred writings, and may have included a limited training in philosophy, astrology, medicine, law, and finance, so that they were able to become advisers to the Great King and his satraps."[6]

At twenty-five the youth was considered a man and he took his place as a citizen of the state and he continued in service till his fiftieth year.

Girls received no education other than that of domestic training, such as was needed in the care of the home, the rearing of the little children, and the other duties that would come to the women. Women held a higher place in the family than was granted to them, for the most part, in other oriental countries.

There was no educational system in Persia. There was no real method of instruction. Perhaps no other nation gave more care to the moral and physical training of the young than did ancient Persia, yet this was to the almost entire neglect of intellectual training. The moral training came through the mingling of the young with their elders and the military training through imitation of the men at the various courts. "We know, however, from Strabo and the general evidence of antiquity that the boys of the higher classes were brought up together under men of gravity and reputation at the court of the great king, and also at the lesser courts of the great nobles and provincial governors."[7]

Persian life and education tended toward individuality.

[6] Graves, History of education, Before the middle ages, 100.
[7] Laurie, Pre-Christian education, 191.

Caste with its repressive influence did not exist in ancient Persia. The national feeling was intense. The government was despotic. The ethical aim was high and the individual was encouraged to high standards of courage, truthfulness, and purity. But in spite of this, the education was faulty in that the individual was trained so strongly in warfare as to overshadow the ethical side. As long as Persia was struggling the ethical standards were maintained alongside the standards of war so that the individual and the nation could keep right. But when conquests came, bringing wealth and power and the lower ethical standards of other nations, the Persians were unable to bear the strain and so degeneration went forward fast and the nation found itself unable to withstand the more vigorous peoples that came against it under Alexander and so the empire fell, leaving but little impress on civilization.

## LITERATURE

1. Benjamin, S. G. W., Persia and the Persians.
2. Dean, Amos, The history of civilization.
3. Fraser, James B., Historical and descriptive account of Persia.
4. Graves, Frank Pierrepont, A history of education, Before the middle ages.
5. Jackson, A. V. Williams, Persia, past and present.
6. Laurie, S. S., Historical survey of pre-Christian education.
7. Letourneau, Ch., The evolution of marriage.
8. McLennan, J. G., Studies in ancient history.
9. Rawlinson, George, The seven great monarchies.
10. Vaux, W. S. W., Persia from the earliest period.

## CHAPTER VIII

### THE CHILD IN JUDEA

**Historical.** We learn from their own writings that the Jews arose from peoples that lived in the region of the Euphrates, a particular tribe of whom, under the leadership of Abraham, near 2000 B.C., migrated to the land of Canaan or Palestine. Here they lived a nomadic life till a portion of them, the descendants of Jacob, migrated to northeastern Egypt, from whence some centuries later they were led forth by Moses and after wanderings and warrings they entered again into Palestine and built up a nation. After some centuries internal dissensions arose and the larger part withdrew and were later forever lost. The smaller portion continued as a nation and later were carried captives into Babylon and then restored again to their own country. Then later they came under the dominion of the Greeks and then under the Romans. Through this contact with the various civilizations, through the effect of their environment of both the country itself and the tribes about them, but more from that something innate in themselves, they developed into a people that evolved the great religious idea which, it seems, will dominate the entire world.

**Women and Marriage.** Woman was held in high esteem by the Jews. She mingled freely in private and in public with others. The Bible is full of the doings of women—as mothers, as wives, as sisters—showing courage and devotion and wisdom. She took a leading part in the life of the nation, especially in religious affairs. She was protected by a religion that did not debase her but which called for a pure home and a happy family. Woman was greatly respected in spite of some of the sayings about her as the following: "It was observed that God formed woman neither out of the head, lest she should become proud; nor out of the eye, lest she should be curious; nor out of the mouth, lest she should be too talkative; nor out of the hand, lest she should be covetous; nor out of the foot, lest she should gad about; but out of the rib, which was always covered. . . . As woman is formed from a rib, and man from the ground, man seeks a wife, and not *vice versa*; he only seeks what he lost. This explains why man is more easily reconciled than woman; he is made of soft earth and she of hard bone."[1]

About eighteen was the age at which men generally married, girls younger. A man under thirteen years and a day was forbidden to marry, and a woman under twelve years and a day. Wednesday was fixed as the day for maidens to marry, and Thursday for widows. If the bride was a maid each party was allowed twelve months after betrothal in which to prepare for marriage, in case of a widow but thirty days were allowed. A widower had to wait over three festivals and a widow three months before re-marrying. A marriage could not take place within thirty days of the death of a near relative, nor on the Sabbath, nor on a feast-day. Marriage was not permitted with those not in their right senses, nor in a state of drunkenness. "The Mosaic law (Lev. XVIII., 7-17; xx., 11, etc.) proscribes no less than fifteen marriages within specified degrees of both consanguinity and affinity. In neither consanguinity and affinity, however, does the law extend beyond two degrees, viz., the mother, her daughter, aunt, father's wife, sister on the father's side, wife of the father's brother, brother's wife (excepting in case of the Levirate marriage), daughter-in-law, granddaughter either from a son or daughter, and two sisters together."[2]

It was generally held that all marriages were arranged in heaven and that it was proclaimed there, forty days before the child's birth, just whom he or she should marry. Upon earth, the parent assumed this part and chose for his child the one he was to have in life as a partner. This duty belonged to the father, and if no father, then the mother. The son might make a personal choice of his bride, so that the son's wishes might be consulted, but all proposals, nevertheless, were made by the father. Girls up to twelve years and a day, minors, could be betrothed by the father and this was true of all women in the earlier times, but later, if of age, the woman had to give her own free and expressed consent, without which a union was invalid. The proposals were offered usually by the parents of the young man, but if there

[1] Edersheim, History of the Jewish nation, 309.
[2] McClintock and Strong, Cyclopedia of biblical literature, V, 774.

was a difference of rank then they were made by the father of the girl.

The betrothal was considered as sacred as marriage and could not be more easily broken. "For a betrothal to be legal, it has to be effected in one of the following three modes: 1. By *money*, or *money's worth*, which, according to the school of Shammai, must be a denar—90 grains of pure gold—or, according to the school of Hillel, a perutah—half grain of pure silver—and which is to be given to the maiden, or, if she is a minor, to her father, as betrothal price. 2. By *letter* or *contract*, which the young man either in person or through a proxy, has given to the maiden, or to her father when she is a minor. 3. By *cohabitation*, when the young man and maiden, having pronounced the betrothal formula in the presence of two witnesses, retire into a separate room. This, however, is considered immodest, and the young man is scourged."[3]

A father was to provide a dowry for his daughter conformable to her station in life, and should the father not be able to do this the bridegroom would, before marriage, give her sufficient for the necessary outfit. In case of an orphan the dowry was provided from public funds. In earlier times, after the giving over of the marriage price and other gifts, the bridegroom took the bride with him. At a later period a marriage-feast was given at the bride's home, and at a later period yet the wedding-feast was furnished at the home of the bridegroom.

Children were very greatly desired by the ancient Hebrews, and especially male children, as the more children a man had the more was he respected. Also the expectance of the Messiah, who might come from any one of the families, made children all the more wished for. Hence marriage was a duty with them, and this desire for children was also a cause for polygamy as thereby more children would be born to a family. Yet polygamy and concubinage was not the rule with the Hebrews but the rare exception, so far as the people generally were concerned, so that they really adopted monogamy and were, probably, the only Semites who did so. Even where polygamy or concubinage did occur the law insisted that each wife or concubine should receive her full conjugal rights, which prevented any extended practice even among the most wealthy.

[3] McClintock and Strong, Cyclopedia of biblical literature, V, 774.

Divorce was allowed for "any shameful thing," which, necessarily, was interpreted in different ways. "In fact, we know that it included every kind of impropriety, such as going about with loose hair, spinning in the street, familiarly talking with men, ill-treating her husband's parents in his presence, brawling, that is, 'speaking to her husband so loudly that the neighbors could hear her in the adjoining house,' a general bad reputation, or the discovery of fraud before marriage. On the other hand, the wife could insist on being divorced if her husband were a leper, or effected with polypus, or engaged in a disagreeable or dirty trade, such as that of a tanner or coppersmith. One of the cases in which divorce was obligatory was, if either party had become heretical, or ceased to profess Judaism."[4] Yet divorces were not so common as might be thought under so loose a statement for procuring them. Rather strict laws were drawn up explicitly stating for what divorce could be allowed, both to man and to woman. Divorce was discouraged and a conciliation was always tried to be brought about before divorce proceedings began. The divorced parties could marry other parties and even could unite again. The bill of divorcement had to be couched in explicit terms, handed to the woman herself, and in the presence of two witnesses. In separation of the parents where there were children, the daughters were placed in charge of the mother and the sons were given to the father; but should the judge consider it of advantage to the children, the sons also were given to the mother.

In order that children might be of the best, prostitution was not allowed and marriage with a prostitute forbidden. "Marriage with a prostitute was contrary to law, and the sons of such a woman were denied the political and religious privileges of citizenship unto the tenth generation."[5]

**Care and Treatment of Children.** Although all children were desired by the Hebrews, yet there was more rejoicing over the birth of a boy than over the birth of a girl. The father was not permitted to be present at the birth of the child, although later the child was given to him, at which time he placed it on his knees. Sometimes the grandfather was permitted to be present at the birth of the child.

In the earliest times the mothers nursed their own children, prolonging this till the child was two and a half and even

[4] Edersheim, Sketches of Jewish social life in the days of Christ, 157.
[5] Thwing, The family, 42.

three years old. In later times the wealthier classes employed nurses for this duty. It was the custom for the boys to be under the care of the women till the fifth year after which the father took charge of them.

Perhaps the most important ceremony in the earlier years of the child was that of circumcision. The child received its name at this time. Only males were subjected to this. It was performed on the eighth day of the child's life, even though it was the Sabbath. If two of the child's brothers had died from the results of the operation, or if he was weakly, this was deferred till such a time as there would be no great danger. This ceremony was of great importance and so the prescribed rules were strictly adhered to, otherwise it was not valid. Usually the father performed the operation, yet it might be done by any Israelite, and even in special cases by women.

The father had full control of his children. He had the power to inflict the severest of punishment, even death. He had greater power over the daughter than over the son, as he could annul a daughter's vow but not a son's. "When a child has attained the age of thirteen years and one day, he is declared of age by his father in the presence of ten Jews, and then he possesses the legal capacity of acting for himself, and can make and perform his own contracts. After that the sins he commits are on his own account. Previously they were on the account of his father. With respect to girls, they are accounted women when they arrive at the age of twelve years and one-half."[6]

**Duties of Children.** "Honor thy father and thy mother," was the great commandment to the Hebrew child. Undutifulness was almost unknown among them. Loving consideration for the parents was one of their strongest marks. Crimes against parents were scarcely heard of. Respect for old age was another great duty and one which was carefully observed. "The general state of Jewish society shows us parents as fondly watching over their children, and children as requiting their care by bearing with the foibles, and even the trials, arising from the caprices of old age and infirmity."[7]

**Dress.** The principal garment worn was a tunic, which encircled the whole body and came down to the knees. Under this was an inner garment that went down to the heels. Over

[6] Dean, History of civilization, I, 597.
[7] Edersheim, Sketches of Jewish life, 99.

all was a mantle, which was a piece of cloth nearly square, several feet in length and breadth, which was wrapped round the body, or tied over the shoulders. A girdle was worn about the waist, some of which worn by the women were of costly fabric and studded with precious stones. A kind of turban was worn on the head. There were three kinds of veils worn. One hung down from the head, so that the lady could see all around; a second was a kind of mantilla, which covered the head and was thrown about the whole person; a third kind was like the modern oriental veil, covering the face and front, leaving only the eyes free. Sandals were worn, and the ladies also wore slippers, some of which were very costly being embroidered or adorned with gems and so arranged that the pressure of the foot emitted a delicate perfume.

The hair was considered a chief point of beauty and so it was well cared for. With the women it was worn long and curled and plaited and adorned with gold ornaments and pearls. Auburn hair being a favorite color, sometimes the hair was dyed and again it was sprinkled with gold-dust. To keep the hair in place, there were hair-pins and combs. Perfumery was greatly in use as were cosmetics, the ladies painting their cheeks and blackening their eyebrows. "As for ornaments, gentlemen generally wore a seal, either on the ring-finger or suspended round the neck. Some of them had also bracelets above the wrist (commonly of the right arm), made of ivory, gold, or precious stones strung together. Of course, the fashionable lady was similarly adorned, adding to the bracelets finger-rings, ankle-rings, nose-rings, ear-rings, gorgeous head-dresses, necklaces, chains, and what are nowadays called 'charms.' As it may interest some, we shall add a few sentences of description. The ear-ring was either plain, or had a drop, a pendant, or a little bell inserted. The nose-ring, which the traditional law ordered to be put aside on the Sabbath, hung gracefully over the upper lip, yet so as not to interfere with the salute of the privileged friend. Two kinds of necklaces were worn—one close-fitting, the other often consisting of precious stones or pearls, and hanging down over the chest, often as low as the girdle. The fashionable lady would wear two or three such chains, to which smelling-bottles and various ornaments, even heathen 'charms,' were attached. Gold pendants descended from the head-ornament, which sometimes rose like a tower, or was wreathed in graceful snake-like coils. The anklets were generally so wrought as in walking to make a sound like little bells. Sometimes the two ankle-rings were fastened together, which would oblige the fair wearer to walk with small, mincing steps. If to all this we add gold and diamond pins, and say that our very brief description is strictly based upon contemporary notices, the reader will have some idea of the appearance of fashionable society."[8]

**Amusements.** It is presumed that Jewish children had games as the children of other nations, yet but slight account is given of such. It is noted that they kept tame birds and imitated marriages and funerals. They also engaged in singing and dancing, but males and females did not dance together, and the dancers performed according to their feelings, wild and fantastic, slow and graceful, nor were there any set forms for dancing. The youth must have taken part in the military sports which took place in public. Another means of entertainment was that of riddles, Samson's well-known one is an illustration. "Riddles are still 'put forth' at weddings. Here is a common one:

> Black as night, it is not night;
> It cuts its wings, it is no bird;
> Damaged the house, it is no mouse;
> It ate the barley and is no donkey.
> *Answer*—The ant."[9]

The following is quoted from Jerome: "It is customary in the cities of Palestine, and has been so from ancient times, to place up and down large stones to serve for exercises for the young, who, according in each case to their degrees of strength, lift these stones, some as high as their knees, others to their middle, others above their heads, the hands being kept horizontal and joined under the stone."[10]

**Education.** "If we take a general, and at the same time, it is to be admitted, a somewhat ideal, view of the education of the Jewish race, we shall find its beginnings and its specific character expressed in the sixth chapter of Deuteronomy: 'Hear, O Israel: The Lord our God is one Lord: And thou shalt love the Lord thy God with all thine heart, and with all thy soul, and with all thy might. And these words, which I command thee this day, shall be in thine heart: And

---

[8] Edersheim, Sketches of Jewish life, 218.
[9] Lees, Village life in Palestine, 203.
[10] McClintock and Strong, Cyclopedia of biblical literature, III, 730.

thou shalt teach them diligently unto thy children, and shalt talk of them when thou sittest in thine house, and when thou walkest by the way, and when thou liest down, and when thou risest up. . . .' Accordingly, we may say that a present God, whom to fear was 'the beginning of wisdom,' the honoring of parents and elders, a sacred family life, the memory of a great history, the practical wisdom of proverbs, and a gradually growing lyric psalmody, constituted the elements of the education of the masses down to the time of the Exile.''[11] Thus the education of the Hebrew child began at a very early age, as it would be taught these essential things as early as it could understand. The parents would begin its training in the home. Higher training, and in fact anything beyond the very rudiments, was given only to the upper classes. The teachers for the most part were highly respected. They were expected to be able men, not too young, and married.

In a general way education among the Hebrews may be divided into two epochs—pre-exilic, from the foundation of the kingdom down to the return from the Babylonian captivity, and post-exilic, from the close of the first period to the fall of Jerusalem and the final dispersion of the Jews.

During the first period there was no public means of education. Instruction was given by the parents, the very young child of both sexes being under the mother's care, but when older the boys went with the father out into his work and so learned from him. The young people were taught the history of their own people, their relation to God, the meaning of the religious feasts, the needed ethical and social training, and the things necessary for making a living and the care of the home. ''Higher education was scarcely known until after the exile. Even the priesthood and scribes were limited to a certain knowledge of law, and of historical and judicial literature. In the schools of the prophets, besides theological interpretation and the law, they apparently learned only the arts of sacred music and poetry, whereby they were to be stimulated to greater ecstasy, and were instructed in the compilation of maxims, narratives, and annals. It has been claimed that they were taught some mathematics and astronomy, to mark off the religious festivals, but this is very doubtful.''[12]

During the Captivity, the Hebrews came in contact with

[11] Laurie, Pre-Christian education, 76-77.
[12] Graves, History of education, Before the middle ages, 124.

the education of Babylon, so that upon their return to their own country education became more general and this continued to grow till contact with the Greeks and Romans brought about more general education and the establishment of schools for the training of the priests and the youth of the upper classes, and later public elementary schools began to grow up and became the most prominent feature of Jewish education. Rich and poor alike attended these schools. Reading and writing and a little arithmetic were taught the younger pupils, the older pupils were given instruction in the law. All pupils were obliged to learn a trade.

In the teaching the children were required to use the memory a great deal so that frequent repetition was the practice and, as in other oriental countries, the pupil was to do this work aloud and should he try to do it quietly he was reproved. In teaching the child to read, he was first given the alphabet, the letters being placed on a board for him so that he could see them. The child had to read aloud to his teacher, who corrected his pronunciation. The Hebrew Bible was begun to be read by the child at an early age. In learning to write, a copy was made in a wax tablet which the child traced with a stylus, and after awhile he followed a copy on papyrus or parchment with a pen. In the more advanced work, interpretation of the law, etc., would be given by the instructor, the youth, would listen attentively and then strive to reproduce in exact words what had been given.

In the early period, at least, discipline must have been severe. If we are allowed to form an opinion based on the old Testament, then we must conclude that the rod took a prominent part in every child's education, and from the authorities given us it is pretty certain that the ancient Jewish parent did not spare the rod whether he spoiled the child or not.

In the early epoch, girls received but little training, only such as was necessary to the carrying on of the domestic duties. At no time did girls receive such training as the boys, but in the second epoch they were taught to read and to write with dancing and music and domestic arts. Yet it would seem that there were some women who showed training beyond the simple subjects and who were able to take a place alongside the educated men of their times.

Jewish education was unsystematic, narrow, and selfish, art and science was scarcely known, and the literature was limited to the ideas connected with their God. Yet there was produced a beautiful family life, a thoughtful and kind treatment of children, a higher position for women than with any other oriental nation, a great reverence for parents, and a true idea of their relation to the Supreme Being.

## LITERATURE

1. Cornill, Carl Heinrich, The culture of ancient Israel.
2. Dean, Amos, The history of civilization.
3. Edersheim, Alfred, History of the Jewish nation.
4. Edersheim, Alfred, Sketches of Jewish social life in the days of Christ.
5. Ellis, G. Harold, The origin and development of Jewish education. *Pedagogical seminary*, IX (1902), 50-62.
6. Graves, Frank Pierrepont, A history of education, Before the middle ages.
7. Laurie, S. S., Historical survey of pre-Christian education.
8. Lees, G. Robinson, Village life in Palestine.
9. Letourneau, Ch., The evolution of marriage.
10. Lewis, Henry King, The child, its spiritual nature.
11. McClintock, John, and Strong, James, Cyclopædia of biblical, theological, and ecclesiastical literature.
12. Milman, Henry Hart, The history of the Jews from the earliest period down to modern times.
13. Thwing, C. F., The family.

## CHAPTER IX

#### THE CHILD IN GREECE

**Physical Characteristics.** The country of ancient Greece, as is modern Greece, was a small peninsula in Southeastern Europe, projecting into the Mediterranean Sea. It was a mountainous country, with no navigable rivers, and a broken coast line with many good harbors. There were differences of climate, varying from the excessive summer heat of the plains on the coast to the chilling atmosphere of the uplands, and yet as a whole the climate tended to be mild and even, with a bracing and pure atmosphere. Although it does seem that the spirit of freedom and independence was innate with the Greeks, yet the character of the country and the climate tended to emphasize these innate propensities and to bring human culture to a high development.

**The People.** In studying the people of ancient Greece, there are found two countries, although in neighboring sections, who were almost the opposite in character and the like. These were Sparta and Athens. In both these countries there were three classes. In Sparta there were first the citizens, who were the owners and the rulers of the land; in the second class were the *periaeci*, who lived in the surrounding towns and country, and although free yet they paid large sums to the citizens for the use of the lands and thus largely supported the Spartans; the third class were the *helots*, who were serfs or slaves and who did all the menial work for the citizens. The first class in Athens were the citizens, who controlled the country and who reserved to themselves the sole right of government and the making of laws; the second class were the aliens, who had settled in Athens for the purpose of engaging in trade or commerce, but who had no part in politics or administration; the third class were the slaves.

The Athenian and the Spartan were almost the opposite in character. The Athenians were refined, patriotic and brave, but at the same time fickle and changing. The Spartans were as patriotic and brave, or even braver, than the Athenians, but they were fixed and knew no change. The Athenians cultivated letters and the finer arts, while the Spartans practiced rigid, practical utilitarianism. The Athenians engaged in employments and amusements, but the Spartans did but little work, had few amusements, and spent their time mostly in military training. The Spartans were cruel in disposition, as was shown in their bearing toward the helots or slaves, as they greatly oppressed them and often put them to death; while the Athenians treated their slaves kindly.

**The Home.** In the early times the private buildings both in Athens and in Sparta were simple, but in later times the houses became larger and more splendid. Yet there were, perhaps, not the extravagances as in other countries, for in Greece much of the time was spent outdoors and away from the home, so that public buildings flourished and they were splendidly built rather than were the private houses.

In the cities the houses were built together, with only party-walls between them. They were narrow in front but extended back to quite a depth. They were, as a rule, built on the street but sometimes there was a small space in front. The door opened out on to the street, instead of inward, and it was a custom for any one going out to knock on the door to avoid opening out against some one passing along the street.

The walls of the houses were a framework of wood, sundried brick, or common stone, and covered with stucco. The roofs generally were flat, made of beams laid close together and covered with cement. In the early period the walls were plain on the inside and the ground served for a floor, but later there were decorated walls and mosaic floors.

There were two principal divisions in the interior of the houses, the one for the men and the other for the women, the women's apartments being back of the men's. The rooms were built around one or more open courts, by means of which light and air were admitted to the house. The homes were furnished with chairs and tables and couches and lamps and other household furniture and the kitchens were provided with pots and pans and bowls and sieves and many other articles.

**Girls and Women.** In the heroic age of Greece, women were accorded much freedom. Yet it would seem that their lot was not much above that found with women in savagery. They had the heavy household cares and duties of savage women. They had the management of the provisions—the grinding of the grain, the preparing of the meals, etc. They had to look after the clothing, doing the spinning and the weaving and the making of the garments. They carried the heavy burdens of domestic life along with the care of the children. Yet the women were well respected and had high standing with the men of that time.

In Sparta the state was everything. Strong and vigorous men were needed to protect the state and so must be provided for military life, and the mothers who were to bear them must be strong and courageous. The girls and women were allowed much greater freedom than in other parts of Greece. The girls received vigorous training, such as was given to the boys, having contests among themselves and even sometimes with the boys. In some of these contests the girls had to divest themselves of their apparel and appear thus before the public. This coming in contact with the males, the great freedom allowed to them, and the vigorous training did not spoil the purity of the girls, for adultery was scarcely known in Sparta. Nor did the training impair their physical appearance, as the Spartan women were noted for their beauty of person, although on account of the vigorous physical training this beauty was somewhat of a masculine type.

Women in Athens were treated quite differently to what they were in Sparta. There was seemingly a contempt by the men for the women and especially so among the leaders and rulers. "The most enlightened of the Greeks limited the duties of a good wife, housewife, and mother, to the following points: 1. That she should be faithful to her husband. 2. That she should go abroad and expose herself to the view of strangers as little as possible. 3. That she should take care of what the husband acquired, and spend it with frugality; and, 4. That she should pay maternal attention to the younger children of both sexes, and keep an incessantly watchful eye upon her grown-up daughters."[1]

In Athens the women were closely watched and carefully guarded. They were usually placed in the back part of the house and in the highest rooms, and for the most part the women and girls passed their time in the apartments allotted to them. There was no intercourse between young men and young women. Women were considered men's inferiors and they were thought little better than the slaves and they had but little more influence with the men. Woman was looked

[1] Dean, History of civilization, II, 176.

upon as an entirely lower being intellectually than man, and so not a fit companion for him in public life. When men outside the household were present in the home, the women were expected to seclude themselves. When a dinner was being given the company consisted entirely of men and the wife kept herself and her children in the women's quarters. The young women rarely went from home. Even if it was necessary for them to appear in public religious ceremonies, they did not take part in common with the other sex but acted apart from them.

Thus the training of the Athenian girl and that of the Spartan girl were quite in contrast and while the Athenian girl grew up to be a pale, slender lady, but little versed in the ways of the world, the Spartan girl grew up to be a vigorous, robust, healthy woman, ready even to take part in public debate if necessary. Yet there was at least one class of women in Athens not secluded, for "in the London market of Billingsgate it is the fishwomen who have been notorious for abusive language; at Athens it was the bread-women." [2]

A discussion of the women of Greece could not be complete without including the much discussed but little understood class known as the *Hetairai*, the stranger-women of Athens. Whether they were simply courtesans or whether they were women seeking freedom from the restraints and seclusion of the wife or whether they were both courtesans and seeking freedom and education, they certainly exercised a remarkable influence in Greece.

There were two classes of women at Athens, the first class being the wives and mothers, the citizen-women of Athens, and the other class being the stranger-women. Athens did not exclude strangers and indeed it was an attractive place to foreigners. "The city itself was full of attractions for the stranger, with its innumerable works of art, its brilliant dramatic exhibitions, its splendid religious processions, its gay festivals, its schools of philosophy, and its keen political life." [3] Although they did not exclude strangers from the city, yet they did exclude them from governing citizenship. Nor was a citizen, male or female, allowed to marry a stranger and severe penalties were inflicted on those who broke this

[2] Tucker, Life in ancient Athens, 122.
[3] Donaldson, Woman, Her position and influence in ancient Greece and Rome and among the early Christians, 56.

law. Since the stranger-women could not marry Athenian men, they had to gain their companionship by other means. The citizen-women, the native women of Athens, were not allowed the company of men nor were they given high accomplishments. "The names of these wives are not to be found in history. But the influence of the Companions came more and more into play. Almost every famous man, after this date, has one Companion with whom he discusses the pursuits and soothes the evils of his life. Plato had Archeanassa, Aristotle Herpyllis, Epicurus Leontium, Isocrates Metaneira, Menander Glycera, and others in like manner. And some of them attained the highest positions. . . . Some were renowned for their musical ability, and a few could paint. They cultivated all the graces of life; they dressed with exquisite taste; they took their food, as a comic poet remarks, with refinement, and not like the citizen-women, who crammed their cheeks, and tore away at the meat. And they were witty. They also occupied the attention of historians."[4] "Thus arose a most unnatural division of functions among the women of those days. The citizen-women had to be mothers and housewives—nothing more; the stranger-women had to discharge the duties of companions, but remain outside the pale of the privileged and marriageable class."[5]

The two most noted of the hetairai were Aspasia and Phryne. "Phryne, the most beautiful woman that ever lived, attracted the eyes of all Greece; Apelles painted her, and Praxiteles made her the model for the Cnidian Aphrodite, the most lovely representation of woman that ever came from sculptor's chisel."[6] "Aspasia, the beautiful, accomplished, and highly gifted woman, a native of Miletus, first the mistress and subsequently the wife of Pericles, exercised an influence and a power in Greece very greatly superior to any ever exercised there by any other woman. She was endowed with a mind more beautiful than her beautiful form. Her genius drew around her all those who had a taste for the beautiful, or a desire to cultivate their minds. At her house, eloquence, politics and philosophy were daily discussed, and ladies of the highest rank resorted thither to acquire some of the accomplishments by which she was distinguished.

[4] Donaldson, Woman, 71-72.
[5] *Ibid.*, 58.
[6] *Ibid.*, 71.

Large concessions must certainly be made to the mind that could be a fit companion for Pericles, and could teach rhetoric to Socrates."[7]

**Marriage.** In most cases Greek marriage was not an affair of the heart, for young people had but little opportunity to be with one another for love-making. Marriage for the man was rather a matter of convenience, for the purpose of the continuation of his family. This was a duty he owed to himself and to the state, for the state must have citizens for its perpetuation. To the Greek public life meant everything, the home counted but little. The wife's duties were considered to be the attending to household affairs and the bearing of children.

Marriage had to be with the consent of the parents. The young woman had no control over her person as she was under the charge of her father, and upon his death of a brother, and in case of no brother then the grandfather, and last her guardian. The father not only had power over his daughter's marriage in his lifetime but also after his death as he could bequeath her by will. And yet more, for upon his deathbed he could betroth his wife to another person and even he could bequeath her in his will to another.

In order for the children to be legitimate both parties had to be citizens of the state, and equality of birth and wealth were the chief considerations. The man could not marry in the direct line of his own descent, yet he could marry his half-sister on his father's side, which was rarely done. There was usually some years of difference in the age of bride and groom, the young woman being from fifteen to twenty and the young man from twenty-four to thirty. Marriages were most frequent in the winter, January being the favorite month, and when the omens were favorable, the most favorable being at the time at which there happened to be a conjunction of the sun and the moon. The selections and arrangements were usually made by the father or the guardian but often a professional matchmaker was employed, who was well informed in regard to the marriageable young people. When the marriage was determined upon, the betrothal took place, which was made by the legal guardian of the young woman and in the presence of friends and relatives of both parties, the dowry of the wife being agreed upon at the time.

In ancient Greece the lover would often write the name

[7] Dean, History of civilization II, 179.

of his loved one on walls and columns and carve it on trees. He would even write the beloved name on the leaves of the trees. The lover would send verses to his lady love. He would decorate her door with flowers and garlands. He would wear a wreath on his head awry or wear it untied, as a token of his being in love. Sometimes the lover would make an image of wax, call it by the name of his loved one, and place it near a fire, as the heat was supposed to melt the hard heart of her he loved as it melted her wax image.

Love potions were in common use as were also antidotes to love. "Some herbs were made use of for this purpose, also insects bred from putrid matter; the lamprey, the lizard, the brains of a calf, the hair on the extremity of the wolf's tail, with some of his secret parts, and the bones of the left side of a toad eaten by ants. The bones on the right side were supposed to cause hatred. Besides these, were also used the blood of doves, the bones of snakes, the feathers of screech owls, and bands of wool twisted upon a wheel, more especially such as had been bound about a person that hanged himself. ... The Greeks also professed to have the means of allaying the passion of love, at least of that species of it which originated from magical incantations. The antidotes were of two kinds. The one consisted of those substances which possessed some natural virtue, to which the production of the effect might be attributed, as the herbs which were supposed enemies to generation. The other included all such as wrought the cure by some occult or mystical power, and by the assistance of demons. As instances of this latter, may be cited the sprinkling of the dust in which a mule had rolled herself, and the confining of toads in the hide of a beast lately slain. Another method of curing love, was to wash in the water of the river Selemnus."[8]

In the Homeric time in Greece, the suitor paid the father for his bride, thus purchasing her. But in later times this was entirely changed and the bride was expected to bring a dowry with her. Among the wealthy this dowry was supposed to consist partly in cash and partly in clothes, jewelry, and slaves. The husband had to give security for it, as in case of divorce it was returned to the bride or to her parents and in case of her death it did not go to the husband but to the nearest of kin. Where there was a daughter of a poor, deserving citizen, and especially if her ancestors had been

[8] Dean, History of civilization, II, 167-168.

serviceable to the state, she was provided a dowry by the state. Sometimes the dowry was given to such a girl by a number of citizens. The dowry was supposed to give the wife better standing and thus bring more respect from the husband and greater freedom. A woman might carry so great dowry to her husband as to make her the stronger partner and so be able to have her husband in submission to her and her money.

The day of the wedding having arrived, offerings were made to the deities that protected marriage, the oath of fidelity was taken, and the father declared that he gave his daughter to the man. The bride and bridegroom both were bathed, at Athens the water being taken from a famous fountain, and they were dressed in their wedding-garments, both bride and bridegroom being richly adorned and wearing upon their heads garlands of various herbs and flowers. The bride was then led from her home and placed in a chariot between the bridegroom and his best man. They then drove slowly through the streets, the bride's mother following them and carrying the wedding torches, kindled at the parental hearth, and a procession of relatives and friends followed. At the bridegroom's home the axle-tree of the chariot was broken or burned, to designate that the bride having found a new home would never return to her old home. The bridegroom's house was decked with garlands and brilliantly illuminated. The couple were met by his mother bearing torches, and surrounded by a group of dancing-girls they came to the door, and at the threshold the bride made a pretense of not wishing to enter, when the bridegroom seized her and carried her inside, seeing that her feet did not touch the sill. All then partook of a feast, consisting of wines, meats, sweetmeats, and wedding-cake, the women with the veiled bride among them sitting apart from the men. The final ceremony consisted in the eating of a quince by husband and wife together, to signify, perhaps, because of the bitter-sweetness, that they should partake of the sweets and bitters of life together, our "for better or worse." Then the guests departed and the couple entered the bridal chamber, where for the first time the bride unveiled herself to her husband. At the last the bridal hymn was sung before their door by a chorus of maidens. The next morning the chorus returned and saluted the married couple with songs. This was the day of "unveiling," as the bride unveiled herself, and the newly married couple spent the entire day in receiving visits with salutations and presents from their friends.

"The marriage ceremonies of the Spartans differed from those of all the other Greeks. Instead of having a public celebration, everything was there done in as private a manner as possible. When everything had been settled between the parties, the bridegroom at night made a secret visit to his bride at her father's house. Before day he returned to his comrades, at the gymnasia, and never, for a long time, visited his wife except at night and by stealth, as it was accounted a disgrace to be seen coming out of his wife's apartment. They sometimes lived in this clandestine manner for years, not unfrequently having children by their wives before they ever saw their faces by daylight." [9]

As citizenship was limited in the states of Greece, it became highly important that the citizens should perpetuate the state by marrying and having children. So the state would encourage marriage and make it honorable and likewise almost compulsory and unmarried men would not be wanted nor would marriage deferred till late in life be considered the best for the state. In both Athens and Sparta bachelors were subject to a legal penalty. In Athens those who held public office and were entrusted with public affairs had to be married, to have children, and to have estates in land. Sparta was quite severe on the bachelors. If a man delayed marriage after a specified age, he subjected himself to a number of penalties. One was for once each winter to go naked around the market-place and sing a song ridiculing his bachelorhood. Such men were not permitted to be present at the contests wherein young women engaged in a nude condition. Upon the celebration of a certain solemnity, the bachelors were dragged around the altar by the women who beat them with their fists. When these men became old they were not accorded that high respect which the young of Sparta was accustomed to pay to the aged.

Monogamy was early established in Greece as the basis of society. There were some instances of polygamy or rather concubinage in the early ages and on some occasions where large number of men were lost in war or from other causes. This might have been resorted to in order to replenish the state but this was of rare occurrence.

In early times in Greece divorce was in the hands of the

[9] Dean, History of civilization, II, 173.

husband and he could exercise it whenever he felt that he was justified but in later times this right was somewhat restricted. The Spartans seldom divorced their wives. In Athens divorce was easy for the man, but a bill of divorce was required to be presented to the magistrate in which the reasons for the divorce were set forth. They would, no doubt, have been more frequent had it not been that in divorce the husband had to restore the dowry to the wife or pay her a sum each month for her support. For a man to divorce his wife was considered a great dishonor to her. It was difficult for a woman to procure a divorce, Athens being more favorable to women in this respect than the other states of Greece. But here she had to present a bill of grievances to the magistrate and it required his action before separation could take place. "The terms expressing the separation of men and women from each other were different. The men were said to dismiss their wives; to loose them from their obligations; to cast them out; to send them away; to put them away. If a woman left her husband, it was termed simply to depart from him." [10]

**Dress.** The articles of dress worn by the Greeks were of two kinds—one drawn on or got into, a tunic, called by the general term *endymata;* the other thrown over the person, a mantle, known as the *epiblemata.* Of the first kind the *chiton* was the representative garment, which was worn next to the body. The chiton in its usual form was an oblong piece of cloth and thrown about the body in such a way as to leave an opening for one arm to go through, while the two ends of the open side were fastened over the other shoulder by means of a buckle or clasp. Sometimes the chiton was made with two sleeves, with one sleeve, or with short sleeves. In some cases, as with workmen, it was thrown across the left shoulder with the right arm and shoulder entirely bare, so as to be left free for action. The chiton was fastened about the waist by a ribbon or girdle. The representative of the epiblemata was known as the *himation.* This was also an oblong piece of cloth, one corner of which was thrown over the left shoulder in front, drawn across the back to the right side, sometimes below the right arm and sometimes over it, and then it was thrown again over the left shoulder.

Boys commonly wore only the chiton. The young men, from the age of seventeen to twenty, called the *ephebi,* in-

[10] Dean, History of civilization, II, 174.

stead of the himation wore the *chlamys,* which was an oblong cloth, thrown over the left shoulder and the open ends were fastened over the right shoulder with a clasp. The himation of Sparta was smaller than that at Athens, scarcely covering the person, and which was called the *tribon.* The women wore the chiton and the himation and in addition they wore another garment over the chiton, called the *crocotos,* which sometimes had sleeves and was of a rich purple or saffron color and frequently had a broad border of embroidery. The Doric maidens usually wore but a single loose woolen garment. It was without sleeves and fastened over the shoulders with clasps. It usually extended about half way to the knees, it was worn with or without a girdle, and the left side was left open, which might or might not have been fastened with a buckle or clasp.

The garments were made of linen, cotton, or wool, and in later times silk also was used. White was, perhaps, the prevailing color and yet many colors were used, as, purple, red, green, yellow, gray, brown, olive, azure, cherry, and changeable colors. If the entire dress was not colored, it might have had colored borders, embroidery, or stripes, worked in or sewed on, and sometimes there were fringes or tassels. The undergarment, in time of mourning, was sometimes black.

The Greeks, both men and women, were especially careful of the hair. The men wore their hair and beard long and they had the hair curled or braided and bound up in a large bunch on top of the head or it might be arranged along the forehead and kept in place with golden grasshoppers. Dandies went to extremes and let their hair grow till it fell down on the shoulders. Most of the men had thick hair. In the cities the men usually went bareheaded but sometimes they wore hats or caps, when at work and on journeys.

The Grecian women for the most part had long, rich hair and, naturally, they took even more care of it than did the men with their hair. Sometimes it was allowed to fall loosely down the back; sometimes the hair was combed over the back in waving lines and a ribbon tied around the head; it might be that the front hair was combed back over the temples and ears and tied at the back of the head in a knot, held in place with hairpins of ivory, bronze, bone, gold, or silver; and there were many other ways of keeping the hair.

The hair of children was carefully attended to. The girls'

hair was often twisted into artistic curls and then drawn together over the forehead and held by a fancy comb. In Sparta the boys' hair was kept short till their majority had been reached, when it was allowed to grow long. Among the Athenians the hair of the boys was permitted to grow till they had reached maturity, when it was cut off and burned to some deity, after which it was allowed to grow long again.

There were oils, perfumes, ointments, and essences for the hair. Curling-irons were in use for curling the hair. Powders were used on the hair and especially the kind that gave it an auburn color. There were dyes for the hair and they were well resorted to. Nets were used by the ladies to enclose their hair, and veils of a light fabric and of transparent texture were worn. On festive occasions wreaths and garlands were worn by both men and women.

Among the Greeks the hands were not usually covered, gloves rarely being worn. The feet were not covered in the house and even sometimes in the street there was no covering to the feet. There was a great variety of foot-wear from the simple sandal to the high boot, the three main kinds being the sandal, the shoe, and the boot.

The sandal was the simplest form of foot-covering. This consisted of a sole of wood or leather, or it might be two pieces of leather with a piece of cork between. This was held on the foot by means of a strap or thong passing between the big toe and the next and running back along the top of the foot and fastened to another strap going over the instep and another that passed round the back of the heel. Occasionally slippers were worn, which among the women were ornamented with needle work.

From the sandal was evolved the half shoe, covering the front part of the foot, and then the shoe, covering all the foot, which arose from the addition of a closed heel and smaller or larger side-pieces sewed to the sole. The working-people of both town and country had the soles studded with iron nails, while the dandy in the city might have had gold or silver nails in his shoes. The women regulated their stature, increasing or diminishing the height, by means of high or low heels and soles of different thickness. The children at Athens began to wear shoes at an early age. In the boot the covering reached to the calf of the leg, open in front, and fastened with laces.

In the footwear was where novelty and taste was shown

by the Greeks. There was fashion in shoes and they often were named for those who originated the styles. They were very careful about neatness of fit and appearance. It was not considered good taste to wear patched or mended shoes. Black, white, and colored shoes were worn. Blacking was used, which was a kind of polish. The material was usually leather but felt also was used and slippers were sometimes made of linen. Socks and stockings seem to have been worn, but they were not in common use.

In the heroic times of Greece, as described by Homer, men wore earrings, necklaces, armlets, fancy girdles, hair ornaments, and finger-rings. In later times all these were discarded except the finger-rings, and these were usually signet rings. The women continued to use all kinds of ornaments. They wore both signet and jeweled rings on their fingers, some of the latter being set with beautiful and costly jewels; they wore necklaces of many patterns, varying from the simple ring to elaborate pendants; they wore armlets, bracelets, and anklets, usually in the form of spiral snakes; they wore a diadem or fillet to keep the hair in place; they wore ornamented girdles. The ornaments mentioned above were usually of gold and adorned with gems, as they used many kinds of precious stones.

The ladies dyed their hair and bleached it and increased its amount by adding other hair; they used tooth-powder; they blackened their eyebrows; a dark complexion was whitened and one too pale was rouged; their lips were touched with vermillion. To aid in this decorating, they had mirrors, which were made of bronze and usually circular, either without a handle or with one richly adorned.

The ladies had parasols, much like the ones at present, which could open and shut by means of wires, and which they carried themselves or had servants to hold over them. They had fans of peacocks' feathers or of thin light wood. Canes were used by the men both in Sparta and Athens, which were mostly of great length and with crook handles.

The ladies of Old Greek times well understood how to adorn, enhance, and remodel the human figure. As was stated above, they hung on to the figure all kinds of ornaments—rings, necklaces, earrings, bracelets, etc.; they could curl and dye and increase the amount of hair; they painted and powdered the cheeks and eyebrows and lips; they knew how to increase or diminish the stature by means of the heels and soles of the shoes; and they knew the art of enlarging or diminishing the figure by means of corsets and padding. Not only did they know all these things, but also they understood how to display to best advantage any part of the figure that was beautiful, as, a woman having pretty white teeth knew how and when to laugh to best display them and the handsome mouth.

**Food.** In the earlier times of Greece, when the food supply was limited to a narrow territory, there was frugality and little variety. As commerce increased the food supply became greater and of a varied character, and yet the Greeks were for the most part frugal and temperate.

There were usually three meals a day—a light breakfast, a heavier meal near midday, while the principal meal was toward the close of the day. When the family ate alone, the father reclined on a couch, the mother sat on a chair near him, and the children sat about them, the younger perhaps on the mother's lap or on the couch by the father.

The bread was made from wheat and barley and also from rye, millet, spelt, and rice. The bread sold by the breadwomen in Athens had a big reputation all over Greece. Among their cakes was one made of wheat and honey, another of rice, cheese, eggs, and honey, and a third of cheese, eggs, and garlic. Beef, mutton, goat's flesh, and pork, were the most common meats. Poultry was abundant and eggs were used in various ways. There was plenty of wild game, as, the partridge, wild pigeons, wild geese, deer, hares, and wild boars. Hot sausages were greatly liked and they were sold on the streets of Athens and perhaps in other cities. Fish were abundant, both fresh-water and salt, and oysters, eels, mussels, and turtles were used as food. Among the vegetables were lettuce, spinach, cabbage, peas, beans, radishes, onions, garlic, turnips, and asparagus. The food was seasoned with salt, mustard, garlic, onions, and herbs. Honey was used as sugar with us and olive-oil and cheese took the place of butter. Of fruits there were figs, apples, quinces, peaches, pears, plums, cherries, grapes, and of nuts there were walnuts, almonds, and chestnuts. Wine was in great use and, perhaps, there was no other beverage but water as milk was not often drunk except in the country.

After being weaned, the child at Athens was fed by its mother or nurse with milk and a weak broth, which consisted mostly of honey. The older Athenian child no doubt had an abundance and a variety of food, but such was not the case in Sparta. Taken to the public tables at seven years of age, the Spartan child was given only very coarse food and not nearly a sufficient quantity of this. He was permitted, however, to steal more food, but if caught he was severely punished.

**Child and Parent.** One of the worst things that could happen to a Greek in the old times was not to have children, and especially not to have a son. Although daughters were not disliked, yet it was through the son that the family name and the worship of family gods and ancestors could be continued after the death of the father. There was more, for the state considered childlessness and especially no sons in a family unfortunate, as it was thought such a condition lessened the ties between citizen and state. So when a boy was born into a family the outer door was decorated with an olive branch, while for a girl a fillet of wool was used.

"The Grecian mothers were subjected to certain rules prior to the birth of their children. Their food and exercises were regulated either by the laws, or by the manners and customs. In most of the Grecian states they were required to lead a sedentary, inactive, and tranquil life. In Sparta, however, it was directly the reverse. There, women while in that condition were required to be abroad, engaged in their usual athletic recreations, eating and drinking as at any other period of time."[11]

**Care of Children.** The newly born child was bathed in water and oil and then it was put into swaddling clothes, a narrow woolen band wrapped tightly round and round the child from the neck to the feet. In Sparta the newly born child was bathed in water tempered with wine, as it was considered strengthening to the child and also that such a bath could be endured only by strong and healthy infants. The baby was not placed in swaddling clothes in Sparta, so that it was allowed the freedom of its limbs and body.

There were two family festivals observed with the young child. The first was of a religious nature, the ceremony of purification, and it usually took place on the fifth day after birth. The child was held in the arms of the nurse, midwife, or some member of the family, who ran round a fire blazing on the family altar, followed by the members of the household. This was done that the child might thus be placed

[11] Dean, The history of civilization, II, 183.

under the care of the household gods. It was ended with a feast. The second festival was that of the name-day, which occurred on the child's tenth day after birth. This was a very important event in the life of the child, as on this occasion the infant was acknowledged by the father as his own and he committed himself to its rearing and education. A feast was held, a special cake was eaten, a sacrifice was offered, chiefly to the goddess of child-bearing, and the baby was given a name. Presents were given to the child, among them being charms or amulets and which were hung around its neck to protect it against magical arts and the evil eye. The favorite name for the eldest son was that of his paternal grandfather. Sometimes the boy was named for his father or there might be a shortened form of the grandfather's or father's name. He might be named for an intimate friend or for some god or for some action or condition or experience in his father's life. Later in life the boy might receive a nickname that would take the place of his real name.

In the earlier times the mothers both of Athens and Sparta nursed their children, but later this was abandoned and nurses were procured. Wet-nurses were employed for the baby's first year or a half year longer and then a regular nurse was obtained for the child. In Sparta the nurses were usually from the women of the perioeci, and the other peoples of Greece preferred the Spartan nurses because they were strong and healthy and also gave the children a vigorous training. "When the child grew to some understanding, the nurse told stories out of the great wealth of Greek mythology and Æsopian beast fables which circulated among the Greeks from the earliest times; also ghost stories, chiefly to frighten and subdue the rebellious: about the horrible bugaboo called Mormo; about Acco, who carried off bad children in a huge sack; or Lamia, once a princess, who ate her own and others' children; or Empūsa, a hobgoblin that took any shape it pleased. If these stories failed to restrain the naughty child, then the sandal was vigorously applied." [12]

The earlier cradle was of basket-work, in the form of a flat swing. A later one was shaped like a shoe, having handles at the sides for carrying and suspending. In yet later times appeared cradles similar to those of modern times.

[12] Gulick, The life of the ancient Greeks, 75.

Lullabies were sung over children as now. One cradle-song has come down to us in this form:

> "Tenderly she touched their little heads and sang:
> Sleep, baby boys, a sweet and healthful sleep;
> Sleep on, my darlings, safely through the night,
> Sleep, happy in your baby dreams, and wake
> With joy to greet the morning's dawning light."[13]

**Infanticide.** If in Sparta the child survived the bath of water and wine, then it was subjected to an inspection by a council of the state to decide whether it was fit to live or not. The strong and robust children were permitted to live, but the weak and sickly and deformed children were thrown down a precipice or exposed on the mountains. If any of the helots or perioeci should find the child and take it they were permitted to keep it, but the child could never become a citizen of Sparta. This custom of destroying or casting out infants was done in order to insure strong citizens for the state. No parent was allowed to pass judgment on the child, such was retained by the state alone.

Infanticide was practiced in Athens, but not by the state. This was wholly in the hands of the fathers. The fathers at Athens were more cruel than the state at Sparta, for not only weak and deformed children were cast aside by the Athenian fathers, but this might be true of other children, as poverty and other causes might be a motive. This was done by placing the infant in a basket or earthenware vessel and leaving it in a temple, or some other public place, so that some one might take it. This was called "potting" the child. The mother usually placed a token as a trinket or an amulet with the child so that possibly afterward the child might be recognized. The party who might take such a child had full power over it and might rear it as a slave or do with it as he might wish. The father was sometimes brutal enough to take the baby to the mountains and leave it to die from exposure or wild beasts.

"From this barbarous custom the Thebans formed an honorable exemption. They rendered the murder of infants a capital offense. Those who were born of parents unable to provide for their maintenance were brought up at the public charge, but in return, when grown up, the public had a right

[13] Laurie, Pre-Christian education, 251.

to their services until they were adequately compensated for what had been expended in bringing them up.'' [14]

**Duties of Children.** The boy at Greece was expected to walk along the street in a quiet manner with head bent, as a sign of modesty, and to speak to no one. At home he was to be careful of his manners and habits. He was to be respectful to his elders, making way for them on the street, keeping silence in their company, and when seated to arise when they entered the room and to give way to them. It was the duty of children to be obedient and respectful to their parents, and to care for them when there was need. But the parents, too, had their duty to perform and if they neglected the children then the children were excused from maintaining their parents.

**Adoption and Inheritance.** People not having children of their own were permitted to adopt other children. If a man had no son he could adopt a young man and have him marry his daughter. Those adopted were accorded all the rights and privileges of any children. The children of an adopted son were regarded as descendants of the adopting father and they preserved the ancestral worship and paid homage at his tomb. If after adopting a son the man should marry and have a son from this marriage, then the two boys received equal shares of the property upon the death of the father. When there were neither legitimate nor adopted sons, the estate went to the nearest relatives. In case of death without heirs, the estate descended to the prince, the commonwealth, or the supreme magistrate, as the laws directed. Sometimes if the children of noted men were left without property, they were provided for by the state. Children could be disinherited, but such had to be done publicly before certain judges appointed for that purpose. When a parent was unable, through age or infirmity, to manage his estate the son could bring this before magistrates, who had the power to turn over the property to the son, who would care for the property and the parent.

**Toys and Playthings.** The children of ancient Greece had quite a number of toys and playthings. The infant's first toy was a rattle, made of metal or wood, having small stones inside. A little older they had painted clay puppets, representing human beings and such animals as tortoises, hares, ducks, and mother apes with their offspring. Dolls were

[14] Dean, History of civilization, II, 185.

plentiful, made of painted clay or wax, often with movable hands and feet. "In more than one instance we have found in children's graves their favorite dolls, which sorrowing parents laid with them as a sort of keepsake in the tomb."[15] The little girls had houses for their dolls and dishes and tables. The children had ships and tops and balls and hoops and carts and swings. They also had pet animals. Sometimes the toys were bought and again they were made by the children, for, through instinct and imitation, they were much given to modeling and making things out of clay or wax or fruit-peel or leather. This is well illustrated by a passage from "The Clouds" of Aristophanes, wherein he has a countryman describing the precocious abilities of his son:

> "He is a lad of parts, and from a child
> Took wondrously to dabbling in the mud,
> Whereof he'd build you up a house so natural
> As would amaze you, trace you out a ship,
> Make you a little cart out of the sole
> Of an old shoe, mayhap, and from the rind
> Of a pomegranate cut you out a frog,
> You'd swear it was alive."[16]

**Games and Plays.** Just as with children in all ages and in all times, the children of Greece had many plays and games. The little boys and girls were in the homes together till they were seven years of age and so they played together. but apart after that. The boys of Athens, just as in other cities in older times and present times, played on the streets and pestered the passers-by and kept the guardians of the peace busy.

The little girls played with their dolls, making houses for them, setting out dishes before them, hauling them in carts, and swinging them and themselves in swings. In some of their plays they were joined by the little boys and they all played in the sand and made mud-pies and had see-saws and swings and they hitched up one another and dogs and goats to carts. The children carried one another pick-a-pack and they rode stick-horses and hobby-horses and they played bob-cherry and hide-the-rope and many other such games.

They rolled hoops, walked on stilts, played running and catching games, such as hide-and-seek; they played leap-frog, hopped and jumped, flew kites; they played games of

[15] Mahaffy, Old Greek education, 20.
[16] Felton, Greece, I, 426.

forfeit, odd or even, how many fingers are held up; the older boys had the tug of war and tossed one another in blankets. In one game the boy had to hop with one foot on a skin-bottle filled with water and greased; they spun coins on the edges; they shot beans from the fingers as the modern boys do marbles; they threw up five small stones and caught them on the back of the hand, as boys do jack-stones now; they played with dice.

There was a game in which a stone was to be so thrown into a circle as to knock out the stones thrown into it by the other boys and itself remain in the circle. They would sharpen one end of a heavy peg of wood and then throw it into a softened place in the earth so that it would stand upright and also knock out another's peg. They would blacken or moisten one side of an oyster-shell and would call one side *day* and the other side *night;* then the boys would divide into two sides with these names and would take turns in tossing the shell up into the air and then note which side was up when it fell to the ground; the winning side would then pursue the others and take prisoners.

The boys, then as now, found great sport with tops, playing in the house as well as in the street. They had different kinds of tops, among them being a humming-top. The Greek boy would tie a long string to the leg of a beetle and then let it loose and guide its flying by holding to the string; sometimes the boys would fix a wax splinter to the beetle's tail and then light it before letting him loose.

The children played blind man's buff. They would bandage a boy's eyes, who would then go about calling out, "I am hunting a brazen fly." This would be answered by the others with, "You will hunt, but you won't catch it." They would then run about and strike him with whips till he caught one, who would then be blindfolded.

The Greeks were very fond of the ball and ball-playing. The balls were of all sizes and colors. Some were stuffed with feathers and wool and others were empty. They were made of leather and of such a size as was suited to the kind of game to be played with them. There was tossing and throwing and juggling with balls and also there were regular games. Mahaffy thinks that he has discovered from the descriptions given that they played games similar to the present foot-ball, hand-ball, and lacrosse. He believes football is shown in this description: "The first is played by two even sides, who draw a line in the center, on which they place the ball. They draw two other lines behind each side, and those who first reach the ball throw it over the opponents, whose duty it is to catch it and return it, until one side drives the other back over their goal line.'' In the following he can see hand-ball: "It consists of making a ball bound off the ground, and sending it against a wall, counting the number of the hops according as it was returned.'' From another writer he finds lacrosse: "Certain youths, divided equally, leave in a level place, which they have before prepared and measured, a ball made of leather, about the size of an apple, and rush at it, as if it were a prize lying in the middle, from their fixed starting-point (a goal). Each of them has in his right hand a racket of suitable length ending in a sort of flat bend, the middle of which is occupied by gut strings, dried by seasoning, and plaited together in net fashion. Each strives to be the first to bring it to the opposite end of the ground from that allotted to them. Whenever the ball is driven by the rackets to the end of the ground, it counts a victory.''[17]

**Sports and Festivals.** Besides the games and plays for the younger people noted above, there was plenty of amusement of youths and adults in the way of sports and festivals. The gymnasium, with its palæstra, and the festivals gave opportunity for exercises and displays of all kinds.

The most common forms of gymnastic exercises were running, jumping, throwing the discus, hurling the javelin, and wrestling, and they formed what was known as the *pentathlon*. They were engaged in at the gymnasium and at the four great national festivals. Beside these there were boxing, the pancration, which consisted of boxing and wrestling, horse racing, and chariot racing.

The gymnasium was originally an athletic ground where all kinds of sports were carried on and it contained the palæstra, which was essentially a building for the purposes of wrestling, although both palæstra and gymnasium came later to stand for other things beside.

There were four great national festivals, known as the Olympian, the Pythian, the Nemean, and the Isthmian. In these festivals contests in races and athletic exercises were held and also sometimes in music, poetry, rhetoric, and the like. The Olympic festival was held at Olympia every four

[17] Mahaffy, Old Greek education, 18-19.

years, in the summer, and lasted for five days; the Pythian festival was also held every four years, near Delphi, in the winter, in the third year of every Olympiad; the Nemean festival was held at Nemea in the second and fourth year of every Olympiad, alternating in winter and in summer; and the Isthmian festival was held at Corinth, in the first and third years of each Olympiad, alternating between spring and summer. These times were thus arranged so that these national festivals did not conflict with one another.

The Olympic festival was the most noted. It was so important that in case of war a truce was entered into among the Grecian states, which lasted probably for three months during the year of the festival. During this time all people journeying to and from the festival were granted protection, and no one was allowed to carry arms within the sacred territory. The official prize was but a crown of wild olive, not valuable in itself, but it was perhaps the most coveted honor in all Greece. Only Greeks were eligible to compete and the winner received the highest honor from his fellow-townspeople. Poets of high renown composed odes in his honor, bronze statues were made of him, he rode home in a triumphal chariot and sometimes a part of the wall of his town was torn down for his entry, he was generally supported for the remainder of his life at public expense, and his honor extended to his parents and to his children, and even to the city of his birth.

Women were not allowed to be present at the Olympian games. The only exception was in permitting the priestesses of Demeter to be present, who remained in a temple built for them near the Stadium. All other women were excluded from the territory for a certain number of days. The penalty of trespassing on the part of a woman was death, the transgressor being thrown from the Typæan rock. "Only one instance is recorded of this rule being broken. Pherenice, a member of the famous family of the Diagoridæ, in her anxiety to see her son Peisirodus compete in the boys' boxing, accompanied him to Olympia disguised as a trainer. In her delight at his victory she leapt over the barrier and so disclosed her sex. The Hellanodicæ, however, pardoned her in consideration for her father and brothers and son, all of them Olympic victors, but they passed a decree that henceforth all trainers should appear naked."[18] But women were per-

[18] Gardiner, Greek athletic sports and festivals, 47.

mitted to enter their horses for the chariot-race, which they did, and won some races, too. The women had their own festival at Olympia, the Heræa, occurring every four years, at which there were races for maidens of various years, the course being one-sixth less than that for men.

Every Greek boy received a thorough physical training. To keep up the spirit for such training, local festivals were held in which was given opportunity for the boys' testing their strength and skill. In the 37th Olympiad were first introduced contests for boys, the names of the victors being inscribed on the records of the events before the names of the adult victors. At first there were only two classes of competition, for boys and for men, later a third class being added, for the beardless or those between boys and men. It would appear as if the ages for boys was between twelve and sixteen and for the beardless between sixteen and twenty. The length of the race-course for boys was but half that for adults and for the beardless it was two-thirds the full length. In the races at the Olympic Heræa the girls were likewise divided into the three ages. In the second century before Christ was introduced the pancration for boys, which shows that the games were becoming more cruel and degraded.

**Other Amusements.** The Greeks of the olden times were much given to entertainments. These might be at the home or on the sea-shore or in the country. They might be given by an individual, or gotten up by parties, each one contributing his part or sharing in the expense. It was not uncommon to have excursions into the country or to the sea-shore, with food and drink packed and taken along for the occasion.

The entertainments in the home were sometimes simply an informal affair, while again they were quite formal. A man wishing to give an entertainment would go out to the market-place or the gymnasium and invite his friends or he might send the invitations by a slave. After entrance into the home and the exchange of greetings, the meal was partaken of and the drinking was entered upon. Toasts were drank to one another and to absent ones, the young men taking the occasion to drink to their loved ones and to sing love-songs. Conversation would be entered upon and jokes and puns made, professional jesters being quite often hired for the evening. There would be games and conundrums and riddles and enigmas. A favorite game for such an evening was called *kottabos,* in which the player would throw the last drops of wine in his cup on to the head of a small brazen figure, which produced a clanging sound and a bobbing of the head; the louder the clang and the more violent the bobbing with the smaller the amount of the wine thrown, the greater the success of the player. There were dancing-girls and flute players and jugglers and contortionists. Recitations of passages from the poets were given and there were pantomimic and dramatic scenes acted. There might have been little of the kind of entertaining as noted above and the evening spent in deep conversation upon the important topics of the day and by the great philosophers and poets and dramatists and the other great men gathered on the occasion.

One of the very greatest amusements of the Greeks was that of the theater. These were usually built along a hillside, the seats being cut into the solid rock. The performances were held in connection with two of the leading religious festivals, the one in the midwinter and the other in the spring. The theaters were public and open to all the citizens and free of expense, the expenses being borne by the state or by wealthy citizens. There were no playbills nor similar kind of announcements of the plays, usually the audience not knowing what was to come till the play opened.

Dancing and music were among the pleasures of the young people. Of these were mimetic dances, representing mythological scenes. There were also warlike and choral dances performed at the feasts of the gods. There were professional dancers and singers and flute-players. There were a number of kinds of musical instruments. The types of the stringed instruments were represented by the lyre, the kithara, and the harp; the wind-instruments were the pipes, clarionets, and trumpets; and the clanging instruments were the castanets, cymbal, and tambourine.

The young men indulged in horse-racing; they frequented gambling places where dice was used; and they placed metal spurs on cocks, pheasants, and quails and fought them thus armed. Hunting was a favorite sport. It was quite fashionable for rich young men to have fine horses and, although they did ride some, yet they preferred to drive their horses to chariots.

The jugglers and acrobats were quite skilful and they were of both sexes. Outside the help of present day science, they seemed to have performed as remarkable feats as at the present time. They gave sword dances; they tossed hoops and balls; they did rope-walking and dancing; they extracted things from their eyes and ears and noses and mouths. They would stand on their hands and head and perform feats with their toes, as filling vessels with water and shooting bows and arrows. In one feat a woman acrobat would bend back her head till it met her heels, then she would clasp her feet with her hands and roll off like a hoop. In one exhibit there was a contrivance, known as the potter's wheel, in which a young woman would be whirled round rapidly and yet she managed to read and write while being so twirled.

**Sickness and Death.** In the earlier times of Greece old age was highly respected in all the states. In Sparta and Thebes this respect was maintained, but among the smart set in Athens this was not the case. In the more remote and primitive districts the aged enjoyed the reverence and affection of the young and middle-aged alike. They were treated with great respect in both public and private and their opinions were sought for in affairs of state and of the home. Yet in all Greece there was a desire for children so that parents might be protected and comforted in advancing age, and those without children were often in a pitiable condition in extreme old age. At the age of sixty a man was recognized to be at least physically old, as he was then exempt from military duty.

Although the Greeks enjoyed an exceptionally fine climate and gave especial care to the body, yet they were subject to diseases as other people. Their houses were not in sanitary conditions, the streets were not in proper order, and the water was not always pure. There were physicians who had quite good skill in the treatment of diseases and both medicine and surgery were in a fair condition, although superstition and folk-lore too often ruled. Athens and other cities employed physicians at public cost to care for the poor free of charge.

Burial of the dead was a very important function and one demanded by both custom and religion. Without this final honor, it was thought the spirit would wander restlessly on forever. So when a man died his family was bound to give him proper burial. This was considered so important that when a man died in a foreign land his body was brought home, or, if that was impossible, then a tomb was erected to him and the burial rites enacted. It was even considered disgraceful not to let enemies in war bury their dead and after battles a truce was entered upon that the dead might be buried.

When dead the body was washed and anointed and clothed in white and placed on a couch. A wreath was placed on the head and garlands about the body, which were given by friends. On the floor about the couch were set pitchers that were to be put into the grave or on the funeral pile. The burial took place early in the morning, at Athens, at least, before sunrise. In the earlier times the dead were buried in the houses, but later they were placed outside the cities, usually along a road, but in Sparta they were kept in the city, while in the country they were buried in the fields. The bodies either were buried or cremated, but as the latter was quite expensive it was used usually by the wealthy only.

In the funeral procession the body was carried in a vehicle or on the shoulders of friends or slaves. The male mourners marched in front of the corpse and the female mourners behind it, all dressed in black with the hair cut short. In the Homeric times there were violent outbursts of grief and abuse of person by the mourners, but in later times laws were passed to prevent such. At the grave if the body was to be burnt it was placed upon the pile and precious ointments and perfumes were poured over it while burning and the ashes were collected and placed in an urn. If it was to be interred, the body was placed in a wooden, earthenware, or metallic coffin and put into the grave, which was usually in the rock. The mourners then returned to the house and partook of the funeral meal. On the third and tenth days sacrifices were offered at the tomb and again on the thirtieth day, which concluded the mourning period. The graves were well cared for and decorated with flowers and plants. "To neglect the tomb of your ancestors was so far a crime that no man could become a chief officer of the state who could be proved to have failed in this respect."[19]

**Religion.** "An Athenian child begins by listening to the 'old wives' tales' of his nurse; then is present at domestic rites and sacrifices, which impress him without his understanding them; afterwards learns his old-fashioned Homer and his poets, before he has any notion of questioning their theology; next moves about among altars and splendid temples and statues of Zeus, Athena, Dionysus, and many an-

[19] Tucker, Life in ancient Athens, 273.

other divinity; is later on initiated into awesome mysteries, which are addressed to his emotions and not to his reason; and is at all times trained to undertake no enterprise, public or private, without first consulting the will of the gods, praying to them, and sacrificing to them.''[20]

The child was introduced into the religious life in the home, as each house had its own altar and its special household deities, to whom prayers were offered and sacrifices made, and on occasions of marriage, birth, death, and the like, special ceremonies occurred. He learned about both the good and the bad, as amulets were hung about his neck to ward off harm and he saw sacrifices made to appease the wrath of the evil ones. In public there were sacrifices and celebrations to the gods, in some of which the child took part.

Old Greek religion was a worship of the beautiful—the ideal in nature and human life, and the gods were ideal expressions of human thought, portraying the divine in man. Religion influenced the old Greek in every way and on every side he was reminded of the gods by temples, altars, statues, sacred trees, etc. But with all his religion, strange to say, the Greek did not connect it closely with his moral life, for his religion was expressed in his attitude toward the gods, while his morality was determined by the laws of the land and the customs of society. This is well shown in his prayers, for these were not offered for inward betterment, but for some definite outward help.

**Education.** In the early times of Greece there were no real schools, the young receiving their training from the life of the family and the community. As this came through contact with living persons and not through dead precepts in sacred books, which demanded strict obedience and following, there was opportunity for growth so that progress might be made by the individual away from fixed and stereotyped ways of doing things. The purpose of the training of those times was to help the boy to become a man who would be wise and eloquent in council and strong and courageous in battle.

Sparta represented a phase of education in Greece. Surrounded as it was by people who were hostile to its ways and customs, it was necessary that the young should be trained to be patriotic to the state and skilled in war. To this end education began before birth, for means were used for having

[20] Tucker, Life in ancient Athens, 206.

strong children born and those not strong at birth were cast aside from the state. If the child at birth was decided by the council to be fit to grow up to be a Spartan, then he was given to his mother and remained with her till his seventh year, when he was taken from her and put under the care and training of state officials.

When at seven years of age the boy was taken over by the state, he was placed in the care of an officer called the paedonomus. This officer had supreme power over all the boys and youth and superintended their moral training and gymnastic exercises and their punishments, having men to assist in the work.

All the education was at public cost and all the young were placed in public buildings, eating and sleeping in common, all being placed together in common, even the younger members of the royal family, the heir-apparent to the throne being alone exempt. Here they were divided into three companies according to age—from the seventh to the twelfth year, from the twelfth to the fifteenth, from the fifteenth to the eighteenth. The elder and stronger boys were placed over them as captains and had them in charge.

When the boy first entered with the others his hair was cut short. The life was one of continued severe discipline and hardship. In summer and winter they went without shoes and with but little clothing, after the twelfth year with only one garment. They slept on pallets of straw without covering and after fifteen their beds consisted of rushes collected by themselves without the use of a knife. They were given but little food. They had permission to steal other food, but if caught stealing they were considered disgraced and received a severe flogging.

The training of the boys consisted in gymnastic exercises, being carefully organized and graded. The younger boys were drilled in running and leaping and ball-playing. The older boys engaged in wrestling, boxing, throwing the discus, and hurling the javelin. Sometimes the *pancratium* was used, consisting of boxing and wrestling and also most anything to win, as biting, kicking, scratching, gouging. The contestants generally were naked. Dancing supplemented the gymnastics, which for the most part were war-dances and also some choral dancing was given to be used in religious festivals. This was all done to prepare the young for warfare.

When a boy reached eighteen years of age, he then left

the buildings for boys and entered upon a more distinctive study of warfare. He was permitted to let his hair and beard grow and was known as a *melleiren,* "budding youth." These youths were drilled in the use of arms and in skirmishing. They were given frequent strict examinations. To test their courage and endurance, there was a custom of each year of whipping a certain number of youth. They were placed at the altar of Artemis Orthia and so severely whipped as to cause the blood to stream from them, their fathers and mothers standing by and urging them to endure it without flinching or murmuring. Sometimes they endured till they died under the severity of the whipping. Also there was another test in the way of a battle of the *melleirenes,* held each year on a small island near Sparta. These youths were divided into two companies, sacrifices to the gods were made, they were lined up against one another, and then commanded to fight. They fought without weapons, but fists and teeth and body and limbs were most fiercely used, and many were the wounds received.

At twenty years of age, the budding youth became known as an *eiren,* "a youth." These remained youths for the next ten years and they lived in barracks to themselves. They took a public oath of loyalty to Sparta and entered the army, thus going into real military life. They entered upon the life of a soldier, lived upon the coarsest fare, were drilled in the usages of warfare, and were sent out to guard and care for some armed camps or fortresses on the border. Each year there were festivals in which was displayed by all the youth their skill in military drill and gymnastic exercises and in music and dancing, such exhibits being before the king and the officers and the public.

At thirty years of age, the Spartan was recognized as being a full-grown man and became a member of the public assembly and was required to marry. But even then he had to remain with the youths and boys and eat at the common table with them, so that he had no home and had to visit his wife secretly in her home. He also continued in military service. It was the custom for each man to select a boy or a youth as a companion and to look after his care and training. These men were expected to be examples to the boys and youths and to correct them in their faults, the men being punished upon failure to do these things.

The girls of Sparta received a public training similar to

that of the boys. It was the aim to train them so as to become strong, healthy women, such as could bear robust sons to the state. They were given gymnastic exercises such as were given to the boys, but not in company with the boys, and also the girls were permitted to remain at home. They were exercised in running, wrestling, leaping, throwing the discus, hurling the javelin, and in dancing and music. On some occasions the young men and young women danced and sang together in public in festivals to the gods. This training did produce strong women and who were as patriotic as the men and who as mothers could give thanks to the gods in the temples when they learned that husbands and sons had died fighting for their country.

It may be seen that Spartan education was public and free and open equally to all free-born children. The Spartan youth received very little intellectual training. No doubt some acquired reading and writing, as such was not forbidden, although not encouraged. They obtained ethical and intellectual training from listening to their elders at meals and on the street. They gained from criticism of their conduct, which criticism was severe at all times. Thus they learned reverence for elders, honesty, and self-respect. All the sufferings and hardships placed upon the youth were that they might receive training to make them good soldiers to go out to battle for their native land. Although Spartan education did produce warriors and patriots, yet it did not bring out individuality, that which makes most for true progress and right living. "The state regulated the individual life, and, by so doing, crushed out individuality, personal initiation, literary and scientific activity, and ethical freedom."[21]

Athens represented another phase in Greek education. A new conception of human life developed here and hence there came forth new ideas in regard to the meaning and end of education. The idea of the significance of the individual took prominence and, although interests centered upon the state, yet the state was considered as being composed of individuals, each of whose free development made the voluntary giving of his life to the state all the stronger and better state. The citizens of Athens were educated for peace as well as for war, so that the aim of education was to produce all-round men who by being trained to be individuals would thus make the best citizens.

[21] Laurie, Pre-Christian education, 248.

At birth the child at Athens was judged by the father and upon his decision it remained in the family or it was taken from the mother and exposed. If it was returned to the mother, whether a boy or a girl, it remained in the home till marriage, when the man or woman went to his or her own home. For the first seven years of the child's life, both boy and girl, he was under the care and training of the mother and the other women of the household. The Athenian boy was well cared for and given plenty to eat and to wear and toys and playthings, so that at least the early years of his life were easy and pleasant. By hearing the nursery-rhymes and the stories from folk-lore, and by having related to him the doings of the gods and god-like men as given in the writings of the times, his emotional nature was stimulated and he became imbued with the poetic feeling and dramatic spirit which invaded Athens and with which later he was to come in close contact through his school training and in his social and political life.

When the boy became seven years of age, he was sent to school. He was then placed under the charge of a male slave, known as a pedagogue, whose duty it was to go back and forth to school with the boy and carry his things and to have care of the boy's manners and morals, having the power of discipline, but he did not impart instruction, that being given by the grammatist (elementary teacher) and the pedotribe (gymnastic teacher). The state did not provide elementary schools, although they were under its supervision. The schools were not only private, but the father had the right to decide what work should be given to his boy, and yet the law did prescribe instruction in gymnastics and music. If the father did not give due education to his sons, in his old age he could not claim support from them. The length of stay in the school and the amount of education obtained depended upon the will and condition of the father, but all the boys did receive elementary instruction in reading, writing, and arithmetic. The physical training consisted in ball-playing, running, leaping, throwing the discus, hurling the javelin, and wrestling, the course being graded to the age and size of the boys. They were also taught dancing and music. Their education was to train the boy to be able to use his body with ease and grace and to increase his intelligence rather than to train him solely to become a soldier.

At fifteen years of age the boy passed out of the elementary training and from the control of the pedagogue, and if of the higher classes he entered upon higher training. He now left the private school and entered the public school, the gymnasium, which was not more than an exercising ground located in a grove just outside Athens. At this time the youth was given much more liberty than when a boy, as now he was allowed to go wherever he wished, that he might become acquainted with what was going on in the city to prepare him for the duties of public life. He was still under the care of his father or guardian and through him he had opportunity for meeting men and hearing the conversations and discussions and thus learn of the political life of the state and the moral obligations of a citizen. At this time the youth began to learn to play a musical instrument and he read and recited poetry and studied drawing and geometry and grammar. The gymnastic training received much more attention at this period than the literary, as beauty of person and health was the great aim. The exercises were about the same as in the previous period but of a more strenuous nature. Boxing was introduced now and sometimes the pancratium was used. Hunting and swimming became a part of the life of the youth.

At eighteen the young man completed the second period of public training and became known as an *ephebus*, ''youth.'' His father or guardian presented him for citizenship, and if he showed proper credentials of legitimate birth, of Athenian parentage, up to standard in body, mind, and morals, he was registered. He also took an oath of fidelity to the state. He then entered into military service and continued for two years. He was thoroughly drilled and then sent to the frontier. At the close of this second year, when he was twenty years of age, he was called to Athens and examined for citizenship, and if he made a proper showing he was then made a full citizen, with all the privileges and duties pertaining to that office.

The pedagogue was not held in high esteem, as he was usually a slave that was unable to work, being too old or crippled. The elementary teacher, too, did not take a high position, as there were no special qualifications, so that any one could fill the position and usually only those entered into this work who were unfitted or unprepared for other occupations, and too often as the last resort. The elementary schools were sometimes carried on in a portico or the sheltered corner of a street, but again there were good buildings and well-equipped for the times. The furniture of these buildings usually consisted of stools for the children and a seat with a back for the teacher. The Athenian boy left home at daybreak for school and he did not get back home till sunset, but this was somewhat offset by the frequent closing of the school for holidays and festivals. The discipline was quite severe, the stick and the strap being much in evidence, and yet the teachers of ancient Greece do not appear to have been more cruel than those of Europe and of the earlier days in America.

In reading, the child was first taught his letters and their sounds, next came the learning of syllables, and this was followed by the learning of words, and the learning of the sentence came at the last. After he had learned to read, the boy was given Homer and other Greek writers. The teacher would recite the selection and the pupil would then repeat it. The poems were carefully explained to the children and questions asked them after such explanation.

Paper made from the bark of the papyrus-plant and parchment were used for writing on. To write on the paper and parchment reeds, split and pointed-like pens were used. Both black and red ink were used in the writing. Such were not used by the school-boy, as he had wax tablets, which were made by covering a small, thin board with a layer of wax. The boy used an ivory or metal pencil for writing on the tablet. One end of the pencil was made pointed for this purpose and the other end was flattened so that the pupil could smooth over the wax when the tablet was to be used again. The teacher would write letters and words, which the boys copied. At times he would guide the hand of a beginner. Also sometimes the copies were made deep in the wax and the children would trace them.

There was no such thing as school education of girls and young women in Athens, no public training whatever. The Athenians held that woman's place was in the home and that she should not take part in public life. Hence, according to their ideas, the girl needed no education beyond what would be required for the life within doors, such as would fit her to perform what they considered the simple duties that would come to her as wife and mother. The education of the girl, therefore, fell solely to the mother, aided by the other women of the household. The girl was taught to sew, spin, knit, weave, etc., and sometimes she learned to read and to write and to play on the lyre and sing. It is true there were women at Athens who were educated, and some of them were most highly learned, but they were not citizens of Athens, being foreigners and known as the hetairai. These women were discussed in a previous section of this chapter, so there is no need of further statements here.

Education in Sparta and in Athens comprehended in a general way much the same, as gymnastic and music were the two basic elements. The gymnastic education consisted not only in the exercising of the muscles, but also in the training for endurance to fit the young men for the fatiguing duties of the life of a soldier. Also music was broadened to include literary and moral training as well as music in its narrower sense. If the Spartan education did crush out much of individuality with the men, yet it did allow advantages to its women as no other education, in that the public training of the girls and the taking part in public affairs by the women gave to them great opportunities for growth. If the Athenian education did allow individual expression to the men, yet in confining the women to the narrow place of the home at Athens and in not allowing them to have any part in public education and public life, it narrowed the life of the woman in Athens more than was narrowed the life of the man in Sparta. There are things to praise and things to condemn in the education of Athens as well as that of Sparta.

## LITERATURE

1. Anderson, Lewis F., History of common school education.
2. Davidson, Thomas, The education of the Greek people.
3. Davis, William Stearns, A day in old Athens.
4. Dean, Amos, The history of civilization.
5. Donaldson, James, Woman, Her position and influence in ancient Rome and Greece, and among the early Christians.
6. Duncker, Max, History of Greece.
7. Felton, C. C., Greece, ancient and modern.
8. Gamble, Eliza Burt, The evolution of woman.

9. Gardner, E. Norman, Greek athletic sports and festivals.
10. Gardner, Ernest Athur, Ancient Athens.
11. Graves, Frank Pierrepont, A. history of education, Before the middle ages.
12. Guhl, E., and Koner, W., The life of the Greeks and Romans.
13. Gulick, Charles Burton, The life of the ancient Greeks.
14. Laurie, S. S., Historical survey of pre-Christian education.
15. Letourneau, Ch., The evolution of marriage.
16. Mahaffy, J. P., Old Greek education.
17. Mahaffy, J. P., Social life in Greece.
18. Tucker, T. G., Life in ancient Athens.

# CHAPTER X

### THE CHILD IN ROME

**Characteristics.** It is one of the world problems to determine just the cause for the origin and building up of a great city from which arose a great nation as Rome. This is one of the great puzzling questions that seems can never be correctly answered. But whatever the cause of the origin of the Romans, there is no question about their accomplishments. From a few mud huts on the bank of the Tiber river filled with savage or semi-civilized people there grew up one of the very greatest ruling forces the world has ever known, conquering the known world and controlling all from the center at Rome with power and wisdom that seem miraculous. The Romans possessed intense pesonality and keen power of organization and control. They believed in the state and that each individual owed it a duty, and yet they conceived that the state existed for the individual and needed each one as well as the individual needed the state. This view of the state and the individual enabled the Romans to base the state on law and to respect law when once established. Through this view they became lovers of law and order. They were essentially practical and from their attacking the problems of the world in a business and thoughtful way they became strong in administrative ability and through which they evolved a sound jurisprudence, which was bequeathed to humanity. The old Romans were men of both moral and physical vigor and of strong thought; they were utilitarian, proud, overbearing, selfish, cruel, and rapacious; with strong self-will they met humanity and nature and conquered both, which is shown on nature by remains of roads, bridges, aqueducts, and other structures, while their language yet dominates a large part of the world and their laws a yet still larger portion.

"Rome was one continual city of noise and bustle. Horace had complained of the turmoil going on night and day, the scurry and crowding of the streets from whose 'torrents and tempests' he hastened to escape into the chaste solitude of the Sabine hills. But during the first century population and activity increased apace, reaching its zenith, perhaps, in the days of Martial and Juvenal. Before daybreak the bakers would be hawking their loaves, and the shepherds, coming into the town from the surrounding districts, their milk: then the infant schools would begin intoning the alphabet, and with hammer and saw the rasping workshops were set going. Creaking wagons would haul huge blocks of stone and trunks of trees, with the weight of which the ground would quake, heavily laden beasts of burden jostled the foot-passenger; on all sides jolting and knocks and trampling, a fine confusion in which pickpockets reap their advantage. Here, says Martial (100 A. D.), the money-changer clatters Nero's bad coin down on his dirty table, and there a workman is hammering Spanish gold on an anvil. A procession of raving priests of Bellona is shrieking uninterruptedly; a shipwrecked sailor, with a fragment of the wreck wrapped up in his hand, is begging alms; a Jewish lad, sent out by his mother to beg; the call of a blear-eyed pedler from the other side of the Tiber, offering sulphur matches for broken glass. Jugglers, some with trained animals (Juvenal speaks of a monkey riding a goat and swinging a spear), Marsian snake-eaters and snake-charmers are calling for spectators for their craft. Peddlers, peddling old clothes, linen and what-not, carriers of pea-flour and smoking sausages, butchers with a reeking quarter of beef, and the foot, the guts and the blood-red lung,—each, to his own screeching tune, proclaiming his own wares."[1]

**The People.** In early Rome the population was divided into three classes, as in Greece, which comprised citizens with full rights and privileges, aliens with no rights of their own, and slaves who were regarded as mere property. But Rome, unlike Greece, did not remain a small territory, but extended its realm to include the parts of Italy about it and then all Italy and then the land about the Mediterranean, and then expanded to other parts of the earth, making a vast territory. Roman citizenship was gradually extended till it reached out into this territory. So the original three divisions did not continue to be maintained closely but there grew up three other divisions of the people. These were the patricians, the equites, and the plebeians, all of whom were

[1] Friedländer, Roman life and manners under the early empire, I, 19.

of the free population, enjoying the citizenship of Rome but not having the same privileges. The patricians, or *ordo senatorius*, were of the governing class; the equites, or *ordo equester*, included the middle class, the business people such as bankers, merchants, contractors, and the like; the plebeians included the great body of citizens, the common people.

**Slavery.** The greatest development of slavery was at Rome, reaching its high point in the last century of the Republic. The Romans had slaves from the earliest history. In the early times those who held slaves usually did not have more than two or three each, but as the years went on civic conditions changed and a great demand for slaves arose and the numbers increased till in the time of Augustus it is estimated that the whole number of free citizens in Rome might have been a half million or more and the slave population half that number, one in every three of the population of Rome at that time being a slave.[2]

The slaves came from the children of slaves, from persons becoming slaves under the law of debt, from importations from other slave-holding countries, from kidnappers who snatched up people from other countries and even from the coasts of Italy, but the great source of all was from captives in the numerous wars waged by Rome upon other peoples. It is claimed that in one campaign there were 150,000 people sold into slavery at its close. Slave-dealers followed the armies and there were slave-markets at Rome and other cities. Slaves were sold in open market just as animals and at hightide prices were very low. There were all kinds of slaves, as they came from many parts of Africa, Asia, and Europe. The greatest number were used in agriculture and in domestic service. There were all kinds of mechanics among the slaves and some most highly skilled. There were educated slaves coming from Greece and other countries of the East, so that they were used for the training of the young and for the carrying on of business for their masters. There even were physicians and surgeons among the slaves, many households having one to look after the needs of the free and the slave. There also were slaves whose duty it was to give amusement and entertainment, such as musicians, dancers, acrobats, jugglers, rope-walkers, and the like. Too, there were poor dwarfs and simple-minded among the slaves, who were

[2] Fowler, Social life at Rome, 213.

used to amuse master and mistress and guests as did the jesters of the courts in Europe later.

In the early times when each family had but few slaves, they were well treated and well cared for, being considered as members of the household. But later, and especially when slaves became so numerous and cheap, they were often treated very badly and neglected. The slaves were the absolute property of the masters and unprotected by the law, but later laws were made for their protection. The punishments were often extremely severe. They were brutally beaten, legs fettered, heavy iron collars put around their necks, thrown into dungeons, put at hard labor till worn out. Their capital punishment was crucifixion, being thrown to the animals of the vivarium, or set to fight the fierce beasts in the amphitheater. They were not always treated badly and even some became greatly esteemed by master and mistress and sometimes master and slave became friends, as some slaves were highly educated and accomplished men. Such slaves were usually set free and thus became freemen.

It is not necessary to discuss here the effect of slavery upon the citizen or the nation, for the world has fully decided that slavery is not good for the slave nor for the master nor for the state.

**The Home.** "The oldest Italian dwelling was a mere wigwam, with a hearth in the middle of the floor and a hole at the top to let the smoke out."[3] As Rome kept growing the houses kept improving until within the city the buildings became among the most wonderful and beautiful in the world. Also the Romans built beautiful country residences, *villas*, out from Rome. Little was known about the houses of the Romans until Pompeii and other cities were discovered in the middle of the eighteenth century, having been buried by an eruption of Vesuvius in 79 A. D. The houses and contents in Pompeii were well preserved, as the city was covered with ashes, while the other places were more or less destroyed by streams of lava.

When Rome became so filled with people, only the wealthy were able to have houses of their own, the well-to-do and the poor had to find place in huge lodging-houses called *insulae* (islands), because they occupied the entire block and so were surrounded by streets. Before the great fire in the time of Nero, the streets were irregular and narrow. In the

[3] Fowler, Social life at Rome, 240.

earlier times of the Republic the houses were three or four stories high and the number of stories grew until the time of Augustus, the maximum height of the frontage of a private building was made 70 feet (Roman measure), which gave room for six or seven stories which height was reduced after the fire of Nero to 60 feet, five or six stories. These houses were erected by speculators and were of poor material and poorly constructed, so that they were continually crumbling and tumbling and burning down. Being cheaply constructed and poorly repaired they did not afford great protection against the weather and so it was fortunate for the poor people that the climate of Italy for the most part favored an out-of-door life.

There were three parts in a Roman house, which were arranged in the same order in almost every house, although there might have been other rooms attached to them. In front was the *atrium*, partly covered; then came a center space, the *tablinum*, which was entirely covered; and adjoining this latter was the *peristylium*, an open court surrounded by columns.

The *atrium* was the essential feature that marked off the Roman house from that of Greece and other countries of the East. In the primitive houses, and in later times with the poor and the middle classes, this was used for both kitchen and sitting-room, while with the wealthier people it was the reception-room. This contained the family hearth and altar. The street door did not open directly from the street but there was a passage from the street and the door was placed at the end of this passage. Usually there was a square opening in the roof of the *atrium* for light and in the floor underneath this opening was a cistern for receiving the water that rained in and there were pipes under the floor for carrying off the water.

The *tablinum* was usually separated from the *atrium* by curtains. This contained the family records and archives; the *peristylium* was a later addition to the Roman house, coming when Greek architecture became to be used in the buildings. This became the ornamental part of the house, with fountains and flowers and shrubbery occupying the center of the court, surrounded by pillars and open to the sky. There were other rooms, among them being the *alae*, small rooms at the right and left of the *atrium*, and from the *peristylium* opened the *triclinium*, dining-room, the *culina*, kitchen, and the *sacrarium*, chapel.

The street door was of wood, having two leaves (a folding-door), moving on pivots, and in private houses opening inward and outward in public buildings. When opening inward the door was secured by a bolt and when opening outward by lock and key. There were but few windows and in general only in rooms above the ground floor. Paper, linen cloth, horn, and mica were used in the windows and glass seems to have come into use under the early emperors. The walls were decorated with paintings. The floors of the primitive houses consisted of clay and then came bricks and tiles and stones and later the houses of the wealthy class had marble and mosaics.

"The Romans resorted to various methods of warming their rooms. They made use of portable furnaces for carrying embers and burning coals to warm the different apartments of the house, and which they seem to have placed in the middle of the room. They also had a method of heating the rooms by hot air, which was conveyed by means of pipes through the different apartments. They also had a kind of stove, in which wood appears to have been usually burned. It has been a matter of much dispute whether the Romans had chimneys to carry off the smoke, but it does not appear that these were entirely unknown to the Romans."[4]

There were four representative kinds of chairs used by the Romans. The first kind was a folding-stool with curved legs placed crosswise; the second kind had four perpendicular legs and were without backs; the third kind were similar to the second but had a back; and the fourth kind was a chair of state, with high or low back, the back and legs being ornamented.

The couches were of three kinds. There was the low dining-couch, upon which they reclined at meals; then there were the beds for sleep at night or siesta by day; and the third kind had usually two arms but no back and which were chiefly used for reading or writing at night. With the bed was the mattress, filled with straw or sheep's wool or the down of geese and swans; bolsters and cushions, stuffed as the mattress; blankets and sheets, of simple material or dyed and embroidered; pillows for propping the head or the left elbow of the sleeping or reclining persons; and footstools.

They had benches of wood and stone and bronze, some of them being semi-circular and large enough to hold quite a

[4] Dean, History of civilization, III, 221.

number of people. There were square, round, and crescent-shaped tables, some being quite large, others smaller with three legs, and a one-legged table, often quite small and made of the rarest material and elegant in design. There were pots and pans of various kinds, and buckets and dishes and drinking-vessels, and other kinds of vessels.

The houses at night were lighted with lamps. The lamp consisted of the oil-reservoir, which contained the oil, the nose, through which went the wick, and the handle to carry it by. The lamps were put on stands or were suspended from lamp-holders or they hung down from the ceiling. The stands and lamp-holders that were used by the poorer people were made of common wood or metal, while those of the rich were of costly material and often most beautifully adorned with figures of all kinds of animals carved upon them. They had lanterns also, which had for covering horn, oiled canvas, and bladder, and later, glass.

**Women.** There were three classes of women at Rome—the citizen-woman, the alien, and the slave. Unlike as in Athens, the foreign woman never rose to prominence at Rome but it was the citizen-woman who took rank always before any other. Nor was a male citizen allowed to marry an alien woman, for citizens were wanted and, therefore, both parents needed to be citizens. But as citizenship was expanded to the parts of the world outside of Rome, the alien woman became a citizen, and so a Roman could marry her and still maintain his own and his offspring's rights.

In the early times the woman remained at home. She engaged in spinning and weaving and other household duties, and she had supreme control of household affairs. She was under the authority of her husband and she had no individual rights in property and she could not make a will. Later she acquired more rights and privileges. The condition of women at Rome was quite a deal better than at Athens or in any other country previous to Roman times. For at Rome women were allowed more freedom and participation in public affairs, they were allowed more to share in the joys and pleasures of the husband and other people, and they enjoyed a greater confidence and esteem of the men.

That Roman women appeared in public and that they were not afraid to stand up for their rights is illustrated in the following. In 215 B. C., when Rome needed resources for the second Punic war, the Oppian Law, was passed which forbade any woman to have gold trinkets of the weight of more than half an ounce, to wear a parti-colored garment, or to ride in a chariot within the city of Rome or a town occupied by Roman citizens or within a mile of these places, except for a religious purpose. Twenty years later, when the war was over and prosperity had returned, the women asked for the repeal of this law. They started a campaign and talked about it in every place, they interviewed men on the street, and they stated the case to every one that had a vote. Women from towns and villages came into Rome to help. On the day of the vote, the women rose early and filled the streets to the Forum and used every means to gain their cause. They finally overcame the opposition, the law was repealed, and the women recovered their liberty of riding and dressing as they had formerly done.

The Roman women would even go to greater extremes than the conducting of a political campaign. Over a hundred years before the event recorded above, when the women had much less privileges, when the despotic actions of husbands became unendurable, the women sought a way of rescuing themselves. At the time a number of men of the upper classes were attacked by an unknown disease, in every case attended by similar symptoms, and nearly all died. No cause could be found until a female slave offered to explain upon promise of freedom and to suffer no harm in consequence. Upon the Senate's guaranteeing such to her, she told them that the deaths were from poison, that the wives met together to compound the poison. She took the officials to the place, where they found the women preparing the ingredients. The women were charged with the matter, and to prove their innocence they partook of the drugs, upon which death followed, and with the same symptoms as with the men. Upon investigation 170 of the women were found guilty and it is held that 300 or more wives had entered into the plot to put their husbands to death. Some doubts are thrown upon this story by some historians but at any rate it is stated that the Romans believed it and told it for the truth.

Another story is told of women's appearing in public. At the time of the second triumvirate, funds being needed, a decree was passed requiring that fourteen hundred of the richest women should make a valuation of their property, under severe penalties against concealment or undervaluation, and that they should turn over such a portion as the triumvirs might require. The women appealed to the sister of one of the triumvirs and to the mother and wife of another but with little success. They then in a body went to the tribunal of the triumvirs, whose acts no man dared question, making for their spokesman, Hortensia, the daughter of the famous orator, Hortensius, and protested against the edict. It is claimed this is the first time to be enunciated the principle of "no taxation without representation." They succeeded in getting the amount reduced to a comparatively small sum.

There are some other instances of the public assembling of women. Under the empire there was an assembly of women known as the *conventus matronarum*, or the "little senate," as one writer of the time named it. The Emperor Heliogabalus built on the Quirinal a meeting-place for this body. This body of matrons met and discussed and voted upon and decided the various points of court etiquette, such as questions of dress, precedence, and the use of carriages.

The public standing of the citizen-woman at Athens has been given in the quotations on pages 179-181, which may be compared with the public standing of the citizen-woman at Rome as given in the following:

"If we take the period of Roman history from 150 B. C. to 150 A. D., we shall be surprised at the number of the women of whom it is recorded that they were loved ardently by their husbands, exercised a beneficial influence on them, and helped them in their political or literary work. Many of these women had received an excellent education, they were capable and thoughtful, and took an active interest in the welfare of the State. It is well known that it was Cornelia, the mother of the Gracchi, who inspired her sons with the resolution to cope with the evils that beset the State, and her purpose did not waver when she knew they had to face death in their country's cause. Julia, the daughter of Julius Cæsar, and the wife of Pompey, kept the two leaders on good terms as long as she lived, and acted with great sweetness and prudence. Cornelia, Pompey's second wife, was a woman of great culture, and a most faithful and devoted wife. Plutarch thus describes her: 'The young woman possessed many charms besides her youthful beauty, for she was well instructed in letters, in playing on the lyre, and in geometry, and she had been accustomed to listen to philosophical discourses with profit. In addition to this, she had a disposition free from all affectation and pedantic display, which such acquirements generally breed in women.' The intervention of Octavia, the wife of Antony, in affairs of state was entirely beneficial and judicious. The first Agrippina displayed courage and energy, herself crushed a mutiny among the soldiers, and was in every way a help to her husband. Tacitus praises his mother-in-law, the wife of Agricola, as a model of virtue, and he describes her as living in the utmost harmony with her husband, each preferring the other in love. And Pliny the younger gives a beautiful picture of his wife Calpurnia, telling a friend how she showed the greatest ability, frugality, and knowledge of literature. Especially 'she has my books,' he says; 'she reads them again and again; she even commits them to memory. What anxiety she feels when I am going to make a speech before the judges, what joy when I have finished it. She places people here and there in the audience to bring her word what applauses have been accorded to my speech, what has been the issue of the trial. If I give readings of my works anywhere, she sits close by, separated by a screen, and drinks in my praises with most greedy ears. My verses also she sings, and sets them to the music of the lyre, no artist guiding her, but only love, who is the best master.'

"These are only a few of the numerous instances that might be adduced, in which wives behaved with a gentleness or courage or self-abnegation worthy of all praise. It is true that they took an active part in the management of affairs, but, on the whole, it must be allowed that they acted with great good sense. And there is a curious proof of this in the times of the Empire. Wives went with their husbands to their provinces, and often took part in the administration of them. Some of the old stern moralists were for putting an end to this state of matters, and proposed that they should not be allowed to accompany their husbands to their spheres of duty; but, after a debate in the Senate, the measure was rejected by a large majority, who thereby affirmed that their help was beneficial.

"No doubt it was their good sense, their kindliness, and their willingness to co-operate with men, that led to their freedom and power in political matters. And this power was sometimes very great. Cicero, in a letter to Atticus, relates an interview which he had at Antium 44 B. C. with Brutus and Cassius. Favorinus was also present, and besides him there were three women—Servilia, the mother of Brutus; Tertulla, the wife of Cassius and sister of Brutus; and Porcia, the wife of Brutus and daughter of Cato. Servilia strikes in twice in the course of the discussion, and it is evident that her words carried weight. On one occasion she promises to get a clause expunged from a decree of the Senate. There must have been many such deilberations where women were present."[5]

Since women entered into public affairs at Rome, it would be natural to conclude they would enter upon some of the public vocations that were occupied solely by men in the earlier times. It would seem that they did enter into the medical profession but, perhaps, not the better class of women and maybe not the citizen-women at all. Since medical art was introduced from Greece, most all the men that followed it were Greek freedmen and likewise the women were likely of the same nationality and standing. Whether there were women lawyers or not, it is true women were permitted to appear in court in their own defense, which some few, at least, did. In religion the cult of Vesta was entirely in their hands, they had the leading part in conducting the rites of Ceres and other female deities, and the wives of priests in some instances held official positions along with their husbands.

Women occupied themselves, too, with literature. Very little is known of their writings and this mostly from the male writers of their period, who did not place a high estimate upon these compositions of the women, either prose or poetry. Many of the women who did not take an active part in literature did interest themselves in the writings of relatives and friends. Other women became critics and took pride in expressing their views, while others directed their energies toward philosophy and science.

"Ladies, when not poets, were critics, and as such, deemed by Juvenal worse than tipplers. Before they had been five minutes at table, they began to discourse æsthetically on Homer and Virgil, monopolizing the conversation, with a hammer and tong-like effect. They paraded their snacks of knowledge, made quotations from forgotten authors; grammar in hand, corrected their friends' slips. A woman, says Juvenal, may have the encyclopædia by heart and yet know nothing. Martial, too, mocks the purist woman, and yearns, as his life-wish, for a not too learned wife."[6]

[5] Donaldson, Woman, Her position and influence in ancient Greece and Rome, 120-123.
[6] Friedländer, Roman life and manners, I, 253.

"In the good old days of the legitimate drama under Plautus, Terence, Accius, and Pacuvius, women never appeared upon the stage. Feminine rôles were taken by men in female dress. But, with the appearance of the mime and the farce in the first century before our era, women began to take part in theatrical and musical performances. Their larger participation in such matters under the Empire is proved by the discovery of the burying place of a guild of women mimes, just outside of Rome, along the highways leading from the city. Women took a very active part in public musical performances, if we may draw an inference from the number of epitaphs which we find in honor of women who had been solo singers and flute players."[7] Women entered, also, into the commoner affairs of public life, as costumers, seamstresses, washerwomen, weavers, fishmongers, barmaids, and the like.

"If we make a general survey of the facts which have been noted above, it is clear that Roman women took an active part in the literary and religious life of the time, and in many of the cults held priesthoods or officially recognized positions from very early times. Their interest in literature, however, was not serious, and they have produced very little of permanent value. In the practice of law they never succeeded in getting a sure foothold. Women of the lower classes entered freely into the medical profession and the trades, but so far as medicine is concerned women confined their practice to members of their own sex. The principal branches of business which they took up were those connected with the manufacture of wearing apparel. The pursuits of the shopkeeper and the artisan were naturally left to the lower classes, but women of standing in society engaged in industries organized on a large scale, as we can see clearly enough in the case of the brick business."[8]

In the early days of Rome, while the people were struggling to maintain themselves and the nation, the virtue of the women stood out strong. But as the days of hardships passed and comfort and ease and luxury came in with the conquests, laxity of morals arose till under the empire, if the writers of the times may be believed, licentiousness and not virtue was the dominant trait of the women as well as the men. Yet there were many good women, as is shown in the quotations a few pages back.

[7] Abbott, Society and politics in ancient Rome, 95.
[8] Ibid., 98-99.

The social vices of Asia found place in Rome and while heretofore only the foreign women were of evil character, at the time of the empire the citizen-women entered into the life, and in 19 A. D. even a woman of prætorian birth registered herself at the ædile's as a prostitute. This created quite a feeling at Rome and a decree was made by the Senate that any woman whose grandfather, father, or husband had been a knight should not be enrolled as a public woman.

The public life of the times, too, tended toward the lowering of the standard of women. The circus, the theater, and the amphitheater were open to them and they attended in great numbers and witnessed the indecent and obscene acts and the debasing fights and slaughters. It became the fashion for women even of the highest rank to interest themselves in the actors, athletes, circus-drivers, gladiators, stage-singers, vocalists, and musicians, and often going into excesses. Pantomime dancers were the favorites with the women as they "were very beautiful young men, whose art lent them fresh grace. About 22 or 23 A. D. they were banished from Italy, on account of the factions they caused, and their relations with women, who must have been of high rank, otherwise no such ordinance would have been passed."[9] Also there were the banquets, which gave further opportunities for the meeting of the women with the men. With their obscene songs and dances and stories added to enflaming food and drinks, they helped to debase women and to arouse their passions.

**Marriage.** In the earlier days of Rome, when religion was purer than in later times, and children were desired to perpetuate the household religion, celibacy was looked upon as an undesired state and deserving censure; but in later times, when high moral and religious tendencies went down, childlessness was preferred to parenthood and celibacy to marriage. Marriage was a very important affair as it meant the bringing of a stranger into the household to enter into the family worship, to take part in the sacrifices to the household gods, the deities which presided over the welfare of that particular family. Thus it was a solemn obligation and one which deserved careful consideration. Up to the time of Augustus, there were no laws in regard to marriage, except as to the disposition of the dowries, as previous to that time it was deemed essentially a private transaction.

To understand marriage at Rome, it is needed to keep in

[9] Friedländer, Roman life and manners, I, 247.

mind that a woman was always considered to be under the control of a man—father, husband, or guardian. Marriage might or might not mean the transfer of this right to the husband, so that there were two general kinds of marriage contracts. By the one, *cum conventione,* the wife passed from her father's family into the family of her husband, *in manum convenit,* and stood in relation to her husband as a daughter, she surrendered her patrimony and became one of her husband's legal heirs. In the second, *sine conventione,* the wife remained under the rule of her father, as before the marriage, and retained her own property and her right of inheritance in her father's estate. In the first case, the wife became a *materfamilias* while in the second she was simply an *uxor.*

In the marriage, *sine conventione,* there was, perhaps, no form required as cohabitation of the man and woman constituted the marriage. In the marriage, *cum conventione,* there were three forms—*usus, coemptio,* and *confarreatio.* Marriage by *usus* prevailed among the plebian, common people; marriage by *coemptio* was the one commonly practised by the middle classes; and marriage by *confarreatio* was the favorite form in the highest social circles.

Marriage by *usus* was the simplest form, in which the wife entered into her husband's *manus,* if she lived a whole year in the man's house, both parties agreeing to the relation. In this case then the father's power was gone and he could not even compel the wife to leave her husband's home. But should the woman absent herself from the man's house for three nights in succession during the year, then the bond was broken. In the times when divorce was denied to the woman, she would often avail herself of this right of remaining away three nights in a year, so that if need arose she could have herself claimed by her father or guardian and in this way she could leave her husband.

In marriage by *coemptio,* there was a kind of mutual purchase, a fictitious sale, which the couple made to each other of their person, in which each delivered to the other a small piece of money and repeated certain words. The father emancipated his daughter in favor of her future husband and she came to sustain to the husband the relation of a daughter, took his name, gave up all her goods to him, and declared that she entered into the union of her own free will.

Marriage by *confarreatio* was the only form that required religious ceremonies. This was the most solemn and stately form of marriage as well as the oldest. By it the wife came into the absolute power of the husband by sacred laws but likewise she became a partner in all his substance and in his sacred rights. In case of the husband's death without will the wife inherited equally with the children and if no children then she inherited his whole fortune. This was a public ceremony, conducted by the pontifex maximus or the flamen dialis, in the presence of at least ten witnesses, and the bridal couple tasted a cake made of a sort of wheat called *far*, which with a sheep, was offered in sacrifice to the gods. The priests themselves had to be married by this ceremony and none but the children of such marriage could ever become flamen of Jupiter, Mars, or Quirinus, or vestal virgins.

A true marriage could be made only between Roman citizens, but as Roman citizenship became widely extended there was thus much latitude for choice. The lowest age for marriage was fixed by law at fourteen for the males and twelve for the female, but usually the girl did not marry before fifteen or sixteen and the boy not till he attained manhood, yet there were a number of instances of early marriages. A woman of twenty or a man of twenty-five who was not a parent became liable to the decree of Augustus against celibacy and childlessness. All within the sixth degree of relationship were originally prohibited from marriage, but later this was lowered to relatives of the fourth degree and when, in 49 A. D., the Senate permitted the Emperor Claudius to marry Agrippina, the daughter of his brother Germanicus, it was lowered to the third degree. But a woman was not permitted to marry her maternal uncle nor a man either his paternal or maternal aunt.

Marriage was a family arrangement, a matter of family convenience, hence, although the law made the consent of the girl necessary, yet really it was wholly in the hands of the parents, for it is well known that children were sometimes betrothed by the parents at a very early age, and the girl was married at the beginning of her thirteenth year, both betrothal and marriage being at an age when the child was wholly under the control of the parent. In the early times, the betrothal was a simple affair but later it became quite formal. This occurred at night or early morning, in the latter case the friends assembling at early dawn at the home of the girl's father or the nearest relative. The amount of the girl's dowry having been agreed upon, a contract was drawn up and signed and sealed by both parties in the presence of witnesses. The boy then gave the girl, as a pledge, an iron ring without ornament or jewels, which the girl placed upon the third finger of the left hand, as from this was believed to be a nerve leading directly to the heart. This was followed by a banquet or feast. The engagement might be broken by either party or by the guardians of either with no legal penalty attached and sometimes this gave the young man or young woman opportunity to escape a union not desired. But as long as a betrothal lasted it imposed certain restrictions, one being that betrothed persons could not testify against one another in the courts. There was usually quite an interval of time between the betrothal and the marriage, but that did not affect the relations of the couple, as they were not together any more than before the betrothal so that really they did not get to know one another till after they were married.

On the night before her marriage the girl put off her *toga prætexta* and her mother placed on her a long white garment called a *tunica recta* or *regilla*, and her loosened hair was confined in a scarlet net. The next day, the wedding-day, the girl put on her wedding-dress, which was a long white robe, gathered in at the waist by a woolen girdle tied in the knot of Hercules, a true-lover's knot, and said to be a charm against the evil eye. The *flammeum*, or wedding-veil, was of a brilliant orange red, or flame-color, quite full, of thin, fine stuff, and it was thrown over the head from behind, leaving the face exposed, and then draped gracefully about her. The bride's hair was divided into six strands or stresses by the bridegroom with the point of a spear, and then ribbons or fillets were bound between the tresses and the hair was braided and confined to the head. On these braids and under the veil was worn a garland of natural flowers which the bride herself had gathered.

"The costume of the bride is a complete allegory. This orange-red veil, this saffron-colored *flammeum*, which covers her head and allows only the face to be seen, is the usual ornament of the flamen's wife, to whom divorce is prohibited; the white tunic represents virginity; the head-dress raised in the form of a tower, almost like that of the vestals, with a javelot which runs through it, indicates that the wife is in submission to her husband; the chaplet of vervain is the symbol of fecundity, and the girdle of wool which is tied round her waist bears witness to her chastity."[10]

Weddings could not take place on any day of the year as there were restrictions in reference to such. As a great number of religious festivals occurred in the early summer, requiring the constant attendance of the priests, marriages were forbidden to take place during the whole month of May and the first half of June. On the *dies parentales*, from the thirteenth to the twenty-first of February, marriages could not take place, as on these days there were memorial services for deceased kindred and offerings to their *manes*. Wedding-days could not be placed upon August 24, October 5, and November 8, as the underworld was supposed to stand open on these days, so they were most unlucky days. Nor could such other unlucky days be used as the kalenda, nones, or ides of any month. Nor was it considered appropriate for young girls to be married on religious holidays, although widows could do so. The best time was considered to be that which followed the ides of June.

The guests having assembled in the early morning at the home of the bride's father, or of her nearest relative, the bride being decked out in her wedding garments and the bridegroom having arrived, the wedding ceremonies began with the taking of auspices. In earlier times this was done by observing the flight of birds, but later by the examination of the entrails of an animal, which was conducted by an *haruspex*, a professional diviner. If the omens were favorable, then the wedding sacrifice was made, usually a sheep, and the skin was spread over stools or chairs, on which the bridal pair sat. The right hands of the pair were then joined by a *pronuba*, a woman who had been married but once and who thus acted as a kind of priestess, and the bride signified her willingness to come into the *manus* of the bridegroom and to take his name by repeating the formula, "*Quando tu Gaius, ego Gaia*," "You being Gaius, I am Gaia." The wedding party then went to a temple or public altar, where offerings and prayer were made to the *flamen dialis* to the gods, especially to June as the patron of marriage. During the offering, the bridal pair sat side by side, while during the prayer they walked together slowly around the altar. These completed, then all returned to the house of the bride's father where a great feast was held.

[10] Duruy, History of Rome, V, 254.

At nightfall the feast ended and then came the *deductio*, the leading home of the bride. The bridegroom and his friends made a pretense of snatching the bride away from her father's house, in commemoration of the rape of the Sabines. In reality the father was the only one who could break the bonds that attached the bride to the hearth of her ancestors, where she was under the protection of the household gods, and so he handed her over to the husband and his family to enter into the new relations with them. The bride was escorted by three boys, sons of living parents, two of them holding her by the hand, the other one going before her bearing the bridal torch of white thorn, to drive away the malevolent spirits. Her way was lighted by four married women bearing pine torches and behind her was borne a distaff, a spindle, and in a basket the instruments for feminine work. The procession went through the streets singing, accompanied by flutes, bonfires were lit in the streets and the streets were lined with people, and specially with children, as the bridegroom threw nuts to them to show that he had given up childish things, the bride also having given up her dolls and playthings by offering them to the household gods who had protected her childhood.

As the bride came to the door of her new home, she rubbed oil on the doorposts and then wound woolen bands around them, in order to keep off baleful spells. She was then lifted up by her companions so that her feet might not touch the threshold, sacred to Vesta, the virgin goddess. In the *atrium*, she received from her husband the symbolic gifts of fire and water. The two then knelt together and with the bridal torch lighted their first hearth fire, offered a sacrifice, and broke the cake of *far*, and ate it together. The husband then presented the keys of the house to the wife to show that henceforth she was to have the management of the household. The day was ended with a feast given by the bridegroom to the relatives and friends.

"No one who studies this ceremonial of Roman marriage, in the light of the ideas which it indicates and reflects, can avoid the conclusion that the position of the married woman must have been one of substantial dignity, calling for and calling out a corresponding type of character. Beyond doubt the position of the Roman materfamilias was a much more dignified one than that of the Greek wife. She was far indeed from being a mere drudge or squaw; she shared with her husband in all the duties of the household, including those of religion, and within the house itself she was practically supreme. She lived in the atrium, and was not shut away in a woman's chamber; she nursed her own children and brought them up; she had entire control of the female slaves who were her maids; she took her meals with her husband, but sitting, not reclining, and abstaining from wine; in all practical matters she was consulted, and only on questions politically and intellectual was she expected to be silent. When she went out arrayed in the graceful *stola matronalis*, she was treated with respect, and the passers-by made way for her; but it is characteristic of her position that she did not as a rule leave the house without the knowledge of her husband, or without an escort." [11]

The wife was expected to lament for her husband upon his death and during the time of mourning certain prohibitions were imposed upon her, but these were not imposed upon the widower. Severe penalties were placd upon a widow who married within ten months after the death of her husband. When a widow married, if the husband went to live in her home, the bed upon which the former husband died was removed, the door of the bed-chamber was changed, and the things in the rooms were moved about, that there might be as few reminders as possible of the former husband.

Concubinage existed, but not polygamy, as monogamy was strictly enforced at Rome. This was so closely guarded that a divorced man could not marry again unless the divorce was an effective one. Concubinage was usually between parties that could not enter into a legal marriage, and thus the concubine was usually a woman of low estate, often a freedwoman. The offspring were considered illegitimate and could not enter into the inheritance.

In the early times there were no divorces in Rome. It is claimed that there were no divorces during the first five hundred years from the founding of the city, the first divorce occurring about 231 B. C., when Spurius Carvilius Ruga put away his wife because she was barren. But divorces increased till in the last years of the republic and under the empire they became very frequent. "Seneca says, some women counted their years, not by consuls, but by their husbands; and Juvenal, that some divorced before the green bays of welcome had faded on the lintels, and they might have had

[11] Fowler, Social life at Rome, 143-144.

eight husbands in five years; Tertullian, that women marry only in order to divorce; these exaggerations must have a foundation in truth. . . . Ovid and Pliny the younger had three wives; Cæsar and Antony four; Sulla and Pompey five; such cases must have been frequent."[12]

There were a number of causes for divorce, in the later days, the most common one being incompatibility of temper. In the divorce, the tablets of the contract were broken in the presence of seven witnesses, all adult Roman citizens. Repudiation was a less solemn act and took place quietly in the family. In the early times, when a woman was divorced she lost her dowry. In later times, a sixth was kept back for adultery and an eighth for other crimes. Then, still later, it came about that if the husband was divorced by the wife he lost the dowry, but if the wife divorced him without a cause the husband retained a sixth of the dowry for each child, but only up to three-sixths.

**Dress.** The Romans had two principal articles of dress—the *toga* and the *tunica*. The toga was made of white woolen cloth. On festival days a new one was worn or one newly cleaned. It was woven in an oblong form and the corners were clipped off till it took the form of an ellipse. Its length was about three times the height of the wearer, exclusive of the head, and its breadth at the middle about twice the same height, although the breadth varied with time and fashion, as, in the early period it was rather narrow, while in later times a fashionable toga was nearly circular. In putting it on, the toga was folded in its long way nearly in the middle and one end was thrown over the left shoulder from behind and allowed to fall to the feet in front. The other end was then brought across the back and under the right arm and the folds were spread out to cover the right side of the body to the calf of the leg and then gathered and carried across the breast and thrown backward over the left shoulder. Thus one-third of the toga would cover the left side and front of the body, the middle third would cover the back and right side, and the remaining third would cover the chest and go over the left shoulder. The diagonal folds across the breast formed the *sinus*, which was often used as a pocket. It would seem that a girdle was not worn with the toga nor pins or clasps to fasten it, but in later fashionable times small pieces of lead were placed in the ends and hidden by tassels which served to

[12] Friedländer, Roman life and manners, I, 243.

preserve the drapery. The white toga, without color, *toga pura*, was the ordinary garment worn. Boys wore the *toga prætexta*, which had a purple border, and which was discarded when manhood was reached at fifteen or sixteen for the *toga virilis, pura* or *libera*. The toga for mourning was black and in later times dark blue also was used. Beside these there were other kinds. Only Roman citizens were allowed to wear the toga.

The tunica was worn indoors, when the toga was thrown off, and also outdoors, when the toga was worn over it. In the later times in cold weather two or more tunics were worn. The tunica was a kind of woolen shirt, at first without sleeves, then with short sleeves reaching to the elbows, and in the time of the empire long sleeves were attached to it. It reached down to the calves and even to the ankles. It was often fastened to the waist by a girdle, which was used as a purse for holding money.

Another garment was the *pœnula*, a kind of cloak made of thick wool and leather, and worn over the toga in traveling in bad weather. Another kind of cloak, worn over the toga or tunica, was the *lacuna*, which was made of lighter and more costly material and was worn for show as well as for use. To both pænula and lacuna could be added a hood (*cucullus*) for further protection from the weather.

The women in the early times wore the toga and the tunica the same as the men. The tunica continued to be worn but there arose as distinct apparel for women, the *stola* and the *palla*. The stola was an oblong garment worn over the tunica and extended to the feet. It was open at the top on either side for the arms to go through and fastened on both shoulders with clasps or brooches (*fibulæ*), which often were quite costly articles. A girdle was drawn around it at the waist and then it was pulled up and allowed to fall over the girdle till the girdle was covered by the folds and then the lower part of the stola was pulled down till it just touched the ground. At the bottom there was an ornamental border. Sometimes there were sleeves to it, which were open below and fastened together with gold or jeweled buttons or clasps. The stola was a special garment that was permitted to be worn only by married women of unblemished reputation. ''The common courtesans were not allowed to appear in the stola, but were compelled to wear a sort of gown, resembling the habit of the opposite sex, and which was regarded as a mark of infamy."[13]

The palla was a kind of cloak worn out of doors over the stola. It was somewhat similar to the toga, as it was a square or oblong piece of cloth. Like the toga, too, it was thrown forward over the left shoulder and let fall to the feet, and then drawn over or under the right shoulder and pulled across the breast and thrown over the left arm or shoulder,. When necessary to protect the head, the palla could be drawn up over it like the toga.

The prevalent material of Roman clothing was always woolen and up to the end of the republic the only materials used were wool and linen. Sheep-raising for wool was one of the very most important industries. Foreign wools, however, were imported, because the supply of native wool was not sufficient to meet the demand and also by importing foreign wool a variety of natural colors could be obtained, as brown, red, black, golden-brown, reddish, and grayish. Goats' wool was not often used for wearing apparel, usually only for coarse cloaks and overshoes. It was woven into rough and heavy cloths for tent-coverings, blankets, and the like, and goats' hair was used for making ropes and cables.

Linen was used for the under-garments of both men and women and for women's belts and girdles and also linen thread was made. In the later times the finer grades of linen for handkerchiefs, table-cloths, napkins, bedding, and suits were all imported. Cotton and cotton fabrics were introduced from the far East into Greece and thence into Rome. Silk began to be used by the women toward the end of the republic and by men under the empire.

The color of clothing was originally white, which was prescribed by law for the toga. Poor people, slaves, and freedmen had their clothing of the natural brown or black color of the wool. The mourning garments of the upper classes were of dark color—black or dark blue. In later periods the women got to using a variety of colors, selecting such as the mode directed or as suited their particular taste, as scarlet, violet, purple, yellow, blue, and many other colors. In imperial times the men adopted a variety of colors for their garments, too. The wearing of genuine purple, however, remained the exclusive privilege of the emperors.

In early times the spinning and weaving was done at home

[13] Dean, History of civilization, III, 214.

under the direction of the mistress of the house. But it was not long till the work of the home did not suffice to supply the demand and large factories (*officionæ*) were established for the weaving of both woolen and linen goods. The garments were prepared with needle and scissors, each wealthy household having several tailors among its slaves. Before they could be used for garments, the woolen cloths had to be finished by the fuller, who not only finished new cloths but also cleansed and restored old garments.

The Romans, usually, whether indoors or out, went bareheaded, both men and women. In case of heat or cold or rain, the men would pull the upper part of the toga up over the head and the women used the palla in the same way. There were times, however, when they did wear coverings upon their heads, as, at the sacrifices, at the public games, at the Saturnalia, upon a journey, or upon a warlike expedition. Also the working-classes exposed to the weather wore a head-covering. These coverings were the *pileus* and the *petasus*. The pileus was a close-fitting felt cap and the petasus was a felt hat with a round brim. Sometimes the *cucullus*, a hood, was worn in place of the pileus. For ornamentation the women would wear a veil, which was fastened to the top of the head and drooped over neck and back in graceful folds. They also wore the *mitra*, which was a cloth wound round the head to form a kind of cap. They also wore a head-covering in the form of a net made of gold-thread.

In the early times men wore their hair long and this was continued for a long time and the wearing of short hair made slow progress and only among the higher classes. In the late empire the close-cropped hair became the fashion. Before the time of cropped hair it was sometimes worn in wavy locks and again, by means of the curling-iron, it was arranged in short curls and perfumed. Also false hair was used. The ancient Romans wore their beards very long. The wearing the beard long continued till the later years of the republic when it became the custom to shave the face, but full beards came into fashion again in the later empire. "The first hair cut from the head of a child, and a youth's first beard, were consecrated to the gods; but the coins of the late republican period show plainly that young men usually wore a beard, though carefully trimmed and dressed, and were seldom cleanshaven before forty."[14] There were barber-shops among the

[14] Preston and Dodge, The private life of the Romans, 99.

Romans and they were the gathering-places of idlers and the centers of male gossip. Among the furnishings were razors, tools to pull out the beard, scissors, pomatums to remove hair where not desired, combs, curling-irons, mirrors, towels, etc.

The ways of arranging the hair by the women varied in the different periods. In the first centuries of the republic, there seems to have been two general fashions. The hair was either parted or unparted and then combed back in wavy lines and gathered together in a knot at the back of the head, low down on the neck, and fastened with ribbons or clasps, or it was wound round the top of the head like a crown. In another way the hair was carried around the head in long curls, or the front hair was plaited and connected with the back hair, etc. These simple ways of arranging the hair gave place to many variegated ways and hair-dressing became a science and the women employed special maid-servants for the purpose or had in their employ female hairdressers. In one fashion there was a tower-like headdress, the natural hair being helped out with artificial hair or with wigs. The hair was frizzled and curled and perfumed and dyed. It was kept in place by means of ribbons and pins and hair-pins of metal or ivory and adorned with gold ornaments and pearls and jewels. The hair was sometimes gracefully adorned with wreaths of flowers or of branches with leaves and blossoms.

The Romans wore shoes (*calcei*) and sandals (*sandalia*). There were several kinds of shoes worn, as every Roman order and every tribe or gens had a distinctive kind of shoe. The *sutor,* or shoemaker, had a particularly respectable calling at Rome. The *pero* was for wet and snowy weather; it was made of raw hide and it was similar to a boot, reaching up to the middle of the leg. The *calceus senatorius* was of black leather with four straps. The *calceus mulleus* was made of red leather, with a high heel, and with straps to fasten it about the ankle. It had on its front a crescent-shaped piece of ivory, the *lunula,* which was of very ancient origin, and, like the *bulla,* may, perhaps, have had the force of a charm. The *caliga* was worn by the soldiers, which was a kind of boot, reaching to the middle of the leg, and the sole was of wood and stuck full of nails. There seemed to have been worn, too, a kind of sock or stocking that reached to the middle of the leg and tied with laces from the instep to the calf. The ladies of the upper classes, for outdoors wore shoes made of fine leather and richly embroidered in silk and gold. In the house both men and women wore sandals (*soleæ*). The sandals and shoes were tied on with straps, which were wound round the foot and the leg upward from the ankle.

The Roman ladies wore many different kinds of ornaments, made of precious metals, ivory, jewels, and pearls. They wore earrings, a very common form being pearls and jewels attached to hooks of gold and then fastened to the ears. There were hair-pins of metal and ivory, made in various forms, some of which contained eyes for the fastening of strings of pearls. They had necklaces of gold with jewels and pearls attached to them. Bracelets, made in the form of snakes, simple ribbons, plaited gold threads, and other styles, were worn at the wrist or above the elbow, with a sleeveless tunic. They had rings adorned with jewels and cameos. They wore chains of gold around the neck, sometimes five or six feet in length. They fastened their girdles and other parts of the dress with buckles and brooches, made of silver and gold and frequently studded with jewels and cameos. Some of these ornaments were also worn by the men, as, rings and bracelets. All the principal precious stones, diamonds, rubies, emeralds, opals, were known to the Romans. They prized the pearl above all other gems and often paid great prices for them. "Julius Cæsar is said to have given to Servilia, the mother of Marcus Brutus, a solitaire pearl for which he paid six million sesterces ($262,500), while Caligula received with his wife, Lollia Paulina a complete *parure* of pearls and emeralds, which was an heirloom in her family; a part of the spoils taken in Eastern war by her grandfather, Marcus Lollius, in the year 2 B. C., and valued at forty million sesterces ($2,180,000)."[15]

"About the mysteries of the toilette of the Roman ladies, mercilessly laid bare by the authors of imperial times, we shall say little. Great care was particularly bestowed on the complexion, and on the artificial reproduction of other charms, lost too soon in the exciting atmosphere of imperial court-life. During the night a mask (*tectorium*) of dough and ass's milk was laid on the face, to preserve the complexion; this mask was an invention of Poppæa, the wife of Nero, hence its name *Poppæana*. Another mask, composed of rice and bean-flour, served to remove the wrinkles from the face. It was washed off in the morning with tepid ass's milk and the face after-

[15] Preston and Dodge, The private life of the Romans, 104.

wards bathed in fresh ass's milk several times in the course of the day. Poppæa was, for the purpose, always accompanied in her travels by herds of she-asses. The two chief paints used for the face were a white (*creta cerussa*) and a red substance (*fucus minium purpurissum*), moistened with spittle. Brows and eyelashes were dyed black, or painted over; even the veins on the temples were masked with lines of a tender blue color. Many different pastes and powders were used to preserve and clean the teeth. Artificial teeth made of ivory and fastened with gold thread were known to the Romans at the time when the laws of the twelve tablets were made, one of which laws prohibited the deposition of gold in the graves of the dead, excepting the material required for the fastening of false teeth."[16]

As an aid in the preparation of the toilet and the like, the Romans had mirrors. These were not made of glass but of polished metal. They were square or round and of various sizes, some being equal in size to a grown-up person. Some of the mirrors had handles for holding with the hand, some were made so as to hang on the wall, and others could be placed upright.

**Food.** The Romans of the early times had a simple fare, living chiefly on pottage, or bread and pot-herbs. They sat at their meals, using a long table. As the nation grew and wealth increased and they came in contact with older nations, they gave up this simple life and entered among the most luxurious nations in their manner of living.

The Romans had three meals a day. The first meal was in the morning, the *ientaculum*, or breakfast, which was simple, consisting of bread flavored with salt or dipped in wine, olives, grapes, eggs, and cheese. The second meal was at midday, the *cena*, or dinner, which with the country people was the principal meal. In the city this midday meal was a lunch, the *prandium*, while the *cena*, dinner, was taken later in the day, toward evening, and often became quite an elaborate affair. There was sometimes a fourth meal, *comissatio*, served late at night, which really was but little more than a drinking-bout.

The meals were usually served in the *triclinium*, or dining-room. In this was a square dining-table, having on three sides one-armed couches, the remaining side being left open for serving. Each of these couches had room for three persons,

[16] Guhl and Koner, The life of the Greeks and Romans, 500.

who reclined upon the left arm, with the feet outward. About the end of the republic, round tables came into use, with semicircular couches. Some of these tables were quite valuable, being made of rare imported woods. The guests used napkins, which they might have brought themselves or were provided by the host. In later times table-cloths came into use. The principal ornament on the table was the *salinum*, or saltcellar, as salt was used not only for seasoning, but also for sacrifices, and the salinum also held the sacrificial cakes. The chief implements for eating were two kinds of spoons, the *ligula*, shaped very much like the table spoon of the present, and the *cochlear*, which had a small circular bowl, flat or slightly hollowed, with a pointed handle. Knives and forks seem to have come into use during the later times of the empire.

The chief dish of the poorer classes was porridge, made of a farinaceous substance and which served them as bread. They had such vegetables as the cabbage, turnip, radish, leek, garlic, onion, cucumber, and pumpkin. Meat was rarely eaten, perhaps only on festival occasions. The market afforded all kinds of foods. Among the animals were the rabbit, pheasant, guinea-fowl, common poultry, peacock, kid, pig, and boar; there were various kinds of fish and oysters and snails; beside the plants mentioned above were rue, lettuce, cress, mallow, and sorrel. It would seem that they had quite a number of different kinds of grain; among the fruits were the apple, pear, plum, cherry, quince, peach, pomegranate, fig, olive, and grape; there were lemons and oranges and nuts of various kinds.

Wine was the only drink of an intoxicating nature that the Romans had. It was customary to mix the wine with water, and to drink the wine without putting water into it was considered a sign of intemperance. For a number of years the water-supply was such as could be obtained from the Tiber, wells, and natural springs, and it was not till the time of the republic that the water was brought from outside of Rome, for which means aqueducts were built and which continued to be built until there was an abundant supply of water.

**Child and Parent.** The Romans practiced the exposure of infants as in Greece. This was begun in the early times and carried down into the later times. The children so exposed were usually feeble or deformed, but the father had the power to use it on any child and this was sometimes done when the father considered the child to be illegitimate. The new-born child was laid at the feet of the father and it was his duty to take the child up into his arms and declare it to be his child and that he would rear it and support it. In case the father did not so claim it, the child was carried away and placed at some cross-roads, where it would die unless taken up by a slave-merchant to rear it to sell.

The relation which existed between the father and the child was known as the *patria potestas*. This power of the father was very great in early times. He could sell his children, disinherit them, select a wife for a son or a husband for a daughter, and he even had the power to put them to death. This power ceased only at death or if the father lost his rights of Roman citizenship. The father himself could emancipate his son. Also this power over the son ceased should he become a *flamen*, or priest, and it ceased over the daughter if she married or took the vestal vows.

**Names.** The Romans had three names: These were the *prænomen*, the individual's own first name; the *nomen*, the name of the *gens* or family to which he belonged; and the *cognomen*, or surname, which distinguished the particular branch or division of the tribe from which he sprung. Thus in the name Marcus Tullius Cicero, Marcus was the prænomen, Tullius the nomen, designating the Tullian family, and Cicero, the cognomen, showing that he was from the Cicerones branch of the tribe.

The boys received the nomen, family name, on the ninth day after birth and girls on the eighth day. On such day the ceremony of purification took place, which was by sprinkling with a branch of olive or laurel dipped in water, the burning of incense, and the offering of sacrifice. The boy was given his prænomen when he put on the toga virilis at sixteen or seventeen and the girl when she was married. The wife at marriage took the nomen of her husband's family, but this was not often a change from her own family as usually marriages were between members of the same gens. In later times, when marriage did not mean so much, and divorces became frequent, the wife did not take her husband's nomen but she was known by the nomen of her father's gens.

**Care and Treatment of Children.** The birth of a son was a happy day in a Roman household and the door of the house was decorated with flowers and green branches. The boy's ninth day after birth and the girl's eighth day was the day of purification, the *lustratio*. A branch of laurel or olive was dipped into water and used to sprinkle the child, incense was burned, a sacrifice was made upon the family altar for the child's welfare, and he was carried to one or more of the temples and placed under the protection of the gods. Also, as stated above, the child's name was bestowed upon him at this time. Usually a private record was made of the time of the lustratio, which was sometimes offered in cases of identification. Under Marcus Aurelius there was begun a public registry of births, as it was decreed that within thirty days after birth the name of each child, born free at Rome, should be placed in the public records in the archives of the treasury in the temple of Saturn. The birthday was religiously observed by every Roman, rich or poor, high or low, at which time the members of his family were brought together and offerings were made to the household gods and a festive time made of the day. Many mothers turned over their children to the care of nurses and the wealthy employed wet-nurses. Each Roman child wore round his neck a *bulla*, which was a small locket of gold or some other metal, sometimes of leather, usually heart-shaped, or circular, and attached to a ribbon or chain. This was a charm against the evil eye. The boy wore his bulla till he put on the toga virilis at manhood and a girl wore hers till her marriage.

"Identical with modern times were the anxious care of mothers, relatives, and nurses, the words of endearment (such as birdie, little dove, little crow, little mother, little lady), and the lisping childish language and the lullabies ('sleep, my child, or suck'), rattles and other means of soothing (such as beating the stone that had hit the child), and the many superstitions, at all ages: such as binding on teeth of horses and boars to alleviate the teething, and old wives' simples and amulets against the evil eye. As a preservative against the *strigæ*, or vampires, garlic was wrapt up in the swaddling-clothes and hawthorn planted in the windows. A mother, who was passing a temple of Venus, would mumble a prayer for her daughter's beauty and make a vow. The figure of the girls was made artificially perfect. They wore tight stays from early childhood, so as to raise the hips into relief, and nurses' carelessness often produced rounded backs or unequal shoulders."[17]

**Citizenship.** At seventeen years of age the Roman boy be-

[17] Friedländer, Roman life and manners, I, 228.

came liable for military duty. In earlier times this was the age at which he assumed the toga virilis. In the later times the age for taking the virile robe varied, usually taking place between the fourteenth and seventeenth years, but there were cases where boys were invested with the toga virilis as early as twelve and where it was withheld until nineteen. The time of year for this ceremony was not fixed, although a favorite date was at the time of the *Liberalia*, or feast of Bacchus, which occurred on March 17th.

"To make the gods propitious, the youth has passed the last night of his infancy covered, like a bride on the eve of her nuptials, with a white material and a saffron-colored sort of net-work. Is not this a betrothal which is now to be completed: the indissoluble union of the new citizen to the city?"[18] The bulla was removed from the boy's neck and the toga prætexta taken off him and both were consecrated to the lares, a sacrifice was made, and then the boy was invested with the toga virilis. Then the boy was conducted to the Forum by his father or guardian, accompanied by relatives and friends, and formally presented to the public. He was, probably, also taken to the *tabularium* under the Capitol and his name enrolled among the list of full citizens.

This was a very important event in the life of the boy, as it freed him from the control of others, as he became by law a man, capable of looking after his own affairs and of holding property. After this he entered upon the affairs of life. If he was of the middle or lower classes, he entered directly into business or work; if of the upper class, he began to prepare for public life or the army.

**Inheritance.** Every citizen had the right to make a will and to leave his property to the ones he wished to receive it. There were two kinds of wills recognized, the one made in civil life before the public assembly, and the other was in military life, made when an army was drawn up ready for battle and while the auspices were being taken.

Instead of a written will there might be an oral declaration, which had to be made before the proper authorities and witnesses and recorded in the city registers. If the will of the soldier dying in battle was unfinished, it was valid if there was no doubt as to his intentions. Those by law who could not make a will, or whose will was invalid, were persons under the power of another, minors, the insane, people not capable of

---

[18] Duruy, History of Rome, V, 242.

managing their own affairs, the civilly dead, and the banished. Where there was no will, the law provided an order of inheritance, the children taking precedence. In case there was neither will nor legal heir, the estate went into the public treasury.

**Adoption.** It was a sacred duty for a Roman family to preserve its name, its domestic sacrifices, and its traditions. These were transmitted from one generation to the next, so in case there was no son, the head of the family was authorized by law to adopt a son. There were three kinds of adoption. The first was adoption properly so-called; the second was the *arrogatio*, adrogation; and the third was adoption made by will or testament, to be confirmed by the proper authorities after the death of the testator.

There were three conditions necessary to adoption. The first requirement was that there were no sons in the family, nor hopes of any, and that the father should be about eighteen years older than the one to be adopted as a son; the second condition was that the honor, religion, domestic worship, or sacrifices of the two families, should not in any way be injured; and the third, that there should be no fraud or collusion.

Adoption proper was for minors. The two fathers, the natural and the adoptive, arranged the matter between them and then, with the child, went before the proper authorities and in the presence of witnesses was legally carried out. The adopted son took the rank and the name of the family into which he entered, he was introduced to the domestic sacrifices, and he became a full heir. If there was a daughter in the family, she became his sister and he could not marry her.

Adrogation was the form of adoption used with citizens who were their own masters. This required the consent of the people assembled for the purpose. Under this act a citizen with his property and all persons subjected to him passed into another's power.

"These adoptions finally led to abuse. The patrician, to obtain the tribuneship, would be adopted by some plebeian, and those who were without children, that they might enjoy office to which only fathers of families could be elected, adopted children, whom, after obtaining the offices, they emancipated. This finally required, to remedy it, a decree of the senate in the reign of Nero."[19]

[19] Dean, History of civilization, III, 250.

**Sickness and Death.** Throughout the time of Rome, medicine was largely in the hands of slaves and freedmen. Those engaged in the medical practice were mostly Greeks and orientals, especially Egyptians. Up to the middle of the republic, they treated their patients according to certain old prescriptions and nostrums. In the later days of the republic, the practice of medicine began to take on more the form of a profession and later the profession became to be divided into physicians, surgeons, and oculists, and also there were dentists, ear specialists, and the like. There were, too, women physicians and midwives. As those engaged in medicine were not required to be examined and were not held by law to much responsibility, quackery prevailed. The practice of medicine was quite remunerative and the physicians who were successful made large salaries.

Among the Romans the duties to the dead were carefully attended to. They believed that the souls of those who had not received the proper honors accorded to the dead were condemned to wander for a long number of years along the banks of the Styx before they were permitted to cross over into the realms of the dead. The dying person was surrounded by his relatives and when he had breathed his last his eyes and mouth were closed by the nearest relative present and the *conclamatio* was made, all calling out loudly three times to the deceased as though he might be in a trance. Upon his not awakening, the relatives and friends retired and left the body to the professional undertaker.

The body was washed, anointed, and clothed, the coin to pay Charon, the ferryman of the Styx, was placed between the teeth, and then the corpse was laid upon a couch in the atrium, with feet turned toward the entrance door. Flowers were placed about the couch and the decorations and crowns, if any, of the deceased were displayed about the body. To show that the house was in mourning, branches of cypress or pine were hung in front. The body lay in state for seven days for visitations of kindred and friends.

The day of the funeral having arrived, the funeral procession took place. In ancient times all funerals were in the night time, but later they were held in the day time, yet still later the procession went with lighted torches.

The order of the procession was arranged by the *designator*, master of ceremonies, and it closely resembled a triumphal procession. At the head marched the musicians, which might have been a single flute-player or a band of musicians with trumpets and pipes and horns; then came the mourning-women, hired for the occasion; next came dancers and mimes, one of whom was dressed up to resemble the deceased, and who acted out his character, imitating his style of speaking, his manner, and exaggerating his peculiarities. Following these came professional actors dressed in the garbs of the ancestors of the deceased and wearing wax masks representing their features, who strove to imitate them in speech and actions. Then were displayed the crowns and rewards the deceased had been honored with and the spoils and standards he had taken in war. Then came the torch-bearers and lictors, with lowered faces, followed by the nearest relatives or friends or slaves set free by the will, bearing upon a lofty bier the corpse extended and exposed in rich garments. Then the family of the deceased followed, the sons with veiled faces and the daughters with heads uncovered and hair loosened. Last came the freedmen, slaves, clients, friends, and the general public.

There were demonstrations of grief displayed by the mourners, the nearest relatives tearing their clothing, pulling out their hair, and covering their heads with dust, the women smiting their breasts, scratching their faces, tearing their hair, and the like.

If there was to be a funeral oration, the procession went to the forum, the bier being set down in front of the rostrum and surrounded by the wearers of the ancestral masks. A near relative, usually, mounted the tribune and delivered a eulogy upon the deceased and his ancestors. An informal eulogy might be given at the place of interment, in which case the procession did not stop at the forum. At the close of the oration the procession passed on. The burial place might have been public, along some one of the great highways leading out of Rome, or it might have been private, upon the suburban estate of the deceased. The vestal virgins had the right of burial within the city itself. The body was placed in the tomb, those present were then sprinkled, in order to purify them, three times with a branch of olive or laurel dipped in pure water, and then all returned from the funeral.

The above description refers to the funeral of the wealthy and illustrious. The bodies of the middle classes were placed in the *columbaria*, which were built up or cut out of rock, being super-imposed niches. These were often built by joint-stock companies who would keep them in order, letting out the niches as they were wanted. The poor were given a place in the common burial-ground, their bodies being carried out at night by the *vespillones,* carriers of corpses. Persons killed by lightning were buried at the place they fell, which was enclosed with a wall. The bodies of malefactors were left unburied, exposed to the elements and to the birds and the beasts.

The earlier Romans interred their dead. Burning the body gradually came into practice and became general near the close of the republic and almost universal under the empire. As Christianity grew, cremation gradually fell into disuse and interment became the practice.

In one way of cremation, perhaps the earlier form, a grave about three and a half feet deep was made and filled with fuel. The body was placed on the fuel and as it burned the bones and ashes of the body fell into the pit with the coal and ashes of the fuel. The remains of the body were gathered up and put into an urn which was set up in the grave and the dirt heaped around so as to form a mound and then a wall was built around the place.

In another way, a funeral pile, made of wood and in the form of an altar, was built up outside the city and near the family burial place. The eyes of the corpse were opened and it was wrapped in a shroud and laid upon the pile. The nearest relative impressed a last kiss upon the lips of the deceased and then with a burning torch and head averted set fire to the pile, the others present raising a *conclamatio.* While the pile was burning there was thrown upon it incense, perfumes, clothing, ornaments, weapons, and other things, as last presents to the deceased. When the body was consumed, the fire was extinguished with wine. The bones and ashes of the body were collected, dried, sprinkled with perfumes, and put into an urn, which was placed in a tomb. The last farewell was spoken, those present were purified with a sprinkling of pure water, and then all departed.

Relatives and friends came together the day after the funeral and partook of the funeral feast. If the deceased had been a great or wealthy man, scenic games were given and raw meat distributed among the people. The mourning continued for ten days, during which time none of the relatives could be summoned to a court of justice. On the ninth day a banquet was held, bringing the whole family together again, and on the tenth day the house was purified and the funeral ceremonies ended.

"The purification of the house ended the funeral ceremonies, but the 'paternal Manes' had three festivals which brought together again families: in March, the three nights of the *Lemuralia,* to appease the Manes whom forgetfulness might irritate; in February, the *Parentalia,* 'the day of the dear kindred,' which Ovid calls also the festival of the *Caristies,* and in the summer, that of roses, *Rosalia,* which were then scattered around the tomb. On this day all the relations were united at the same table, *socias dapes,* in order that the festival might lead to forgetfulness of quarrels: 'This is the time,' says the poet, 'when concord takes pleasure in descending among us.'"[20]

**Industries.** Agriculture was the most important industry of the early Romans. The farms were small and many of the leading citizens followed the calling of farming. Later there arose large landed estates, which greatly changed the manner of farming. The proprietors did not work themselves and most of the work was done by slaves. Large tracts of land were used for parks and pleasure grounds and others were kept in pasturage. Thus agriculture decreased or changed and as the population grew the people of Rome were no longer able to supply their own food and food-stuffs were imported from other countries. The time came when immense supplies of grain were brought in by the government and distributed free among the people or sold at a nominal price.

On a great estate the dwelling of the master, the villa proper, stood apart from the other buildings, which were built around a court-yard and all were enclosed with only one entrance which was guarded by a porter with a fierce watch-dog. The slaves that could be trusted worked out in the fields and the others were kept within the enclosure, often in underground chambers, and did indoor work. A great deal of the farm work was done by hand and for which they had a number of implements, such as spades, mattocks, rakes, hoes, and forks. They had different kinds of plows to suit the nature of the soil. They usually used oxen for plowing.

The Romans understood about fertilizing and drainage and rotation of crops. It seems they had many different kinds of grain and practiced both fall and spring sowing. Next in

[20] Duruy, History of Rome, V, 285.

importance to the grains were various kinds of pulse, the most useful being the *faba*, some variety of bean. They raised turnips as food for cattle and sheep.

Among the animals raised on the farms were cattle, bred mostly for draught rather than for beef; horses and mules, race-horses commanding the highest prices; sheep and goats and hogs. Poultry-raising was quite important. Doves and thrushes and peacocks were raised and for which there was quite a demand. Since honey took the place of sugar, great attention was given to bee-culture.

Two of the greatest industries were the raising of grapes for wine and olives for oil. Market-gardening employed quite a large number and it was quite profitable, especially near cities and large towns. There were various kinds of fruit-trees and grafting was a common practice. Beside fruit-trees other trees were raised, in particular trees for shade and ornament.

"In considering the Roman farmer's year as a whole, we find that he computed rainy days and festivals at forty-five and reckoned on thirty days after the sowing when there was no field labor to be done. But on these thirty days, and on the stormy ones, there were ropes to make, baskets to weave, and other home-made utensils to prepare; while all the other instruments of the husbandman—his 'mute servants,' as Verro calls them—had to be repaired and thoroughly cleaned. Even on feast-days certain kinds of work were allowed, such as the cleaning of drains and the mending of highways, so that only the December Saturnalia seem to have afforded a complete holiday to the slaves.

"On New Year's day, a little work of every kind was done for good luck; but then followed a time of complete relaxation. In the latter half of January, the ground was cleared of brambles, and the trimming of the vineyards completed; while the autumn-sown grain and the beans, if they were sufficiently grown, were hoed for the first time. Early trees were now grafted, and the stock was planted. Vineyards were also cultivated, and young orchards set out, grass sown and ground broken, fields manured and osier-beds renewed. Vine-sets were also transplanted, if needful and the late fruit trees grafted.

"In March, the vegetable garden was prepared, the autumn grains received their second hoeing, and the spring grains were sown. In April, came weeding, sheep-washing, the setting out of new vineyards, the trimming of old vines, and the olive-grafting.

"May brought the earliest mowing, and in this month the earth was first spaded up about the olive-trees, and the vineyards dug over, this latter process being repeated each month until cold weather. The olives were also trimmed, the vine-shoots nipped; in warmer latitudes the sheep were shorn, and the lupins, which had been sown as fertilizers, were ploughed in. In June the first ploughing was finished and the second done, the threshing-floor was made ready, vetches mown, beans picked, and honey taken from the hives.

"Grain-harvest took place in July, and the cutting of the straw and gathering of leaves for the winter fodder of cattle. In August, figs and grapes were dried for winter use, and brakes cut for litter.

"September was, *par excellence*, the month of the vintage, and then, too, turnips were planted, and the later grains harvested. In October, winter grains were sown and harrowed in, trees trimmed, and the olive-picking begun.

"November was devoted to a general cleaning-up of autumn work. The making of oil was finished in December, and the vines trimmed, and we may close the brief *résumé* of the work of the Roman agricultural year by a few general precepts from the natural history of the elder Pliny: 'He is no farmer who buys what his estate can supply. He is a bad head of a household who does by day what can be done by night—except in case of foul weather; he is a worse who does on working-days what is permitted on holidays; the worst of all is he who on a pleasant day chooses to work within doors rather than in the field.''[21]

The upper classes in Rome held in low esteem, and even in contempt, the tradesmen and mechanics. This might have been because these people performed for the masses the duties that slaves did for the higher classes, and so all were put on the same footing. These people were, with few exceptions, debarred from serving in the legions and in consequence they became cowardly and likewise at times unruly. Yet the laboring class, as everywhere and in all times, were greatly needed at Rome and did perform a large amount of honest and useful labor. The great commerce carried on needed a large number of sailors and in the ports dock hands and porters and clerks. The city, too, needed a large number in the trades,

[21] Preston and Dodge, The private life of the Romans, 132-134.

as, bakers, tailors, shoemakers, potters, carpenters, and various kinds of smiths. There were needed plenty of small shops where the people could procure the things necessary for life and such shops would call for the employment of many people.

People of the same trades would naturally associate together and attachments would be formed, so that guilds came into existence at an early date, both from this natural instinct of association and for the protection of their trades. Among the crafts represented in the guilds were weavers, carpenters, dyers, leather-workers, tanners, smiths, porters, and a number of others. They were modeled after the gens or family, with a religious center and a patron deity. They had separate inns for their meetings. They had festive days at which times they went in procession through the streets carrying their emblems and banners. They provided for the funerals of their members, they had their widow's fund, and in other ways they looked after the interests of the ones belonging to the guilds.

Rome had an extensive commerce. Traders went along with the soldiers or quickly followed after them to open trade with the conquered provinces. Thus London in 61 A. D., only eighteen years after the conquest, had a large number of Roman merchants among its people. The roads built from Rome into all parts of the world greatly promoted commerce. The traders did not stop with the boundaries of the empire but went out among peoples not under Roman sway. As an instance of this was their going out into the North of Europe to the Baltic for amber and at one time there was quite a trade in this and in other articles. Even before Cæsar's conquest of Gaul, Roman traders had entered it over the St. Bernhard pass and had even gone among the Belgæ. The Mediteranean, the Black Sea, and the Atlantic were full of Roman ships trading with the various provinces and countries. The conquest of Egypt opened up a great trade, not only with that country but through it also with Arabia, Ethiopia and even India.

**The Spectacles.** The public games, or Spectacles, were the greatest amusements the Roman people had. Originating in early times as religious celebrations, they became so fixed as to make them a public necessity, a means of keeping the mass of the people busy so as to keep their attention away from affairs of state. As it became a duty of the government to provide grain free or at a nominal cost, so it became its duty to furnish free entertainment for the masses. These games were provided by the officials and made free to the public. There were four phases of the spectacles. Horse and chariot races were held in the circus, gladiatorial fights and fights with animals and also sea fights in the amphitheater, scenic representations in the theater, and athletic and musical contests in the stadium.

The Circus Maximus was located in Rome in the valley between the Palatine and Aventine hills. It was of an oblong circular form, about a mile in circumference, and seated 150,000 or more people. Among the displays were exploits on horseback, such as leaping from horse to horse while running, picking up things from the ground with the horse in full gallop, and the like. Young men in full armor gave mock-fights, and sometimes there would be military drills, and again boys from senatorial families and young princes went through cavalry exercises in glittering armor. The greatest displays of all were the chariot races. Factions arose with their colors, at first but two with white and red, and then four with white, red, blue, green, and later gold and purple were added but soon dropped out, leaving the four factions and colors. Heavy bets were made by the factions and there were fierce contests and often fights between them. Sometimes two chariots raced, usually four, and again at times six, and there were two or four horses to each chariot, rarely three. The victor in the race was crowned and received a cash prize and he was greeted with great applause.

The amphitheater was an elliptical building with an arena in the center and with tiers of seats leading up all around. The Coliseum at Rome was the greatest of all, being computed to have contained 87,000 seats. In the amphitheater were held the gladiatorial fights. Just how these originated is unknown but the first public exhibition of gladiators at Rome was given in 264 B. C., by the brothers Marcus and Decimus Brutus at their father's funeral. Such continued at funerals and then they were given at other times, the number of days and number of fighters gradually increasing, till Trajan, upon his return after a victorious campaign on the Danube, gave gladiatorial games for 123 days, in which 10,000 fighters took part. The gladiators were captives, slaves, and criminals, and under the empire knights and senators and even women were enrolled among them. There were schools for the training of gladiators. Emperors, senators, and all classes of people attended these fights and although women at first were excluded, later they were admitted freely. The gladiators wore helmets and had leather coverings for their legs and they carried shields. Their weapons were the lance, dagger, sword, and rapier. There were others who used the trident and the net for entangling their opponents. They were usually matched by pairs and when one was overcome his life depended upon the people, who would turn down their thumbs for his life to be spared and upon the turning up of their thumbs the wounded gladiator was slain by his opponent. The victor received a palm crown, sometimes money, and he might be given his freedom.

"These gladiatorial exhibitions proclaim the true nature of the Roman character. When the vestal virgin, the Roman matron, and the young lady could find amusement in such scenes of human slaughter, it can certainly surprise no one that the Roman character, in its constituent elements, possessed so much hardihood, and could remain such firm proof against every tender feeling of humanity. The school of blood in which the young were reared, and the old matured, was eminently calculated to form precisely the character which the Roman possessed. It is thus that the manners and customs of a people are influenced by, and in their turn, influence the character from which they originate."[22]

Another great amusement of the Romans was the *venatio,* or exhibit of wild animals. The first known display of wild animals at Rome was given by Marcus Fulvius Nobilior, the conqueror of Ætolia, in 186 B. C., eighty years after the first gladiatorial exhibit. These displays grew until all parts of the world were searched to find animals. There were bears, elephants, deer, hares, stags, boars, bulls, crocodiles, hippopotamuses, rhinoceroses, lynxes, apes, giraffes, tigers, ostriches, hyenas. They were made to fight with one another. They were starved to make them fierce with hunger and then driven into the arena against one another with whips, pricked with lances, burnt with hot irons, and in other ways tormented to make them extremely angry. There were also fights between men and beasts. These were often captives and criminals compelled to fight, but there were others, *bestiarii,* who were trained, as the gladiators, in schools to fight against animals. These men sometimes were assisted by dogs trained to hunt

[22] Dean, History of civilization, III, 240.

and to fight wild animals. In some exhibits, captives and criminals were bound to stakes and animals set upon them or they were sent unarmed or poorly armed against the wild animals. There were, too, exhibits of trained animals and animal-training became a regular profession under Augustus.

Another form of the spectacle for the entertainment of the Roman public was the *naumachia*, or naval battle. As in the other contests, usually the combatants were captives and criminals. These were held in the amphitheater, in which case the arena was flooded with water, or great ponds were dug for the purpose. The first naval battle on a large scale was given by Julius Cæsar in 46 B. C., the two sides having biremes, triremes, and quadriremes, with 1,000 marines and 2,000 oarsmen on each side. Claudius in 52 A. D. gave a naval contest in which there were 100 triremes and quadriremes and 19,000 warriors and oarsmen. Other large naumachiæ were produced by Augustus, Nero, Titus, and Domitian. In these conflicts real fighting took place and large numbers were killed.

There were no theatrical entertainments in the early times of Rome. In 364 B. C., during a plague which could not be stopped, to appease the wrath of the gods scenic performances were first introduced into Rome. Actors from Etruria were brought to Rome, who gave mimic dances to the accompaniment of a flute. For a long time there were no theaters erected at Rome, a temporary wooden stage being erected for the occasion. Later wooden theaters were built and then torn down after the performances were over, being used but one time. The first stone theater was built on the Campus Martius in 55 B. C. by Pompey, and which was large enough to hold 40,000 people. Comedies, tragedies, and pantomimes were given. Tragedy was never popular with the masses as they were too much used to seeing real tragedies enacted in the arena for any great impression to be made upon them by the imitations of the stage. Pantomime attained to the most significance of all performances upon the Roman stage and especially under the empire. The professional actors were mostly slaves and freedmen or natives of other countries, as there was a prejudice against the profession in Rome. Noted actors were paid high fees for their performances. Many of the most famous actors belonged to the imperial households.

The last of the great spectacles were the athletic, literary and musical contests. These contests were not common under the republic but they grew on the people till they became popular under the empire. Athletic contests were first introduced into Rome at the same time as the exhibit of wild animals and by the same person, in 186 B. C., by Marcus Fulvius Nobilior, who brought athletes from Greece for the purpose. These contests continued to be given and they increased in popularity till a stadium for them was built in 28 B. C. on the Campus Martius and the demand from the people became so great that the officials who provided the state games included athletic contests with the other games. The Capitoline Agon was instituted by Domitian in 86 A. D., and it took rank with the Olympian. For these contests he built a stadium large enough to accommodate 30,000 or more spectators. There were contests in oratory and poetry, in music, and in athletics. The oratorical contests ceased in later times, but those in poetry increased in importance and the most talented poets in the empire competed for the prize of oak-wreath, bestowed by the emperor upon the winner after the decision of the judges. The gymnastic contests for men and boys were the same as in Greece. The Spartan custom of races for girls was introduced but soon discontinued because of the feeling against it.

**Other Amusements.** Among the sports of the Romans was that of hunting. They kept parks for this purpose and they also hunted in fields and forests. They used dogs in hunting and they were trained for hunting various kinds of animals, as, the lion, the bear, the stag, the hare, and the like. Boar-hunting was one of their most common pastimes. They had hawks and other birds of prey trained for hunting. Fishing was another sport and they made use of rod and line and net. In winter when the water was frozen over they would cut holes through the ice for fishing. They had large fish-ponds on their country estates.

Walking was used as a means of exercise and as a pastime. This was done in the open air and also there were covered walks built at different places and in particular about the Campus Martius and the Forum. There were also places provided for horseback riding and for pleasure driving in vehicles.

There was a game similar to chess in which the chess men were glass, ivory or metal colored. Dice were in great use and gambling with dice prospered in spite of laws against it. Under the empire there arose an entertainment similar to a lottery, in which tickets were distributed free to the guests or sold to them and a drawing was made for the prizes. At their banquets and elsewhere the guests were entertained with musicians, mimics, dancers, jugglers, acrobats, rope-dancers, and other kinds of performers.

**The Bath.** The Romans in early times took their baths in the Tiber. Later, the *lavatrina*, or washhouse, connected with the kitchen by a heating apparatus, served as a bathroom. In those days they bathed only for health and cleanliness. Under the empire, bathing became a fashion and it was carried to excess. When the supply of water became abundant by means of the aqueducts, baths multiplied rapidly and public baths were established. The public baths were at first arranged for and used only by the common people, but their importance grew gradually until all classes used the public baths and they were enlarged and beautified and different kinds of baths provided, as, hot, tepid, cold, and shower. The usual time for the bath was in the afternoon shortly before the evening meal. It also became the custom to take a bath after the meal and then the number was often increased till the bath was taken seven or more times during the day and evening.

The *thermæ*, baths, at Rome, under the empire, covered large spaces, with magnificent structures adorned with paintings and sculptures, the walls lined inside with marble, with marble columns, and silver mouthpieces for the water pipes. There were rooms not only for bathing, but also large halls for swimming, and rooms for places of meeting for conversation, for listening to the reading of poems by their authors, for gymnastic exercises, and the like, and provided with libraries and museums. Thus these thermæ became centers for gatherings of various kinds and places of amusement.

**Games and Plays.** Children in Rome played a great deal, just as do children everywhere. They had their dolls and hobby-horses and toy-houses. They played with carts and used them very much as the children of the present. They skipped stones and walked upon stilts and spun tops. They used nuts for playing a number of games, one being called *ludus castellorum*, in which three nuts were to be so arranged that a fourth nut could be placed upon them without displacing them, the winner receiving all the four nuts. They played *par impar*, odd or even. The boys and even sometimes the young men would roll a large iron hoop, which had iron or brass rings fastened around it and kept up quite a clatter while the hoop was rolling. Some of these hoops were five or six feet in diameter and required quite a little skill to roll them, being rolled and guided by means of an iron rod.

Ball was a game especially liked by the boys and young men of Rome. There were three kinds of balls used—a large hollow ball, a small hollow ball, and a ball stuffed with feathers. At the country villas about Rome there was usually a place for ball-playing. The boys used the streets and squares of Rome for ball-playing, particularly before the butchers' shops in the Forum Romanum. They played ball alone or with a few or with many. In one game the ball was thrown up into the air and all tried to catch it. The *trigon*, or *pila trigonalis*, was a favorite way of playing ball, the players being placed in a triangle and they were to fling the ball at one another, the one failing to catch it and return it being the loser. There was a game in which they would choose sides and have the ground marked out as for lawn-tennis.

**Religion.** The Romans were of a deeply religious nature even down into the times of the empire. Religion entered into the life of the Romans in a practical way and touched upon the civic duties and social relations, as the events of life were held to be of a sacred nature. The Roman life was closely connected with religion, as every activity of life was presided over by a deity, whom it was necessary to worship properly in order that the activity might prove successful.

The child came in contact with religion at his very earliest life in the home in the worship of the household gods, the Penates and Lares, the former being the gods of the hearth, who guarded the stores and provisions of the family, and the latter were the spirits of departed ancestors, who were the protectors of the family. In the atrium was the image of the chief lar between two penates, to whom were offered sacrifices each morning by the father as priest, and birthdays and marriages and the putting on of the toga virilis by the boy and the return of a member of the family after a long absence were occasions of special religious exercises. The young people, too, were led further into religion as the gens and the state carried on similar sacrifices and ceremonies for the common good, for the state had its common hearth, presided over by the Vestal Virgins, who guarded the sacred fire upon the altar, which symbolized the home.

**Vestal Virgins.** In Rome was a worship in which was

preserved a common hearth, having always burning on it the domestic fire of the whole nation. This was in the temple of Vesta, the goddess of the home. The goddess being herself a virgin, it was considered necessary that this fire should be cared for by virgins.

This temple of Vesta went through a purification on June first of each year and a renewal of the fire was made on March first. In case the fire went out it was kindled again by the rubbing together of two pieces of "lucky wood," thus producing a fire, and in later times by use of a concave mirror to focus the sun's rays. This was the most sacred of all worship at Rome and the letting this fire go out was considered a great evil, as this was emblematic of the state and its extinction meant the extinction of the nation, hence the Virgin who, through carelessness or negligence, permitted this was severely scourged in the dark by the pontifex.

There were six Vestal Virgins. When chosen, the girl was not to be younger than six nor older than ten; she was to be the daughter of freeborn parents, alive at the time of her selection and residing in Italy, and not engaged in any dishonorable calling; she was to be free from mental and physical defects.

At the time of the admission of a Vestal, her hair was cut off, and a very solemn ceremony was gone through with, after which she was dressed in white and admitted to the work of the Virgins. It appears that her hair was allowed to grow again and to be worn long. Her dress was always white and she wore round her forehead a broad band which had ribbons fastened to it. In processions and at sacrifices she wore a white veil, buckled under the chin.

The term of service was thirty years, the Vestal being a novice during the first ten years, an active priestess the second ten, and a teacher of novices the remaining period. At the end of the term of service of thirty years, the vestal could go back to her family and even get married, but most of them remained in the service of the goddess.

The Virgins had four important duties to perform: (1) Tending the sacred fires; (2) Bringing water daily from the sacred spring, for ceremonial sprinkling and sweeping; (3) Offering sacrifices of salt and cakes, and pouring libations of wine and oil on the sacred fire; (4) Guarding the seven sacred objects on which the stability of Roman power was supposed to stand, the chief of these being the Palladium.

The Vestals were very jealously guarded. Death was inflicted on any one committing an offense against one of them. No man was allowed to go near the temple of Vesta at night nor at any time permitted to enter the dwelling of these Virgins. If a breach of chastity occurred on the part of one of them, she was severely punished by being cruelly beaten and then buried alive. The one sharing her disgrace met a violent death. Twelve Vestals were so punished.

The privileges of a Vestal were very great. She was entirely free from the control of her parents; she could make a will; could give evidence without taking an oath; had the seat of honor at banquets and games; one who was convicted of a crime, if he accidentally met her, was given his liberty. She was treated with the utmost respect and reverence; a consul meeting her on the street, always made way for her; and all the people gave great homage to her. In all the troublesome times between patricians and plebeians neither party disturbed the Vestal Virgins but on the contrary greatly respected them.

**Education.** As long as Rome was in its full strength, education was wholly of a practical nature, its aim being to prepare its young that in manhood they might be of most service to the state. It was more of the Spartan idea than the Athenian, but unlike Sparta the Roman state did not undertake the education of the young but left that wholly to the home, and it was not till the time of the empire that education was taken up by the state, for before that time the state did not even assist in education, let alone control it. Although the state did not concern itself with education, yet love of country and obedience to its laws were so instilled into the minds of the young that no other nation has ever got its citizens to quite so high a pitch of patriotism as the Roman people reached under the republic. As conquest grew and wealth increased under the empire, the Romans came more and more under the influence of Greece until Greek methods and models and ideals dominated Roman education.

In the early times of Rome there were probably no public schools, education being wholly in the hands of the parents. The early years of the child were under the mother, and he received his training from her. These early years of the child could not have been passed better than under the care and training of the old Roman mother, for she was a woman of purity and dignity and industry, qualities fitted for the training of the child's younger years. As the boy grew older he would be permitted to be in the atrium of a morning when his father received his clients and so the boy would receive training in custom and law as he would hear the counsel given by his father to the clients. The boy would also gain much from the discussions of the men at the banquets and other gatherings as he would attend with his father. The child of these times did not learn through instruction so much as by informal training and in imitation of his elders.

Reading and writing were taught to the boy by the father and also simple calculations, such as would be needed in everyday affairs. Ballads, national songs, and religious hymns and deeds of the men of the past were learned by the Roman boys. Physical training of the boys came mostly through games while the young men practised gymnastic exercises, but only to prepare them for military life. Such training made warriors and loyal citizens but also made these Romans selfish, overbearing, cruel, and rapacious, without lofty ideals or enthusiasm for the higher things of life.

Literary education may have said to have begun at Rome during the third century before Christ. In 260 B. C., according to Plutarch, a school was opened by Spurius Carvilius at which fees were charged, the first of the kind. This man was a freedman and he had been a domestic tutor to the consul of the same name, Spurius Carvilius, who, as mentioned before, was the first man at Rome to divorce his wife. From this time education increased and there became three kinds of schools—elementary, grammar, and a higher school, the rhetor's school. The first was presided over by the literator, or ludus magister; the second by the literatus, or, grammaticus; and the third by the rhetor. Added to these kinds of schools were those of the various philosophies, which were given to the adherents in form of lectures. The child entered the elementary school at about the seventh year of age. Near his twelfth year he went into the grammar school and at fifteen or sixteen, if he had determined on politics or law, he would enter the rhetor's school.

As stated above, the child entered school at about seven years of age. The term *ludus* was used to designate the elementary school and *schola* the higher school. In the elementary schools, reading, writing, and arithmetic of a very elementary nature were taught. In learning to read, the child was first taught his letters and then syllables, which were followed by words and then came the sentences. At the first of the elementary schools the reading was taught by means of exercises given by the teacher on account of the scarcity of books. But during the second century before Christ large numbers of slaves were put to copying books so that from this time there were plenty of copies to be had at reasonable cost, and no doubt each child had his own reading book, which contained, perhaps, a Latin version of the Odyssey and the standard Latin poets. Special attention was given to correct pronunciation and intelligent expression. After the child had learned to read he was then taught to write. In the beginning the teacher would make the letters with a stylus on a waxen tablet and then he would give the stylus to the child to trace the letters, the teacher guiding the child's hand. In arithmetic but simple calculations were taught in the elementary schools, the children learning to count and to calculate on the fingers or by means of pebbles and after using these means till they gained some facility an abacus with pebbles was used. Also the waxen tablet with the stylus was used for calculation.

It is quite probable that for a large number of the children school education ceased with the end of the training in the elementary schools. At twelve years of age the boy who went on with his education entered the grammar school. There were two kinds of these schools—the Greek and the Latin. In the Greek schools the language used was Greek with Greek literature and methods of instruction, and at first the teachers were Greek. The Latin schools differed in that the language used was Latin and while at first the literature was Greek translated into Latin later there was a Latin literature. Too, the Latin schools laid more stress upon the practical side of the work rather than the theoretical. The head of each grammar school determined what the curriculum should be but these were quite uniform after all, as all were striving for the same end. The principal studies were grammar and literature, but also were included mathematics, geography, history, and music.

In the study of grammar there were studied the divisions of the letters into vowels and consonants with the divisions of the vowels, the sounds of the letters or phonics, philology in a simple way, the parts of speech, the inflections of the parts of speech, and the like. In literature in the Greek schools, the study of Homer took the leading part as did the study of

Vergil in the Latin schools, and also other authors were studied. Geometry was studied along the practical lines of mensuration and astronomy. Likewise geography and history were entered into for practical purposes. Music was taken up to aid in getting proper intonation and rhythm in oratory and for learning the religious chants. There was but little training in gymnastics, only for hygienic purposes and as an aid to military training. Dancing was not taught in the schools but in the home. This was not as with us, but more of the form of calisthenics. There was nothing such as the round dance with us, which would have been thought shockingly vulgar by the Romans.

When the youth, at about sixteen years of age, assumed the toga virilis, his further education depended upon what his life's work was to be. If it was to be war, then he at once entered the army. If he was to enter public life, then he attended the rhetorical school and studied oratory and law. Also he frequented the places where he could hear the public orations and he might have attached himself to some orator or jurist.

In the rhetor's school those things were studied which would help the young man in his public career. Oratory and rhetoric were the leading studies, and, as he sought, too, to gain a wide knowledge, mathematics, philosophy, law, and literature would be included in the course. The youth usually remained in these higher schools for two or three years. Then he might go on with his studies through travel and attendance at centers outside of Rome.

"Youths of higher intelectual ambition did not rest satisfied with the instruction obtainable at Rome, but (at least after 80 B. C.) resorted to Athens and other philosophical and rhetorical centers. In the last decade of the Republic there were many famous schools of this higher class. In addition to Athens, the mother city, we have the great university schools of Rhodes, Apollonia, Mitylene, Alexandria, Tarsus, Pergamus, and afterwards, in imperial times, Smyrna and Ephesus. In the time of Cicero Marseilles also was already a widely known school."[23]

The elementary schools were poorly provided for, as they were not held in regular school houses for there were no buildings for such educational purposes. The school-rooms were sometimes on the street or in the market-place, wherever a

[23] Laurie, Pre-Christian education, 342.

quiet, convenient corner was found; they were, too, in sheds or booths in front of a house like a lean-to; again they were in places similar to a veranda of a house. If the school-room was the street, the children sat on the stones; in buildings, they sat on the floor, or they might have had benches. The grammar schools were better cared for, as they were generally in covered places attached to large buildings and opening on the street. They had benches for the children and the teacher sat on a chair on a raised place. There were often placed in grammar schools sculptures of marble or plaster and also paintings. All school-rooms were open to the public and frequently the parents and friends went in to see the work and at times there were great "speech days."

The pedagogue was used in Rome, as in Greece, to have charge of the boy and to accompany him to and from school. Although the Romans used the Greek term *pedagogue*, yet the Latin terms *custos*, guardian, and *pedisequus*, attendant, were, perhaps, most commonly used and, too, were used *comes*, companion, and *rector*, governor. The Romans were more careful in the selection of a slave for pedagogue than were the Greeks, and yet he was too often too old or too much physically disabled for the best performance of his duties. These slaves often were manumitted when their duties were completed in a satisfactory manner.

The elementary teacher, litterator, was usually a slave or freedman, and too often quite ignorant, in consequence these teachers were held in little esteem and almost with contempt. Although the grammaticus was better educated and received more esteem yet he did not have a high standing. It was only the rhetor who was respected and praised in Rome. The elementary teacher received very poor pay and the grammar teacher did not fare much better. Yet in later times the grammaticus and rhetor were both well paid and there were some who even became wealthy.

The school year, at least for the elementary schools and probably, also, for the grammar schools, consisted of eight months, with a vacation from July to October inclusive. There was a holiday in whole or in part every eighth day, market day, and there were numerous other holidays throughout the school year. The school day began at daylight, often before, and continued till evening, with a recess for dinner. There were, however, no home lessons.

The discipline at school was very severe. The ferule, whip,

strap, and rod were very liberally used. There must have been quite a good deal of such punishment, as many wrote protests against it, Quintilian, perhaps, most of all.

"Roman boys, like boys in our times, occasionally shirked school, or contrived to feign illness in order to avoid reciting their lessons. The master hung up, where all might read it, a board with names of pupils who absented themselves or had run away. Persius tells us that when a boy he used to rub his eyes with olive oil to give him the appearance of illness, though how oil would have that effect is not apparent. Pliny says that school children took cumin to make them pale."[24]

In the early days the education of the girls was for the most part that gained from the mother in the home. They were taught spinning and weaving and sewing and other household arts, and, no doubt, they also learned to read and write, the same as the boys. When education became common, girls had about the same studies as the boys but whether they attended the same schools with the boys is a disputed question. It is, perhaps, true that the girls of the common people attended the elementary schools with the boys, while the girls of the higher classes had tutors at home. It was more difficult for women to get higher education as they must have obtained it through private instruction and possibly, after marriage, from their husbands.

## LITERATURE.

1. Abbott, Frank Frost, Society and politics in ancient Rome.
2. Abbott, Frank Frost. The common people of ancient Rome.
3. Anderson, Lewis F., History of common school education.
4. Church, Alfred J., Roman life in the days of Cicero.
5. Clarke, George, The education of children at Rome.
6. Dean, Amos, The history of civilization.
7. Dill, Samuel, Roman society from Nero to Marcus Aurelius.
8. Donaldson, James, Woman: Her position and influence in ancient Greece and Rome and among the early Christians.

[24] Clarke, Children at Rome, 67.

9. Duruy, Victor, History of Rome and the Roman people.
10. Fowler, W. Warde, Social life at Home in the days of Cicero.
11. Fowler, W. Warde, The Roman festivals of the period of the republic.
12. Friedländer, Ludwig, Roman life and manners under the early empire.
13. Graves, Frank Pierrepont, A history of Education, Before the middle ages.
14. Guhl, E., and Koner, W., The life of the Greeks and Romans.
15. Ihne, W., Early Rome.
16. Lanciani, Rodolpho, Ancient Rome in the light of recent discoveries.
17. Laurie, S. S., Historical survey of pre-Christian education.
18. Letourneau, Ch., The evolution of marriage.
19. Mommsen, Theodor, The history of Rome.
20. Payne, George Henry, The child in human progress.
21. Preston, Harriet Waters, and Dodge, Louis, The private life of the Romans.
22. Shumway, Edgar S., A day in ancient Rome.
23. Wilkins, A. S., Roman education.

## CHAPTER XI

#### THE CHILD IN EARLIER AND MEDIEVAL EUROPE

**Historical and Critical.** We come now to a time in Europe when there is an overturning of the greatest nation, perhaps, that has ever arisen in this world and with the highest civilization the world had reached up to its time and we enter upon a period where barbarians rule and where civilization lies stagnant for a long number of years. The question ever arises why these great civilizations should be overthrown and pass away as it would seem with their preservation the world would go on toward higher progress and better living while their tearing down leaves the world in ignorance and darkness till another civilization gradually arises.

Yet the very fact that these civilizations are overthrown would imply that the people themselves are weakened or else they could not be overcome. So it would seem that the nation has reached a place where it no longer can prove most useful to the people composing it or to the people of the world, and it must be overthrown and caused to cease to exist in order that new, fresh elements may be allowed to enter into the life of the people that stagnation may not come upon the whole race of people.

The old Romans disappear and a new race enters upon world activity, a race of barbarians, and not only a new people but likewise a youthful people, which must promise much for the race. But this new people begin at quite a lower plane of civilization than the old nations of Greece and Rome had reached and so there is entered upon a long, slow upward climbing but there is a civilization attained that not only reached to that of Greece and Rome but even surpassed these nations and it is still going upward.

It would seem that it does a world good at times to slow down and even to lie dormant for in the end it will surpass its former self. Humanity is the same always and the dominant traits, though they may be checked and held passive for a long time, in the end will show themselves, strengthened by the rest. The best things that a nation produces are not lost in the nation's passing away for the conquering people will in a slow way absorb and work over the essentials and they will come forth among the new people all the better and stronger for race progress. What if the time be long and the regeneration slow, the world can pass away its time in no better way than in getting ready for progress and it has plenty of time for such.

"The larger part of all that the ancient world had gained seemed to be lost. But it was so in appearance only. Almost, if not quite, every achievement of the Greeks and the Romans in thought, in science, in law, in the practical arts, is now a part of our civilization, either among the tools of our daily life or in the long-forgotten or perhaps disowned foundation-stones which have disappeared from sight because we have built some more complete structure upon them, a structure which never could have been built, however, had not these foundations first been laid by some one. All of real value which had been gained was to be preserved in the world's permanent civilization. For the moment it seemed lost, but it was only for the moment, and in the end the recovery was to be complete. By a long process of education, by its own natural growth, under the influence of the remains of the ancient civilization, by no means small or unimportant, which worked effectively from the very first, by widening experience and outside stimulus, the barbarian society which resulted from the conquest was at last brought up to a level from which it could comprehend the classic civilization, at least to a point to see that it had very much still to learn from the ancients, and then, with an enthusiasm which the race has rarely felt, it made itself master in a generation or two of all that it had not known of the classic work—of its thought and art and science—and from the beginning thus secured, advanced to the still more marvelous achievements of modern times."[1]

**Feudalism.** Feudalism was a form of society and government which arose during the Middle Ages and became one of the great institutions of that time, whose legal principles and social ideals are still prevalent in the fundamentals of law and society of the present. "It is itself a crude and barbarous form of government in which the political organization is based on the tenure of land; that is, the public duties and obligations, which ordinarily the citizen owes to

[1] Adams, Civilization during the middle ages, 9-10.

the state, are turned into private and personal services which he owes to his lord in return for land which he has received from him."[2] The feudal system was not confined to Europe, for it existed as well in Japan and in Central Africa and among the Mohammedans, for if the conditions that underlie this system arise then human nature, whatever the place or time, is likely to take on this form of government.

The feudal system grew up from the conditions of society of the time, which caused the people to organize themselves about earlier institutions whose remains still existed among them. In Rome there had grown up a system where the great man had clients attached to him, who consulted him, who helped him and in turn were helped and directed by him. This system must have somewhat been taken up by the conquerors and carried through the years in a modified form, so that when there was no longer a strong central power able to care for the people as a whole, it was natural for them to turn to the strong men about them and to attach themselves to the ones who could bestow upon them land to hold in tenure and likewise who was strong enough to protect them in the use of this land or of their own land. The constituent elements of feudalism were those referring to land and its tenure and to the relations which existed between the protector and the one protected, or, vassalage, beneficies, and immunities.

The term vassal was originally applied to servants not free, but it gradually grew to mean a free man and a vassal was of the same condition as his lord, so that the term held an honorable meaning. The relation of the vassal to the lord was that of homage and fealty. There were two parts to the ceremony of vassalage. In the first ceremony, the man kneeled before the lord, laid his hands in those of the lord, and promised homage to him, upon which the lord lifted him up and gave him the kiss of peace. In the second ceremony, an oath of fealty to the lord was taken upon the Gospels or upon some relic or relics of saints. At the time of this ceremony the lord performed the ceremony of investiture, when he handed to the vassal some material object to symbolize that the man was invested with a fief. The vassal owed to his lord military, civil, and financial duties. He had to give military service for a certain length of time each year, usually forty days, at his own expense, which, if continued, was at

[2] Adams, Civilization during the middle ages, 197.

the expense of the lord. The vassal was bound to attend the court of his lord and to aid him in administering justice. In cases where the lord was taken prisoner in war and a ransom was demanded or his son was knighted or his eldest daughter married, or if he went to the Crusades, the vassal was to give financial aid. The lord owed the obligation to his vassal to support him in his fief and to defend him against every enemy.

On the death of the lord the inheritance passed to his children. At first only male heirs could inherit lands, but later the daughter shared with the son all the privileges of succession except that of primogeniture.

The benefices were bestowed by the lord upon the vassal, the land to be held by tenure, and thus the vassal was placed under obligation to the lord. There were some lands that were held freely and not by tenure, such being known as allodial lands, but these freeholds decreased until finally they wholly disappeared and all the land was held by tenure.

The immunities were grants of privileges to churches or to private individuals. These included the exemption from certain dues or certain obligations.

In his domain the lord was a kind of sovereign. He administered justice, levied taxes, coined money, and declared war for himself and for his own benefit. The revenues of the lord were of various kinds. He received a certain part of the crops from his vassals and he received the judicial fees and other fees of various kinds. Property left after death where there were no heirs went to him.

**The Feudal Castle and Its Life.** As has been stated, when the central power became weak and no longer able to protect the common people, they began to cluster about strong men for protection. These men occupied places that could be defended or else they sought out places of strength and security, usually, heights and places which were difficult of access. Here they built castles and fortified them. These were at first wood, making a kind of wooden blockhouse, but gradually stone came to be used and they were built exceedingly strong, and often considered impregnable.

The feudal village lay beneath and about the castle. There was a complete social separation between the life in the castle and that in the village surrounding it. They pursued a different life, as the lord and his retainers were engaged in war or the chase or lived in idleness, while the people of the village were laborers. There became a wide separation between the village and the castle and special privileges grew up about the dwellers of the castle and, through inheritance, a nobility arose that lived in idleness and came to looking down upon and really despising the common people.

This isolation of the castle did, though, bring a closer relation between the members composing its family. However much the lord might go out for war or for adventure, in the end he must return to his castle, as it was his home. Here he found his wife and children, with whom he must spend his time, mostly alone with them, so that close relations grew. When the lord was away from the castle, his wife must, naturally, have had charge of affairs and this would produce in her characteristics which would cause her to be respected by her lord and often to be considered his equal. It thus arose that domestic life came to mean much in that time and the family became the center of social relationship. The importance of the woman increased and the value of wife and mother became to be recognized beyond what had been known up to that time.

**Chivalry.** Chivalry arose in the Middle Ages, reaching its height during the Crusades. It constituted the moral and social law and custom of the ruling classes in Europe between the eleventh and sixteenth centuries.. It grew out of old Teutonic customs, was modified by the feudal system, and brought into existence a distinction between men of noble rank and the common people about them. The chivalric person was expected to devote himself to the service of God, to his feudal lord, and to his lady. The knight was trained to service and obedience. He was to give his services to the weak, especially of his own rank, to give himself over to the protection of the church, to be reverent and obedient to his superiors, and to hold womankind in high esteem.

In the training of a knight, the boy remained at home till his seventh or eighth year under the care of his mother, who began his religious education and gave him his early training in respect and obedience to his superiors. He was then placed under the care of some nobleman or churchman, in whose castle he lived and took his place with the members of the household. He was known as a *page* and he waited upon his lord and lady. He learned to play chess and other games and in most cases to play the harp and to sing and likewise to read and write. He was trained in running, wrestling, boxing, and riding and some knightly exercises that went with the riding. At fourteen or fifteen the youth became a *squire* and entered into more intimate relations with the knight and his lady. With other squires he played chess and walked and hunted with the lady of the castle, and they attended to the personal wants of the knight, such as caring for his bed, helping him to dress, grooming his horse, and attending upon him at the tournament and in war. During this time the youth learned the arts of war—to exercise in armor, to ride and to use the shield, and to handle the sword and lance and battle-axe. As he neared the end of his squireship, the young man chose his lady-love, to whom he was ever to be devoted. She was usually older than he and often married and he was expected to remain devoted to her even though he should marry.

At twenty-one the young man became a knight, after the ceremony of knighthood. When the time for the ceremony arrived, the candidate put in a season of fasting and purification and prayer, and then he passed the night in a church in prayer and meditation. In the morning came the confession and the absolution and the eucharist. He then placed his sword upon the altar, the priest blessed it and returned it to him, after he had taken the solemn oath of knighthood. His armor was placed upon him and his sword buckled about him and then he knelt before his lord, who laid his sword upon the candidate's shoulder and dubbed him knight. The new knight then arose and mounted his horse and displayed his skill and strength in handling his horse and in the use of his weapons.

The knight's great occupation was that of war. For this he lived and for this he trained throughout life. For practical training in war the tournament came into existence, wherein there were actual combats waged with the weapons of war, and when there were good numbers on each side it became a real battle, even to the wounding and killing. This gave opportunity for displaying knightly powers and courage, for gaining the smiles and good-will of the ladies, and likewise for the settling of private quarrels. The tournament, too, was the greatest of all amusements during feudal times and brought together the largest gatherings and the greatest displays. Fairs were held in connection with them in which there was great merry-making, where jugglers and strolling players and musicians found place and drunkenness and gambling and the like prevailed.

A level piece of ground was chosen on which an oval enclosure was made, with rows of seats and covered galleries all round. The knights who were to engage in the fights pitched their tents at either end, where they stationed themselves with their squires. Heralds had charge of affairs and arranged the ceremonies and rules of procedure. There were jousts, in which two opponents met one another on horseback with lances, and after the jousts was a general fray, in which there were a number of champions on each side who fought with swords and sometimes even with battle-axes, usually on horseback, but on some occasions some on horse and some on foot. The evening before the tournament there was a try-out of arms of squires and young knights, blunt weapons being used, the winners being allowed to enter the general fray of the next day.

All being ready, the lists were cleared and the two knights, on horseback with lances, were placed at some distance opposite each other. At a signal from the herald they lowered their lances and rushed at each other, each striving to knock the other from his horse. In case both knights kept their seats unhurt, they tried it again, till one or both were unhorsed. Then they fought on foot with swords till one was overcome. At the close of all the jousts the general fray took place. In the jousts sometimes one or the other knight was badly wounded and sometimes even killed. In the general fray the fight might have become so fierce that a number would be wounded and killed on both sides. In the evening after the close of the tournament a great feast was held, which was attended by the ladies and the knights who participated in the tournament and other members of the nobility.

The mounted knight was a great fighter and could overcome quite a number of unarmed and unarmored peasants. As long as fighting was done at close quarters no other fighter could equal him or expect to overcome him. But when the common people began to be armed with the bow and the pike an army could be raised that did not always have to fight at close quarters and so armor did not mean so much. War, too, was becoming a mercenary trade and a king could obtain an army by paying for mercenary cavalry and by arming his yeomen and peasants and forming them into pliant infantry. While the barons wasted their strength in fighting and robbing one another, the king swept down upon them with his army of infantry and mercenary cavalry and defeated them one by one, thus doing away with petty baronies and their private quarrels and uniting them under one strong power. When gunpowder came into general use, the knight and his armor vanished in smoke and the chivalry of the middle ages passed away and through the transforming influences of the printing press and steam power and the many other arts of modern times it was refined and became the basis of the civilization of the present day. Chivalry is still extant, but it has a different meaning than that of feudal times, for where the feudal system had its *knight* the present age has its *gentleman*.

The age of chivalry most naturally aroused poetic and musical fancies and during that time arose the trouveurs of Northern France, with whom may be placed the minstrels of the British Isles, and the troubadours of Southern France and the minnesingers of Germany. These poets and singers were from all classes—nobility, artisans, clergy—and although most of them were of noble rank, yet there were some noted ones from the common people. They would go about the country reciting and singing their poems and they were welcome everywhere. They would sing of war and of love, many of the productions being based upon heroes of the past and again others being of imaginary characters.

**The Peasantry.** During feudal times there arose a great distinction between noble and ignoble service. The noble service was that performed by the knight in armor on horseback, that of the unpaid warrior, while ignoble service was that of the field laborer. Since feudal life was mainly agricultural, the artisan, the dweller in the town, counted but little, but there came a time when he did count much for the overthrow of feudalism. The mass of the laboring people were serfs and they were treated sternly by their masters, the noblemen, and they were not much more than slaves.

Slavery, so prominent under the Roman rule, gradually disappeared during the middle ages. Yet the serf at first was but little better off, for, although he could not be sold, he could not leave the land. He did have some control of his person, for he had allotted to him a bit of land upon which he could work without being driven by an overseer. Later he was permitted to go out elsewhere for work, but for this he must possess a legal permit. This led to the custom of allowing him to pay his lord in money for his services in lieu of work upon the land or returns from the land, and then followed his being permitted to purchase his freedom, so that the serf could become a freedman.

During the early part of the period the laboring and the trading classes did not count as political, military, or social factors. They are scarcely mentioned in the records of the time. They were robbed by the nobles, their persons maltreated, and their wives and daughters dishonored. There were exactions of all kinds. They had to pay annual dues for the use of the land, they had to give a certain number of days free each year to the repair of the public roads and to the cultivation of the lord's domains, and they had to be ready, when called upon, to render military service of such an inferior kind as they could do. "He was bound to bake his bread at the lord's oven, grind his grain at the lord's mill, and press his grapes in his lord's wine-press, paying, of course, for the privilege; if he wanted to chase or cut wood in the forest, or fish in the stream, or feed his cattle in the pasture, all of which were reserved seigniorial rights, he must pay his tax. He must pay the lord for the use of his weights and measures, or for a guarantee against changes in his coinage. He may not even sell the remnant of crops which survived this accumulation of taxes until those of the lord have been sold at the highest market price. After the lord had squeezed the peasant almost to the point of extinction, came the church with its even more effectual agencies of terror and superstition. Its principal exaction was the tithe, a tax of one-tenth upon the products of agriculture, a burden sufficient, if rigidly enacted, to ruin any field industry. But not content with this, the church, like the feudal seignior, profited by every special occasion, birth, baptism, marriage, death, to collect new contributions."[3]

Even in the seventeenth century the life of the laboring man was very hard, as is shown in the following in reference to the British peasant of that time. "At the first setting out of the plough after Christmas, which was the time to begin fallowing, or breaking up the pease earth, the teamsman rose before 4 a. m., and after thanks to God for his

[3] Emerton, Medieval Europe, 518.

night's rest, proceeded to the beast house. Here he foddered his cattle, cleaned out their booths, rubbed down the animals, currying the horses with cloths and wisps. Then he watered his oxen and horses. He next foddered the latter with chaff, dry pease, oat hulls, beans, or clean garbage, such as the hinder parts of rye. While they were eating their meal, he got ready his collars, hames, treats, halters, mullers, and plough gears. At 6 a. m. he received half an hour's liberty for breakfast. From seven till between two and three in the afternoon he ploughed. Then he unyoked, brought home his oxen, cleansed and foddered them, and, lastly, partook of his dinner, for which he was again granted another half-hour's spell of leisure. By 4 p. m. he was again in the stable. After rubbing down his charges and re-cleansing their stalls, he went to the barns, where he prepared the fodder for the following day's bait. He carried this to the stable, and then watered his beasts and replenished their mangers. It was now close on 6 p. m. He therefore went home, got his supper, and then sat by the fireside, either mending his and the family's shoe-leather, or knocking hemp and flax, or picking and stamping apples and crabs for cider or vinegar, or grinding malt on the quern, or picking candle rushes, till 8 p. m. He then lighted his lanthorn and revisited the stable, where he again cleansed the stalls and planks, and replenished the racks with the night's fodder. Then, returning to his cottage, he gave God thanks for benefits received during the day, and went to bed."[4]

**The Town People.** In the early part of this period the artisans, like the field serfs, were grouped under a lord to whom their products belonged. Later they grouped themselves into communities and began to deal with the lord more as a body and not as separate individuals, although at first there was not much organization. There was a continuous growth, though, toward closer organization till there arose the great free city with its charter of freedom obtained from the lord for services rendered or funds furnished in a time of his great need.

The growth of commerce, too, aided in the formation of these cities, as for the carrying on of trade it was necessary to have centers where the people might come together. These places might at first have been a fair, a temporary affair, but gradually these centers became permanently established or

[4] Garnier, Annals of the British peasantry, 141.

old ones revived. For the carrying on of trade it was necessary to have a medium of exchange and the amount of money was increased by the cities through accumulation and coinage. This gave to the cities a strong means for obtaining freedom, as the lord was ever in need of funds and the cities by accumulating money and having the power to raise a general fund could from time to time buy rights from the lord as his need of money became urgent.

In Italy and Germany the cities formed themselves into corporations, the most noted perhaps being the Hanseatic League. In England, however, the cities did not join together, but each stood apart and cared for itself alone. They became really more interested in the welfare of the town itself than in that of the nation and the prosperity of the town was of the most importance. The town could not set aside the law of the land, but it could add to it as far as the government of the town itself was concerned and ordinances were passed relative to the welfare of the town. The officers of these towns considered themselves as very important personages and on occasions of state they arrayed their persons in gorgeous robes and carried themselves with great dignity. These towns erected stately churches and other public buildings and adorned them magnificently.

A striking feature of town life of the Middle Ages was the formation of guilds. This was not original with this period for, as told under the chapter on Rome, there were organizations at Rome similar to the guilds of the middle ages and likewise there were similar organizations in Greece. In the medieval period there were two kinds of guilds. The first kind was of a general nature and it was organized for mutual protection or aid, such as protection against thieves and aid in times of sickness, old age, and the like. The second kind was the trade guild, such as formed by merchants and craftsmen. Guilds formed a very important element in the town life of the Middle Ages, as almost all professions and occupations had guilds.

The craft guild embraced all the members of a craft—the apprentice, who was bound for service for a number of years to learn the trade; the journeyman, or skilled laborer, who received wages for his work; and the master, who controlled the journeyman and the apprentice. The function of the guild was to regulate and protect the craft and also to help one another and to care for the orphan and the widow and the aged. Officers from their own body were appointed to carry out the regulations and to have general oversight of the organization.

"The medieval townsman was very narrow in his aims, very selfish, and sometimes very cruel in his exclusiveness, but his whole-hearted affection for his town, his anxiety for its welfare, and his pride in its beauty are delightful: they must have made his life very real and absorbing to him, and they make it very attractive to us."[5]

**The Aristocracy.** As was stated before, during the middle ages in Europe there grew up a sharp distinction between the noble and the commoner, which was strongly emphasized by inheritance till there became the grouping of people into hard and fast classes. The nobility possessed two characteristics that distinguished them from the common people which were the right to inherit landed estate and the right to knighthood. Thus arose a class born to estate and chivalry which hardened into an aristocracy that was almost impossible for the man born of the public to enter. Yet there were two ways by which he might enter into nobility, by the purchase of an estate to which the quality of nobility was attached, which his children inherited, and through the creation of new nobles by the king, which, though, was rarely done during medieval times.

The love of show and magnificence was great during the middle ages and was greatly displayed by the aristocracy of the period. The most impressive and lavish displays were centered round the person of the king. This was shown in the gorgeous ceremonies and settings of his coronation, in court etiquette and regulations, and in the large establishment of his household. Some of the great nobles had establishments that rivaled and even excelled that of the king. The great lord had a large body of retainers who wore his livery and badge, a great number of whom were members of his household and ate at his table. These great lords were lavish in their entertainment and sometimes impoverished themselves through their hospitality, and were thereby compelled to obtain money, which, as mentioned before, gave to the cities the opportunity of securing privileges from them. In England such nobles sometimes repaired their fortunes by marrying the daughters of rich merchants or by engaging in trade, but in France the old noblesse, whose social stand-

[5] Abram, English life and manners in the later middle ages, 30.

ing depended upon their ancient origin, preferred poverty to such means of enriching themselves, which they would regard with holy horror, and they kept their respect and dignity through all the vicissitudes of misfortunes, without thus endangering their pure strain of noble blood by mixing it with that of the common herd or soiling their sacred persons with the vulgar touch of trade.

**The Home.** As time went on in the Middle Ages, the houses built as a means of defence grew less, so that the castle began to disappear and the home to take its place. The houses began to assume proportions of grandeur and forms of beauty, the outgrowth of the love of magnificence and display of the times. In England the manor houses were grouped around a courtyard with the entrance through a gate-house. In the house was a great hall, made to accommodate a large number of people. The kitchen was a large room, sometimes having three or four large fireplaces. Leading from the hall were chambers for the lord and lady and guests. There were also the bake-house, brew-house, stables, granaries, ox-stalls, pig-sties, and other buildings.

The town houses had usually been no higher than two stories, but later went up to three or four stories in height. They often had gardens about them. They were built of stone, brick, or wood, sometimes having a cellar of stone while the upper part was wood. They were thatched with straw, but often tiles were used. Thin horn, talc, and canvas were placed across windows, but glass was coming into more common use, so that many houses had glass in their windows. The rooms were lighted by candles, sometimes torches were used, the candles being set in standing or hanging candlesticks of iron, wood, or latten. The heating was done by a fire built in the center of the hall, the smoke escaping through an opening in the roof, or there was a fireplace in the corner or the side of the room. The fuel used was wood, charcoal, ling, peat, or coal.

In the hall the furniture consisted of tables, seats, and a cupboard. In the chamber was a bedstead with curtains around it and the bedding consisted of a straw mattress, a feather bed, bolster, pillows, sheets, and blankets. There were chairs in the room, a table, and a clothes chest. The walls were painted or hung with tapestry. The floors were bare or strewn with rushes or straw, some floors being of tiles, and carpets came into use late in the period.

**Women.** At the time of the beginning of Christianity women had reached a high position at Rome, having great freedom, power, and influence. At the first women played an important part in the activities of the Christians, but later they were relegated to quite a subordinate place. The old church fathers even went farther and claimed that woman was a source of evil and that she should live in continual penance on account of the curses she had brought upon the world. So it became her duty to remain at home secluded, going out into public only when visiting the sick or attending church, and then she must be veiled. Nor should she enhance her beauty, which was only a snare, by dress but such should be simple and grave and of plain color, not for the purpose of ornament but for protection alone.

"The influence of Christianity tended at once to elevate and to narrow the position of women. It elevated her position, for, while the pagan ideal of life is essentially masculine, the Christian ideal is in part feminine. Justice, energy, strength, are the pre-eminent qualities of the pagan ideal; and mercy, love, gentleness, and humility, of the Christian. The coincidence of the characteristics of Christianity with the characteristics of the female heart resulted in the elevation of woman. This result was also achieved in other ways. In the realm of the emotions, and especially of the religious emotions, woman is superior to man. If she is inferior to him in her power of apprehending a system of truth, she is his superior in respect to her loyalty to individuals. Christianity demanded personal loyalty to a personal Christ as the first and comprehensive condition of admission to its church. Thus the influence of Christianity ennobled the position of woman. This increased power was manifest in various ways. Women flocked to the Church in large numbers, and were important factors in the conversion of the Empire. They embraced martyrdom with unflagging zeal and fortitude. Although not usually admitted to the priesthood, they performed ecclesiastical functions of minor importance. As deaconesses—an order for which may justly be claimed apostolic sanction—they were of peculiar usefulness in the great and arduous work of charity and of philanthropy. Of the asceticism which so early sprang up they were ardent defenders. In their households, their influence was more pervasive than in the Church. For the conversion of their husbands and sons and daughters they labored with constancy, if not always with wisdom, and often with success. The wife of Theodosius the Great was one of the most distinguished defenders of the faith. Augustine writes of the influence of his mother in the formation of his Christian chaarcter. The mother of Constantine bore an important part in the conversion of her royal son. In dignity and in useful influence, in social rights and family prestige, Christianity tended to elevate the place of woman. For force or passion as the basis of marriage—elements which when exercised degrade the husband more than the wife—was substituted love. The New Testament teaching was the foundation of practice.

"But in one respect the position of the married woman was narrowed by Christianity. It has been already noticed, that in the civil marriage of the period of the later Republic and Empire, the wife remained in the guardianship of her own family. She did not pass into the control of her husband. The consequence of this method was that the power of her guardian became less and less, and that the power of her husband did not increase. She, therefore, came to occupy a situation of great independence as to both person and property. Against the loose marital bond of the civil marriage, which was indeed a mere species of wedlock, the Church uttered its protest. It was contrary to the teachings of the New Testament; it was opposed to Christian practice. In their repudiation of the civil marriage, the Christian moralists also repudiated that liberty and independence of the wife which were among its essential elements. Thus the legal position of the married woman was narrowed by the Church." [6]

Among the early Germans, women were greatly respected. Woman was considered man's inferior only in physical nature and this very physical weakness was the one great cause of her being so well respected. The wife was not thought inferior to the husband in morality, courage, prudence, and wisdom, but his equal. Although this was somewhat changed by contact with the Romans, yet it appears to be the basis for the building of the high honor paid to women in chivalry. During the time of feudalism the wife tended to become the husband's peer and companion. In the age of chivalry women were held in high esteem, or at least women of the noble class,

[6] Thwing, The family, 56-57.

and they were subjects of great devotion by the knights and squires.

During the Middle Ages many women possessed property and because of this they had a social standing they would not otherwise have had. But riches brought disadvantages as well, as heiresses were in danger of being carried off and compelled to marry their captors or to give them large sums of money. If single a woman's property was more or less under the control of her guardian and when married her husband had control of her belongings. On the other hand, the wife had a certain right in her husband's possessions and upon his death she had her portion as dower.

Women entered into industrial affairs, as they engaged in the manufacture and sale of many articles. They occupied themselves in spinning and weaving, in making ribbons and laces, in making shoes and candles, and other articles; they sold fruit, bread, fish, poultry, and wares of different kind; they were employed in farm work and in unskilled labor such as carrying clay and water, gathering moss and heath, and waiting on thatchers and masons. Women carried on foreign commerce, in England exporting goods to France, Spain, and other countries. They were permitted to become members of guilds, although they did not take a very prominent part in them.

**Marriage.** In the early Christian church marriage was made to mean a great deal. Surrounded as the Christians were by the moral rottenness of the decaying Roman state, it became necessary for the sustenance of their religion that the marriage vow should be a sacred obligation. To this end marriage became a religious ceremony. A Christian could not marry a pagan, as this vow could only be properly taken between parties of the same religious belief and could thus receive the benediction of the bishop. This idea of marriage made chastity the all-important thing in woman and thus created the home and gave to children a pure parenthood and made childhood mean more to children than the world had given before.

Among the Germans, and likewise other northern nations of earlier Europe, monogamy was prevalent and almost the universal practice. There was a kind of purchase of the wife, as the man in the presence of her parents offered a dowry to the bride, which if accepted sealed the match. The parties to the contract both had to be mature people, the bridegroom having to be old enough to be invested with arms and to become a member of the state. Before the woman could marry she had to have the consent of her father or nearest relative, and if a widow, having been purchased, she had to have the approval of the relatives of her deceased husband.

"Marriage ceremonies (among Anglo-Saxons) consisted in the assemblage of friends, the consuming of the great loaf (made by the bride as an introduction into house-keeping, and the ancestor of our wedding-cake); some special barrels of beer were brewed—the 'bride ale,' hence our modern 'bridal.' This beer was drunk to her health and to that of the bridegroom (originally *brydgumma*, bridesman). The Anglo-Saxons paid a regular sum, agreed upon beforehand, to the father before the wedding; the consent of the lady being obtained, the bridegroom then gave his promise and his 'wed.' 'Nor,' adds Sharon Turner, 'was this promise trusted to his honor merely, or to his own interest. The female sex was so much under the protection of the law that the bridegroom was compelled to produce friends who became security for his due observance of the covenant.' In this we have the origin of 'groomsman,' or 'best man,' of our time. The parties being betrothed, the next step to take was to settle by whom the *fosten-léan*, or money requisite for the care of the children, was to be supplied. The bridegroom pledged himself to do this; his friends became security for him. These preliminaries being arranged, he had to signify what he meant to give her for choosing to be his wife, and what he should give her in case she survived him. This was the *morgen gifu*, being given by the Anglo-Saxon husbands to their wives on the morning after the wedding.[7] The old law says that it is right that she should halve the property, or the whole of it should become hers if she had children, unless she married again. The friends of the bridegroom became surety for his conduct and those of the bride for hers. A priest—when Christianity was introduced—blessed the union; and after many points of law had been settled for the protection of the wife under all circumstances, 'her relations wedded her to him.' But in all these instances no mention

[7] Hallam, Middle Ages, II, 179, quotes from Palgrave the following, coming under Norman times: "By the declaration of the husband at the church door, the wife was endowed in the presence of the assembled relations, and before all the merry attendants of the bridal train."

is made of the wedding-ring, which came later. The English, regarding the wife in her capacity of ruler of the household, placed a ring upon her finger as a badge, not of servitude, but of authority, as in the case of the consort of Ethelred the Second, who before receiving the crown was anointed and distinguished by this symbolic act of adornment."[8]

There was a time during the Middle Ages when betrothal and even marriage took place at a very early age, even between quite young children. In England boys could be married at fourteen and girls at twelve, but these ages were sometimes disregarded and children were married at even younger ages. Betrothals were made by parents or guardians for children of very young age, one such case is on record as having been entered into when the little girl was but four years of age, the child having been given in charge to her future father-in-law. This custom was by far most common among the upper classes, for, as a rule, the men and women of the middle classes did not enter upon marriage till of more mature age. These early marriages or betrothals were probably the result of guardians having under their charge children who were heirs and so they arranged the marriage to their own advantage or sold their rights for a sum of money, and even parents were known to have sold the marriage of their children to gain money.

The idea of the early Christians that marriage should not be civil but religious gradually prevailed till not only was the ceremony performed by the church alone, but also breaches of marriage vows were punished not by the state but by the church. But this did not prevent marriage from becoming a business affair, where the material advantages to be gained were closely looked into and the amount of property or money to be gained on either or both sides was the most important and chief consideration. Nor did this prevent informal marriages, for men and women did join themselves together without priest or religious ceremony by a simple declaration that they would take each other as husband and wife. This was not accepted by the church nor always recognized by the state, but such unions did take place nevertheless.

"It is sometimes thought that in the Middle Ages men were always obliged to hold to their wives for better or worse to

[8] Traill, Social England, I, 215-216.

their lives' end. There are some grounds for this opinion, but it is not quite correct. The Church did not allow divorce in the modern sense of the word; that is to say, she taught that a valid marriage could not be dissolved; but marriages could be, and often were, annulled on the ground that some impediment existed which rendered them invalid."[9]

There was no regular marriage among the serfs of the earliest times. As marriage became more a church ceremony, this institution established, about the twelfth century, the legality of this ceremony among the serfs. This, of course, caused difficulties when the serf of one lord married the serf of another, and especially so when such parties had children. Sometimes money satisfied this, sometimes other marriages, and even sometimes the children were divided among the two estates.

**Dress.** The simple and beautiful dress of the Greeks and Romans was displaced during the Middle Ages by changing costumes, which sometimes were of the most fantastic designs and colors, sometimes ugly, and sometimes beautiful. It is impossible to give here in detail the dress of all the nations or even in a general way to depict the changes that took place, and but one nation, England, will be considered, and that only in a hurried way.

The early Britons used a mantle that covered the whole body, which was fastened in front with a clasp or with a belt about the waist. These mantles were of skins of animals, the hair being left on for the outside of the garment. Sometimes also they wore a woolen jacket. Their shoes were made of coarse skins, the hair being left for the outside as with the mantle. The women wore chains and rings and bracelets, and their hair was left loose upon the shoulders without braiding or tying.

The Anglo-Saxons had a linen undergarment over which they wore a linen or woolen tunic, reaching to the knees, with long, close sleeves, the tunic being fastened at the waist with a belt. Over these garments they wore a short cloak, fastened with clasps. They wrapped bands of cloth, linen, or leather about the leg from the ankle to the knee, and their shoes opened down the instep and were fastened with a thong. The women wore a long, loose garment, like a tunic, reaching to the ground, and over this a mantle. They wrapped about the head and neck a kind of veil made of a

[9] Abram, English life and manners in the later middle ages, 119.

long piece of silk or linen. The men wore the hair and beard long.

The Normans made quite a display in dress. They wore a long, close gown, reaching to the feet, often embroidered with gold at the bottom, and fastened at the waist with an ornamental girdle. Over this they wore a cloak with a hood, fastened across the breast by a gold or silver brooch. The women wore a loose dress, trailing on the ground, with girdle round the waist, and a cloak over the dress. The men wore their hair long, sometimes curling it like women, but they wore no beard, shaving the face clean.

During the Middle Ages dress was a distinguishing mark of very great importance. The king needed to be arrayed in gorgeous robes of rich texture and color, as his dignity require such; the city officers, in keeping with the pride of the city, must be clothed in brilliant attire; the sign of power and greatness of the nobles was displayed in the showy livery of their retainers; and the uniform of the craft-guilds was a badge of their importance in the life of the people and of the nation. During the most of this period there was great luxury in dress among the noble and wealthy. Silks, satins, velvets, scarlet cloths, fine cloths of gold and silver, and rich furs were used in the apparel of both sexes, and not only was the finest and best of their own land used, but also fine materials were brought in from other countries. Not only was the clothing very costly, but also there was a striving for a large amount, so that the expenditure for dress was very great.

The men dressed as fanciful and elaborately as did the women and the styles changed quite as often and as differently. At one time they wore a close-fitting tunic with tight or short sleeves and a short cloak; at a later time they wore a long gown with long, full sleeves, and again their clothing was padded, the shoulders being made as broad as possible. Sometimes the colors of the garments would be of one hue or well matched, and again there would be one garment of one color and another of an entirely different color, and even the parts of the same garment would not be of the same color. "A dandy of the fourteenth century is thus described: 'He wore long pointed shoes, fastened to his knees by gold or silver chains; hose of one color on one leg, and of another color on the other. Short breeches, not reaching to the middle of the thigh; a coat, one-half white, and the other half black or blue; a long beard, a silk band buttoned under his chin, embroidered with grotesque figures of animals, dancing men, etc., and sometimes ornamented with gold, silver, and precious stones.'"[10]

The women wore long dresses reaching to the ground and sometimes with long trains. At times the bodices fit closely and were low in the neck, while in another time the body was encased in whalebone to the hips and the shoulders supported an enormous ruff, as much as three feet or more in width. Men also wore the ruff. The ladies used paint on their faces and adorned them with black patches as "beauty spots."

Men and women of the working classes dressed more simply than the upper classes, usually wearing short tunics with small sleeves and with hoods for outdoors. But they, too, dressed up for special occasions and at times they were arrayed in highly-colored and costly garments and even at times vied with the upper classes, in spite of laws passed to prevent people from dressing above their stations.

Children were clothed in about the same manner and the same styles as their elders, their being no great distingushing marks in the dress of the younger and older people.

The girdles, which were so necessarily an important part of the dress, were often highly ornamental and very costly. They were sometimes made of silk, lined with fine leather, and ornamented with gold and silver and precious stones. The garments of both men and women were at times embroidered, having armorial devices, mottoes, initials of the owners, and other designs. They were also lined and trimmed with fur, many kinds of fur being used.

The men wore their hair long and then again very short; it was cut off short at the forehead and at another time allowed to grow long till it almost fell into the eyes. Sometimes they wore a full beard and sometimes they were clean shaved. At a late time in the period wigs came into use, and they were thought to be indispensable by every man of social standing. They wore hoods and then caps and hats of various styles. The women wore their hair loose down the back or braided and coiled and put into a net of gold wire. At one time great headdresses were the fashion, one style rising up horn-like from the head, another being like a steeple, running to a high point. There were also heart-shaped erec-

[10] Dean, History of civilization, VI, 203.

tions, turban-shaped, crescent-shaped, one like an inverted lamp-shade, and still another shaped like a butterfly.

Shoes were of various styles, one style having very sharp-pointed toes and even projecting far beyond the foot and then turned up and fastened to the knee with a silver or gold chain. Then the shoes were changed from length to breadth, till Parliament passed a law limiting the width of the toes to six inches. There was one kind made of fine, soft leather cut into beautiful designs and worn over bright-colored stockings that showed through the openings.

Jewelry was used quite a great deal. Caps and girdles and other garments were sometimes decorated with precious stones. They wore chains about the neck with pendants in the shape of crosses, medallions, and the like. Reliquaries (little cases containing relics) were also sometimes hung on neck-chains. There were beads of gold and silver and ivory. Brooches and clasps and rings of gold and silver studded with jewels were quite common and other jewelry was worn.

"Very extraordinary ideas were current as to the properties of jewels; talismanic and medicinal powers were attributed to many of them—it was thought that the jaspar, agate, and toad-stone neutralized or detected poisons, that pearls dissolved in powder cured stomachic complaints, and that coral acted as a charm. Great importance was attached to engraving, because it was held that if a gem were engraved by a skilful person under the right planetary influence its virtue was greatly increased. If, for example, an engraving depicting Ophinclius, the constellation which had the power of resisting poison, were cut on an agate its efficiency would be doubled. Even substances which had in themselves no talismanic qualities could acquire them if they were inscribed with words or symbols possessing them, and consequently sacred names and mystic signs were frequently placed not only upon gems, but also upon all kinds of jewelry, and sometimes upon other things, such as drinking cups, as well." [11]

Food. Eating and drinking was a most important function of the middle ages. Banquets were held to celebrate great events and feasting occurred on all occasions, both public and private. Good things to eat were so well thought of that it was the custom to send gifts of food to friends and patrons and the very highest in the land, as was often shown in

[11] Abram, English life and manners in the late middle ages, 167.

England, did not think it undignified to give or to receive such presents, from whomever they might come. Towns in order to gain favors would send out as presents large quantities of food to royal personages, and loyalty shown by towns and individuals was sometimes rewarded by the king in the same way.

As artificial light was hard to get, the meals were usually partaken of during daylight. The cooks of the time showed great skill in the preparation of foods and in decorating their dishes, being fond of coloring all kinds of food and displaying branches and flowers about the food and table. The table was covered with a cloth and each guest furnished with a napkin, knife, and spoon but no fork, the fingers being used instead. Good manners prohibited the putting of the knife into the mouth, but it was all right to dip sops or morsels into soups or sauces, and it was a mark of good breeding to be able to carry such to the mouth without letting any drops fall upon the tablecloth or the person.

There were many different kinds of bread; among the meats were beef and pork, poultry and game of all sorts, among such eaten being peacocks, gulls, swans, herons, and cranes; many varieties of fish were to be had; there were many different kinds of fruits and vegetables used, among the fruits being quinces, pears, cherries, strawberries, apples, peaches, plums, and grapes, and of the vegetables, peas, leeks, cabbages, onions, turnips, parsnips, and beets. Soups and broths were very common, and the mixing of ingredients in dishes was much in use, as, meat was cut up into small pieces, boiled, ground in a mortar, passed through a strainer, and then mixed with spice, salt, sugar or honey, almonds, dates, raisins, and grated bread, all being blended together with the yolk of eggs.

The poorer classes sometimes fared badly, but usually in England the peasants had sufficient food, although often of the cheaper sort and not of great variety. "The methods of preparing the raw material for baking differed in various parts of this island. For a very long period it was imperative on the manorial populations in both England and Scotland that they should take their corn to be ground at the lord's mill. But when this regulation fell into disuse, all sorts of contrivances for grinding crept in. The most primitive was undoubtedly that of the Highland peasant. The first process was the separation of the grain from the ear. This was not threshed, but graddaned—that is to say, it was burned out of the ear in much the same fashion as the parched corn of Boaz. Either whole sheaves or several ears were fired on the cottage floor. Though the burning of the entire sheaf was the most expeditious process, it was a sad waste of manure and thatch. Sometimes oats were beaten out of the straw with a rude mallet, and kiln-dried. But usually both they and barley underwent the burning treatment. The housewife knelt before the fire, holding a few stalks in her left hand. Setting the ears alight, she deftly beat out the grain with a stick, just when the husk was quite consumed. The grains, blackened like coal, were picked off the floor with the hand and placed in the quern. This consisted of two stones, 1½ ft. in diameter, the lower slightly convex, the upper slightly concave. In the middle of each was a round hole, and on one side of it a long handle. The Scotch housewife shed the grain into the hole with one hand, and worked the handle round with the other. The corn slid down the convexity of the lower stone, and by the motion of the upper one was ground in the passage.''[12] ''Hasty pudding was a great favorite among the poorer sort. Indeed, all spoon meat of a sweet description was popular, as Houghton proves by a delightful little anecdote. Two Norfolk boys once were overheard discussing the kind of treat in which either of them would indulge if he became King of England. The one decided that he would have pudding every day for dinner; the other burst into tears, because his comrade's wish had left him nothing good from which to choose.''[13]

**Children of the Ancient Britons.** "It seems to have been the custom of the Celts to plunge their new-born infants into some lake or river in order to try the firmness of their constitutions and to harden their bodies—this even in the winter season. The Scandinavians used, it is said, to pour water upon the heads of their children as soon as they were born, and this long before the introduction of Christianity; but there is no certainty that this custom was observed in Britain. Before the introduction of Christianity the inhabitants of the northern part of Britain did not give names, it is said, to their sons before they had performed some brave action, or given some indication of their disposition and character. . . .

[12] Garnier, Annals of the British peasantry, 196.
[13] Ibid., 201.

"The early British matron, even of the highest rank, always nursed her infants, and would have resented in the greatest degree the delegation of this parental office to another woman. We know little of the bringing up of the children. There is a story of Solinus to the effect that his first morsel of food was put into the infant's mouth on the point of the father's sword, with a prayer that he might prove a great and brave warrior and die on the field of battle. This seems more likely to apply to the races who succeeded them and the Roman occupation than to the veritable Britons. . . . The Ancient Britons were accustomed almost from infancy to handle arms and to sing the glorious actions of their ancestors. The young were thus inspired to feats of strength and to be engaged in war. As they advanced in years they were, while being instructed in martial exercises, also taught that everything in life depended on their valor —the praises of the bards, the favor of the great, and the applause of the people, and that happiness after death was the reward only of those who were daring in war. It may be considered certain that the youth of Britain at this period were not delicately nurtured; a rough and hardy people would not educate their children in a manner unfitting for their surroundings and way of life, and doubtless—as in Germany—the families of the nobler sort were brought up with no more delicacy or tenderness than the common people. Tacitus says of the Germans, 'In every house you see the little boys, the sons of lords and peasants, equally sordid and ill-clothed, lying and playing promiscuously together on the ground and among the cattle, without any visible distinction. In this manner they grow up to that prodigious strength which we behold with admiration.' The sons of the ancient Germans, Gauls, and Britains of all ranks were allowed to run, wrestle, jump, swim, climb, and to engage in vigorous exercises at their will and without restraint until they approached manhood. To this continued exercise, together with the simplicity of their diet, is ascribed by Cæsar the great strength of body and boldness of spirit to which these nations attained. Cæsar says that when the youth of Germany, Gaul, and Britain began to approach the manly age, some more attention seems to have been paid to them by the public and their parents than previously, for when the son was younger it was accounted a shame for a father to be seen in his company. Children who were designed for the priestly order were then put under the direction of the Druids for their instruction in the sciences and in the principles of law, morality, and religion, while those who were intended for a warlike life—according to Cæsar—had arms put into their hands by their fathers, or nearest kinsmen, in a public assembly of the warriors of the state or clan. Some vestiges of this custom continued till later times—especially with respect to the eldest sons of the lairds or chieftains—in some parts of the Highlands and western isles of Scotland.''[14]

**Children among the Early Christians.** The old church fathers were so much given to ascetism that it would appear as if there was really an antagonism to marriage in their time and which must have had a great influence on family life. Donaldson states[15] that children are seldom mentioned in the Christian writings of the second and third centuries, and that almost nothing is said of their training, as if there were but litle attention given to their instruction. And yet infants were considered with a much higher standard than among the Greeks and Romans, for, as given in the chapters dealing with children among these nations, infanticide was practiced by them, as the father had the right to expose his children, so that infants on their birth might be abandoned and left to perish, and this was particularly the case with weakly and deformed children and often with female children without blemish. From the very first Christianity condemned the practice and denounced it as murder. They even went further, for the church forbid the practice of the destruction of children before birth. Thus Christianity protected the lives of infants and especially of female infants.

**Child and Parent.** In England at least there did not at times seem to have been a great, strong affection between parents and children. This may have been caused in part from the custom of boarding out the children or sending them out to be servants or ladies-in-waiting to the persons with whom they were sent to live, as children who would thus go out from parents at an early age and not getting to see them often would not have the opportunity of showing affection for them and they would naturally take up with the people with whom they came in daily contact. The children who were sent to boarding-school were there throughout the en-

[14] Traill, Social England, I, 106-108.
[15] Donaldson, Woman, 180.

tire year, being at home only a few days at a time, on holidays. Another cause for the lack of affection between parents and children may have been from the custom of the remarriage of parents, the new husband or the new wife drawing the affection away from the children. Although the children showed outward respect to their parents, which was well portrayed in the letters they wrote to them, yet it would seem there was not so deep an inward respect.

**Care and Treatment of Children.** Children were brought up quite strictly during the Middle Ages. They were punished very much, minor offenses often bringing a severe punishment, for it was held that every child needed correction and that quite frequently. The children of the poor were usually put to work when very young and had to undergo much suffering. Orphans had the hardest lot of all, for if parents cared so little for their own children and often neglected them, they would care still less for the children of other people, and so would neglect them or treat them cruelly. If the orphans were heirs, they were often despoiled of their possessions by their guardians or married to parties unfit for them in order to have control of their estate. Of course, all parents were not lacking in affection and all guardians were not knaves. Yet it would seem that children during the Middle Ages did not have the happiest of times and they often lived miserable lives.

**Apprenticeship.** There arose during the Middle Ages a belief that every child should be trained to do something. As was stated under feudalism, it was the custom for boys of the upper classes to be sent into the homes of nobles and churchmen to serve a number of years in order to become learned in chivalry and to acquire the use of arms. In like manner there grew up for the boys of the common classes the apprenticeship system, whereby they were placed under a master to spend a number of years to learn a trade or to carry on agriculture.

It was held, at least in England, that all able-bodied men should work and to that end they should be trained as boys, so that when grown up they would be able to work at a trade or farming and thereby earn their own living and not become a burden upon the state. During the sixteenth century it became a law that every child should have such training as would fit him for business or a calling. Some were apprenticed to trades and some to agriculture. If a parent could prove that he was able to furnish a maintenance for his children they were not apprenticed, but otherwise, if the children were found to be growing up in idleness, the authorities had the power to apprentice them.

There was a fee charged for apprenticeship to a trade, sometimes only an entrance fee and again an annual due, but not very large in either case. The term of service varied, in France being from three to thirteen years, while in England it generally lasted seven years. The apprentice probably secured no pay at any time, but was cared for by the master in the way of food, lodging, clothing, and other needs. After he had completed his years of service, the apprentice became a journeyman and then entered regularly into the trade, receiving wages for his labor. In the earlier times the journeyman could easily become a master, but later when capital began to be amassed and the carrying on of the manufacture of goods required much capital, the journeyman did not have very good opportunity for becoming a master. In the early days master, journeyman, and apprentice all lived and worked together and were in the same guild, and so there was not any great separation among them. But later when a large amount of capital was required to carry on business and a large number of men used, there became a wide difference between master and workmen and strife grew up betwen them and journeymen formed guilds for themselves alone, which guilds were sometimes suppressed by the authorities. Such a guild came in time to prohibit aliens from becoming apprentices, and thus from learning the trade, and even to restricting apprenticeship to the children and relatives of its members who were working in the trade.

**Military Training for the Young.** In order to bring back the old military training in England, in 1511 an act was passed "that every man being the king's subject, not lame, decrepit, or maimed, being within the age of sixty years, except spiritual men, justices of the one bench and of the other, justices of the assize, and barons of the exchequer, do use and exercise shooting in long bows, and also do have a bow and arrows ready continually in his house, to use himself in shooting. And that every man having a man child or men cihldren in his house, shall provide for all such, being of the age of seven years and above, and till they shall come to the age of seventeen years, a bow and two shafts, to learn them and bring them up in shooting; and after such young men shall come to the age of seventeen years, every one of them shall provide and have a bow and four arrows continually for himself, at his proper costs and charges, or else of the gift and provision of his friends, and shall use the same as afore is rehearsed."[16]

**Amusements.** The people of medieval times were much given to amusements. This was particularly true of the people of England and what follows here is for the most part about that country.

The greatest pastime of the nobility was that of war, and the joust and the tournament were the most attractive amusements because they most resembled war. The young men engaged in a sport known as tilting at quintain, which was designed to prepare them for warfare. The figure of a Saracen with a saber or club in its right hand and a shield on the left arm was hung up so that it would turn about very radily. A young man on horseback with a lance or something similar, as in a joust, would ride at the figure and strive to strike it between the eyes or on the nose, for if some other part was struck the figure would be turned round so as to give the rider a blow on the back with the saber or club, which not only brought a laugh at his expense, but also helped to teach the young candidate for knighthood to aim accurately another time. This was practiced on other objects, as, tilting at a tree or post or at a ring. Another military exercise was throwing the spear or javelin, which might be at the quintain or some other object or to throw it to the greatest distance. Learning to throw with the sling was also another military exercise. Another great sport in the early times of this period was that of archery. Footraces took place and likewise wrestling.

Hunting has ever been a great sport in England. The ancient Britons were hunters, as were the Saxons and also the Danes in England. But it remained for the Normans to bring hunting to a system, for they were not content to hunt in an open country, but took up thousands of acres and enclosed them in parks and stocked them with game and prohibited the common people from hunting within them, passing severe laws against such. There was a form of hunting that is most striking and became a great rage, which was hawking or falconry. This was greatly indulged in by both men and women and the birds they used for taking the

[16] Froude, History of England, I, 70.

other birds were highly trained and brought great prices. This was *the* sport of the gentility and common people were not at all allowed to partake of it. Fishing was another sport, as was horse-racing and bull-baiting and cock-fighting. Throwing at cocks was another brutal amusement, wherein a heavy stick was thrown at a bird and if knocked over it belonged to the thrower if he could run and catch it before it could get to its feet.

The people managed so as to get quite a bit of pleasure out of their religion. One pastime was the wakes. On an evening preceding a saint's day the people went with lighted candles to the church, which was originally for the purpose of worship, but later it came to be a time for dancing and singing and eating, hawkers and peddlers congregating about the church to serve the crowd. Another church affair was the church ales. The church officials would brew a large quantity of ale before a holiday when there would be gatherings of people who bought and drank the ale, the profits being used for the good of the church. Another amusement was hocking, which took place on the Monday or Tuesday following the second Sunday after Easter. Men would hold a rope across a road and take toll of every woman passing or else women would have charge of the rope and collect toll off the men, the receipts going into the church treasury. The miracle and morality plays and the like, too, though intended as a means of instruction, became really a form of amusement for the masses.

Christmas was a great time for merry-making. One of the affairs at the time was mumming. Masks were used and disguises put on so as to impersonate all kinds of people and even animals. These mummers would make calls on people and sometimes even on high personages, making their entrances and exits without saying anything. May-day was a great occasion. Upon this day the houses would be decorated with flowers and branches from trees. There would be the dance about the May-pole and many games and plays. There were fair days, when people came together for traffic and for sports. There were sack races for the young men and smock races for the young women. Also there were wheelbarrow races and other kinds of races and contests. One such contest was the grinning match, where each person in the contest would thrust his head through a horse's collar and they would then vie with one another in grinning.

In the yawning match, they would wait till late at night when all were tired and sleepy and then each would try to yawn the greatest. The one that yawned the widest and the most naturally and would thereby cause the most yawns from all present would win the prize.

It was a custom during this period for kings and great nobles to have Fools, who were the butt of all and who made all the butt of their jokes. They also kept minstrels in their households. Sometimes these minstrels played on different kinds of musical instruments and formed a musical band. Among the musical instruments were the ruible (a two-stringed instrument played with a bow), the veille (an instrument somewhat like a violin), the gitern (a kind of guitar), the harp, bagpipe, trumpet, pipe, lute, dulcimer, tambourine, and cymbals. There were a number of other kinds of entertainers, as, acrobats, rope-walkers, jugglers, contortionists, and conjurers. There was wire-dancing, rope-dancing, ballet-dancing, and sword-dancing. There were dancing bears and trained monkeys. There were entertainers who disguised themselves as birds and other animals and imitated their actions and cries. Dancing was, also, an amusement of the middle ages and it was indulged in by the nobility and all classes of the people.

There were plays acted in the castles and the towns and the colleges and the schools and even in the churches in the way of mysteries and moralities. There were strolling bands of players that attended wakes and fairs and played in barns and taverns and even in the farmhouse kitchen, wherever they might find place. "I shall transcribe out of Hall a description of a play which was acted by the boys of St. Paul's School, in 1527, at Greenwich. The occasion was the despatch of a French embassy to England, when Europe was outraged by the Duke of Bourbon's capture of Rome, when the children of Francis I. were prisoners in Spain, and Henry, with the full energy of his fiery nature, was flinging himself into a quarrel with Charles V. as the champion of the Holy See.

"At the conclusion of a magnificent supper 'the king led the ambassadors into the great chamber of disguisings; and in the end of the same chamber was a fountain, and on one side was a hawthorne tree, all of silk, with white flowers, and on the other side was a mulberry tree full of fair berries, all of silk. On the top of the hawthorne were the arms of

England, compassed with the collar of the order of St. Michael, and in the top of the mulberry tree stood the arms of France within a garter. The fountain was all of white marble, graven and chased; the bases of the same were balls of gold, supported by ramping beasts wound in leaves of gold. In the first work were gargoylles of gold, fiercely faced, with spouts running. The second conceit of this fountain was environed with winged serpents, all of gold, which griped it; and on the summit of the same was a fair lady, out of whose breasts ran abundantly water of marvellous delicious savour. About this fountain were benches of rosemary, fretted in braydes laid on gold, all the sides set with roses, on branches as they were growing about this fountain. On the benches sate eight fair ladies in strange attire, and so richly apparelled in cloth of gold, embroidered and cut over silver, that I cannot express the cunning workmanship thereof. Then when the king and queen were set, there was played before them, by children, in the Latin tongue, a manner of tragedy, the effect whereof was that the pope was in captivity and the church brought under foot. Whereupon St. Peter appeared and put the cardinal (Wolsey) in authority to bring the pope to his liberty, and to set up the church again. And so the cardinal made intercession with the kings of England and France that they took part together, and by their means the pope was delivered. Then in came the French king's children, and complained to the cardinal how the emperour kept them as hostages, and would not come to reasonable point with their father, whereupon they desired the cardinal to help for their deliverance; which wrought so with the king his master and the French king that he brought the emperour to a peace, and caused the young princess to be delivered.' " [17]

The game of dice was found in England from an early period, as the Saxons, Danes, and Normans were much given to it, and during the Middle Ages dice were in great force and much used in gambling. There were also chess and draughts and domino and backgammon. Cards came into use late in this period, perhaps not earlier than the latter part of the fourteenth century, and seem not to have been much used in England before the middle of the fifteenth century. Gambling was very common among all classes, so much so that one of the restrictions in the indenture of apprentices was

[17] Froude, History of England, I, 76-77.

that they should keep from places where gambling was carried on. Some of the guilds had to pass laws that no help would be given a member who got into trouble or fell into poverty through playing dice.

Ball-playing was engaged in during the Middle Ages, just as in all ages and in all countries. The ball was, perhaps, more of a favorite in England than in any other country in Europe. They had club-ball, one player throwing the ball and another striking it with a straight club; cambuc or bandy-ball was probably a kind of golf, as the ball was struck on the ground with a curved club, called a bandy; pall-mall must have been a kind of croquet, as a wooden ball was used which was struck with a mallet and driven through arches of iron, there being an arch at each end of the grounds; in hand-ball the ball was struck with the palms of the hands against a wall or over something, being somewhat like tennis without a racket, and then later tennis with net and racket came to be played; there was foot-ball, the ball being kicked about by the foot.

Tip cat was a game played with a piece of wood called a cat, pointed at each end much like a double cone, which was laid on the ground in the center of a large ring; the player would strike one end of the cat with a stick, causing it to fly upward, which he then tried to strike to knock it out of the ring. There was bowling, many villages having bowling-greens. They also played quoits, fox and geese, and other kinds of outdoor games.

Young people played in the games and indulged in the sports mentioned in the foregoing and children played many of them, and also they had many other sports, such as spinning tops, catching butterflies and beetles, playing blind man's buff, and the like.

**Education.** The early Christians, surrounded as they were with pagan thoughts and ideas found it necessary to withdraw themselves from such influences, and, as they were without schools of their own, they became largely illiterate, having no training beyond what was obtained through their religion. Although they received but little literary education, yet they were given moral training of the very highest and best. As the church grew there was found the necessity of instructing those who were being brought into it, as well as the young, and so there arose what were known as the catechetical schools.

These schools began more and more to come under the influence of the old pagan culture and to drift away from their original purpose of giving religious instruction and to enter more upon the intellectual side. To counteract this they were finally taken away from the laity and brought under the influence of the clergy and came to be established in connection with the churches and then these schools became to be known as cathedral schools. They then gradually grew to become used for the training of the clergy. When monasteries arose in connection with the Christian church, there grew up in them schools for the training of those who were to become monks or priests. Thus education became to be less common than under Roman civilization and the schools to be used mostly for those who were to enter more directly into the work of the church.

One of the marked characteristics of the Middle Ages was the growth of the idea of education for all classes. In the early part of the period education was not considered highly important for any one, then came the idea of education for those who were to enter into clerical duties, and then last of all began to grow up the idea of education for all, whatever the future life work might be. That classical learning in its essential features was preserved to Europe was due to the Christian church, for keeping up the use of the Latin language the churchmen were thus given access to the written works of Roman culture and through them much was retained, especially in the monasteries. While the Roman civilization was almost annihilated in the central part of the empire, the extreme eastern and western parts were relatively undisturbed and classical learning was maintained in them, Ireland being the chief center in the West, from whence later this learning was returned to the central part of Europe. There were three distinct outbursts of learning following the darkest time of the period, the first being under Charlemagne (742-814) in France and Central Europe, the second in England under Alfred the Great (849-901), and the third under the Mohammedans in Spain.

The course of study in the schools of the Middle Ages was primarily designed to train the clergy to be able to participate in the church services and also to conduct them. The instruction was given in the elementary or song school which was followed by the grammar school and then by higher instruction. In the elementary school reading, writing, music, arithmetic, and Latin were taught. In reading the beginner was taught by the alphabetic method and when reading was begun careful attention was given to enunciation and accent and often boys were taught to read well without knowing the meaning of the words of the Latin they were reading. In writing wax tablets were used in the earlier times and then there came into use pen, ink, and parchment. This was an important phase of education because of the need of copying books. Music was an important subject because of its use in the church service. Arithmetic was begun by counting and then simple operations on the fingers, adding, subtracting, multiplying, and dividing being drilled into the pupils through oral work, but little written work being done. Latin was only of an elementary form, a beginning in conversation being made. The student who went on with his studies took up the subjects of the trivium—grammar, rhetoric and dialectic. If he wished to pursue his studies further he entered into the subjects of the quadrivium—arithmetic, geometry, music, and astronomy.

There were three kinds of medieval church schools—the monastic school, the cathedral school, and the parish school. The monastic school occupied a place within the monastery and it was primarily intended for those who were to enter into monastic life; there were no charges for tuition, the school being maintained through gifts from pupils, sometimes such being quite large; the poor pupils were supported by charity or they paid their way by copying books or by doing other things. In the cathedral school there was usually a song school, for elementary instruction, and a grammar school, for those who should want more advanced education. As assistants in the smaller churches needed instruction, parish schools were established, in which there was but little training given beyond that needed for participation in the church services.

Lay education arose in this period in three ways. In the first place it came through the education and training of those intended for knighthood, as such produced standards of deportment that impressed themselves upon the upper classes in such a way that as civilization advanced and means of intercourse widened there came a need of systematic instruction so that there arose the great public schools of England and similar schools upon the continent. In the second place the growing importance of the cities in industry and commerce led to the establishment of schools for the training of the city youth, so that the burgher school was produced. Under the guild system there arose a kind of industrial education and the need of means of instruction of the young of the guild members so that guild schools were formed.

During the period following the fall of Rome, the culture and learning of Greece and Rome were almost entirely lost to central and western Europe. Only here and there was a little retained, usually in some monastery where some of the old manuscripts were stored away. Yet learning was never entirely lost, and when the Crusades arose and the people of the West came in contact with the old Greek culture in eastern Europe and with the scientific learning of the Moslems, and who brought learning again into Spain, they brought back with them a widening interest in learning. Too, as commerce grew and wealth increased there became more leisure for learning and there grew up a desire for further knowledge and, so to the education as discussed in the foregoing paragraphs there was added a still higher form, that of the university.

The university arose during the Middle Ages. In its beginning it came neither directly from church or state. The awakening of a scientific spirit and the spreading abroad of discussion through scholasticism caused to arise centers around which learned men gathered about them the young men of the times. The earliest of these were the universities of Bologna and Salerno in the twelfth century. The former was for the study of law and the latter for medicine. The University of Paris originated near the same time and in it arose the four faculties—theology, philosophy, law, medicine—which are still extant to-day in the universities. Oxford, Cambridge, Vienna, and many other universities were formed during this period.

From the very first, special privileges were conferred upon the universities by the authorities. Sometimes they were allowed to have full control of their own affairs, having their own special courts. Again those connected with the universities were exempt from military service, except in time of great need, and from paying taxes. There were a number of other privileges granted. These privileges were not always granted because of the high regard in which the university was held but sometimes they were gained by the university threatening to remove to another place and even doing this, for there were no great plants in those days demanding permanent residence as now, as professors and students were about all there was to a medieval university as the buildings usually were furnished for them and there were no great libraries or laboratories or other equipment. These privileges often led to abuses on the part of the students for many of them led dissolute lives and others became bullies and adventurers. Whatever may have been the cause, it is too true that the moral tone of the medieval university was low.

The medieval university in its organization was similar to the guild, the term signifying a company of persons that were joined together for study. There came to be a natural grouping together of the students from the same part of the world so that there arose the *nations*, and each year each nation elected a councillor, who was to be the chief to act for the nation. The university was organized into faculties, the complete number being four, of arts, law, medicine, and theology. Each faculty elected a dean, as its representative, and then deans and councillors elected the rector, the head of the university. In the South the rector was usually a student while in the North he was generally elected from the body of professors.

At first the courses offered differed in the various universities, but later the courses were fixed either by a papal decree or by the faculty. The student was not only to acquire the subject, but to be able to debate upon it. He was expected to memorize the professor's lecture and to prepare himself in debate so as to be ready to cope with students taking the other side of the question.

Usually the courses in arts were taken by the younger students as a preparation for the professional training. At first the bachelor's degree meant only that the one receiving it was granted the privilege to enter upon the work leading to the other degrees, but later it became a separate degree. Master and doctor at first were about of equal rank, and then later doctor represented a higher period of learning.

The Church Fathers were quite severe in their ideas of education. The most famous writings among them on the subject are by Saint Jerome on the education of girls, being letters to a mother. Some of the admonitions are as follows:

"Do not allow Paula to eat in public, that is, do not let her take part in family entertainments, for fear that she may desire the meats that may be served there. Let her learn not to use wine, for it is the source of all impurity. Let her food be vegetables, and only rarely fish; and let her eat so as always to be hungry.

"For myself, I entirely forbid a young girl to bathe.

"Never let Paula listen to musical instruments; let her even be ignorant of the uses served by the flute and the harp.

"Do not let Paula be found in the ways of the world (emphatic paraphrase for *streets*), in the gatherings and in the company of her kindred; let her be found only in retirement.

"Do not allow Paula to feel more affection for one of her companions than for others; do not allow her to speak with such a one in an undertone.

"Let her be educated in a cloister, where she will not know the world, where she will live as an angel, having a body but not knowing it, and where, in a word, you will be spared the care of watching over her."[18]

Whatever we may think of the foregoing, we must agree that the following advice is most wholesome:

"Do not chide her for the difficulty she may have in learning. On the contrary, encourage her by commendation, and proceed in such a way that she shall be equally sensible to the pleasure of having done well, and to the pain of not having been successful. . . . Especially take care that she do not conceive a dislike for study that might follow her into a more advanced age."[19]

There is not very much given on education of women during the medieval period. It is no doubt true that girls received even less education than did boys. During the time of chivalry the young women, like the young men, were often educated in the castle of some knight or lord, being trained in household management, music, and gentle manners. It would seem that sometimes girls had in their own homes governesses for training them. Sometimes girls and little boys were sent together to nunneries to be educated. Here and there are found references which imply that some women were well educated for their times and particularly so in languages, reading and writing and speaking English, French and Spanish. But in the main it was considered that all the training necessary for the girls was a little elementary education and such knowledge of housework and management as would fit them for wives.

[18] Compayré, History of pedagogy, 65-66.
[19] *Ibid.*, 67.

**The Children's Crusade.** Among the greatest events in medieval Europe were the Crusades, and perhaps the most striking was the Children's Crusade. This occurred in 1212 A. D., in France and Germany. The early Crusades had been successful in taking Palestine away from the Saracens and a Christian kingdom had been established with Jerusalem as its center. But at the time of the Children's Crusade, Palestine had nearly all again fallen into the hands of the Mohammedans. It is true there had been three later crusades, but they were not successful and they had for a time ceased against Palestine and had been turned against parts of Europe. One such was made on Germany, a second was against the Saracens in Spain, and a third was against the Albigenses in southern France. People became indifferent in reference to Palestine, so the church sent out chosen ones to arouse enthusiasm and to strive to bring about another Crusade. Amid such scenes arose the Children's Crusade.

Never was there at any other time such an arousing of children. All classes of children were included. Children came from the hovel of the peasant, the hut of the shepherd, the home of the merchant, and the castle of the lord. Most of them enrolled in the Crusade from religious fervor, but many went only to get away from the restraints of home. Sad it is, too, that many worthless characters, both men and women, flocked to the standard of the children. Many girls were included in this movement, but the very greater part were boys under twelve years of age. The children seemed to be filled with the fervor and nothing could restrain them. When the procession of children went along it made the others wild to join. If by any means children could be detained by their parents, they pined so that they had to be given their freedom and be allowed to join the throng.

In France the leader was Stephen of Cloyes, who at the time of the Crusade was about twelve years of age. He was the son of a poor peasant, a shepherd. When old enough, Stephen was sent out to tend sheep and for some years he spent his summers upon the plains near his home. As in other parts of Europe, so at Cloyes means were taken to arouse the people to another crusade into Palestine. Among such were processions in which was shown the condition of the Christians in Palestine and with entreaties for the people to strive to redeem the Holy Land. As with all the others, Stephen must have witnessed these scenes and have listened to the portrayals of affairs in Palestine, which he must have greatly considered while tending his sheep.

One day a stranger appeared before him and stated that he was a pilgrim from Palestine, and asked for food. Stephen fed the stranger and asked in return to be told about the Holy Land. The stranger told his stories and he must have seen that Stephen was greatly affected as he finally declared himself to be Jesus Christ and to have come to appoint Stephen to lead the children in a crusade, and gave him a letter to the king of France. Stephen at once entered into his holy mission and told his story to parents and neighbors, showed the letter he had to the king, and declared himself to be called to go forth as a leader in the Crusade.

Stephen called the children to his crusade and there flocked about him the children of his neighborhood, but he soon saw that he could not arouse the nation from this out-of-the-way place. So he determined to go to the greatest religious center in France, the city of St. Denis, the place of burial of the martyr Dionysius, whose tomb was the great shrine of the land, to which great crowds went on pilgrimages. To this place Stephen went, attired in his shepherd's dress, crook in hand, and wallet by side. He went from crowd to crowd, before the church door and in the market place, showing his letter to the king and preaching his Crusade. It was not long before he attracted attention and aroused enthusiasm in the young. The people carried news of him throughout France as they returned to their homes and the young people gathered together their fellows and returned with crowds of children to Stephen. As the numbers increased, Stephen led them through the towns and villages till he had all the children wild to join him. This did not go on without some opposition. Some of the more intelligent men, among them some from the clergy, thought it should not go on, and even the king, Philip Augustus, was in doubt about it. He asked an opinion concerning it from the University of Paris, and after due deliberation its members advised the king that the movement should be stopped even if vigorous means had to be used. The king then issued an edict, commanding the children to give up the enterprise and to return to their homes. This edict had but little effect, as the movement went right on, and the king did not dare enforce the edict.

The crowds of children gathered more and more over France and Stephen designated Vendôme as the central place in which to assemble and to get ready to depart for Palestine. This was a good selection as it was an important place and with roads coming into it from all directions. The bands of children came into Vendôme in great numbers, one chronicler stating that there were fifteen thousand children under twelve years of age from Paris alone, and although in all probabilities this is an overestimation, yet it shows there was a vast assembly of children, so much so that Vendôme could not contain them and they had to encamp outside its walls, each band to itself so that those from the same city or community were together. The children were from all parts of France, varying in language and dress, but not in zeal. Whether they all wore a uniform is not known, but they did put on the Cross of the Crusaders, made of red woolen cloth and sewed on the right shoulder of the coat by some one of the leaders, and of which emblem the children were all very proud. Finally all the bands had gathered and Stephen was ready to make the start for the sea, which was to open and let them march through to the Holy Land. The number assembled at Vendôme was about thirty thousand.

The message of the pilgrim delivered to Stephen must have come the last of April or the first of May, 1212, as it occurred shortly after Stephen had observed in the city of Chârtres the procession to commemorate the sufferings of those who had died in defense of the Holy Land and which was held on St. Mark's day, April 25th. He went to St. Deny's in the month of May and to Vendôme, perhaps, the last of May or the first of June and the start for the sea was made the last of July or the first of August, all of the same year.

And now all was ready for the departure from Vendôme. Their leader Stephen had become so great that there was provided for him a carriage, decorated with flags and tapestries of brilliant colors, and over him was a canopy of rich draperies as a protection from the heat of the sun. About his carriage was a band of youths of noble blood, on horseback, and equipped as knights, acting as his body guard. Good-byes were said and the procession, singing their songs, with flags and oriflammes, started. At the beginning of the journey Stephen was given great honor and gladly obeyed, they even vied with one another in showing him adulations and tried to secure a piece from his clothing or from the trimmings of the carriage or from the trappings of the horses which was kept as a relic and used as a charm. But as days went on and hardships and sufferings came upon them and their journey lengthened out, they became little more than a straggling crowd without order or discipline, and then Stephen's authority was no longer regarded by them. Their journey was to Blois, where they crossed the Loire, and then to Lyons, where the Rhone was crossed, and thence to Marseilles. As they were asked on the way where they were going they all answered: "To Jerusalem." This was an unusually hot summer and the children suffered greatly from heat and thirst and many of them from hunger, although the people along the way sympathized with the movement and aided them. At last they came to Marseilles. They asked for shelter in the city for the night only, as on the morrow God was to open the sea for them and they would proceed on their way to the Holy Land.

The city granted their request and the children entered the gates and went into the city, singing their songs as they marched through the streets. They passed the night and in the morning they went to the sea to go on with their journey. The sea did not open that day nor the next day nor on any day. This discouraged them and many gave up, but others remained, hoping for a way to Palestine. And a way did come, for two merchants of Marseilles, Hugo Ferreus and William Porcus, so their Latin names read, offered "for the cause of God, and without price," to provide ships for their transport. Preparations then were made, and seven ships furnished and it is estimated that about five thousand children went on board these ships to proceed on their way to Palestine. Nothing further was heard of these children who sailed from Marseilles on that August day in 1212, till in 1230, eighteen years afterward, when a priest came to Europe from Palestine and told that he was among those who were on the vessels with the children. He stated that two of the ships were wrecked off the coast of the island of San Pietro and all on board perished. The other five ships were taken to Bujeiah and Alexandria and the children were sold to the Saracens. Upon learning of this, Pope Gregory IX. had a church built on the island where the wreck occurred and had the remains of the children interred in it and named it the ECCLESIA NOVORUM INNOCENTIUM—*The Church of the New Innocents.*

The story of Stephen at St. Denys was not only carried all over France, but likewise to the neighboring countries, spreading to the Rhine provinces in Germany. It reached a village near Cologne where lived a boy who was about the same age as Stephen and by the name of Nicholas. Like Stephen he, too, was a shepherd boy, and he had heard the stories about the Crusades. When he learned about Stephen there arose a desire to do as he, and aided by his father, some say induced by him, he took upon himself the preaching of a children's crusade for Germany. He, too, had been called to the work, as he stated while with his flocks he saw a blazing cross in the sky and there came to him a voice that told him the cross was to lead him to victory in his undertaking to recover the Holy Land. Like Stephen, too, Nicholas went to a great religious center, the city of Cologne, as at this time this city was a great center for pilgrimages, as in its cathedral rested the bones of the "Three Kings of the East" who came "with a great multitude of camels to worshippe Christ, then a little childe of thirteen dayes olde," so the old legend ran.

Nicholas related his story and preached his crusade before the cathedral to the pilgrims who came to view the relics. These pilgrims carried the story of Nicholas back to their homes and there soon came a number of children to him at Cologne. He also sent out assistants to preach the crusade in different parts of the land. The excitement became even greater than in France for bands of children came into Cologne in even greater numbers than to St. Denys. This was a more mixed crowd than that of Stephen, as there were more girls and more adults and especially more lewd women, so many of these latter that the chroniclers referred to them often and attributed to them the greater part of the evils that came upon the multitude. These crusaders had a uniform, which consisted of a long gray coat, with a cross sewed upon the breast, and they wore broad brimmed hats and carried a palmer's staff. In about a month the host had gathered and was ready to start for the sea, which was to let them pass through to the Holy Land, as with the army of Stephen. But there arose a division and only a part started under the leadership of Nicholas.

Those who remained with Nicholas left Cologne for Genoa in June or July, 1212. The number that started was said to have been twenty thousand, the majority being boys under twelve years of age. Nicholas took his place at the head and at a signal the start was made, with banners flying and the singing of hymns. But this was not true of all the parents and friends, for many of them were in great distress over the leaving of their children, and they followed for some distance pleading for them to give up and return to their homes. One of the songs of this band comes down to us. Gray [20] states that an account of the discovery of this hymn may be found in a magazine, the *Evangelical Christendom* for May, 1850. and that Hecker asserts it was used by the children. It was in German, coming from Westphalia, and had been used before by Crusaders on their journey to Palestine. The English translation is as follows:

> "Fairest Lord Jesus,
> Ruler of all nature,
> Thou of Mary and of God the Son!
> Thee will I cherish,
> Thee will I honor,
> Thee my soul's glory, joy, and crown!
>
> "Fair are the meadows,
> Fairer still the woodlands,
> Robed in the blooming garb of spring;
> Jesus is fairer,
> Jesus is purer,
> Who makes our saddened heart to sing.
>
> "Fair is the sunshine,
> Fairer still the moonlight,
> And the sparkling, starry host;
> Jesus shines brighter,
> Jesus shines purer,
> Than all the angels heaven can boast."

They took their way along the Rhine, they entered into Switzerland going by way of Geneva, their route through the Alps was over Mont Cenis, entering Italy in what is now Piedmont, and from thence to Genoa. At that time the region along the Rhine was not much peopled, a feudal castle rising here and there on some prominent crag with hamlets below, but most of the way was almost a wilderness and with plenty of wild animals such as stags and boars and wolves and bears. The children suffered much, especially from lack of food and shelter. The children also were carried off by the robber barons. The children were preyed upon by the hangers-on and thieves and the degraded men and women and they were soon without control, and the band became but little more than a rabble. But their sufferings along the Rhine were quite small as compared with what took place in traversing the Alps. The trials and sufferings were so great that many

[20] Gray, The children's crusade, 78-80.

of them succumbed and a large number gave up and turned back. The summit was reached and in the monastery there they were helped with food and shelter and afforded a time to rest before going on with their journey. They went on and came into Italy where they had hoped to receive kind treatment, but instead they were treated harshly, robbed, refused entrance into the towns, seized by the lords and carried away as slaves. Finally they came to a place where they saw Genoa from a mountain and then they felt that their sufferings were over. They again recognized Nicholas as their prophet and leader and with crosses aloft, banners unfurled, and hymns sung in praise, they hurried down to the sea to enter the path that surely would be opened to them to go over to the Holy Land.

As was stated, twenty thousand started with Nicholas at Cologne, but after the hard journey of seven hundred miles, there were only seven thousand that reached Genoa in August, 1212. But these were the very best for only the strongest kept on and could endure the hardships. Like the children at Marseilles, they asked to remain in Genoa but one night as on the morrow God was to open the sea to them that they might continue on their journey. The authorities at first granted them permission to remain six or seven days but on the very same day this time was shortened to one day, as it was feared they might become lawless and again there was fear of famine, but most of all the Genoese feared the displeasure of the Pope, who at that time was in conflict with the German Emperor, and of course these children were subjects of the Emperor. The children agreed to this, as they said they wanted but one night as they would go on through the sea in the morning. The gates were then opened and the children entered and marched through the streets singing, with crosses uplifted and banners flying. The night was passed and in the morning they rushed to the seashore, but as with the other children so with these, for they waited in vain for the sea to open.

When the senate at Genoa had taken back their offer to let the children remain six or seven days and gave them permission to remain but one day, they did extend an invitation to all those who would like to make Genoa their permanent home to do so, and they would be received as citizens. At the time the offer was made it was rejected by all as they were anticipating that on the morrow the sea would open and a path would be provided for a way to Palestine. After the sea did not open, many of the children were convinced that their journey was ended and they decided to accept the offer and to remain at Genoa. There were quite a number that so decided, and they became citizens and some of the youth grew to become wealthy and prominent men and some joined themselves with patrician families, being of noble German birth, and several great families were so founded, among such being one great princely house.

Those who did not wish to remain at Genoa left on the following day after their entry. Outside the gates a council was held and they decided to go on their way by land to Palestine as far as they could. After this there was no further organization, and Nicholas is not heard of again. They went to Pisa and from here two shiploads of children set sail for the Holy Land, but there is nothing known of them further. The remnant went on to Rome and were received by the Pope who talked to them kindly and advised them to give up their march, but he held them to their vows and told them that when they reached manhood they should go forth to fight for the redemption of the Holy Sepulcher. These young people then gave up their enterprise and prepared to return home.

It is not known who was the leader of the band that separated from that one led by Nicholas. It is thought that when this band left Cologne it was as large as that which went out with Nicholas. They took a different route, going through Swabia to Switzerland and crossing the Alps at the Pass of St. Gotthard and entered Italy in Lombardy. They traversed the entire length of Italy to Brindisi. This company was composed of about the same elements as the other one and they met with even greater difficulties and hardships and became even more lawless. They were treated very badly everywhere in Italy. At Brindisi a number of them embarked on ships and sailed away for Palestine and that was the last ever heard of them.

The return of the German children was sadder than their going. In Italy, having to obtain food and clothing in any way possible, they contracted the worst of vices. So on their return they were no longer a religious throng hurrying on to save the Cross, but a rabble, with no respect for any one and no one had respect for them. Hence they were treated badly on the way back and only found a refuge when arriving each one in his own home.

This Crusade shows the great danger to which child-nature may be subjected in times of great excitement and teaches the need of the careful guarding of children from such. In this Crusade it is estimated that more than thirty thousand children never saw their homes after leaving. In all near a hundred thousand children went from their homes, leaving sixty thousand sorrowing families behind them. Perhaps not one of these children who returned home came back with the purity with which he or she started.

**Other Child-pilgrimages.** "The *second children's pilgrimage* falls only twenty-five years later; so that the assumption of a morbid excitability of the child-world at all this time appears to be justified. It was confined to the city of Erfurt, and the phenomenon was very transient, but not the less presents all the distinctive marks of a religious convulsion, and exhibited more of disease than other child-pilgrimages, as far at least as has come down to posterity. On the 15th July, 1237, there assembled, unknown to their parents, more than 1,000 children, left the town by the Löber Gate, and wandered, dancing and leaping, by the Steigerwald to Armstadt. A congress such as this, as if by agreement, resembles an instinctive impulse as in animals, when, for instance, swallows and storks collect for their migration; the same phenomenon has doubtless taken place in all children's pilgrimages, it was also remarked by eye-witnesses of the first of them, in a manner characteristic of the Middle Ages. It was not till the next day that the parents learned the occurrence, and they fetched their children back in carts. No one could say who had enticed them away. Many of them are said to have continued ill some time after, and in particular to have suffered from trembling of the limbs, perhaps also from convulsions. The whole affair is obscure, and so little account has been taken of it by contemporaries, that the chronicles only speak of the fact, and say nothing of its causes. The only probable conjecture is that the many noisy and pompous festivities connected with the canonization of St. Elizabeth, the Landgravine of Thuringia, had excited in the child-world of Erfurt this itch for devotion, which sought to relieve itself by displays of spinal activity. For this child-pilgrimage is in very near proximity to the Dancing Mania.

"Still much more obscure is a child-pilgrimage of 1458, of which the motives were quite clearly religious. It is probably, at present, almost impossible to trace the chain of ideas which occasioned it; it is enough that it was in honor of the Archangel Michael. More than 100 children from Hall, in Suabia, set out, against the will of their parents, for Mont St. Michel in Normandy. They could not by any means be restrained, and if force was employed, they fell severely ill, and some even died. The mayor, unable to prevent the journey, kindly furnished them a guide for the long journey, and an ass to carry their luggage. They are said to have actually reached the then world-renowned Abbey, and to have performed their devotions there. We have absolutely no other information of them, and it appears that this child-pilgrimage, which falls to the time when chorea was very frequent and widely spread in Germany, has excited even much less attention than the migration of the children of Erfurt in the year 1237.''[21]

## LITERATURE.

1. Abram, A., English life and manners in the later middle ages.
2. Adams, George Burton, Civilization during the middle ages.
3. Anderson, Lewis F., History of common school education.
4. Bémont, Charles, and Monod, G., Medieval Europe.
5. Bury, J. B., A history of the later Roman empire.
6. Compayré, Gabriel, A history of pedagogy.
7. Cornish, F. Ware, Chivalry.
8. Davidson, Thomas A., A history of education.
9. Davis, H. W. C., Medieval Europe.
10. Dean, Amos, The history of civilization.
11. Donaldson, James, Woman: Her position and influence in ancient Greece and Rome and among the early Christians.
12. Emerton, Ephraim, Medieval Europe.
13. Finck, Henry F., Romantic love and personal beauty.
14. Froude, James Anthony, History of England from the fall of Wolsey to the death of Elizabeth.
15. Garnier, Russell M., Annals of the British peasantry.
16. Graves, Frank Pierrepont, A history of education, During the middle ages.
17. Gray, George Zabriskie, The children's crusade.

[21] Hecker, Epidemics of the middle ages, 353.

18. Guizot, Francis Pierre Guillaume, General history of civilization in Europe.
19. Hallam, Henry, View of the state of Europe during the middle ages.
20. Hecker, J. F. C., The epidemics of the middle ages.
21. Laurie, S. S., The rise and early constitution of universities.
22. Lacroix, Paul, Manners, customs, and dress during the middle ages.
23. Letourneau, Ch., The evolution of marriage.
24. Michaud, Joseph François, The history of the crusades.
25. Mullinger, J. B., The schools of Charles the Great.
26. Neal, Daniel, The history of the Puritans.
27. Payne, George Henry, The child in human progress.
28. Rait, Robert S., Life in the medieval university.
29. Sheldon, Henry D., Student life and customs.
30. Thwing, Charles Franklin, The family.
31. Traill, H. D., Social England.

## CHAPTER XII

#### THE CHILD IN EARLIER UNITED STATES

**Customs Relating to Land.** The settlers in the United States brought with them many of their old-world customs and some of these early customs relating to land seem to us now most curious. Society has ever been influenced by the manner of holding, transferring, and inheriting land, and this all the more in a new country and especially where greatly influenced by customs and laws transferred from other countries.

One very old and peculiar custom was brought over from England and used by the first colonists. This was the transferring of land under the old ceremony of the *livery of seizin*, a feudal ceremony. When land was being sold, the owner would stand upon it and he would pluck a twig from the tree or bush and place it in the hand of the purchaser, or he would take a small piece of the turf and stick a twig in it and give over to the purchaser. If a house was sold, the owner would take hold of the ring or latch of the door and formally give over the house to the purchaser.

In Virginia once every four years between Easter and Whit Sunday, the owner of a piece of ground had to go over the boundary and renew the marks, and when a piece of land had been thus traced three times, the right to possess it by the owner was never afterward disputed. Another custom was feudal in its nature. The land of the new country was given out in grants by the King and the owners acknowledged allegiance to him and paid annual dues and these proprietors established a system of land-tenure in which they let out the land, and an annual due was always expected. This was sometimes paid in money and again in produce from the land, sometimes being a very small amount, just sufficient to show acknowledgment of feudal service, it might be a few pounds of butter or a couple of loads of wood or a pair of chickens. In Virginia the first tenants were little better than villains of feudal times, as when they received land they were bound to remain seven years on it and to pay one-half of the whole produce as rent.

In New England and also in some parts of New York and New Jersey, there was the custom of holding land in common—upland, meadow, and woodland were apportioned out for use to the different members of the community. The church was a great binding force among them, so that the meeting-house was the center about which the people settled, and they were kept all the more closely together by the hostile savages.

But in a new country where land was plentiful and easy to obtain and laws difficult of enforcement, the customs of an old and thickly peopled country could not long hold, and particularly so if unsuited to the needs of the new country. Yet such were enduring enough in this country as to have wielded quite an influence.

**The People.** Only a fringe along the eastern part of this country was settled at this time. Too, this part was not all peopled by the same nationality as there were English, Dutch, Swede, German, and French, and there was not much if any mixing among them. When all this territory came under England, then there was more intercommunication but not even then a great deal on account of the difficulties of travel. There, too, grew up quite a distinction between the people of the northern part and those of the southern part. The southern part was much better suited for cultivation under the systems of that time and it became a farming community, with large farms and the people were not close together and there were not many towns and cities. In the northern part farming could not be carried on nearly so successfully, and so manufacturing and commerce grew, both of which demanded that people should live in towns and cities. The separation of the people in the South and the wealth obtained through agriculture made them most generous and hospitable. In the North and especially in New England the hard struggle for maintenance and the living together in communities narrowed the people, till there was a selfishness displayed by each town for its own. In the South strangers were welcome and really wanted as there often was not great opportunity for the people being much together or of learning of outside affairs, so that the stranger could tell them of the doings of the outside world and thus give entertainment for hospitality. In New England, especially among the early people, there grew up a suspicion of all newcomers and particularly strangers, and often it went so far that a stranger could not acquire property in a town and so could not gain a legal residence. It went yet further in some places, for the people of a town were not encouraged even to have their relatives from outside visit them.

"The primitive land systems lasted long enough to exert a considerable influence upon the people. If we consider extreme examples this becomes evident. The inhabitant of the town community was trained to association with his fellows. Measures were taken to promote village life; laws were made in Connecticut, in 1650, against consolidating house-lots, and the dwellers in Andover were forbidden to live upon their plow-land, lest their hogs and cattle should injure the common meadows. Artisans were secured by the community. Newark, for example, reserved a lot for the miller, another for the town's tailor, another for the boatman, and so on. A town in one case kept a flock of sheep for the public benefit. The habit of coöperation promoted voluntary associations. We find one New England mill owned by seven shareholders, another by thirteen, and a third by fourteen. The towns in New England and New York made by-laws, and regulated their internal concerns in field and town meetings. The system was productive of no end of petty wrangling and neighborhood feuds, but it cultivated a democratic feeling and taught each man to maintain his right.

"On the other hand, the Southern planter lived in some isolation, but his public interests were as extensive as his county or his province. This state of society begot self-reliance, and produced more leading statesmen than the other; but the people lacked the New England cohesion and susceptibility to organization, without which the statesmanship of the Revolution would have been in vain. The Southerner, from his isolation and from other causes, became hospitable, eager for society, and in general spontaneously friendly and generous; the New England people became close-fisted and shrewd in trade, it is a trait of village life. But the benevolence of New England was more effective than that of the South, because it was organized and systematic. The village life of the extreme North trained the people to trade, and led to commercial development; and it made popular education possible. The sons of the great planters at the South were averse to commerce; they were also the most liberally educated and polished in manners of all the colonists; but the scattered common people could have no schools, and were generally rude and ignorant, even when compared with the lower class of New Englanders, who stood a chance of getting some rough schooling, besides a certain education from the meeting-house and the ever-recurring town debates."[1]

**Slavery.** In 1619 the first negroes were brought to the colonists. They were carried to Jamestown by a Dutch ship and fourteen of them were bought by the people and remained at Jamestown. They were kept as slaves and their work proved so profitable that more were brought in and this continued till there were quite a number in the colonies. Not only in Virginia, but in all the colonies, both North and South, slaves from Africa were used. At the beginning of the eighteenth century, the colonies tried to put a check on the slave-trade but it had proved so profitable to the English ship owners who carried on the traffic in African slaves, that the mother-country favored them and would not allow laws of the colonies against the slave trade to be enforced.

For a long time but a few women were brought over in the slave ships and many of the slaves were from wild tribes in Africa and so they were fierce and dangerous. They committed many crimes and were severely punished. Some of the punishments were most cruel, as the hanging in chains, and burning. Other punishments were whipping, cropping the ears, hamstringing, branding in the face, and slitting the nose. As slavery could be much more profitably used in the South, there were, of course, more negroes taken there, and so it was the home of much of the cruel treatment. But the North had it share in such, as is shown in the following quotations:

"In colonies where the statutes did not warrant extraordinary penalties on slaves, the administration of law went to the limit of severity. In Massachusetts hanging was the worst penalty for murder, but the obsolete common-law punishment specially assigned to women who were guilty of petty treason was revived in 1755, in order to burn alive a slave-woman who had killed her master in Cambridge; earlier still the old *lex talionis* had been put in force, that a negro woman might die by fire in Boston for arson causing death. In New

[1] Eggleston, Social conditions in the colonies, Century magazine, VI, 852.

Jersey, even in that part of the province in which Quakerism should have softened the spirit of the people, negroes were burned in many instances. New York, without the excuse of serious danger—for her negroes were not more than a sixth of the population—had a code barely less fierce than that of South Carolina, where the multitude of the slaves was a perpetual danger to the whites. Some of the revolting penalties inflicted on slaves in New York with the sanction of law-courts are striking proofs of the small advance the men of that time had made from positive barbarism."[2]

"Though in the beginning he refused to harbor or tolerate negro-stealers, the Massachusetts Puritan of that day, enraged at the cruelty of the savage red men, did not hesitate to sell Indian captives as slaves to the West Indies. King Phillip's wife and child were thus sold and there died. Their story was told in scathing language by Edward Everett. In 1703 it was made legal to transport and sell in the Barbadoes all Indian male captives under ten, and Indian women captives. Perhaps these transactions quickly blunted whatever early feeling may have existed against negro slavery, for soon the African slave-trade flourished in New England, as in Virginia, Newport being the New England center of the Guinea trade. From 1707 to 1732 a tax of three guineas a head was imposed in Rhode Island on each negro imported—on 'Guinea blackbirds.' It would be idle to dwell now on the cruelty of that horrid traffic, the sufferings on board the slavers from lack of room, of food, of water, of air. But three feet three inches was allowed between decks for the poor negro, who, accustomed to a free, out-of-door life, thus crouched and sat through the passage. No wonder the loss of life was great. It was chronicled in the newspapers and letters of the day in cold, heartless language that plainly spoke the indifference of the public to the trade and its awful consequence. I have never seen in any Southern newspapers advertisements of negro sales that surpass in heartlessness and viciousness the advertisement of our New England newspapers of the eighteenth century. Negro children were advertised to be given away in Boston, and were sold by the pound as was other merchandise. Samuel Pewter advertised in the *Weekly Rehearsal* in 1737 that he would sell horses for ten shillings pay if the horse sale were accomplished, and five shillings if he endeavored to sell and could not; and for

[2] Eggleston, Social conditions in the colonies, Century magazine, VI, 863.

negroes '*sixpence a pound* on all he sells, and a reasonable price if he does not sell.' "[3]

The Dutch of New Netherlands had negro slaves but it would seem they differed from the English colonists in that they treated their slaves with kindness. Masters were placed under bonds and they were not permitted to whip their slaves without authorization from the government.

When more slave-women were brought in and negro families were established, the slaves became less fierce and more willing to accept their lot. Too, the children born to them learned to use the English language as their own and took up the ways of their masters and families and the old savage doings were for the most part forgotten. Cruelty to the slaves then decreased and new and less cruel laws were made for their government and control or the old laws and barbarous punishments were not enforced or used against them. The revolutionary movement did a great deal toward giving the negroes a better legal standing. This was particularly true in reference to free negroes and Indians, for many of the discriminations against them were abolished.

**Servants.** With the settlement of this country, there came a great need for laborers. As was given in the foregoing, the slave trade arose and negroes were brought over and sold as slaves, and also Indians taken in war were used as slaves. But these sources were not sufficient to meet the demand for laborers and this caused the importation of white help from Europe. These people were brought to America and bound out for a term of service, which, before 1650, was sometimes as long as ten years and often for seven or eight years, and then the time was made four or five years for all the colonies. These people were of three classes—those who because of debt in the old country or of poverty or from other causes bound themselves out for a term of years in which they were to pay their way, and were known as "redemptioners"; the second kind were those who had been trapped or induced to go on board ship and then carried off to America, and were known as "kids"; and the third class were criminals, convicted and transported for crime.

In the first class, the redemptioners, were found English laborers who bound themselves to service in America, hoping thereby to better their condition. Men and women in domestic trouble, men having wives with whom they could not or

[3] Earle, Customs and fashions in old New England, 88-89.

would not live and women having unbearable husbands, placed themselves in this number. Men who were in debt and threatened with imprisonment sold themselves out to save themselves. Beside these there were many others who wished to go to America, but did not have the funds for the passage, who bound themselves out for service and thus secured the passage and a place for work, with the opportunity to redeem themselves within four years.

The second class, "kids," were obtained through people who were called "spirits." These parties had been engaged in spiriting away men who were turned over to the military authorities to become soldiers, and when the demand for laborers for America became such as to offer opportunities for great profit, these "spirits" turned their trade into procuring people to satisfy this want of the new county. These men were particularly active in kidnapping children. Among a shipload of such children offered for sale in Boston one day in 1730, there was a boy who had sailed from America with his uncle who was the captain of the ship. The uncle died at sea and the mate and crew sold the boy to a transport-ship which was passing them bound for this country. The boy served out his term and later became an officer in the wars with the Indians. One noteworthy case was that of James Annesley, son and heir of Lord Altham. When thirteen years of age he was taken from Dublin, at the instigation of his uncle, and carried to America and he served twelve years of bondage in Pennsylvania. After this service he returned to his native land and brought suit to recover his father's titles and estates. This suit was successful but it was appealed to the House of Lords and the young man died before the decision was reached.

Not only were criminals that were convicted sent to America, but when a man was on trial for a small crime the officers of the court would make him believe that he would suffer severe punishment, perhaps hanging, so that he would beg for transportation. Then these prisoners were sold and the money would be kept by the officers. They even went further, for innocent persons were arrested and condemned that they might be sold into the colonies. However strong were the needs of the colonists for laborers, yet they did not want these convicts and protested against their coming in. Some of the colonial assemblies passed laws against such importation but England would not accept such laws as this course afforded too good a way of getting rid of criminals. "The hardest words said against the mother country in colonial prints, a quarter of a century before the Revolution, sprang from the bitter resentment excited by this practice of forcing criminals on the plantations in spite of their utmost endeavor to keep them out. One of the most pungent newspaper writers of the time compared England to a father seeking to spread the plague among his children, or emptying filth upon their table; and Franklin proposed to send a present of rattlesnakes for the king's garden, as a fit return for the convicts out of English jails."[4]

Not only were English laborers sent to the colonies, but also great numbers of Germans were got to sell themselves, sailing from Dutch ports to Philadelphia. Some of these Germans were of such a saving turn that though they had sufficient funds to pay their fare to America, they preferred to sell themselves out for a number of years in order to get free transportation. Others would pay half their fare, while still others would pay their passage by selling some of their children to service during their minority. As the country developed out from Philadelphia, these Germans with others would be taken out in droves of fifty or more by the "souldrivers," men who would peddle them out to those needing such service. Also there were a large number of Irish imported.

The colonists themselves helped to meet the demand for help, as they would sell the town-poor out to the lowest bidder, the one who would agree to take the least from the town for their support. They, too, sold the criminals into service to work out their sentences. Children from the almshouses were likewise bound out for a term of service. Beside all these kinds of help, there were servant-girls and serving-men, sometimes from well-to-do families, and this was particularly true before there were so many slaves and bondsmen sent into the colonies from over the sea.

The laborers that were brought into the colonies from Europe were not altogether the most desirable persons. Even if not from the criminal classes they were too often people not of great account in their old homes and they carried to their new homes the elements that made them shiftless and

[4] Eggleston, Social conditions in the colonies, Century magazine, VI, 856.

continued so to keep them. Too, they were often a source of moral corruption, the degradation of the women-servants being a continued source of evil. The thrifty New Englanders complained a great deal about these servants, as being lazy and trifling and of a thieving and lying disposition, anything than worthy help. Too, there were many runaways. Yet among these there were many who were valuable and of good disposition and upright in character. This class gave to this country some families of honorable distinction. As women were scarce in the new country, many of these bondmaids married those who purchased them or married into their families. The larger part of these people, when their time of bondage was completed, entered into the class of small farmers or free laborers. There was another element that pushed out across the frontier of settlements to get away from law and civilization and built up centers where lawlessness has ever prevailed. Still others became the ancestors of shiftless and pauper and criminal families which prevail in different sections of this country, both North and South.

It is surprising at the number of bond-servants that were in the colonies. They were used in all kinds of business and it seemed impossible to do without them. It is stated that in Virginia in 1670 there were six thousand English servants and but two thousand negroes. When it is considered that these bondmen served but for four years, the importations must have been great to keep up the numbers.

When there were not a great number of bond-servants, they became well known to the families with whom they lived and they were well treated and well cared for. As the numbers increased, and especially when convicts and other evil characters were brought in, the treatment changed and often was quite cruel. As flogging was one of the main punishments of the world at that time, it was greatly used in the colonies, the servants being whipped naked with hickory rods and then rubbed with brine. There were also other ways of punishment, one being the use of thumb-screws.

The sick servant, too, might not be cared for, especially if quite ill and likely to die, as he was not considered worth the physician's bill. Often the slaves were treated better than the servants, for the slaves were property while the servants were freed at the end of four years. Later laws were enacted in the colonies for the protection of the servants and cruel punishments prohibited. There were plenty of instances of fair treatment of servants by masters and sometimes even they were treated quite kindly and generously.

**The Home.** When the first colonists came to America, they were poorly equipped for preparing dwelling places for themselves. There were plenty of trees for boards, abundance of clay for brick, limestone in plenty for plaster and mortar, and rocks of all kinds for building purposes, but the settlers did not possess implements with which to put these natural materials into forms for their use. Consequently they lived at first in primitive fashion. Some would take for their home the dense foliage of a tree, living under its protection, while others dwelt in hollow trees. Some made for themselves caves, by digging into a bank or hill, supporting the sides with brush and poles, and covering it with poles over which were laid sod or bark or rushes.

It was natural for the early settlers to imitate the dwellings of the native inhabitants, and so wigwams were used by them. They made them of bark or of plaited rush or grass mats or of deerskin, all placed over a frame, or even they might simply pile brush about the frame, and in the far South these frames were covered with layers of palmetto leaves. In the Middle and Southern states, with their milder climate, these wigwams sometimes were left open on one side—the "half-face camp"—the fire being built in front of the opening. Sometimes this half-face camp was made more substantial by being built of logs, and again in some cases it was only a booth, with sides and roof of palmetto leaves.

The early settler did have one implement which became wonderfully useful to him, which was the ax. He soon learned to use this in making for himself and family a more permanent dwelling-place, the log cabin. At first the log cabin was of round logs, notched at the ends, and fitted together at the corners, roofed with logs or with bark on poles, having a door of rough slabs and hung on wooden hinges or straps of hide, and if a window, with a shutter similar to the door, and without floor or loft. Then came a floor of rough puncheons hewn out with ax and the cracks between the logs were chinked with pieces of wood and daubed over with clay. A chimney was made at one end out of sticks of wood with ends crossed and held together with clay and well plastered inside with clay, called in New England, a "katted" chimney. It was not very long till better houses were built. The logs were hewn and squared, clapboards were made for covering, and oiled paper was used in the windows. Then came the use of boards and stone and brick and plaster and nails and, later, paint and glass, and some substantial houses were built. There grew up a style of home for the different parts of the country, corresponding to the needs of each section and, no doubt, aided by imitation of the old country, as, in the South, in Pennsylvania and neighboring parts of New Jersey and Delaware, with the Dutch in New York and in New England.

The most notable Southern home was that of the wealthy planter, which would seem to have been fashioned somewhat after the old English manor. This Southern home was in a spacious home-lot or yard, with a large lawn in front and usually with fine trees about it. There was a large, pretentious house, the home of the owner, and grouped about it were more or fewer smaller buildings, as, kitchen, overseer's house, negro cabins, stable, coach-house, hen-house, smoke-house, dove-cote, milk-room, tool-house, brew-house, spinning-house, and not far away, a cider-house.

The Quakers and Germans of Pennsylvania and neighboring parts were quite different people from the Southerners and lived quite a different life. The manor style of home did not exist with them. The country houses were substantial but not pretentious, made of hewed logs and some of stone or brick, while the barns were large, sometimes vast. By each house was a clay oven and nearby a smoke-house. There was usually a small building enclosing a spring, known as the spring house, for caring for the milk and butter and other things during warm weather. Often there was no shade about the dwelling-house, being open to the sun.

In New York the homes took the form of those the Dutch were used to back in Holland. The houses were built near the sidewalk with the gable-end to the street, the top of the gable showing in corbel-steps. They were built of brick, or at least the gable-ends were, imported from Holland, and the date of erection and the owner's initials were shown by bricks of different colors from the others. The roof was quite steep and at first thatched but later tiles were used, and with a metal gutter projecting well out into the street. There was a weather-vane at the top of the house, which might have been a horse, lion, goose, or fish, but the prevailing fashion was a rooster. The front door was usually divided in the middle horizontally, making an upper and a lower half, hung on leather hinges and, later on, heavy iron hinges, and in the upper half were placed two bull's-eyes of heavy greenish glass. Often the front door had a knocker of iron or brass. The Dutch farmhouse was similar to the town house, as described above, but the cellar was built more carefully as it was necessary to be cool in summer and warm in winter to care for the great supply of food that was stored in it. After the English came to New York, the Dutch styles were changed to English styles and the houses of the landed gentry became quite similar to those of the Southern planters.

After the primitive sheltering as described in the first paragraphs under this section, "The Home," the people of New England built log houses, as in the other colonies, and for near a half century, there was scarcely any house larger than a cottage. These houses were thatched and had the katted chimneys. Oiled paper was used for admitting light, glass coming into use later. Paint was not used at all at first and very little used for quite awhile, either without or within the house.

After half a century, particularly in the older settlements in New England, they began to build larger houses—many of two stories and also an attic story. In building these the second story was made to project a foot or two out over the first story and the attic story also projected out over the second story, which was like their old homes in England. Later came another form of house, which was almost peculiar to New England. In this the house was two and a half stories in front, with a sharp gable, then with a long slope back to a low story. The low back part of the house was called the "lean-to" or *linter*. A later style of house was that with the gambrel roof, in which the upper part of the roof was of a rather flat slope and then there was a change to quite a steep slope for the lower part of the roof. There was usually a chimney in the center of these larger houses, of whatever style of house, made of stone or brick. "Some of the dwellings of the rich were very commodious; the house of Eaton, the first governor of New Haven colony, had nineteen fire-places, and that of Davenport, the first minister of New Haven, had thirteen."[5]

In the very early times of the colonists there was but little furniture in their homes and that of the rudest kind. As wealth came to them and their houses grew in size and splen-

[5] Eggleston, The colonists at home, Century magazine, VII, 877.

dor, the furniture increased in amount and value. The following well portrays this.

"The inventories of the household effects of many of the early citizens of New York might be given, to show the furnishings of these homes. I choose the belongings of Captain Kidd to show that 'as he sailed, as he sailed' he left a very comfortable home behind him. He was, when he set up housekeeping with his wife Sarah in 1692, not at all a bad fellow, and certainly lived well. He possessed these handsome and abundant house furnishings:

One dozen Turkey work chairs.
One dozen double-nailed leather chairs.
Two dozen single-nailed leather chairs.
One Turkey worked carpet.
Three suits of curtains and valances.
Four bedsteads.
Ten blankets.
One glass case.
One dozen drinking-glasses.
Four tables.
One oval table.
Three chests of drawers.
Four looking-glasses.
Four feather beds, bolsters, and pillows.
Two dressing boxes.
One close stool.
One warming pan.
Two bed pans.
Three pewter tankards.
Four kettles.
Two iron pots.
One skillet.
Three pairs of fire irons.
One pair of andirons.
Three chafing dishes.
One gridiron.
One flesh fork.
One brass skimmer.
Four brass candlesticks.
Two pewter candlesticks.
Four tin candlesticks.
One brass pestle.
One iron mortar.
Five carpets or rugs.
One screen frame.
Two stands.
One desk.
2½ dozen pewter plates.
Five pewter basins.
Thirteen pewter dishes.
Five leather buckets.
One pipe Madeira wine.
One half-pipe Madeira wine.
Three barrels pricked cider.
Two pewter salt-cellars.
Three boxes smoothing irons.
Six heaters.
One pair small andirons.
Three pairs tongs.
Two fire shovels.
Two fenders.
One spit.
One jack.
One clock.
One coat of arms.
Three quilts.

Parcel linen sheets, table cloths, napkins, value thirty dollars.
One hundred and four ounces silver plate, value three hundred dollars.''*

The floors were not carpeted in colonial times till late in the period, and, really, a carpet in those days was not to place on a floor but it was a cover for a table or cupboard. Sometimes sand was placed over the parlor floor and marked off

* Earle, Colonial days in Old New York, 102-103.

into ornamental figures. The walls of the rooms were wainscoted and painted. In some of the houses of the wealthy, there were hung on the walls rich cloths and tapestries and sometimes leathern hangings and in later times there were paper-hangings of strong and heavy material. The ceilings were usually left entirely open, showing the beams and rafters, often rough hewn. Prints were placed on the walls, beings pictures of ships, battle scenes, and the like, and there were paintings, usually portraits of ancestors.

Cupboards were found in all the houses and they were of various kinds and sizes, to fit into different places and for many uses. One parlor piece was a kind of writing-desk, the scrutaire, spelled in many ways in old inventories and at present time secretary. There were tables of many kinds. There were dressers and dressing-glasses in frames of walnut and olive-wood and with gilt and japanned frames. The chest was an indispensable piece of furniture and there were all kinds and sizes and of different woods and some had most beautiful carvings and inlayings. These chests were greatly needed for each household had an abundance of household linen and many a goodly quantity of silver. The time was told by means of sun-dials and hour-glasses, but there were also numbers of watches and clocks among the colonists and later there were all kinds of clocks for sale.

Chairs were in use very little, if at all, in early colonial days, as stools and benches took their place. Later chairs were greatly in use and of many kinds. There were three general kinds—turned chairs, in which the seats were often of flags and rushes; wainscot chairs, being all of wood, including backs and seats; and covered chairs, sometimes covered with leather and again with rich cloths, velvets, etc. Cane chairs were not introduced into the colonies till quite a late period.

The one piece of furniture that more than any other was a distinguishing mark of class was the bed, which graded from none at all in the cabin of the very poor to the great bed of state in the parlor of the very wealthy. There was, sometimes from poverty, sometimes from other causes, no bed in the house of a colonist, all sleeping on the floor, usually though, having placed on it deer, buffalo, or bear skins. Sometimes a pallet of bed-clothing was spread on the floor. In other homes there was but one bed for the father and mother, the rest of the family sleeping on the floor. Sometimes the bed was nothing more than a wooden box with bedding on it. The primitive fashion of sleeping on the floor might have occurred in any or all of the homes of the very early settlers and especially so when they lived in caves and wigwams and under trees, but it was not very long till beds were brought in from Europe or made in this country and there became a great variety in style and price.

The trundle-bed was used, being pushed under a high bedstead in the daytime. There were sometimes two standing and two trundle beds in one room. A common form of bed in the early times of the colonists was one that was built into an alcove or recess in a room, somewhat like a bench, with doors about it, which were kept closed to shut the bed off from view when not being used. Another form of bed was the slawbank. The slawbank was a frame with a cord bottom, fastened to the wall of the room on one side with hinges and on the other side having two legs to hold it up from the floor. When not in use this bed could be pulled up and hooked against the wall and there were closet-like doors to shut it in or curtains to drop down over it to hide it from view. The bed of all beds was the state-bed, the household idol, kept in the parlor, and not even shown to vulgar eyes and used only on very rare occasions. This was a great carved four-poster, very costly, with richly embroidered coverlets and hangings of brilliant hues.

There was no lack of bedding after the early struggles, as there were good feather beds with coverlets of all kinds, an abundance of linen sheets, and also flannel sheets were used, but cotton sheets were not plentiful. There were bolsters and pillows and coverings for them. "Such poor people in the colonies as had tastes too luxurious to enjoy a deerskin on the hearth were accustomed to fill their bed-sacks and pillows with fibrous mistletoe, the down of the cat-tail flag, or with feathers of pigeons slaughtered from the innumerable migrating flocks. The cotton from the milkweed, then called 'silkgrass,' was used for pillows and cushions. In the houses of the prosperous, good feather and even down beds were in use. The Pennsylvania German smothered and roasted himself between two of these even in summer nights and sometimes without sheets or pillows." [7]

The furniture of those early days was usually set up from the floor on legs, as, chests of drawers, dressing-cases, side-

[7] Eggleston, The colonists at home, Century magazine, VII, 877.

boards, and the like were often a foot off the floor, so that they could be thoroughly swept under. Cooking utensils, too, were often set on feet, such as pots, kettles, gridirons, skillets, and the other sorts, which was for the purpose of placing them above the coals and ashes of the open fireplace.

The early dining-table was a board placed on trestles, which was called a table-board. As boards were quite scarce, often these table-boards were made from boxes and chests which came from England containing goods. It was not long, however till there were tables of different kinds. One kind, called a drawing-table, had leaves so that it could be extended, a kind of extension-table. Another kind had flaps at either end which could be turned down on hinges or held up by means of brackets. There was another kind in which by the use of hinges the top could be fixed for a table or turned about to form the back of a chair. Usually a long, narrow bench, without a back, was used with the table-board instead of stools or chairs, and the children did not always get to use this bench as they often had to stand behind the older people while eating.

As the table was called a table-board so the table-cloth was called a board-cloth. Although the table-cloth might have been coarse it was bleached out as white as any at present and later there were quite a variety imported from the old country. Napkins were in plenty, as many or more were in use as at present. The principal article on the table was the trencher, which ordinarily was a block of wood about a foot square and three or four inches thick and hollowed out in the middle into a sort of bowl. Into this the food was placed—porridge, meat, vegetables, etc.—and two people ate from one trencher, or there was a trencher for each person if the family were quite extravagant in their ways. The next important article was the salt-cellar, which was set in the center of the table and quality folks were seated "above the salt," that is, toward the end where sat the host and hostess. The abundance of napkins may be accounted for by the fact that forks were not known to the early colonists. Spoons were in general use and took the place of forks, as most of the food was prepared for the use of the spoon. Porringers, little shallow dishes with handles, were in great use and especially by the children, and there was a kind, often without a handle, called a posnet.

The cooking of the early times was done in fireplaces.

There were various kinds of utensils for cooking, as pots, kettles, gridirons, skillets, toasting-forks, frying-pans, and the like. A very important utensil was the Dutch oven, with which was used a long-handled shovel, the peel or slice, for placing the food to be cooked well within the oven. One important function of cooking was the proper roasting of meats. At the first the roast was suspended from a string over the fire, the string being given an occasional twist, usually the task of a child. Then there was invented a metal suspensory machine, which had clockwork to turn the roast regularly. Also the turnspit dog was introduced into the colonies, this dog being trained to work in a revolving cylinder and thus keep the roast turning before the fire.

Many of the articles for the table were made of wood, such as trenchers, tankards, bottles, cups, and dishes. The shells of cocoanuts were made into goblets and dippers and often mounted in pewter and sometimes even in silver. Horn was used for spoons and drinking-cups. Pitchers, bottles, drinking-cups and jugs were made of leather, which sometimes were tipped with silver. Gourds were used for drinking-cups and dippers. There were very few tin vessels among the colonists and even iron was not so greatly in use, being used for andirons and pots and pans and some other vessels. There were brass and copper pots and kettles, which were quite costly and highly prized by the owners and well cared for. Silver was not greatly in use and yet quite a number of the families had silver spoons and others also had silver drinking-cups, salt-cellars, candle-sticks, and other kinds of silver vessels. Pewter was *the* metal of the colonists. Much of the tableware was made of this metal and found in each household. There were spoons and plates and dishes and cups and porringers and many other vessels of pewter. Often a family prided itself on having a full pewter set and would keep it as bright and shining as they would silverware, if they had such. A good thing about pewter was that when dishes and plates became worn they could easily be recast into new pewter spoons. Glass was but little in use among the early colonists, perhaps nothing beyond bottles, which though were of different shapes and kinds and the glass was of a very coarse, poor quality. Little chinaware, if any at all, was found among the early colonists, and this, perhaps, only among the Dutch settlers. Later, china was brought in and it increased in use till in Revolutionary times it became to be common and to take the place of pewter. In the earlier times there were some vessels of stoneware, such as drinking-jugs.

The colonial houses were heated by means of fireplaces and in the kitchen the fireplace was also used for cooking. Some of these fireplaces were very large, "sometimes wide enough to drive a cart and horses between the jambs. . . . Logs were sometimes drawn on to the ample hearth by a horse."[8] "In the old Phillips farmhouse at Wickford, Rhode Island, is a splendid chimney over twenty feet square."[9] As fuel grew scarce, sometimes these fireplaces were made smaller by closing them up in part and building a "little chimney" within them. For holding the fuel in the fireplace were andirons, which sometimes were of three sizes to hold logs at different heights, and there were fire-dogs or creepers, which were smaller than the andirons and were placed between them. In the kitchen fireplace there also were cob-irons, on which were hooks to hold the spit and dripping-pan, and a crane or chain with pot-hooks to hold kettles. In Pennsylvania the Germans had stoves. While the English colonial house would have two chimneys, one at either end and with a fireplace in each, the German house would have a single chimney in the middle and use stoves. These stoves were of different kinds. One kind was built from the outer wall into the house, with the opening for feeding the stove on the outside of the house and the back of the stove inside the house. In the second story they sometimes had drums, connected with the stoves, for heating the rooms there. Stoves were later introduced into the other colonies, and especially so as fuel became scarce. In 1742 Benjamin Franklin brought out his "New Pennsylvania Fireplace," a rather complicated affair, in which both wood and coal could be used, and which later grew into the form now known as the "Franklin Stove." As the bedrooms of the colonists were freezing cold in winter, a warming-pan was used to heat up the bed before getting into it for the night. The warming-pan was round, about a foot wide and four or five inches deep, with a perforated metal top and a long wooden handle. This was filled with hot coals from the fireplace and placed between the bed-linen and moved rapidly about for warming without scorching the bedding. Wood, of course, was very plentiful at first and it was used quite freely, the immense

[8] Eggleston, The colonists at home, Century magazine, VII, 879.
[9] Earle, Home life in colonial days, 68.

fireplaces consuming vast quantities of it. As the forests disappeared and wood became scarce, especially in the towns, coal was brought from across the ocean as it sometimes was found to be cheaper when used with stoves than was the wood.

"The discomfort of a colonial house in winter-time has been ably set forth by Charles Francis Adams in his 'Three Episodes of Massachusetts History.' Down the great chimneys blew the icy blasts so fiercely that Cotton Mather noted on a January Sabbath, in 1697, as he shivered before 'a great Fire, that the Juices forced out at the end of short billets of wood by the heat of the flame on which they were laid, yett froze into ice on their coming out.' Judge Sewall wrote, twenty years later, 'An Extraordinary Cold Storm of Wind and Snow. Bread was frozen at Lord's Table. . . . Though 'twas so Cold yet John Tuckerman was baptized. At six o'clock my ink freezes so that I can hardly write by a good fire in my Wives Chamber'—and the pious man adds (we hope in truth) 'Yet was very Comfortable at Meeting.' Cotton Mather tells, in his pompous fashion, of a cold winter's day four years later. ' 'Tis Dreadful cold, my ink glass in my standish is froze and splitt in my very stove. My ink in my pen suffers a congelation.' If sitting-rooms were such refrigerators, we cannot wonder that the chilled colonists wished to sleep in beds close curtained with heavy woolen stuffs, or in slaw-bank beds by the kitchen fire.

"The settlers builded as well as they knew to keep their houses warm; and while the vast and virgin forests supplied abundant and accessible wood for fuel, Governor Eaton's nineteen great fireplaces and Parson Davenport's thirteen, could be well filled; but by 1744 Franklin could write of these big chimneys as the 'fireplace of our fathers'; for the forests had all disappeared in the vicinity of the towns, and the chimneys had shrunk in size. Sadly did the early settlers need warmer houses, for, as all antiquarian students have noted, in olden days the cold was more piercing, began to nip and pinch earlier in November, and lingered further into spring; winter rushed upon the settlers with heavier blasts and fiercer storms than we now have to endure. And, above all, they felt with sadder force 'the dreary monotony of a New England winter, which leaves so large a blank, so melancholy a death-spot, in lives so brief that they ought to be all summer-time.' Even John Adams in his day so dreaded the tedious bitter New England winter that he longed to hibernate like a dormouse from autumn to spring."[10]

The early settlers learned from the Indians to use for light the pine-knots of the pitch-pine. This was called *candlewood* in New England and *lightwood* in the South. This wood was split into pieces so as to be used as a kind of torch and because of the smoke and the pitch droppings as it burned, it was usually placed in a corner of the fireplace. As fish was abundant in the streams, oil was obtained from them and used in a rude kind of lamp, but it would seem that this fish oil was not greatly used for light. Wax from bees was also used, which was made into a kind of candle by heating the wax and pressing it around a wick. Tallow and grease were used in making rush lights, wherein the pith from the common rushes was used, the outer covering being stripped off, and then the pith was dipped into the heated tallow or grease and this was then let harden. Deer suet, moose fat, and bear's grease were saved and tried out for candles, but they were not greatly used. Quite a good deal of wax from the wax myrtle tree was gathered and used for candles, whose berry has a thick coating of wax, and this tree was also called the bayberry tree, tallow shrub, and candle-berry tree. One great source for light came from the whale-fisheries, the oil from the spermaceti whale furnishing quite an important material for the making of candles. The most common of all material and the greatest used was the tallow from the cattle, which increased in number and became quite an important industry in the colonies.

In the making of tallow candles there were candle-rods, sticks about fifteen to eighteen inches long, and to each stick were tied six to eight candle-wicks. The tallow was melted and the wicks in the rods allowed to drop down and then were dipped into the melted tallow. The rod was then placed across the backs of two chairs or hung across two poles placed across chairs or stools, and then a second stick would be dipped and hung up to drip, and so on, and when the first rod had dried sufficiently it was dipped a second time and it was so continued to be dipped till the required sized candle was made. Later moulds came into use, made of tin or pewter, a half dozen individual moulds being joined together, sometimes a dozen and a sometimes as many as two dozen. The wick was fastened to a nail or wire and then let down into

[10] Earle, Customs and fashions in old New England, 128-129.

the center of the mould, the nail holding across the top, and the melted tallow was then poured in around the wick. The making of candles in the first way required a good deal of care and skill and it was slow work, two hundred candles a day being considered an extra good day's work. When moulds came into use, there were candle-makers who would go from house to house with their moulds to make the needed supply for the home. On account of the trouble in making candles, the colonists were very careful of them. They were carefully packed away and all pieces saved and also a little contrivance, called a save-all, made of pins and rings, was used to hold up the candle to the last till all was used. The candles were sometimes placed in a rough candlestick made of four pieces of wood fastened to a small piece of board so as to form a receptacle for the candle, and also in rude chandeliers, candle-beams, made of crossed sticks of wood. There were candlesticks of pewter, iron, brass, and silver. There also were sconces, called candle-arms or prongs. Snuffers were used, and snuffers trays.

Lamps were in use by the colonists but the early ones were of rude form. Among the earliest in use was the betty-lamp, which consisted of a shallow basin, two or three inches wide and an inch deep, with a nose or spout an inch or two long. They were rectangular, oval, round, or triangular in shape. They were set on the table or stand but often suspended from a nail on the wall by a hook and chain attached to the lamp. They were filled with tallow, grease, or oil and a cotton rag or a coarse wick was placed in the contents and hung out from the nose of the lamp. The phœbe-lamp was similar to the betty-lamp, but some had a nose at either end and used a double wick. The lamps were made of iron or pewter and some of brass. Later glass lamps came into use and were of various shapes and sizes.

The colonists had to be quite careful not to let the fire go out in the fireplace for there were very poor means for striking a light. In case there was no fire or light in the house, some one would go to the home of a neighbor with a shovel or covered pan, and sometimes with only a piece of green bark, and get coals to bring back for relighting the fire. This was usually the task of a small boy. For striking a light, a flint and steel with tinder were used. By striking the flint with the steel a spark was produced which was caught by the tinder and was then blown into a flame.

Another means was by setting off powder in the pan of a gun of that time which would set a piece of tow on fire. Later, matches were made by dipping small pieces of wood into melted sulphur, which could be set on fire by placing them in contact with the blaze on the hearth or of a light and then they could be carried about to light fires and candles and lamps. Such means of obtaining light were in use down to a late time, for friction matches did not come into use until the nineteenth century.

**Women.** During the earlier times in the settlement of America, the women had a hard time. They had to endure the hardships of a new country and to forego many of the things that in an old country make women's lives the more easy. They were never thought to be quite the equals of men and the following well portrays how they were looked upon by the men of the time:

"If some of our foremothers were intelligent and thoughtful, it was rather by natural gift than from instruction. Men of cultivation seem to have found it a little irksome to get down to the level of topics deemed sufficiently simple for the understanding of women. 'Conversation with ladies,' says William Byrd, 'is liked whipped syllabub, very pretty, but nothing in it.' The most accomplished gentlemen of that time thought it necessary to treat their lady friends to flattery so gross that it would not be bearable now. Byrd, great lord that he was, repaid his lady friends for courteous and hospitable entertainment at their houses by kissing them at his departure, and excused himself for leaving one gentleman's house by assuring the lady that her beauty would spoil his devotions if he remained."[11]

"Yet tho colonial usage kept women in retirement, the colonial South had notable women that vied with their assertive sisters of the North in the world of affairs. There was no marked difference between the sections in the extent to which women took up independent careers, or assumed responsibilities beyond housewifery."[12]

"In South Carolina women took an active part in all sorts of affairs and seem to have enjoyed a certain standing not gained by women elsewhere in the colonies. The men often had to be absent and it was not uncommon for a woman to be alone for several months in charge of a great plantation

[11] Eggleston, Social life in the colonies, Century magazine, VIII, '403.
[12] Calhoun, Social history of the American family, I, 276.

with hundreds of slaves with no white man to assist her save the overseer. Women often taught their own children. Eliza Lucas studied law and while studying it drew up two wills and was made trustee in another. In the Revolution the women were often more stalwart than the men, urging husbands and fathers not to give in in order to save their property and bearing cheerfully hardship and banishment. In all the Southern colonies there were keen gentlewomen that took up tracts of land and cleared and cultivated their estates. Southern women were not outdone by the business women of the North."[18]

In the old Dutch times in New York, possibly women touched closer to equality with men than in any other colony or at any other time. They occupied so high a place that they sometimes sat on juries. They engaged in business of various kinds. They traded with the Indians, they engaged in commerce with other colonies and the old country, they conducted stores, and they entered into other kinds of businesses. They proved themselves quite as shrewd as the men and well able to look after their own affairs.

At least there was one woman of a scientific turn of mind. "Jane Colden, the daughter of Governor Cadawallader Colden, was of signal service, not in trade, but in science. A letter written by her father explains her interest and usefulness:

'Botany is an amusement which may be made agreeable to the ladies who are often at a loss to fill up their time. Their natural curiosity and the pleasure they take in the beauty and variety of dress seem to fit them for it.

'I have a daughter who has an inclination to reading, and a curiosity for Natural Philosophy or Natural History, and a sufficient curiosity for attaining a competent knowledge. I took the pains to explain Linnæus' system, and to put it into an English form for her use by freeing it from technical terms, which was easily done, by using two or three words in the place of one. She is now grown very fond of the study, and has made such a progress in it as, I believe, would please you, if you saw her performance. Though she could not have been persuaded to learn the terms at first, she now understands to some degree Linnæus' characters—notwithstanding she does not understand Latin. She has already a pretty large volume in writing of the description of plants. She

[18] Calhoun, Social history of the American family, I, 278.

has shewn a method of taking the impression of the leaves on paper with printer's ink, by a simple kind of rolling press which is of use in distinguishing the species. No description in words alone, can give so clear an idea, as when assisted with a picture. She has the impression of three hundred plants in the manner you'll see by the samples. That you may have some conception of her performance, and her manner of describing, I propose to enclose some samples in her own writing, some of which I think are new genera.'

"Peter Collinson said she was the first lady to study the Linnæan system, and deserved to have her name celebrated; and John Ellis, writing of her to Linnæus in 1758, asks that a genus be named, for her, Coldenella. She was also a correspondent of Dr. Whyte of Edinburgh, and many learned societies in Europe. Walter Rutherfurd enumerates her talents, and caps them with a glowing tribute to her cheese-making."[14]

**Marriage.** There never occurred in the colonies the very early marriages of children, such as had ben in vogue in England some years before the colonies arose in America but which had grown very much less in England at this time. Yet they occurred early enough in the colonies, as there were marriages at fifteen and sixteen and less, for being a new country women were scarce and they were rarely allowed to become very old before they were in demand as wives. A young woman who passed twenty years of age without being married was rare indeed and it could not be understood why such should be the case.

Wooing in those days was done under much difficulties. In Boston a young man had to be very particular to get the consent of the young woman's parents or guardians before he entered upon his wooing, and even then he had to proceed cautiously or else fines, imprisonments, or the whipping-post would be applied to him. Yet it was not always demurely done in Old New England, as, in 1660 in New Haven, one day, "they sat down together; his arm being about her; and her arm upon his shoulder or about his neck; and hee kissed her and shee kissed him, or they kissed one another, continuing in this posture about half an hour, as Maria and Susan testified."[15] In New London in 1670 two lovers were accused and tried for sitting together on the Lord's Day under an

[14] Earle, Colonial days in old New York, 164-166.
[15] Earle, Customs and fashions in old New England, 42.

apple tree in an orchard. On account of the difficulties of wooing, there came into use two most peculiar modes of courting, known as "bundling" and the "courting-stick."

The courting-stick was six feet or so long, about an inch in diameter, hollow, and with an enlargement at each end for speaking into and for hearing from. A picture in Harper's Weekly for November 29, 1900, no doubt historically correct, represents the father seated in the fireplace, the mother busy spinning, by the mother the daughter sitting on the bench knitting, while the young man is sitting across the room, with cider mug and pitcher beside him, and he is just in the act of raising the courting-stick to his mouth, the other end of which is lying in the lap of the young lady. To complete the picture, a younger sister is crouched behind the high back of the settee upon which her sister is sitting, ready to overhear what the young man would send over through the stick, so as to be prepared to tease her sister on the morrow.

According to the only one who has given us a general history of the subject "bundling was practiced in two forms; first between *strangers*, as a simple domestic make-shift arrangement, often arising from the necessities of a new country, and by no means peculiar to America; and, secondly between *lovers*, who shared the same couch, with the mutual understanding that innocent endearment should not be exceeded."[16] Webster's New International Dictionary gives the following: "To bundle—To sleep or lie in the same bed without undressing:—said of a man and woman, esp, lovers." The Century Dictionary defines it thus: "To bundle—In New England (in early times) and in Wales, to sleep in the same bed without undressing; applied to the custom of men and women, especially sweethearts, thus sleeping."

Writers upon the subject are at a loss to account for bundling having been permitted among a people so austere as were the early New Englanders; who highly esteemed virtue and severely punished unchastity. Yet bundling was openly practiced and perhaps "in its open recognition lay its redeeming feature. There was no secrecy, no thought of concealment; the bundling was done under the supervision of mother and sisters."[17] It is a question whether such a custom showed coarseness and viciousness in the people or if it

[16] Stiles, Bundling: Its origin, progress, and decline in America, **13.**
[17] Earle, Customs and fashions in old New England, 64.

really showed a hospitality in that the guest was thus found a place to rest for the night, nevertheless the smallness of the dwelling or the crowded condition of the rooms. Again, the severe New England climate would make it next to impossible for the lover otherwise to have been made comfortable through the night without a great outlay of fuel, and a corresponding waste of lights, which would be carefully considered by the frugal colonists. Yet this custom was not altogether confined to the lower and poorer classes. In all probabilities this did not originate with the colonists but was brought over from the mother country, as it existed in Ireland, Scotland, and Wales, and in a form in Holland.

Bundling, it would seem, did not exist among the colonists outside of New England and Pennsylvania, while among the Dutch in New York the somewhat similar form of "questing" was known. It was not considered to any great extent wrong until the young colonial soldiers returning to their homes after the French and Indian wars took with them the vices of the camp and thus brought this practice into disrepute. Jonathan Edwards preached against it and other ministers joined in and the custom finally died out. It was at the greatest height among the colonists in the middle of the eighteenth century, and yet it reached down into the nineteenth century, being found in the region of Cape Cod as late as 1827, and in Pennsylvania even as late as 1845, such being shown by a court record, "and where it probably still lingers in out-of-the-way places among people both of English and of German extraction." [18]

Wooing was not always so difficult as to need the courting-stick or bundling to help it along, for some times it was done in a hurry and in most any place. There were cases in New England where a man would seek out a woman, call at her home, tell her his need of a wife, get her consent, and send in their desire for marriage to the town clerk to be published, and all this accomplished in one day or even a few hours. In the time of the Dutch in New York, one day a widower saw a young lady milking and falling in love with her told his love at once. Before she had finished milking, he jumped on his horse and rode in a great hurry to town, obtained his license, and hurriedly returned and took off his bride.

[18] Eggleston, Social life in the colonies, Century magazine, VIII, 290.

Love was not the only motive for marriage in New England, for it was quite customary to make inquiries concerning the bride's portion, and before marriage to arrange what should go with her. Sometimes a father-in-law was sued by his son-in-law for this portion.

There were, too, other ways of getting wives beside wooing them, as is shown by the following advertisement, which appeared in the *Boston Evening Post* for February 23, 1759:

"To the Ladies. Any young Lady between the Age of Eighteen and twenty three of a Midling Stature; brown Hair, regular Features and a Lively Brisk Eye; Of Good Morals & not Tinctured with anything that may Sully so Distinguishable a Form possessed of 3 or 400£ entirely her own Disposal and where there will be no necessity of going Through the tiresome Talk of addressing Parents or Guardians for their Consent: Such a one by leaving a Line directed for A. W., at the British Coffee House in King Street appointing where an Interview may be had will meet with a Person who flatters himself he shall not be thought Disagreeable by any Lady answering the above description. N. B. Profound Secrecy will be observ'd. No Trifling Answers will be regarded." [19]

Among the New England colonists there was a formal ceremony of betrothal, called a pre-contract or contraction. There was made a solemn promise of marriage between the couple before two witnesses and often there was a sermon preached in the church upon it by the minister, wherein it was the custom to permit the bride to select the text. The wedding-bans in New England were published three times in the meeting-house. This might be at any of the meetings—Sunday service, lecture, or town meeting. The names of the parties and their intention to marry were read by the minister, the town clerk, or the deacon at any of the meetings and on the church door or on a "publishing post" was placed a notice containing this information. In New York, under the English, this custom was considered not genteel and was very little practiced, as there a marriage license was issued. In Virginia both customs were in practice, as a license was required and also the bans had to be published for three several Sundays in the parish church where the contracting parties dwelt.

In the early days of the colonists in New England, mar-

[19] Earle, Customs and fashions in old New England, 66.

riage was considered a civil contract and the minister was not permitted to perform the marriage ceremony, the law requiring that all marriages should be conducted by a civil magistrate. But even as it was, the marriage ceremony was really of a religious nature as psalms were sung by the guests and prayers offered. Gradually the prejudice against ecclesiastical rites passed away and by the close of the seventeenth century ministers were authorized by law to perform the marriage ceremony. In the early times the wedding occurred in the home and was quietly conducted, but after a time feasting was added to the singing of psalms and the offering of prayers. In Virginia the custom was just the opposite, for civil marriage was not permitted by law, the ceremony having to be of a religious character and according to the rites of the Church of England. There was never a civil marriage before a magistrate permitted by law till near the close of the eighteenth century and then only allowed in very exceptional cases.

Among the Puritan colonists in New England the rude and really brutal wedding customs of the old country were entirely suppressed or greatly modified. Sack-posset was drunk at weddings and although this might have occurred within the bridal chamber, yet a psalm was sung before partaking and the drinking was followed with a prayer, which made a rather solemn affair out of it. There must have been, though, some weddings that were not so solemn, as in 1651 a law was passed that there should not be dancing at taverns at the time of a wedding on account of abuses and disorders that had occurred at such times. Among the Germans in Pennsylvania at a wedding the guests strove to steal a shoe off the bride's foot and the groomsmen tried to prevent this and if they did not the shoe was redeemed with a bottle of wine. In some parts the guests tried to obtain a garter of the bride as it brought luck and a quick marriage to the one getting it. In the Connecticut Valley the custom prevailed of stealing the bride. This was done by a group of young men, usually made up of those not invited to the wedding, who would rush in at the close of the marriage ceremony and seize the bride and carry her off to the tavern, where she was redeemed by the groom and his friends with a supper to the abductors. In some places it was the custom to tie wild grape-vines across the path of a wedding-party or to fell trees across the road to delay them, while at other times they would be greeted by a sudden volley fired from ambush.

"Isolated communities retained for many years marriage customs derived or copied from similar customs in the 'old country.' Thus the settlers of Londonderry, New Hampshire—Scotch-Irish Presbyterians—celebrated a marriage with much noisy firing of guns, just as their ancestors in Ireland, when the Catholics had been forbidden the use of firearms, had ostentatiously paraded their privileged Protestant condition by firing off their guns and muskets at every celebration. A Londonderry wedding made a big noise in the world. After the formal publishing of the bans, guests were invited with much punctiliousness. The wedding day was suitably welcomed at daybreak by a discharge of musketry at both the bride's and the groom's house. At a given hour the bridegroom, accompanied by his male friends, started for the bride's home. Salutes were fired at every house passed on the road, and from each house pistols and guns gave an answering 'God speed.' Half way on the journey the noisy bridal party was met by the male friends of the bride, and another discharge of firearms rent the air. Each group of men then named a champion to 'run for the bottle!' —a direct survival of the ancient wedding sport known among the Scotch as 'running for the bride-door,' or 'riding for the kail' or 'for the broose'—a pot of spiced broth. The two New Hampshire champions ran at full speed or rode a dare-devil race over dangerous roads to the bride's house, the winner seized the beribboned bottle of rum provided for the contest, returned to the advancing bridal group, drank the bride's health, and passed the bottle. On reaching the bride's house an extra salute was fired, and the bridegroom with his party entered a room set aside for them. It was a matter of strict etiquette that none of he bride's friends should enter this room until the bride, led by the best man, advanced and stationed herself with her bridesmaid before the minister, while the best man stood behind the groom. When the time arrived for the marrying pair to join hands, each put the right hand behind the back, and the bridesmaid and the best man pulled off the wedding-gloves, taking care to finish their duty at precisely the same moment. At the end of the ceremony everyone kissed the bride, and more noisy firing of guns and drinking of New England rum ended the day."[20]

[20] Earle, Customs and fashions in old New England, 74-75.

One peculiar custom was that of the "coming out" of the bride. On the Sunday after the wedding, the bride and groom and, sometimes, also the other members of the bridal party, would attend church in their wedding clothes. It was a common and an expected thing for the bridal couple to occupy some conspicuous place and in the midst of the sermon stand and slowly turn about to show their clothing. The peeking of the congregation can well be imagined when the groom was dressed in a velvet coat, lace-frilled shirt, and white broadcloth knee-breeches and the bride in a gorgeous peach-colored silk gown and a bonnet with sixteen yards of white ribbon on it. One groom was not content with showing off on one Sunday when he came out in white broadcloth for the next Sunday he was attired in brilliant blue and gold and the third Sunday in peach-bloom with pearl buttons.

An engagement of marriage was a very important matter and when once properly entered into it could not be lightly broken. There are records of a good number of breach of promise suits in New England and New York. Sometimes the suit was brought by the woman or her father against the man; sometimes, too, it was the man that brought the suit against the woman. Although the father had great control over his daughter in reference to her choice of a husband, yet if he permitted a contract to be entered into with his daughter he could not break off the engagement without good reason, such as a court would accept. There are a number of cases on record where the young man brought suit against the girl's father for breach of contract, sometimes for loss of time in paying court to the daughter. In some cases the young man in his suit included both the father and the mother and also the girl, claiming that all joined in against him.

Since there was civil marriage in New England it would seem naturally to follow that there would be civil divorce, which was the case. Not only were church courts not established in New England but also there were none in any of the colonies. As in Virginia marriage was by the church and as there were no church courts, there were no statutes on divorce enacted in that colony. There were separations, though, and the courts acted upon them when brought before them. The causes allowed for divorce in New England were such as desertion, cruelty, and breach of the marriage vow. Usually the husband and wife were dealt with as equals before the law. "Female adultery was never doubted to have been sufficient cause; but male adultery, after some debate and consultation with the elders, was judged not sufficient."[21] This has reference to Massachusetts, being from Governor Hutchinson.

The bearing of husband and wife was rather carefully regulated by law in New England. A husband could not keep his wife on frontiers where there was much danger, nor could he leave her for any long while, nor could he whip her, and he was not even allowed to use harsh words with her. A wife must not scold her husband too much nor strike him, lest she be put in the public stocks or pillory. Nor could they be too publicly demonstrative. "Captain Kemble of Boston sat two hours in the public stocks (1656) for his 'lewd and unseemly behavior' in kissing his wife 'publicquely' on the Sabbath upon his doorstep when he had just returned from a voyage of three years."[22] In old New York it was the custom to strive to reconcile all difficulties and even in some cases it seems that force was almost, if not quite used to have the husband and wife live together. In no case was the father of the wife to permit his daughter to have refuge in his home against the wishes of her husband.

"In spite of the hardness and narrowness of their daily life, and the cold calculation, the lack of sentiment displayed in wooing, I think Puritan husbands and wives were happy in their marriages, though their love was shy, almost somber, and 'flowered out of sight like the fern.' A few love-letters still remain to prove their affection: letters of sweethearts and letters of married lovers, such as Governor Winthrop and his wife Margaret:

" 'MY OWN DEAR HUSBAND: How dearly welcome thy kind letter was to me, I am not able to express. The sweetness of it did much refresh me. What can be more pleasing to a wife than to hear of the welfare of her best beloved and how he is pleased with her poor endeavors! I blush to hear myself commended, knowing my own wants. But it is your love that conceives the best and makes all things seem better than they are. I wish that I may always be pleasing to thee, and that these comforts we may have in each other may be daily increased so far as they be pleasing to God. I will use that speech to thee that Abigail did to David, I will be a servant

[21] Howard, History of matrimonial institutions, II, 331.
[22] Calhoun, Social history of the American family, I, 92.

to wash the feet of my lord; I will do any service wherein I may please my good husband. I confess I cannot do enough for thee; but thou art pleased to accept the will for the deed and rest contented. I have many reasons to make me love thee, whereof I shall name two: First, because thou lovest God, and secondly, because thou lovest me. If these two were wanting all the rest would be eclipsed. But I must leave this discourse and go about my household affairs. I am a bad housewife to be so long from them; but I must needs borrow a little time to talk with thee, my sweetheart. It will be but two or three weeks before I see thee, though they be long ones. God will bring us together in good time, for which time I shall pray. And thus with my mother's and my own best love to yourself I shall leave scribbling. Farewell my good husband, the Lord keep thee.
'Your obedient wife,
'MARGARET WINTHROP.' " [23]

In the good old colonial days of New England it was not only a man's duty to marry but also a necessity, so a widower did not remain single as a usual thing nor was it usual to remain in that condition very long, as for instance, "the father and mother of Governor Winslow had been widow and widower seven and twelve weeks respectively, when they joined their families and themselves in mutual benefit, if not in mutual love. At a later day, the impatient Governor of New Hampshire married a lady but ten days a widow." [23a] "Peter Sargent, a rich Boston merchant, had three wives. His second had had two previous husbands. His third wife had lost one husband, and she survived Peter, and also her third husband, who had three wives. His father had four, the last three of whom were widows." [23b]

One poor widower had quite a time after his wife's death as depicted in his diary, and to the cares and troubles of this poor old man, Judge Sewall of Boston, Mrs. Earl devotes thirteen pages of her *Customs and Fashions in Old New England*, and they are truly most unlucky pages. The Judge lost his wife on October 19, 1717, with whom he had lived forty-three years and they had seven sons and seven daughters, and on February 6th, of the following year (he was 66

[23] Earle, Customs and fashions in old New England, 79-80.
[23a] *Ibid.*, 36.
[23b] Calhoun, Social history of the American family, I, 70.

at the time) is found in his Diary: " 'Wandering in my mind whether to live a Married or a Single life.' Ere that date he had begun to take notice. He had called more than once on Widow Ruggles, and had had Widow Gill to dine with him; and looked critically at Widow Emery, and noted that Widow Tilley was absent from meeting; and he had gazed admiringly at Widow Winthrop in 'her sley.' " [24] Nor were the good old Dutch of New York far behind their Yankee neighbors in this matter, although they didn't want to allow their wives the same privileges without encumbrances, as, "John Burroughs, of Newtown, Long Island, in his will dated 1678 expressed the general feeling of husbands towards their prospective widows when he said: 'If my wife marry again, then her husband must provide for her as I have.' " [25] In 1673 a husband in making a joint-will with his wife enjoined loss of property if his wife married again. "Perhaps he thought there had been enough marrying and giving in marriage already in that family, for Brieta had had three husbands—a Dane, a Frieslander, and a German—and his first wife had had four, and he—well, several, I guess; and you couldn't expect any poor Dutchman to find it easy to make a will in all that confusion." [26]

"The precocity of colonial marriage allowed time for repetitions of the act. Many of the Virginia girls that married in childhood and assumed the burdens of family at so immature an age became broken in health and after bearing a dozen children died, leaving their husbands to marry again and beget new broods perhaps as large as the first. On the eastern shore of Virginia in the seventeenth century it was not remarkable for a man to have three or four successive wives. There were instances of Virginians married six times. It is not unusual to find a colonial dame that was married four times. Few conspicuous colonial men in Virginia, at least, lived beyond middle life; most died short of it. The malarial climate, exposure, and reckless habits cut them off. The young and attractive widows need not remain long forlorn in a country with a preponderance of males, at least if the feminine charms were supplemented by a fine plantation. Sometimes the relay was so close that the second husband was granted the probate of the will of the first. In one case

---

[24] Earle, Customs and fashions in old New England, 43.
[25] Earle, Colonial days in old New York, 54.
[26] *Ibid.*, 54.

funeral baked meats furnished the marriage table. One husband left all the estate to his wife's children by her next marriage. Quickness of remarriage does not indicate callousness but rather the woman's need of protection on the plantation and of an overseer for the work.

"A noticeable feature of colonial Virginia was the belleship of widows. Maidens seem not to have been 'in it.' As we come toward the Revolution the widows still reign supreme. It may be that the larger social experience of the widows magnified their charms or made them more adept at handling bashful lovers. Washington belonged in this class if we may trust the sentimental poems that he wrote to the unknown maiden that he loved when he was fifteen. After several unsuccessful affairs he probably was sufficiently experienced not to dally in his wooing of Mrs. Custis. Patrick Henry's father married a widow; so did Jefferson and James Madison."[27]

In New Netherlands there prevailed a custom, borrowed from Holland, that when a man died and left a number of debts the widow could be relieved from all demands or claims of his creditors by giving up her rights of inheritance. In one form this giving up of rights was shown by the widow's laying a key and a purse on the coffin of the deceased husband. There was another peculiar custom in both New England and New York for the purpose of getting out of paying debts. In this the widow was married in her shift, often at cross-roads, and sometimes at midnight. Later the custom was for the widow to be in a closet with no clothing on and put out her hand through a hole in the door for the marriage ceremony. Under such a marriage it was held that the new husband was exempt from paying the debts of the former husband and even of those of the wife contracted before her marriage to the new husband. After her marriage, whether on road or in closet, the new bride would deck herself out in clothing furnished by the new husband, usually these were with her in the closet, and then she would come forth resplendent and unencumbered to her new man.

As in all new countries, in the early times of the United States, women were fewer than men and very few women remained unmarried. Too, it was quite necessary for a woman to marry as she needed some one to care for her and

[27] Calhoun, Social history of the American family, I, 247-248.

protect her more than would be the case in an old and well-settled country. Yet there were some few women who preferred maidenhood to marriage, but for the most part such women had a hard time, for they were not well considered by the colonists as they believed it to be the duty for every man and woman to marry. At least one such woman persevered in this state for quite a time as there is a record of her death in her 91st year.

"The state of old maidism was reached at a very early age in those early days; Higginson wrote of an 'antient maid' of twenty-five years. John Dunton in his 'Life and Errors' wrote eulogistically of one such ideal 'Virgin' who attracted his special attention.

"'It is true an *old* (or superanuated) Maid in Boston is thought such a curse, as nothing can exceed it (and looked on as a *dismal* spectacle) yet she by her good nature, gravity, and strict virtue convinces all (so much as the fleering Beaus) that it is not her necessity but her choice that keeps her a Virgin. She is now about thirty years (the age which they call a *Thornback*) yet she never disguises herself, and talks as little as she thinks, of Love. She never reads any Plays or Romances, goes to no Balls or Dancing-match (as they do who go to such Fairs), to meet with Chapmen. Her looks, her speech, her whole behavior are so very chaste, that but once (at Governor's Island, where we went to be merry at roasting a hog) going to kiss her, I thought she would have blushed to death.

"'Our *Damsel* knowing this, her conversation is generally amongst the women (as there is least danger from that sex), so that I found it no easy matter to enjoy her company, for most of her time (save what was taken up in needle work and learning French, &c.) was spent in Religious Worship. She knew time was a dressing-room for Eternity, and therefore reserves most of her hours for better uses than those of the Comb, the Toilet and the Glass.

"'And as I am sure this is most agreeable to the Virgin modesty, which should make Marriage an act rather of their obedience than their choice. And they that think their Friends too slowpaced in the matter give certain proof that lust is their sole motive. But as the Damsel I have been describing would neither anticipate nor contradict the will of her Parents, so do I assure you she is against Forcing her own, by marrying where she cannot love; and that is the reason she is still a Virgin.' "[28]

Even if the Puritan did tolerate the unmarried woman he scarcely did the unmarried man, for it was considered almost a crime for a man to remain single. They went so far that to encourage bachelors to marry they were given home lots upon which to build if they married. Whatever the cause, there were very few bachelors among them. Bachelors were treated almost as criminals as they were spied upon by the constable, the watchman, and the tithing-man. In some places they had to pay a stipulated sum per week, or other time, for the privilege of remaining single, while in other places they were not permitted to live alone. An order issued in 1695 in Eastham, Mass., reads: "Every unmarried man in the township shall kill six blackbirds or three crows while he remains single; as a penalty for not doing it, shall not be married until he obey this order."[29] "Bachelors were not in good standing among the Dutch, at least in Albany. The colony had no laws, as in New England, to regulate these misfits and they shared in the benefit of Dutch tolerance toward misguided folk. But where marriage was so spontaneous, bachelors were almost pariahs. They did manage to find shelter but not home. Mrs. Grant describes them as passing in and out like silent ghosts and seeming to feel themselves superior to the world. Their association was almost exclusively with one another though sometimes one took part in the affairs of the family with which he lived."[30]

**Dress.** In the very early days there was quite a difference of feeling in reference to dress among the various colonies. In Virginia there was no horror of fine clothing and they dressed as far as they could as in the home country. In New England and Pennsylvania this was different, as in the former the Puritans were much against fine dress and in the latter the Quakers dressed demurely. In New York saving was such a grace with the Dutch that the clothing was quite durable, whatever the style. Yet even among the early colonists there was a disposition to dress according to rank and hence finery was not altogether excluded from any of the colonies. This is shown in the laws, as, in Virginia in 1623 only those of the governor's council were allowed to wear

[28] Earle, Customs and fashions in old New England, 38-39.
[29] Ibid., 37.
[30] Calhoun, Social history of the American family, I, 165.

silk, and, in 1651 the General Court of Massachusetts set forth its "utter detestation and dislike that men or women of meane condition, educations and callings should take uppon them the garbe of gentlemen, by the wearinge of gold or silver lace, or buttons, or poynts at theire knees, to walke in greate boots, or women of the same ranke to weare silke or tiffany hoodes or scarfes."[31]

As the colonies grew and wealth increased, display in dress grew and continued up through the seventeenth and eighteenth centuries. There was a constant succession of rich and gay fashions patterned after those of Europe. This was not only true of women's clothing but of men's as well. There were importations from Europe, among which were gauzes, silks, laces, velvets, and fine cloths of bright colors. Too, when trade widened, goods were brought from China and the East Indies. Although the colonists might wear rich clothing they were not wasteful, for the gowns and ribbons were turned and dyed and well cared for, and much of the clothing was passed on to other generations. This passion for dress was not even stopped by the Revolutionary War as is shown from a letter by a Hessian officer of that time:

"They are great admirers of cleanliness and keep themselves well shod. They friz their hair every day and gather it up on the back of the head into a chignon at the same time puffing it up in front. They generally walk about with their heads uncovered and sometimes but not often wear some light fabric on their hair. Now and then some country nymph has her hair flowing down behind her, braiding it with a piece of ribbon. Should they go out even though they be living in a hut, they throw a silk wrap about themselves, and put on gloves. They also put on some well made and stylish little sunbonnet, from beneath which their roguish eyes have a most fascinating way of meeting yours. In the English colonies the beauties have fallen in love with red silk or woolen wraps. The wives and daughters spend more than their incomes allow. The man must fish up the last penny he has in his pocket. The funniest part of it is the women do not seem to steal it from them, neither do they obtain it by cajoling, fighting, or falling in a faint. How they obtain it is a mystery, but that the men are heavily taxed for their extravagance is certain. The daughters keep up their stylish dressing because their mothers desire it.

[31] Eggleston, The colonists at home. Century magazine, VII, 887.

Nearly all articles necessary for the adornment of the female sex are very scarce and dear. For this reason they are wearing their Sunday finery. Should this begin to show signs of wear I am afraid that the husbands and fathers will be compelled to make peace with the Crown if they would keep their women folk supplied with gewgaws.''  [32]

This growth in the richness of apparel did not escape the eyes of the lawmakers, for sumptuary laws were passed in order to restrain and even prohibit luxury and extravagance in dress, but needless to say all such laws failed in the end. In 1634 the General Court of Massachusetts gave out the order:

"That no person either man or woman shall hereafter make or buy any apparel, either woolen or silk or linen with any lace on it, silver, gold, or thread, under the penalty of forfeiture of said clothes. Also that no person either man or woman shall make or buy any slashed clothes other than one slash in each sleeve and another in the back; also all cutworks, embroideries, or needlework cap, bands, and rails are forbidden hereafter to be made and worn under the aforesaid penalty; also all gold or silver girdles, hatbands, belts, ruffs, beaverhats are prohibited to be bought and worn hereafter.'' [33]

"In 1639 'immoderate great breeches, knots of ryban, broad shoulder bands and rayles, silk ruses, double ruffles and capes' were added to the list of tabooed garments.'' [33a] In 1651 came the utterance of the Court as given before.

Nor were these idle laws, for many people were tried and punished. In Northampton in 1676 there were thirty-eight women brought up at one time before the court for their "wicked apparell.'' Not only did the courts and lawmakers try to stop the increase for showy clothing but also the ministers took up the refrain and preached against the display of finery.

"After a while the whole church interfered. In 1679 the church at Andover put it to vote whether 'the parish Disapprove of the female sex sitting with their Hats on in the Meeting-house in time of Divine Service as being Indecent.' In the town of Abington, in 1775, it was voted that it was 'an indecent way that the female sex do sit with their hats

---
[32] Earle, Costume of colonial times, 31-32.
[33] Earle, Customs and fashions in old New England, 316.
[33a] Ibid., 316.

and bonnets on to worship God.' Still another town voted it was the 'Town's Mind' that the women should take their bonnets off in meeting and hang them 'on the peggs.' We do not know positively, but I suspect that the bonnets continued to grace the heads insteads of the pegs in Andover, Abington, and other towns.''[34]

In the early times in New England the men wore breeches of leather or of heavy woolens lined with leather with waistcoats, jackets, and doublets of leather, being plain and durable. But even at that early time there were scarlet caps and scarlet coats. In the country the clothing of the men was usually plain and made by the people themselves, the cloth being spun, dyed, and woven at home. Sometimes trousers were worn instead of the conventional short-clothes and shoes and hose dispensed with, the men going barefooted. Among the frontiersmen there were suits of deer-skin and coats made of bear-skin and raccoon-skin.

"The frontiersmen and hunters did not quite escape the prevailing fondness for the decorative and fanciful in dress. That some of them clubbed and some of them queued their hair, I have already remarked. Their 'hunting-shirt,' which served for vest and coat also, was of linsey-wolsey or buckskin in winter and of tow-linen in the summer. It had many fringes and a broad belt about the middle. The hunter wore either breeches of buckskin or thin trousers; over these he fastened coarse woolen leggins tied with garters or laced well up the thigh, as a defense against mud, serpents, insects, and thorns. He wore moccasins, and covered his head with a flapped hat of a reddish hue, or a cap. The sharp tomahawk stuck in his belt served for a weapon, for hatchet, for hammer, and for a whole kit of tools besides. The shot-bag and powder-horn completed his outfit; the powder-horn was his darling, and upon it he lavished all the resources of his ingenuity, carving it with whimsical devices of many sorts. And there was probably less that was in false taste in the woodman's outfit than in any costume of the period.''[35]

Whatever way the New England Puritan may have dressed himself in the early colonial times, he did not hesitate to bedeck himself in the later times. "Picture to yourself the garb in which the patriot John Hancock appeared one noonday in 1782:

[34] Earle, Home life in colonial days, 286.
[35] Eggleston, The colonists at home, Century magazine, VII, 891.

" 'He wore a red velvet cap within which was one of fine linen, the last turned up two or three inches over the lower edge of the velvet. He also wore a blue damask gown lined with velvet, a white stock, a white satin embroidered waistcoat, black satin small-clothes, white silk stockings and red morocco slippers.'

"What gay peacock was this strutting all point-device in scarlet slippers and satin and damask, spreading his gaudy feathers at high noon in sober Boston Streets!—was this our boasted Republican simplicity? And what 'fop-tackle' did the dignified Judge of the Supreme Court wear in Boston at that date? He walked home from the bench in the winter time clad in a magnificent white corduroy surtout lined with fur, with his judicial hands thrust in a great fur muff.

"Fancy a Boston publisher going about his business tricked up in this dandified dress—a true New England jessamy.

" 'He wore a pea-green coat, white vest, nankeen smallclothes, white silk stockings and pumps fastened with silver buckles which covered at least half the foot from instep to toe. His small-clothes were tied at the knees with riband of the same color in double bows, the ends reaching down to the ancles. His hair in front was well loaded with pomatum, frizzled or creped, and powdered; the ear locks had undergone the same process. Behind his natural hair was augmented by the addition of a large queue, called vulgarly the false tail, which, enrolled in some yards of black riband, hung halfway down his back.' " [36]

The dress of the women among the colonists is shown in such lists as in the will of Jane Humphrey, who died in Dorchester, Mass., in 1668:

"Ye Jump. Best Red Kersey Petticoate, Sad Grey Kersey Wascote. My blemmish Searge Petticoate & my best hatt. My white Fustian Wascote. A black Silk neck cloath. A handkerchiefe. A blew Apron. A plain black Quoife without any lace. A white Holland Appron with a small lace at the bottom. Red Searge petticoat and a blackish Searge petticoat. Greene Searge Wascote & my hood & muffe. My Green Linsey Woolsey petticoate. My Whittle that is fringed & my Jump & my blew Short Coate. A handkerchief. A blew Apron. My best Quife with a Lace. A black Stuffe Neck Cloath. A White Holland apron with two breadths in it. Six yards of Redd Cloth. A greene Vnder Coate. Stan-

[36] Earle, Customs and fashions in old New England, 327.

ing Kersey Coate. My murry Wascote. My Cloake & my blew Wascote. My best White Apron, my best Shifts. One of my best Neck Cloaths, & one of my plain Quieus. One Calico Vnder Neck Cloath. My fine thine Neck Cloath. My next best Neck Cloath. A square Cloath with a little lace on it. My greene Apron."[37]

"Vrouentje Ides Stoffelsen, the wife of a respectable and well-to-do Dutch settler in New Netherlands, left behind her in 1641 a gold hoop ring, a silver medal and chain and a silver undergirdle to hang keys on; a damask furred jacket, two black camlet jackets, two doublets—one iron gray, the other black; a blue, a steel-gray lined petticoat, and a black coarse camlet-lined petticoat; two black skirts, a new bodice, two white waistcoats, one of Harlem stuff; a little black vest with two sleeves, a pair of damask sleeves, a reddish morning gown, not lined; four pairs pattens, one of Spanish leather; a purple apron and four blue aprons; nineteen cambric caps and four linen ones; a fur cap trimmed with beaver; nine linen handkerchiefs trimmed with lace, two pair of old stockings, and three shifts."[38]

The list of the wardrobe of the widow of Dr. Jacob De Lange, of New York, in 1682, showed the following:

"One under petticoat with a body of red bay; one under petticoat, scarlet; one petticoat, red cloth with black lace; one striped stuff petticoat with black lace; two colored drugget petticoats with gray linings; two colored drugget petticoats with white linings; one colored drugget petticoat with pointed lace; one black silk petticoat with ash gray silk lining; one potto-foo silk petticoat with black silk lining; one potto-foo silk petticoat with taffeta lining; one silk potoso-à-samare with lace; one tartanel samare with tucker; one black silk crape samare with tucker; three flowered calico samares; three calico nightgowns, one flowered, two red; one silk waistcoat, one calico waistcoat; one pair of bodice; five pair white cotton stockings; three black love-hoods; one white love-hood; two pair sleeves with great lace; four cornet caps with lace; one black silk rain cloth cap; one black plush mask; four yellow lace drowlas; one embroidered purse with silver bugle and chain to the girdle and silver hook and eye; one pair black pendants, gold nocks; one gold boat, wherein thirteen diamonds & one white coral chain; one pair gold stucks

[37] Earle, Customs and fashions in old New England, 319.
[38] Earle, Costume of colonial times, 28-29.

or pendants each with ten diamonds; two diamond rings; one gold ring with clasp beck; one gold ring or hoop bound round with diamonds.'' [39]

There was no ready-made clothing in the colonies till late, for men appearing about the middle of the eighteenth century and for women not till near the close of the same century. The women's clothing was made by themselves or by dressmakers, who had establishments in the town and went from home to home in the country. Sometimes the women would send to the home country for garments, which would be passed about among themselves as models. A rather striking way of introducing the new styles was by importing dolls fully and carefully dressed in Europe in the newest fashions. The notice of the arrival of such a doll is found in an advertisement in the *New England Weekly Journal* of July 2, 1733.

"To be seen at Mrs. Hannah Teatts Mantua Maker at the Head of Summer Street Boston a Baby drest after the Newest Fashion of Mantues and Night Gowns & everything belonging to a dress. Latilly arrived on Capt. White from London, any Ladies that desire to see it may either come or send, she will be ready to wait on 'em, if they come to the House it is Five Shilling & if she waits on 'em it is Seven Shilling.'' [40]

They did not have a great deal of jewelry. Bracelets and lockets were worn by a few of the women and some of the men had gold and silver sleeve-buttons, and also men sometimes wore thumb-rings, which seems in keeping with their using muffs. Rings were common, which were for the most part mourning-rings, as these were given to all the chief mourners at funerals. Silver buckles for the knees and ankles were quite common among the men. Paste brilliants were very much in use, being worn on shoe buckles by the men, and women wore paste combs and paste pins. Watches appeared in England about the middle of the seventeenth century, but it was quite a little later before they were found among the colonists, and even then they were used only by the wealthy. Umbrellas, made of oiled linen, came into use late in the colonial period, but before that the ladies had learned to protect their faces from the sun by sun-fans of green paper, and green masks were worn while riding. In New England black velvet masks were used as a shield from the cold, being held in place by means of a silver mouth-

[39] Earle, Costume of colonial times, 26-27.
[40] Earle, Customs and fashions in old New England, 322.

piece. Hoopskirts came into fashion and they became quite big affairs about the middle of the eighteenth century. To set off the coats and breeches of gaudy colors the men wore shirts with highly ruffled bosoms. The stylish shoes of the women were frail affairs, being of very thin material and with paper soles which were protected by overshoes known as goloe-shoes, clogs, pattens, etc.

In the colonies the customs in reference to the wearing of the hair prevailed as in use in the old country, the Puritans in New England keeping their hair short, as did their brethren in England, and so nicknamed Roundheads, while in Virginia the hair was worn long, as was the custom with the Cavaliers of England. As hard as the New Englanders fought against long hair, going as far as to offer men under sentence release from punishment if they would cut off their long hair, the Virginians went further and made short hair disgraceful by making it a brand and a mark of identification for indentured servants when caught and returned to their masters after running away before their time of service had expired.

But Puritan and Cavalier and Quaker all succumbed to the wig. The rage for wearing wigs by the beginning of the eighteenth century seemed to have possessed the colonists, as wigs were worn by men of all ranks and conditions, by children, servants, prisoners, and even sailors and soldiers. The styles varied greatly, sometimes they swelled out at the side, sometimes they hung in braids or in curls or in pigtails, and again they were in great puffs or were turned under in heavy rolls. They were made of human hair, horsehair, goat's-hair, calves' and cows' tails, thread, silk, and mohair. Some of them were quite costly, even as much as the equal of a hundred dollars today. There were a great variety of styles of wigs, known as the tie, the brigadier, the spencer, the major, the albemarle, the ramillies, the grave full-bottom, the giddy feather-top, the campaign, the neck-lock, the bob, the lavant, the vallaney, the drop-wig, the buckle-wig, the bag-wig, the Grecian fly, the peruke, the beau-peruke, the long-tail, the bob-tail, the fox-tail, the cut-wig, the tuck-wig, the twist-wig, the scratch.[41]

"Soon after 1750, perhaps, the decline of the wig set in; but the exuberant fancy of the age still made the heads of gentlemen to blossom. The wig-maker's tortures fell upon

[41] Earle, Customs and fashions in old New England, 300.

the natural hair: it was curled, frizzled, and powdered; it was queued or clubbed. The man of dignity, even the fashionable clergyman, sat long beneath the hands of the barber every day of his life. Side-locks and dainty little toupees were cultivated. The 'maccaroni'—type and pink of the most debauched English dandyism—made his appearance in 1774 in the fashionable assemblies of Charleston, and even in Charleston there were two varieties of these creatures: the one wore the hair clubbed, the other preferred the dangling queue. The rage for growing the longest possible switch of hair infected the lower classes; sailors and boatmen wrapped in eel-skin their cherished locks, and the back-countryman in some places was accustomed to preserve his from injury by enveloping it in a piece of bear's-gut dyed red, or clubbing it in a buckskin bag.''[42]

The women of the colonies, like the men, tried to keep up with the fashions of Europe. The manner in which they wore their hair brought upon them the wrath of the parsons, one of whom, Increase Mather, even included a notice of such in his great sermon upon the comet in 1683: ''Will not the haughty daughters of Zion refrain their pride in apparell? Will they lay out their hair, and wear false locks, their borders, and towers like comets about their heads?''[43] These towers grew out of style, but they came back again near a century later, in Revolutionary times. At this later time the front hair was drawn up over a roll or cushion and stiffened with powder and grease and then the back hair was drawn up in a similar way. The pile was then built up with ribbons, pompons, aigrettes, jewels, gauze, flowers, and feathers till it arose near a half yard in height. This process took a long time, as is told in 1771 by a bright little Boston school girl, eleven years of age, who saw a hairdresser at his work. ''How long she was at his opperation, I know not. I saw him twist & tug & pick & cut off whole locks of grey hair at a slice (the lady telling him she would have no hair to dress next time) for the space of a hour & a half, when I left them, he seeming not to be near done.''[44] ''One may judge of the vital necessity there was for all this art from the fact that a certain lady in Annapolis about the close of the colonial period was accustomed to pay six hundred dollars

[42] Eggleston, The colonists at home, Century magazine, VII, 888.
[43] Earle, Customs and fashions in old New England, 290.
[44] Earle, Diary of Anna Green Winslow, 19.

a year for the dressing of her hair. On great occasions the hairdresser's time was so fully occupied that some ladies were obliged to have their mountainous coiffures built up two days beforehand, and to sleep sitting in their chairs, or, according to a Philadelphia tradition, with their heads inclosed in a box."[45]

The contents of such a tower is shown in a description of an accident to a young woman in the streets of Boston, as found in the *Boston Gazette* of 1771. "In an infaust moment she was thrown down by a runaway, and her tower received serious damage. It burst its thin outer wall of natural hair, and disgorged cotton and wool and tow stuffing, false hair, loops of ribbon and gauze. Ill-bred boys kicked off portions of the various excresences, and the tower-wearer was jeered at until she was glad to escape with her own few natural locks."[46]

These dressings of the hair called for material to use and they had powdering puffs and powdering bags and powdering machines and several varieties of powder to use in them, such as brown, maréchal, scented, plain, and blue. Pomatums came into use, one of which in a book dated 1706 is shown to be made thus: "The Dutch way to make Orange-butter. Take new cream two gallons, beat it up to a thicknesse, then add half a pint of orange-flower-water, and as much red wine, and so being become the thicknesse of butter it has both the colour and smell of an orange."[47] There were hair-restorters and hair-dyes, all promising much to those using them correctly and carefully, one such formula coming down to us from 1685: "A Metson to make a mans heare groe when he is bald. Take sume fier flies & sum Redd wormes & black snayls and sum hume bees and dri them and pound them & mixt them in milk or water."[48]

In early colonial times not much attention was given to the teeth. The following is in line with their knowledge and care of the teeth. "If you will keep your teeth from rot, plug, or aking, wash the mouth continually with Juyce of Lemons, and afterwards rub your teeth with a Sage Leaf and Wash your teeth after meat with faire water. To cure Tooth Ach. 1. Take Mastick and chew it in your mouth until

[45] Eggleston, The colonists at home, Century magazine, VII, 889.
[46] Earle, Customs and fashions in old New England, 294.
[47] Earle, Colonial days in old New York, 182.
[48] Earle, Customs and fashions in old New England, 296.

it is as soft as vvax, then stop your teeth with it, if hollow, there remaining till it's consumed, and it wil certainly cure you. 2. The tooth of a dead man carried about a man presently suppresses the pains of the Teeth."[49] The tooth powders were such as to be quite injurious to the teeth. One such had in its combination cuttle-bone, brick-dust, and pumice-stone. Another was to contain coral reduced to a powder, and if no coral was to be had, then coarse earthenware might be broken up and powdered for use. Their instruments for pulling teeth were crude and caused the greatest of pain, often breaking the jaw. The artificial teeth of that time may have helped the looks, but they were of very little value in eating, if any at all. There was used an ingrafting process wherein sound teeth were extracted from one person and inserted in another person's mouth. "I cannot find any notice of the sale of 'teeth brushes' till nearly Revolutionary times. Perhaps the colonists used, as in old England, little brushes made of 'dentissick root' or mallow, chewed into a fibrous swab."[50]

After the first years of hardships, and wealth began to come to the colonists, there not only arose among the women the desire for fine dress, but also a love of cosmetics. As early as 1686 it was said of a woman of Boston, "to hide her age she paints, and to hide her painting dares hardly laugh." One of the ministers of New England about that same time stated to his congregation: "At the resurrection of the Just there will no such sight be met as the Angels carrying Painted Ladies in their arms." In the newspapers are advertisements of washes for the skin, face powders, face paints, compositions to take off "Superficious Hair," face patches, and the like. One of the leading cosmetics was the wash-ball, a substitute for soap. They loved perfumes and not only used them about their persons, but also to scent their linen chests, closets, and rooms.

"With regard to the bathing habits of our ancestors but little can be said, and but little had best be said. Charles Francis Adams writes, with witty plainness, 'If among personal virtues cleanliness be indeed that which ranks next to godliness, then judged by the nineteenth century standards, it is well if those who lived in the eighteenth century had a

[49] Earle, Customs and fashions in old New England, 302.
[50] Ibid., 304.

sufficiency of the latter quality to make good what they lacked of the former.' He says there was not a bathroom in the town of Quincy prior to the year 1820. And of what use would pitchers or tubs of water have been in bedrooms in the winter time, when, if exposed over night, solid ice would be found therein in the morning? The washing of linen in New England homes was done monthly; it is to be hoped the personal baths were more frequent, even under the apparent difficulties of accomplishment. I must state, in truth, though with deep mortification, that I cannot find in inventories even of Revolutionary times the slightest sign of the presence of balneary appurtenances in bedrooms; not even of ewers, lavers, and basins, nor of pails and tubs. As petty pieces of furniture, such as stools, besoms, framed pictures, and looking-glasses are enumerated, this conspicuous absence of what we deem an absolute necessity for decency speaks with a persistent and exceedingly disagreeable voice of the unwashed condition of our ancestors, a condition all the more mortifying when we consider their exceeding external elegance in dress. This total absence of toilet appliances does not, of course, render impossible a special lavatory or bathroom in the house, or the daily importation to the bedrooms of hot-water cans, twiggen bottles, bathtubs, and basins from other portions of the house; but even that equipment would show a lack of adequate bathing facilities. Nor do the tiny toilet jugs and basins of Staffordshire ware that date from the first part of this century point to any very elaborate ablutions.''[51]

**Infants' Clothing.** Some articles of clothing of infants of colonial times have been preserved. These are not the common every-day dress, as they were worn out or not thought nice enough to lay away, but these remaining are the finer sort such as their christening robes and their finer shirts, caps, and petticoats, such as would not be worn very much and kept put away till baby outgrew them and they were so pretty that they were still preserved and have come down to us to show us what beautiful apparel our baby forefathers wore.

All the undergarments of the colonial baby were made of linen—little low-necked shirts with short sleeves, made of thin, fine linen. The little hands were enclosed in linen

[51] Earle, Customs and fashions in old New England, 308-309.

mitts, one pair, though, that comes down to us were made of fine lace and there were some of silk, and some even of stiff yellow nankeen. The baby-dresses are little, straight-laced gowns for display, or, rather shapeless large-necked sacks and drawn into shape at the neck with narrow cotton ferret or linen bobbin. The poor little head was covered summer and winter with a cap, which must have been quite warm in summer as they were often warmly padded. Mrs. Earle states that she had never seen a woolen petticoat which was worn by an infant of pre-Revolutionary days. But there were infants' cloaks of wool. There were also beautifully embroidered long cloaks of chamois skin. The baby was kept warm by little shawls placed around the shoulders and the body was enveloped in quilts and shawls, which also included the head and shoulders.

**Boys' Clothing.** In the early colonial times as soon as the boys became old enough to get about, they were dressed like their fathers. In Massachusetts the boys' clothing consisted of doublets, which were warm double jackets, leather knee-breeches, leather belts, knit caps, while in Virginia, because of the warmer climate, their clothing was of lighter material. Sometimes the boys had deerskin breeches.

When cotton goods became to be imported from Oriental countries, about the latter part of the eighteenth century, the clothing of children, as well as of grown-folks, were made of it. This became so important in dress that it was worn in winter as well as in summer. We find that boys wore nankeen suits the entire year and that jackets and trousers for the boys were made of calico and chintz. It is hard for us to believe that boys in New England ever wore nankeen suits in winter and even calico pants in snow time.

"There is an excellent list of the clothing of a New York schoolboy of eleven years given in a letter written by Fitz-John Winthrop to Robert Livingstone in 1690. This young lad, John Livingstone, had also been in school in New England. The 'account of linen & clothes' shows him to have been well dressed. It reads thus:

"Eleven new shirts.
4 pr laced sleves.
8 plane cravets.
4 cravets with lace
4 stripte wastecoats with black buttons.
1 flowered wastecoat.

3 pr silver buttons.
2 pr fine blew stockings.
1 pr fine red stockings.
4 white handkerchiefs.
2 speckled handkerchiefs.
3 pair gloves.
1 stuff coat with black buttons.

4 new osinbrig britches.
1 gray hat with a black ribbon.
1 gray hat with a blew ribbon.
1 dousin black buttons.
1 dousin coloured buttons.
3 pr gold buttons.

1 cloth coat.
1 pr blew plush britches.
1 pr serge britches.
2 combs.
1 pr new shoes.

Silk & thred to mend his clothes.''[52]

In 1759 George Washington ordered from England for his step-son—Master Custis—six years of age, the following:

6 Pocket Handkerchiefs, small and fine.
6 pairs Gloves.
2 Laced Hats.
2 Pieces India Nankeen.
6 pairs fine Thread Stockings.
4  "   Coarse    "    "
6  "   Worsted   "    "
4  "   Strong Shoes.
4  "   Pumps.
1 Summer suit of clothes to be made of something light and thin.
1 piece black Hair Ribbon.
1 pair handsome Silver Shoe & Knee Buckles.
1 light duffel Cloak with Silver Frogs.[53]

**Girls' Clothing.** The little girl of the early settlers must have been dressed very plainly, as was her mother. As the colonists grew wealthy and cities arose, the little girl's dress grew to be quite elegant and stiff and formal and hampering, nearly as much so as that of her mother.

In 1759, in the same list mentioned above for his step-son, George Washington ordered from England for his step-daughter—Miss Custis—four years of age, as follows:

8 pairs kid mitts.
4  "    gloves.
2  "    silk shoes.
4  "    Calamanco shoes.
4  "    leather pumps.
6  "    fine thread stockings.
4  "     "    worsted    "
2 Caps.
2 pairs Ruffles.
2 tuckers, bibs, and aprons if Fashionable.
2 Fans.
2 Masks
2 bonnets.

[52] Earle, Colonial days in old New York, 37.
[53] Earle, Costume of colonial times, 13.

1 Cloth Cloak.
1 Stiffened Coat of Fashionable silk made to packthread stays.
6 yards Ribbon.
2 Necklaces.
1 pair Silver Sleeve Buttons with Stones.
6 Pocket Handkerchiefs.[53a]

"A little girl four years of age, in kid mitts, a mask, a stiffened coat, with pack-thread stays, a tucker, ruffles, bib, apron, necklace, and fan, was indeed a typical example of the fashionable follies of the day."[54]

The school girl in a fashionable boarding-school dressed extravagantly fine. One of the daughters, twelve years of age, of General Huntington of Norwich, Conn., was placed in a boarding-school in Boston. She had twelve silk gowns but her teacher wrote that the girl must have another gown of a "recently imported rich fabric," which was got for her so that she might dress "suitable to her rank and station."

Another Boston school girl, twelve years of age, in 1772, describes her own evening dress thus:

"I was dress'd in my yellow coat, black bib & apron, black feathers on my head, my past comb, & all my past garnet marquesett & jet pins, together with my silver plume—my loket, black mitts & 2 or 3 yards of blue ribbin, (black & blue is high tast) striped tucker and ruffels (not my best) & my silk shoes compleated my dress."[55]

This same school girl, in her diary four months later, tells us of her famous headdress:

"I had my HEDDUS roll on, aunt Storer said it ought to be made less, Aunt Deming said it ought not to be made at all. It makes my head itch, & ach, & burn like anything Mamma. This famous roll is not made *wholly* of a red *Cow Tail*, but is a mixture of that, & horsehair (very course) & a little human hair of yellow hue, that I suppose was taken out of the back part of an old wig. But D—— made it (our head) all carded together and twisted up. When it first came home, aunt put it on, & my new cap on it, she then took up her apron & mesur'd me, & from the roots of my hair on my forehead to the top of my notions, I mesur'd above an inch longer than I did downwards from the roots of my hair to the end of my chin. Nothing renders a young person more

[53a] Earle, Costume of colonial times, 12.
[54] *Ibid.*, 13.
[55] Earle, Diary of Anna Green Winslow, 17.

amiable than virtue & modesty without the help of fals hair, red *Cow tail* or D—— (the barber).'' [56]

The little girl's complexion had to be protected by a mask of cloth or velvet from the healthy coloring of the sun. "Little Dolly Payne, who afterwards became the wife of President Madison, went to school wearing 'a white linen mask to keep every ray of sunshine from the complexion, a sunbonnet sewed on her head every morning by her careful mother, and long gloves covering the hands and arms.' " [57]

These little girls wore vast hoop-petticoats. They wore high-heeled shoes made of silk, morocco, or light stuff. They wore stays and corsets, and even the poor little boys had to wear them.

"I have seen children's stays, made of heavy strips of board and steel, tightly wrought with heavy buckram or canvas into an iron frame like an instrument of torture. These had been worn by a little girl five years old. Staymakers advertised stays, jumps, gazzets, costrells, and caushets (which were doubtless corsets) for ladies and children, 'to make them appear strait.' And I have been told of tin corsets for little girls, but I have never seen any such abominations. One pair of stays was labelled as having been worn by a boy when five years old. There certainly is a suspicious suggestion in some of these little fellows' portraits of whalebone and buckram." [58]

"From the deacons' records of the Dutch Reformed Church at Albany, we catch occasional hints of the dress of the children of the Dutch colonists. There was no poorhouse, and few poor; but since the church occasionally helped worthy folk who were not rich, we find the deacons in 1665 and 1666 paying for blue linen for *schorteldoecykers,* or aprons, for Albany *kindeken;* also for *haaken en oogen,* or hooks and eyes, for warm under-waists called *borsrockyen.* They bought linen for *luyers,* which were neither pinning-blankets nor diapers, but a sort of swaddling clothes, which evidently were worn then by Dutch babies. *Voor-schooten,* which were white bibs; *neerstucken,* which were tuckers, also were worn by little children. Some little Hans or Pieter had given to him by the deacons a fine little scarlet *aperock,* or monkey-jacket; and other children were furnished linen *cosynties,* or night-caps

---

[56] Earle, Diary of Anna Green Winslow, 71.
[57] Earle, Home life in colonial days, 290.
[58] Earle, Child life in colonial days, 58.

with capes. Yellow stockings were sold at the same time for children, and a gay little yellow turkey-legged Dutchman in a scarlet monkey-jacket and fat little breeches must have been a jolly sight."[59]

**Food.** The early colonists in the United States fared poorly at first in the way of food and there was a scarcity of food among them for some time. Yet there was an abundance of fish and oysters and clams and wild nuts and berries and wild game. After they had learned how to gather these in and also what to plant and how to plant there was a plenty if not abundance. Not having a great number of cooking utensils, they learned from the Indians and devised ways of cooking without utensils. They broiled meats and fish on the bare live coals; they roasted Irish potatoes, sweet potatoes, green corn, and squashes by burying them in the hot ashes; apples and eggs and green corn were baked by laying them on the hearth between the andirons; they would bake cakes of Indian corn meal and of buckwheat and rye flour before the fire on a flat stone, a hoe, an oak board, or a pewter plate. The breakfast was usually a frugal one, consisting of a porridge of peas and beans, with a savor of meat, cheese, maybe beer or tea, but often milk and bread. One peculiar custom with the dinner, generally served exactly at noon, was that usually there was a pudding and which was eaten first. This might have been an Indian pudding, made of Indian corn meal mixed with dried fruit. Among some of the more frugal the supper was often of mush and milk. In some parts of the country at least, it was a custom on the occasion of a dinner to which guests were invited to send to those who could not be present a "taste" of the different dishes, and this was done particularly to sick neighbors.

Wheat did not do well at first but oats grew all right and quite a good deal was raised, so that oatmeal was used and oatmeal porridge became a rather popular dish. Indian corn, maize, was the staple grain of the colonists. When they first came to America they found this grain growing and they learned from the Indians how to plant it, raise it, grind it, and cook it. The foods made from this corn still retain their Indian names, as samp, supawn, pone, succotash, hominy.

Samp was the corn pounded to a coarsely ground powder. Supawn was a thick corn-meal and milk porridge. Another way of preparing the corn by the Indians was called *nocake*

[59] Earle, Colonial days in old New York, 183-184.

or *nookick*, in which the corn was parched in the hot ashes, then taken up and the ashes sifted out, and then beaten into a powder. This was used on journeys, being put into a pouch, and it was quite sustaining as a small amount of it sufficed for a meal. Johnny-cake was made of corn-meal boiled with water, probably the same as our mush now. They also roasted the green corn, roasting-ears, and parched the dried corn.

A corn-husking of 1767 in Massachusetts is thus described in a diary of that time. "Made a husking Entertainm't. Possibly this leafe may last a Century and fall into the hands of some inquisitive Person for whose Entertainm't I will inform him that now there is a Custom amongst us of making an Entertainm't at husking of Indian Corn whereto all the neighboring Swains are invited and after the Corn is finished they like the Hottentots give three Cheers or huzza's but cannot carry in the husks without a Rhum bottle; they feign great Exertion but do nothing till Rhum enlivens them, when all is done in a trice, then after a hasty Meal about 10 at Night they go to their pastimes."[60]

The corn was shelled by hand or by raking the ear across the edge of a shovel or other piece of sharp iron and then ground in stone mortars with pestles or in wooden mortars. Later came "querns," hand-mills, which from the descriptions, must have been similar to the ones used by the Scotch housewives of the earlier times, as described in another place in this book. Then in Massachusetts came the first wind-mill in 1631 and the first water-mill in 1633.

When the colonists came to this country, they found the rivers and seas abounding with fish. It is stated that some of the rivers were so full of fish that horses ridden into them would step on the fish and kill them. The Indians killed them in the brooks by striking them with sticks and the colonists scooped them out alive with pans. In 1614, after having left Virginia, John Smith went to New England for whale and he found cod instead and in one month he caught sixty thousand of the cod. Two popular fish today, the shad and the salmon, were so common that the colonists were really ashamed to be seen eating them in their homes. A writer in 1636 stated that, "I myself at the turning of the tyde have seen such multitudes of sea bass that it seemed to me that one might goe over their backs dri-shod."[61]

[60] Earle, Home life in colonial days, 136.
[61] *Ibid.*, 120.

Not only were there great numbers of fish, but also a great many different kinds, one writer of 1672 told of over two hundred kinds that were caught in the waters of New England. Not only was there great quantity and great variety but also great size. Writers of these early times tell of lobsters weighing twenty-five pounds and five and six feet long, and of oysters that were a foot or more across.

At the first the settlers were poorly provided with fishing-tackle, but it was soon brought in from across the sea and a great industry arose. Fishing-vessels were fitted out and the product sold to the colonies and Europe. "With every fishing-vessel that left Gloucester and Marblehead, the chief centres of the fishing industries, went a boy of ten or twelve to learn to be a skilled fisherman. He was called a 'cut-tail,' for he cut a wedge-shaped bit from the tail of every fish he caught, and when the fish were sorted out the cut-tails showed the boy's share of the profit."[61a]

There was likewise a great abundance of wild game. Deer were found everywhere. They were at first without fear and came in droves near to the colonists. But this was not for long as the colonists began to kill them in great numbers, both for the food and for the hides. Wild turkeys were likewise plentiful at first and of great size, as they weighed thirty and forty and even sixty pounds. They came in flocks of a hundred or more and were destroyed as the deer, and in a short time they had disappeared from the settled parts, by 1690 rarely found near the coasts of New England. Wild geese were found in flocks of thousands. Doves were very plentiful. There were wild pigeons in vast quantities, so much so that in their flight the sun would be obscured and the sky darkened for some length of time, and where they roosted the limbs were broken off the trees and sometimes even the largest limbs and again the trees might be almost stripped of their limbs by the weight of the pigeons. There were many other kinds of game birds, as the pheasant, quail, woodcock, plover, snipe, curlew, and the like. Rabbits and squirrels were so numerous as to be a very great pest and in many places bounties were paid for their heads. "The Swedish traveler, Kalm, said that in Pennsylvania in one year, 1749, £8,000 was paid out for heads of black and gray squirrels, at three pence a head,

---

[61a] Earle, Home life in colonial days, 122.

which would show that over six hundred thousand were killed."[62]

There was an abundance of wild nuts which could be gathered and used, such as walnuts, hickory-nuts, chestnuts, hazelnuts, and the like. There were plenty of wild berries, as huckleberries, blackberries, and strawberries, and likewise wild grapes. The colonists used the pawpaw and other wild fruits found in the woods. "The North Carolinians even made puddings and what they called tarts of the American pawpaw."[63] They planted out apple-trees and peach-trees and other kinds of fruit trees and it was not many years till there was plenty of these cultivated fruits. The apples were especially valuable to them and used in various ways, applesauce, and apple-butter were made in great quantity by each family. "They made preserves and conserves, marmalets and quiddonies, hypocras and household wines, usquebarbs and cordials. They candied fruits and made syrups. They preserved everything that would bear preserving. I have seen old-time receipts for preserving quinces, 'respasse,' pippins, 'apricocks,' plums, 'damsins,' peaches, oranges, lemons, artichokes, green walnuts, elecampane roots, eringo roots, grapes, barberries, cherries; receipts for syrup of clove gillyflower, wormwood, mint, aniseed, clove, elder, lemons, marigolds, citron, hyssop, liquorice; receipts for conserves of roses, violets, borage flowers, rosemary, betony, sage, mint, lavender, marjoram, and 'piony;' rules for candying fruit, berries, and flowers, for poppy water, cordial, cherry water, lemon water, thyme water, Angelica water, Aqua Mirabilis, Aqua Cœlestis, clary water, mint water."[64]

The natives not only gave to the colonists the valuable Indian corn, but also with it three vegetables that are yet to this day raised in the field with this grain, being the pumpkin, the squash, and the bean. They also got the potato, both Irish and sweet, from the natives, but the colonists did not learn for quite a time how to prepare the Irish potato properly and so at first it was not liked and not greatly used. They supplemented the native list of vegetables with those grown in Europe, and so it was not long till they had growing peas and turnips and parsnips and carrots and cucumbers and many others.

[62] Earle, Home life in colonial days, 110.
[63] Eggleston, The colonists at home, Century magazine, VII, 883.
[64] Earle, Customs and fashions in old New England, 155.

Another product which they obtained from the natives, although not food, almost seemed to take its place as food, which was tobacco. This became about as great a necessity with the colonists as food and its use became general in all the colonies and among all classes of people, and even with women. If there was one people above all the other colonists in the use of tobacco it was the New York Dutch, who smoked incessantly, and yet the New Englanders were not far away from the lead. "Boston was the best market for snuff. The early lawmakers of Massachusetts had sought to put tobacco under ban, or at least to hamper it, after the example set in England, where tobacco was forbidden in ale-houses because it was believed to excite a thirst for strong drink. But revered preachers became fond of the pipe, and the restrictions were quite broken down by their example. Groups of New England ministers were wont to fill a room so full of smoke that it became stifling. Long before the close of the seventeenth century, ladies of social standing in New England 'smoked it,' as the phrase ran; and in 1708 one finds the Governor of Massachusetts showing friendly feeling by sociably smoking a pipe with the wife of Judge Sewall."[65]

The colonists found another food in the woods that helped them out greatly and that was wild honey, which helped to fill the need of sugar which was very scarce with them. They also got a supply of sweetening from the sugar-maple tree, whose sap they learned to use in making sugar and syrup. This became quite an important industry and helped to give a greater variety of cooked foods. This sugar making was important enough in Virginia to have it written about by Governor Berkeley, wherein he called the maple the sugar-tree. "The Sugar-Tree yields a kind of Sap or Juice which by boiling is made into Sugar. This Juice is drawn out, by wounding the Trunk of the Tree, and placing a Receiver under the Wound. It is said that the Indians make one Pound of Sugar out of eight Pounds of the Liquor. It is bright and moist with a full large Grain, the Sweetness of it being like that of good Muscovada."[66]

But the colonists did not altogether rely upon honey and maple-sugar for their sweetening as many families did keep a supply of sugar, and especially to sweeten the tea. This was in the form of a loaf or cone, called loaf-sugar, which

[65] Eggleston, The colonists at home, Century magazine, VII, 886.
[66] Earle, Home life in colonial days, 111.

weighed nine or ten pounds, and one cone would usually last a family an entire year. The sugar was cut up into lumps of equal and regular size by the women of the household, for which purpose they had sugar-shears or sugar-cutters.

The colonists began to raise cattle and hogs and sheep and so when wild game became scarce the domestic animals furnished the meat. There were no ways for keeping meat fresh for any length of time after it was killed and so it had to be preserved by being salted and pickled. They had smokehouses for smoking and curing beef, ham, and bacon. They made sausage and head-cheese and rendered out the lard and the tallow. "Sausage-meat was thus prepared in New York farmhouses. The meat was cut coarsely into half-inch pieces and thrown into wooden boxes about three feet long and ten inches deep. Then its first chopping was by men using spades which had been ground to a sharp edge."[67]

With the raising of Indian corn and the clearing of ground so that grass might grow abundantly, the number of cows increased till in the eighteenth century milk and its products became quite an important industry. Mrs. Earle concludes that butter was not made by many families in the seventeenth century because of there being so few churns, as she states that in the inventories of the property of the early settlers of Maine there is but one churn named. But by the eighteenth century the care of cream and butter-making went on in every household in the country and with many in the town. Cheese, too, became a leading product and one of the staple foods.

**Drink.** At the time of the settlement of America, water was not used in Europe as a constant drink, and hence the colonists were used to other drinks and one of their greatest complaints upon their first living in the new country was on account of their being deprived of the old country drinks. Governor Bradford of the Pilgrims in Massachusetts complained loudly and frequently of this deprivation while the Salem minister, Higginson, in 1629, boasted of his ability to drink water. "Whereas my stomach could only digest and did require such a drink as was both strong and stale, I can and ofttimes do drink New England water very well."[68] The colonists were not long without their beverages for one of their very first importations from England was beer, and soon they were manufacturing ale and beer themselves, and in 1675

[67] Earle, Home life in colonial days, 154.
[68] Earle, Customs and fashions in old New England, 163.

Cotton Mather stated that every other house in Boston was an ale-house.

Although for a short time the colonists might have had to use water, yet that did not change their taste for other drinks, and through manufactures and importations, the country became flooded with liquors and the drink-habit became universal. There was no class of people among the colonists that would be considered temperate according to present-day standards. Drink was a part of every transaction, of every doing in both public and private life, as, auctions, buyings and sellings, signing a deed, drawing up a contract; house-raisings, the moving into a new house, the arrival and departure of friends; the election of officers, the assembling of a court, the arbitration of a suit; funerals, weddings, the birth of a child; the ordaining of deacons, the induction of a new minister, the assembling of a body of clergymen, the opening of a yearly Quaker meeting, and even religious meetings in private houses.

"In Boston, and perhaps elsewhere, the great punch-bowl came on the table first of all; the master of the house, after setting an example, sent around the table the cup that he had drunk from, that each guest might drink in turn. A 'generous bottle' of fiery Madeira topped off every dinner among the gentry in New York. In Virginia a host now and then showed his hospitality by locking the door and cheerily notifying his guests that no man might depart until all were drunk."[69]

As was stated above, before coming to this country the colonists were unaccustomed to the use of water as a constant beverage and upon arriving in America they complained bitterly at having to drink water. They not only considered it a hardship to be deprived of their accustomed drinks, but also they had been trained to consider it dangerous to health to drink water. Water was believed to contain matter injurious to health and so they really seemed to have dreaded its use and all the more so because in those days there was no analyzing of the water to learn of its ingredients and the mystery and lore surrounding it made it seem all the more dangerous. Being compelled to use water upon their arrival in America, the Puritan settlers were greatly surprised that instead of being injurious it was found to agree with them and that there was improvement in health instead of deterioration. This fact so impressed Governor Winthrop that he continued

[69] Eggleston, The colonists at home, Century magazine, VII, 885.

water as a constant drink in his family and in 1630 he stopped the custom of drinking healths at his table. This example of their chief officer must have had its influence, for laws were passed against excessive drinking and drunkenness and against drinking healths in public and thus was tried to keep down so great drinking. These laws had some good effects for during the seventeenth century, judged at least by the standards of their times, it would appear for the great part that the New Englanders were sober and law-abiding.

It must be recognized that at the time of the settlement of America by European colonies, alcoholic stimulants were considered a necessary part of living, about as necessary a provision as bread, and, further, that water was looked upon as really dangerous to health. So it need not be so greatly wondered at that the colonists were so much given to drink almost anything and everything but water and also it may account somewhat for the many kinds of drinks, for not only were they seeking drinks that were palatable but also that were healthful. They not only imported all kinds of drinks but manufactured them here and likewise experimented with materials that were found here but not in Europe, as the Indian corn and other plants. Yet the above does not hide the fact that the colonists were great drinkers and that they drank because they wanted to and would have drank, excuse or no excuse. Nevertheless, there were efforts made against drunkenness even in those days and some good starts made, too.

The colonists made whisky from rye, wheat, barley, and also from potatoes and Indian corn. They imported rum from the West Indies and, too, imported the molasses and made the rum themselves. "The making of rum aided and almost supported the slave-trade in this country. The poor negroes were bought on the coast of Africa by New England sea-captains and merchants and paid for with barrels of New England rum. These slaves were then carried on slave-ships to the West Indies, and sold at a large profit to planters and slave-dealers for a cargo of molasses. This was brought to New England, distilled into rum, and sent off to Africa. Thus the circle of molasses, rum, and slaves was completed."[70] Beer was the first drink, and even among the very first articles imported from England by the Puritan settlers. They soon learned to make beer from the Indian corn and "the pious

[70] Earle, Home life in colonial days, 163.

Puritans quickly learned to cheat in their brewing, using molasses and coarse sugar.''[71] The Dutch established breweries at New York and Albany and they were great beer-drinkers. The English colonists, both in New England and in Virginia, were not such great users of beer, but found other drinks to take its place. One such drink was metheglin or mead, made from honey, yeast, and water in England, while in this country it was learned as well to make it from the sweet-bean of the honey-locust and also by a concoction of honey and a liquid from a mixture of various herbs, and which was considered a fine drink. In Virginia a home-made beer was made from Indian corn meal, from the green stalks of the Indian corn, from baked cakes of a paste of persimmons, from potatoes, and from artichokes. In New England the small beer was made by a mixture of a decoction made from spruce or birch or sassafras twigs and molasses and water or by boiling the twigs in the sap of the sugar maple. There were plenty of wines imported and vineyards were planted and wines were made by the colonists. Also brandies were imported and manufactured.

As apple orchards increased and apples became plentiful, cider became the great drink in New England. It became the common drink of the people and it was made in vast quantities. It was very cheap and used everywhere, being used in large amounts by students at college, given to children at meals, furnished to travelers and to Indians, and indeed to any one who wished it. ''Beverige'' was another common drink, mild in its character, made in various ways, one way being of water flavored with molasses and ginger. Another such drink was sillabub, in one form made of cider with sugar, nutmeg, and cream added. There were many other kinds of drinks, as, switchel, similar to beverige, ebulum made from the juice of the elder and juniper berries mixed with ale and spices, perry made from pears, peachy made from peaches, apple-jack distilled from cider, flip made of small beer and sweetened with sugar or molasses or dried pumpkin and rum added and also made in other ways. Beside all the drinks enumerated here there were various other kinds.

''A terrible drink is said to have been popular in Salem—a drink with a terrible name—whistle-belly-vengeance. It consisted of sour household beer simmered in a kettle, sweet-

[71] Earle, Customs and fashions in old New England, 164.

ened with molasses, filled with brown-bread crumbs and drunk piping hot."[72]

In the early years of the colonists, they did not have tea or coffee or chocolate as drinks since they were not in use in England at the time. It was not till about the last third of the seventeenth century that these drinks were introduced into the colonies and it was not till the first part of the eighteenth century that their use had become any ways general. About this time came the porcelain ware specially designed for the use of tea and lacquered tables on which to serve it and tea-drinking became fashionable throughout the country. In Virginia upon the calling of the young men of afternoons the young ladies served them with tea. The Dutch of New York served tea with a lump of sugar at each cup, which was placed in the mouth and kept there while the tea was being sipped. In the early introduction of tea into New England, it was not understood just how to prepare it. Sometimes the tea was boiled quite a while till it was bitter and then drank without milk or sugar. Again, after the boiling of the tea the liquid was poured off and the cooked leaves eaten and to make them more to the taste the leaves were buttered and salted. It is unexplainable how people who were not afraid of any drink whatever providing it was not water should have feared to drink tea, and yet such was the case. When tea-drinking began to be general there were many utterances against it, such terms being used as "detestable weed," "base exotick," "rank poison far-fetched and dear bought," "base and unworthy Indian drink." Many ill effects were ascribed to tea-drinking, such as the frequent decay and loss of teeth in America and ill-health in general and as being especially injurious to the mind. During the time just before and at the Revolution tea was proscribed by the women loyal to the cause of America and many substitutes arose, as, the raspberry, loose-strife, goldenrod, dittany, blackberry, yaupon, sage, strawberry, currant, thoroughwort, ribwort, and many others. Of all the substitute tea-drinks, Liberty Tea was the most esteemed. "It was thus made: the four-leaved loose-strife was pulled up like flax, its stalks were stripped of the leaves and boiled; the leaves were put in an iron kettle and basted with the liquor from the stalks. Then the leaves were put in an oven and dried. Liberty Tea sold

[72] Earle, Customs and fashions in old New England, 179.

for sixpence a pound. It was drunk at every spinning-bee, quilting, or other gathering of women."[73]

"At the time of the Stamp Act, when patriotic Americans threw the tea into Boston harbor, Americans were just as great tea-drinkers as the English. Now it is not so. The English drink much more tea than we do; and the habit of coffee-drinking, first acquired in the Revolution, has descended from generation to generation, and we now drink more coffee than tea. This is one of the differences in our daily life caused by the Revolution."[74]

In 1670 a license to sell coffee and chocolate was granted for an inn in Boston, which seems to be the first mention of the use of coffee. From this time on, other innkeepers obtained license to sell coffee and then came the establishment of regular coffee-houses. This drink also came into use in private families and coffee-pots and coffee-mugs and coffee dishes were brought in expressly for this use. As with tea, some people did not know at first how to prepare the coffee and so sometimes the whole beans were boiled without being crushed or ground. It is presumed that then the liquor was poured off and the cooked beans eaten as in the case with the leaves of the tea, but no statements are made that such was really the fact. Chocolate, too, came into use at this time, and it soon became quite a popular drink and mills to grind the cocoa were established in Boston.

Whatever prejudice the colonists may have had against the use of water as a drink, they certainly had none against the use of milk. Milk was used from the first and cows were increased in number and milk became very cheap, as in 1630 the statement was made by a minister of that time that milk cost but a penny a quart in Salem. It is found that writers among the colonists placed as being used together milk and bread, milk and hasty pudding, milk and baked apples, and milk and berries.

**Food and Drink of Children.** There is not a great deal left to us in the writings preserved from colonial times in reference to the food and drink of children of those days. But it is safe to judge that very much what the adults had the children would have had, modified to suit the needs of the different ages and added to such would be some things that are used mostly in childhood, as sweetmeats and the like.

[73] Earle, Customs and fashions in old New England, 181.
[74] Earle, Home life in colonial days, 165.

There was an abundance of food for children but not so great a variety. Among the good things were the cereal foods, which were plentiful and varied, many of such having been made from the Indian corn, as, samp, hominy, supawn, pone, succotash, described in another part of this chapter. Beans also were common and made good food for children. There were fruits, as, pears, apples, peaches, and cherries, and also prunes, figs, currants and raisins. There were several kinds of berries, some ripening in the summer and others in the fall, which the children gathered, and, too, there were plenty of nuts for them to gather in.

Sweetmeats for children were plentiful among the colonists even in the early days. There were sugar and molasses from which to make sweet things for the children, not omitting maple sugar. Raisins were brought in by the ships in large quantities for they were quite a dainty with the colonial children and in great demand. There was not a great variety of candy, among such being lemon-peel candy, angelica candy, rock candy, sugar candy, Black Jack, and Gibraltar Rock. It would be surmised that this latter named candy must have had lasting qualities like the all-day sucker of the present-day child. Rock-candy was the favorite and great amounts of it were brought in from China by the ships, one vessel having brought in at one time sixty tubs of this candy. There were candied eryngo-root, candied lemon-peel, and sugared coriander-seeds. The children had plenty of cakes those days and each city had some one confectioner or baker who was noted for his cakes. Boston had Meer's cakes. There were cookies, crullers, egg cakes, marchpanes, maccaroons, and other kinds.

Much less is given about the drink of children of colonial times than even about the food. Mrs. Earle found in an old almanac of the eighteenth century, where advice was given on the "Easy Rearing of Children," that young children should never be allowed to drink cold drinks, but should always have their beer a little heated. Children were given all the cider they wanted, even very little children drank it. Fortunately for the colonial children milk was very plentiful and cheap so they had plenty of that to drink. That children were given the drinks of their elders is shown in the following:

"This picture has been given by Sargent of country funerals in the days of his youth: 'When I was a boy, and was at an academy in the country, everybody went to everybody's funeral in the village. The population was small, funerals rare; the preceptor's absence would have excited remarks, and the boys were dismissed for the funeral. A table with liquors was always provided. Every one, as he entered, took off his hat with his left hand, smoothed down his hair with his right, walked up to the coffin, gazed upon the corpse, made a crooked face, passed on to the table, took a glass of his favorite liquor, went forth upon the plat before the house and talked politics, or of the new road, or compared crops, or swapped heifers, or horses until it was time to *lift*. A clergyman told me that when settled at Concord, N. H., he officiated at the funeral of a little boy. The body was borne in a chaise, and six little nominal pall-bearers, the oldest not thirteen, walked by the side of the vehicle. Before they left the house a sort of master of ceremonies took them to the table and mixed a tumbler of gin, water, and sugar for each.' " [75]

**Infancy.** It would be expected that a child born in any new country would have to undergo hardships, and this was particularly true of a child born in a rugged climate as in New England and among the early settlers who were so poorly prepared to withstand the rigors of a winter of that region. In a severe climate, with houses not very warmly built and so poorly heated that within a yard of the fire-place on a very cold day water would freeze, it could not be possible for a baby always or even ever to be kept comfortable.

Both in Dutch New York and Puritan New England the babe of a few days old was taken to the meeting-house to be baptized. This usually occurred among the Puritans on the first Sunday following the child's birth, whether summer or winter, whatever the weather, and it must take place in the meeting-house. As these meeting-houses had no fires in them, often on many a cold day the water in the christening-bowl froze and the ice had to be broken and the icy water was used on the child of less than a week old. The weather might be too cold for some of the adults to attend the ceremony but never too cold for the baby, as is shown in the following record made on January 22, 1694, in the diary of Judge Samuel Sewall of Boston. "A very extraordinary Storm by reason of the falling and driving of Snow. Few women could get to Meeting. A Child named Alexander was baptized in the afternoon." [76] Worst of all, one Puritan parson

[75] Earle, Customs and fashions in old New England, 371.
[76] Earle, Child life in colonial days, 4.

is recorded as immersing the infants and he only stopped the dangerous and cruel practice when his own little babe nearly lost its life by such.

There was great mortality among infants in the colonial times and especially in the earlier days. In one family of fourteen children, but three outlived the father, the majority of the children dying in infancy; in another family of fifteen children but two survived the father, and of these, too, the greater number died in infancy; in a third family five children in succession died in infancy, so that when the mother had been married nine years she had one living child and there were five little graves to tell the story of her life and sufferings.

In the seventeenth century medicine was yet being influenced by astrology and necromancy, there being quite a strong belief in occult influences. Consequently there was recorded the birth not only in the year, month, and day, but as well the hour and minute, so that it might be ascertained under what planet the child was born and thus be reckoned what influences for good or evil were ascendent at his birth.

The most common diseases of infancy at the time were worms, rickets, and fits, to use their plain Anglo-Saxon terms. The most famous medicines for the cure of rickets used snails as the basis of its formation, one noted receipt for making this snail water comes down to us as follows:

"The admirable and most famous Snail water.—Take a peck of garden Shel Snails, wash them well in Small Beer, and put them in an oven till they have done making a Noise, then take them out and wipe them well from the green froth that is upon them, and bruise them shels and all in a Stone Mortar, then take a Quart of Earthworms, scowre them with salt, slit them, and wash well with water from their filth, and in a stone Mortar beat them in pieces, then lay in the bottom of your distilled pot Angelica two handfuls, and two handfuls of Celandine upon them, to which put two quarts of Rosemary flowers, Bearsfoot, Agrimony, red Dock roots, Bark of Barberries, Betony wood Sorrel of each two handfuls, Rue one handful; then lay the Snails and Worms on top of the hearbs and flowers, then pour on three Gallons of the Strongest Ale, and let it stand all night, in the morning put in three ounces of Cloves beaten, sixpennyworth of beaten Saffron, and on the top of them six ounces of shaved Hartshorne, then set on the Limbeck, and close it with paste and so receive the water by pintes, which will be nine in all, the first is the strongest, whereof take in the morning two spoonfuls in four spoonfuls of small Beer, the like in the Afternoon."[77]

For worms and fits snails also were used, with senna and rhubarb and prunes. For teething there was a famous Anodyne Necklace, which was warranted to cure all disorders from teething, providing it was properly used. There were other remedies for teething, one of which was to scratch the child's gums with an osprey bone, and another was to hang a string of fawn's teeth or wolf's fangs around the baby's neck.

There was a custom that prevailed in which a dinner was given to the midwife, nurses, and the other women who had given help in the way of work or advice during the first week or two of the child's life. This occurred about the end of the child's second week. This was a good substantial meal, at one place consisting of "rost Beef and minc'd Pyes, good Cheese and Tarts," and another dinner was of "Boil'd Pork, Beef, Fowls, very good Rost Beef, Turkey, Pye and Tarts." There was also a custom of visiting the young babe and mother at which presents of money, clothing, or trinkets were given to the nurse. A usual gift to the young babe was a pincushion. This was quite fancifully made and the child's name with a welcome was made with pins stuck in the cushion or sewed on in steel beads, the pins being stuck about it.

"The baby was carried upstairs, when first moved, with silver and gold in his hand to bring him wealth and cause him always to rise in the world, just as babies are carried upstairs by superstitious nurses nowadays, and he had 'scarlet laid on his head to keep him from harm.'"[78]

There were cradles for these early babies, among the Puritans and Dutch, each with a deep hood to protect the child from the chilly drafts that were constantly occurring in the poorly heated houses, and for twins there were hoods at both ends of the cradle. There were wooden cradles, which often were paneled or carved. There were also wicker cradles, one of which still preserved, Mrs. Earle states, is one of the few authentic articles still surviving that came over on the *Mayflower*, and which cradle was used by Peregrine White, the first white child born in Plymouth. There was also used

[77] Earle, Customs and fashions in old New England, 6.
[78] *Ibid.*, 5.

as a cradle an Indian basket with handles at the ends whereby it was hung up on a wooden standard or frame. But perhaps the cradle most common in the earlier colonial years was one made of birch bark by the Indian women and obtained from them by the white mothers. The covering for the babe in the cradle was a homespun blanket or a pressed quilt. The blanket or "flannel sheet" was made of the finest whitest wool, usually having the baby's initials marked on it.

"A finer coverlet, one of state, the christening blanket, was usually made of silk, richly embroidered, sometimes with a text of Scripture. These were often lace-bordered or edged with a narrow home-woven silk fringe. The christening blanket of Governor Bradford of the Plymouth Colony still exists, whole of fabric and unfaded of dye. It is a rich crimson silk, soft of texture, like a heavy sarcenet silk, and is powdered at regular distances about six inches apart with conventional sprays of flowers embroidered chiefly in pink and yellow, in minute and beautiful cross-stitch. It is distinctly Oriental in appearance. . . . Another beautiful silk christening blanket was quilted in an intricate flower pattern in almost imperceptible stitches. These formal wrappings of state were sometimes called bearing-cloths or clothes, and served through many generations. Shakespeare speaks in *Henry VI.* of a child's bearing-cloth." [79]

In New England a go-cart or standing-stool was often used in teaching a baby to walk. As the mother must go to church and as, of course, the baby must go along, there was sometimes a little wooden cage, or something similar, to hold the young baby, while in the church.

**Number and Names of Children.** It is, perhaps, true that in a new country the average number of children to a family is greater than in older settled places. Although there were many instances of quite large families among the colonists of the United States, yet, as was noted under Infancy, there were so many deaths among the little ones that there were many families with a small number of children. Children were welcomed by the colonists and there was plenty of room for them and each child could find work about him to make himself helpful and not burdensome.

There are records of very large families. One mother had twenty-six children, one man was the father of thirty children, and families of fifteen children were not rare. Cotton

[79] Earle, Child life in colonial days, 23.

Mather states that, "One woman had not less than twenty-two children, and another had not less than twenty-three children by one husband, whereof nineteen lived to man's estate, and a third was mother to seven and twenty children."[80]

There seemingly was no particular trouble about finding names for all these children. Except among the Puritans double names were rarely given before the time of the Revolution. There were various reasons for naming the children and often the poor little babe was burdened with a name that must, as looked at nowadays, have caused it when older much pain and anger at its parents for inflicting such a punishment so unjustly deserved in its helpless state. Often the God-fearing parents sought out names of deep significance, such as they thought would affect the child's life and be productive of good upon its career. An expectant mother being widowed by the death of her husband in a snowstorm, upon the birth of her child named it Fathergone. A child named Seaborn told its place of birth in its name. Among the Puritans of New England names as the following were common and show by their significance why the children were so named: Deliverance, Temperance, Endurance, Patience, Silence, Submit, Rejoice, Comfort, Hoped For, Peace, Joy, Faith, Love, Hope, Charity.

"The children of Roger Clap were named Experience, Waitstill, Preserved, Hopestill, Wait, Thanks, Desire, Unite, and Supply. Madam Austin, an early settler of old Narragansett, had sixteen children. Their names were Parvis, Picus, Piersus, Prisemus, Polybius, Lois, Lettice, Avis, Anstice, Eunice, Mary, John, Elizabeth, Ruth, Freelove. All lived to be three-score and ten, one to be a hundred and two years old. Edward Bendall's children were named Truegrace, Reform, Hoped for, More mercy, and Restore. Richard Gridley's offspring were Return, Believe, and Tremble."[81]

**Child Welfare.** There is no doubt that the welfare of their children was considered by the colonists, as with any body of people, but the hardships of a settling people would react upon child life as well as upon adult life. Much of the seeming harshness of the Puritan settlers toward their children was brought forth by the stern necessities under which they had to live as well as the sternness of their religious ideas. They did not try to find for themselves easy paths

[80] Earle, Child life in colonial days, 12.
[81] *Ibid.*, 16.

of going and they did not always see that these paths were extremely rough for young and tender feet. This is illustrated in the writings of one of them who was giving advice on the rearing of children, in which he urged that boys should go without hats to harden them and children's feet should be wet in cold water and also they should wear thin-soled shoes in order to toughen the feet. Whether following the suggestions of this writer or not, the parents of Josiah Quincy did act in accord with them for when he was but three years of age, in winter and summer, they would take him out of his bed of a morning and carry him to a cellar kitchen and dip him three times in a tub of cold water fresh from the pump, and also no attention was paid to the care of his feet, so that in his boyhood his feet were wet for half the time or more.

This rough treatment of children is likewise shown in reference to their position at meals. In those old days children were often not permitted to be seated at their meals but they were to stand and eat as rapidly as possible, so as to get out of the way and troubling of the adults, and to keep quiet and make no complaint at their treatment. Sometimes the children had to stand at the side of the table and eat their food standing, while the parents and the other adults were seated. Again, the children would stand behind their parents and the other grown people and receive such food as would be handed back to them from the table, just as with the household animals. In other families the children stood at a sidetable and they would take their trenchers to the large table to receive the food to take back to their own table to eat.

That these early people were deeply interested in their children's welfare and appreciated their hardships is shown by the following statements from the writings of Governor Bradford:

"As necessitie was a taskmaster over them, so they were forced to be such, not only to their servants, but in a sorte, to their dearest children; the which, as it did not a little wound ye tender hearts of many a loving father and mother, so it produced likewise sundrie sad and sorrowful effects. For many of their children, that were of best dispositions and gracious inclinations, haveing lernde to bear ye yoake in their youth, and willing to bear parte of their parents burdens, were often times so oppressed with their hevie labours, that though their minds were free and willing, yet their bodies bowed under ye weight of ye same, and became decreped in their early youth; the vigor of nature being consumed in ye very budd as it were. But that which was more lamentable and of all sorrowes most heavie to be borne, was, that many of their children, by these occasions, and ye great licentiousness of youth in ye countrie, and ye manifold temptations of the place, were drawn away by evil examples into extravagante and dangerous courses, getting ye raines off their neks and departing from their parents. Some became souldiers, other took upon them for viages by sea, and other some worse courses, tending to disoluteness and the danger of their soules, to ye great greef of their parents and dishonor of God. So that they saw their posteritie would be in danger to degenerate and be corrupted.'' [82]

**Manners and Courtesy of Children.** One of the characteristics of the age of chivalry in Europe was the bearing of the young people toward their elders and superiors and parents, and this idea was carried down through the ages and even was brought to America, so that the character of the colonial child was greatly influenced by those old laws of courtesy. Such often made little boys and girls act as older people and to be dressed in an oldish way. Little girls were frequently addressed with the stiff term Mistress, even the term Miss not being strong enough as it was deemed to be lacking in dignity, designating childishness and flippancy and lack of character. In a written funeral tribute to a little girl of seven, she was designated as "Mrs. Rebeckah Sewall," and another child was written of as "Mrs. Sarah Gerrish, a very beautiful and ingenious damsel seven years of age."

There were books of etiquette for children offering rules for their guidance, among the things found in them being the following:

"Never sit down at the table till asked, and after the blessing. Ask for nothing; tarry till it be offered thee. Speak not. Bite not thy bread but break it. Take salt only with a clean knife. Dip not the meat in the same. Hold not thy knife upright but sloping, and lay it down at right hand of plate with blade on plate. Look not earnestly at any other that is eating. When moderately satisfied leave the table. Sing not, hum not, wriggle not. Spit no where in the room but in the corner.''

"Eat not too fast nor with Greedy Behavior. Eat not

[82] Earle, Customs and fashions in old New England, 16.

vastly but moderately. Make not a noise with thy Tongue, Mouth, Lips, or Breath in Thy Eating and Drinking. Smell not of thy Meat; nor put it to Thy Nose; turn it not to the other side upward on Thy Plate.''

"When any speak to thee, stand up. Say not I have heard it before. Never endeavor to help him out if he tell it not right. Snigger not; never question the Truth of it."[83]

Children were taught to be considerate of the old and afflicted and to respect and honor their parents. This often led to a stiff and formal manner as is shown in the following letter written by a girl of eleven residing on Long Island:

"EVER HONORED GRANDFATHER;

SIR: My long absence from you and my dear Grandmother has been not a little tedious to me. But what renders me a Vast Deal of pleasure is Being intensely happy with a Dear and Tender Mother-in-Law and frequent oppertunities of hearing of your Health and Welfair which I pray God may long Continue. What I have more to add is to acquaint you that I have already made a Considerable Progress in Learning. I have already gone through some Rules of Arithmetic, and in a little Time shall be able of giving you a Better acct of my Learning, and in the mean time I am Duty Bound to subscribe myself
    Your most obedient and
      Duty full Granddaughter
        PEGGA TREADWELL."[84]

Another little girl of eleven, in this same manner closes a letter written at Boston in 1771 to her parents in Nova Scotia:

"With Duty, Love & Compliments as due, perticularly to my Dear little brother (I long to see him) & Mrs. Law, I will write to her soon.
    I am Hon$^d$ Papa & mama,
      Yr Dutiful Daughter
        ANNE GREEN WINSLOW."[85]

Yet withal there were boys in those old colonial days who were as boys in all times and among all peoples. They played

[83] Earle, Child life in colonial days, 215, 216, 217.
[84] Earle, Colonial days in old New York, 16.
[85] Earle, Diary of Anna Green Winslow, 8.

and shouted and raced in the streets and were reprimanded by the authorities; they worried the poor night patrolman in New Amsterdam by setting dogs on him and by getting behind trees and fences and shouting out to him "The Indians!" they made disorder in the churches of the Puritans and were knocked on the head with the hard knob of the long stick of the tithing-man; they robbed orchards, tore down gates, frightened horses, and threw stones at dogs and cats and at each other; they beat and kicked one another and produced bloody noses; "worse yet, when the girls went forth to gather 'daisies and butter-flowers,' the ungallant boys kicked the girls 'to make them pipe.' "[86]

**Diary of a Boston School Girl of 1771.** Of the quaint and delightful things that are preserved to us of those old days of our country, to me there are none others more attractive than the writings of a little Boston school girl, gathered up and put in book form by Mrs. Alice Morse Earle.[87] These writings are the diary of Anna Green Winslow, who in 1770, at the age of ten years, was sent from her home in Nova Scotia to Boston, the birthplace of her parents, to "finish" her education in the schools of that city. I shall not attempt to analyze these writings, that is thoroughly done by Mrs. Earle in her *Foreword*, but simply give a few extracts, without comment, to show somewhat the thoughts and feelings of a girl who lived in Boston during those stirring times, 1771-1773, and whose father was a paymaster in the English army and loyal to his king.

In her *Foreword* Mrs. Earle tells of the condition of the diary. "It covers seventy-two pages of paper about eight inches long by six and a half inches wide. The writing is uniform in size, every letter is perfectly formed; it is as legible as print, and in the entire diary but three blots can be seen, and these are very small. A few pages were ruled by the writer, the others are unruled. The old paper, though heavy and good, is yellow with age, and the water marks C. J. R. and the crown stand out distinctly. The sheets are sewed in a little book, on which a marbled paper cover has been placed, probably by a later hand than Anna's. Altogether it is a remarkably creditable production for a girl of twelve."

"My Aunt Deming says I shall make one pye myself at

---

[86] Earle, Child life in colonial days, 226.
[87] Earle, Diary of Anna Green Winslow, A Boston School Girl of 1771.

least. I hope somebody beside myself will like to eat a bit of my Boston pye, thou' my papa and you did not (I remember) chuse to partake of my Cumberland performance. ... My aunt Deming gives her love to you and says it is this morning 12 years ago since she had the pleasure of congratulating papa and you on the birth of your scribling daughter. She hopes if I live 12 years longer that I shall write and do everything better than can be expected in the *past* 12. ... Dear mamma, you don't know the fation here— I beg to look like other folk. You dont know what a stir would be made in sudbury street, were I to make my appearance there in my red Dominie & black Hatt. ... My aunt also says, that till I come out of an egregious fit of laughterre that is apt to seize me & the violence of which I am at this present under, neither English sense, nor anything rational may be expected of me. ... Elder Whitwell told my aunt, that this winter began as did the Winter of 1740. How that was I don't remember but this I know, that to-day is by far the coldest we have had since I have been in New England. (N. B. All run that are abroad.) ... I began my shift at 12 o'clock last monday, have read my bible every day this week & wrote every day save one. ... Unkle is just come in with a letter from Papa in his hand (& none for me) by way of New bury. I am glad to hear that all was well the 26 Nov$^r$ ult. I am told my Papa has not mention'd me in this Letter. Out of sight, out of mind. ... My cloak & bonnet are really very handsome, & so they had need be. For they cost an amasing sight of money, not quite £45 tho' Aunt Suky said, that she suppos'd Aunt Deming would be frightened out of her Wits at the money it cost. I have got *one* covering, by the cost, that is genteel, & I like it much myself. ... I heard Mr. Thacher preach our Lecture last evening Heb. II. 3. I remember a great deal of the sermon, but a'nt time to put it down. It is one year last Sep$^r$ since he was ordain'd & he will be 20 years of age next May if he lives so long. ... I have now the pleasure to give you the result, viz., a very genteel well regulated assembly which we had at Mr. Soley's last evening, miss Soley being mistress of the ceremony. We had two fiddles, & I had the honor to open the diversion of the evening in a minuet with miss Soley. Our treat was nuts, raisins, Cakes, Wine, punch, hot & cold, all in great plenty. We had a very agreeable evening from 5 to 10 o'clock. For variety we woo'd a widow, hunted the whistle, threaded the needle, & while the company was collecting, we diverted ourselves with the playing of pawns, no rudeness Mamma I assure you. . . . Hon$^d$ Mamma, My Hon$^d$ Papa has never signified to me his approbation of my journals, from whence I infer, that he either never reads them, or does not give himself the trouble to remember any of their contents, tho' some part has been address'd to him, so, for the future, I shall trouble only you with this part of my scribble. . . . My fingers are not the only part of me that has suffer'd with sores within this fortnight, for I have had an ugly great boil upon my right hip & about a dozen small ones—I am at present swath'd hip & thigh, as Samson smote the Philistines, but my soreness is near over. I have read my bible to my aunt this morning (as is the daily custom), & sometimes I read other books to her. So you may perceive, I *have the use of my tongue* & I tell her it is a good thing to have the use of my tongue. . . . My honor'd Grandma departed this vale of tears 1-4 before 4 o'clock wednesday morning August 21, 1771. Aged 74 years, 2 months & ten days. . . . I went to meeting & back in Mr. Soley's chaise. Mr. Hunt preached. He said that human nature is as opposite to God as darkness to light. That our sin is only bounded by the narrowness of our capacity. His text was Isa. xli. 14. 18. . . . Saterday I din'd at Unkle Storer's, drank tea at Cousin Barrel's was entertain'd in the afternoon with scating. . . . This day Jack Frost bites very hard, so hard aunt won't let me go to any school. I have this morning made part of a coppy with the very pen I have now in my hand, writing this with. . . . Papa I rec'd your letter dated Jan. 11, for which I thank you, Sir, & thank you greatly for the money I received therewith. . . . It has been a very sickly time here, not one person that I know of but has been under heavy colds. . . . Very cold, but this morning I was at sewing and writing school, this afternoon all sewing, for Master Holbrook does not in the winter keep school of afternoons. . . . We had the greatest fall of snow yesterday we have had this winter. Yet cousin Sally, miss Polly, & I rode to & from meeting in Mr. Soley's chaise both forenoon & afternoon, & with a stove was very comfortable there. . . . Boast not thyself of tomorrow: for thou knowest not what a day may bring forth. Thus king Solomon, inspired by the Holy Ghost, cautions, Pro. xxvii. 1. My aunt says, this is a most necessary lesson to be learn'd & laid up in the heart. I am quite of her mind. . . . Mr.

Stephen March, at whose house I was treated so kindly last fall, departed this life last week, after languishing several months under a complication of disorders—we have not had perticulars, therefore cannot inform you, whether he engag'd the King of terrors with christian fortitude, or otherwise. . . . This minute I have receiv'd my queen's night cap from Miss Caty Vans—we like it. Aunt says, that if the materials it is made of were more substantial than gauze, it might serve occationally to hold any thing mesur'd by an 1-2 peck, but it is just as it should be, & very decent, & she wishes my writing was *as* decent. But I got into one of my frolicks, upon sight of the Cap. . . . April 1st.—Will you be offended mamma, if I ask you, if you remember the flock of wild Geese that papa call'd you to see flying over the Blacksmith's shop this day three years? I hope not; I only mean to divert you. . . . Yesterday was the annual Fast, & I was at meeting all day. . . . I have now before me, hon$^d$ Mamma, your favor dated Jan. 3. I am glad you alter'd your mind when you at first thought not to write to me. I am glad my brother made an essay for a Post Script to your Letter. I must get him to read it to me, when he comes up, for two reasons, the one is because I may have the pleasure of hearing his voice, the other because I don't understand his characters. . . . I went a visiting yesterday to Col. Gridley's with my aunt. Col$^n$ brought in the talk of Whigs & Tories & taught me the difference between them. . . . Visited at uncle Joshua Green's. I saw three funerals from their window, poor Cap$^n$ Turner's was one. . . . I learn't three stitches upon net work to-day. . . . Last Wednesday Bet Smith was set upon the gallows. She behav'd with great impudence. . . .Yesterday I heard an account of a cat of 17 years old, that has just recovered of the meazels. This same cat it is said had the small pox 8 years ago. . . . Sept. 1.—Last evening after meeting Mrs. Bacon was brought to bed of a fine daughter. But was very ill. She had fits. September 7.—Yesterday afternoon Mr. Bacon baptiz'd his daughter by the name of Elizabeth Lewis. It is a pretty looking child. . . . Dear Mamma, what name has Mr. Bent given his Son? something like Nehemiah, or Jehosophat, I suppose, it must be an odd name (our head indeed, Mamma.) Aunt says she hopes it a'nt Baal Gad, & she also says that I am a little simpleton for making my note within the brackets above, because when I omit to do it, Mamma will think I have the help of somebody else's head but, N. B. for herself she utterly disclames having either her head or hand concern'd in this curious jurnal, except where the writing makes it manifest. So much for this matter.''

**Inheritance.** "The leadership of the great families was sustained in New York and in the colonies south of Pennsylvania by primogeniture—the prerogative of the eldest son to inherit the landed estate in case the father left no will. Custom followed the law, and fathers who willed their property usually left the most or all of the land to the oldest son, as belonging to him by prescriptive right. This inequitable practice had its use in the warlike ages of feudalism, when the first son to grow up must take his father's place at the head of his troop of dependents; but in the American colonies it was only the result of that remarkable and often stupid bondage to tradition in which the Anglo-Saxon peoples contrive to exist and advance. To primogeniture the aristocratic colonies added the dead hand of entail, by which the land was sent down for generations in the line of the oldest male. Even a clumsy fiction, called in law 'common recovery,' by which the entail might be broken in England, was forbidden by statute in Virginia, and was not accounted applicable to the other colonies.

"The pilgrims at Plymouth and the Massachusetts Puritans had belonged to that politico-religious party in England which sought the abolition of certain old abuses. As early as 1636 Plymouth enacted that land should be held after 'the laudable custom, tenure, and hold of the manor of East Greenwich,' that is, in an ancient Saxon way preserved at the coming of William the Conqueror by the county of Kent. One characteristic of this tenure was that it divided the lands equally among the sons in case there was no will. Massachusetts, which expressly abolished many of the worst features of feudal tenure by name, gave to the oldest son a double portion according to the Mosaic code, but divided the rest among daughters as well as sons. This system prevailed throughout New England. Primogeniture had come to be esteemed a natural right, and the Massachusetts leaders felt obliged more than once to defend themselves from the charge of having 'denied the right of the oldest son.' Pennsylvania took the same middle course of sheltering innovation under the law of Moses by giving the oldest son a double portion. The laws of some of the colonies made the land liable, to a greater or less extent, with personal estate for the debts of the deceasd—which robbd the oldest of a part of his 'insolent prerogative'; but it was not until the shock of the Revolution that primogeniture and entail were swept away, under the leadership of Jefferson and others. The oldest son's double portion in New England survived the Revolution for some years. A very ancient mode of inheritance prevailed in some English boroughs, called among lawyers 'borough English.' By this custom the lands descended to the youngest son. It found no lodgment in the laws of the colonies, so far as I know; but in New Hampshire it was a widespread custom to leave the homestead to the youngest, who remained at home and cared for the old age of his parents. This reasonable form of the custom of 'ultimogeniture' lingers yet in certain parts of the country, as, for example, in some of the northern counties of New York."[86]

**Sickness and Death.** There was great mortality among the early colonists and especially of children. There was nothing in the way of sanitation, drainage was not considered necessary, there was scarcely any disinfecting, and isolation in contagious diseases was but poorly carried out. There were various kinds of diseases, such as colds, fevers, malignant sore throats, scurvy, rickets, fluxes, and many others, and contagious diseases, smallpox having been very prevalent, almost as pneumonia now, and being epidemic six times in a century.

In the earlier times the ministers took up medicine and practiced healing as well as preaching, also compounding and selling drugs to the people. Also other persons entered into healing and selling medicines, as, innkeepers, magistrates, grocers, and schoolmasters. There were, of course, plenty of quacks and quack medicines. Even those who really practiced medicine were not very well prepared. Such a person did not prepare himself by long and arduous study in some school of medicine, in fact there were none in the early days, but he joined himself to an established physician to learn the business from him. "He ground the powders, mixed the pills, rode with the doctor on his rounds, held the basin when the patient was bled, helped to adjust plasters, to sew wounds, and ran with vials of medicine from one end of the town to the other. In the moments snatched from duties such as these

[86] Eggleston, Social conditions in the colonies, Century magazine, VI, 853.

he swept out the office, cleaned the bottles and jars, wired skeletons, tended the night-bell, and, when a feast was given, stood in the hall to announce the guests."[89] But even with this little training he became a power for good in his community for "Sunshine and rain, daylight and darkness, were alike to him. He would ride ten miles on the darkest night, over the worst of roads, in a pelting storm, to administer a dose of calomel to an old woman, or to attend a child in a fit. He was present at every birth; he attended every burial; he sat with the minister at every death-bed, and put his name with the lawyers to every will."[90] The pay of the physicians was often quite meager and "in many communities a bone-setter had to be paid a salary by the town in order to keep him, so few and slight were his private emoluments, even as a physic-monger."[91] There was the practice of midwifery in those days and in New Amsterdam, at least, it was a much respected calling.

Among a people who feared to use water as a constant drink, as given under "Drink" in a foregoing part of this chapter, it is not to be wondered at that water was denied the patient tormented with fever, and clam-juice in small quantities given instead. Bleeding and purging were resorted to on every possible occasion. Salve was one of the leading remedies and there were many different kinds used. But the great remedies were those compounded and concocted from the plants and the minerals and the animals that went into the medical preparations of those times. They tried about every weed and flower and most everything else to find remedies and it did not seem to matter what the preparation or the mixture was for they often went in as a jumble regardless of the effect of one upon another. Earth-worms, snails, toads, fishes, sowbugs, wood-lice, spiders, vipers, and adders among the animal life were used; there was a great array of plants, such as plantain, dandelion, dock, catnip, jimson-weed, horehound, mint, garlic, elder, sage, saffron, tansy, and wormwood; and of the mineral substances were quicksilver, verdigris, brimstone, alum, and copperas. It did not seem to matter greatly about the doses as there was no close exactness as the quantity was given as "the bigth of a walnut," "enough to lie on a pen knifes point," "the weight of a shilling,"

---

[89] McMaster, History of the people of the United States, I, 27.
[90] Ibid., I, 29.
[91] Earle, Customs and fashions in old New England, 361.

"enough to cover a French crown," "as bigg as a haselnut." "take a little handful," "take a pretty quantity as often as you please," and other similar lax directions.

There was scarcely an affliction for which there were not several remedies. Here is a cure for insomnia:

"Bruise a handful of Anis-seeds, and steep them in Red Rose Water, & make it up in little bags, & binde one of them to each Nostrill, and it will cause sleep."[92]

For defective hearing is given the following:

"To Cure Deafness.—Take the Garden Daisie roots and make juyce thereof, and lay the worst side of the head low upon the bolster & drop three or four drops thereof into the better Ear; this do three or four dayes together."[93]

For melancholy the following is "A pretious water to revive the Spirits:"

"Take four gallons of strong Ale, five ounces of Aniseeds, Liquorish scraped half a pound, Sweet Mints, Angelica, Eccony, Cowslip flowers, Sage & Rosemary Flowers, sweet Marjoram, of each three handfuls, Palitory of the VVal one handful. After it is fermented two or three dayes, distil it in a Limbeck, and in the water infuse one handful of the flowers aforesaid, Cinnamon and Fennel-seed of each half an ounce, Juniper berries bruised one dram, red Rosebuds, roasted Apples & dates sliced and stoned, of each half a pound; distil it again and sweeten it with some Sugarcandy, and take of Amber-greese, Pearl, Red Coral, Hartshorn pounded, and leaf Gold, of each half a Dram, put them in a fine Linnen bag, and hang them by a thread in a Glasse."[94]

Perhaps next to the wonderful Snail-Water for rickets, given on page 497 of this chapter, the Water of Life was the great remedy, used for fevers and also as a tonic in health:

"Take Balm leaves and stalks, Betony leaves and flowers, Rosemary, red sage, Taragon, Tormentil leaves, Rossolis and Roses, Carnation, Hyssop, Thyme, red strings that grow upon Savory, red Fennel leaves and root, red Mints, of each a handful; bruise these hearbs and put them in a great earthen pot, & pour on them enough White Wine as will cover them, stop them close, and let them steep for eight or nine days; then put to it Cinnamon, Ginger, Angelica-seeds, Cloves, and Nuttmegs, of each an ounce, a little Saffron, Sugar one pound,

---

[92] Earle, Customs and fashions in old New England, 343.
[93] Ibid., 344.
[94] Ibid., 340.

Raysins solis stoned one pound, the loyns and legs of an old Coney, a fleshy running Capon, the red flesh of the sinews of a leg of Mutton, four young Chickens, twelve larks, the yolks of twelve Eggs, a loaf of White-bread cut in sops, and two or three ounces of Mithradate or Treacle, & as much Muscadine as will cover them all. Distil al with a moderate fire, and keep the first and second waters by themselves; and when there comes no more by distilling put more Wine into the pot upon the same stuffe and distil it again, and you shal have another good water. This water strengtheneth the Spirit, Brain, Heart, Liver, and Stomack. Take when need is by itself, or with Ale, Beer, or Wine mingled with Sugar." [95]

Small-pox was such a dreadful scourge to the colonists, causing death, disfigurement, and misfortune, that after inoculation was introduced and accepted as reliable, small-pox hospitals arose and it became quite the fashion for entire families and even parties made up of friends and acquaintances to resort to them together and be inoculated all at the same time, these parties being called classes. Sometimes these gatherings were held at private homes and special invitations were sent out to friends. "These brave classes took their various purifying and sudorific medicines in cheerful concert, were 'grafted' together, 'broke out' together, were feverish together, sweat together, scaled off together, and convalesced together. Not a very prepossessing conjoining medium would inoculation appear to have been, but many a pretty and sentimental love affair sprang up between mutually 'pock-fretten' New Englanders." [96]

The small-pox hospitals were of various kinds and prices, ranging as low as three dollars per week for lodging, food, medicine, care, and inoculation. The following advertisement of one such hospital appeared in the *Connecticut Courant* of November 30, 1767:

"Dr. Uriah Rogers, Jr., of Norwalk County of Fairfield takes this method to acquaint the Publick & particularly such as are desirous of taking the Small Pox by way of Inoculation, that having had Considerable Experience in that Branch of Practice and carried on the same the last season with great Success; has lately erected a convenient Hospital for that purpose just within the Jurisdiction Line of the Province of

[95] Earle, Customs and fashions in old New England, 337.
[96] *Ibid.*, 353.

New York about nine miles distant from N. Y. Harbour, where he intends to carry said Branch of Practice from the first of October next to the first of May next. And that all such as are disposed to favour him with their Custom may depend upon being well provided with all necessary accommodations, Provisions & the best Attendance at the moderate Expense of Four Pounds Lawful Money to Each Patient. That after the first Sett or Class he purposes to give no Occasion for waiting to go in Particular setts but to admit Parties singly, just as it suits them. As he has another Good House provided near Said Hospital where his family are to live, and where all that come after the first Sett that go into the Hospital are to remain with his Family until they are sufficiently Prepared & Inoculated & Until it is apparent that they have taken the infection.''[97]

Upon a death in a town in New York state in colonial times, notice was given by the ringing or tolling of the church-bell and the funeral inviter was sent out, a man paid for his services, who was dressed in gloomy black with long streamers of crape hanging from his hat. The ones to be invited were visited by him and notified of the day and hour of the funeral. The funeral-inviter usually combined in himself along with this office those of schoolmaster, bell-ringer, chorister, and grave-digger. Later the funeral-inviter was made a public officer and the fees were regulated by law. The corpse while lying at the home was watched over through the night by intimate friends of the family and these watchers were well supplied with drinks and cakes and tobacco and pipes. The body lay in state in a large room which was rarely used for other occasions than this.

There were rare occurrences of night-burials in the colonies, confined to people belonging to the English Church, the funeral procession and burial taking place by torch-light. In the earlier times in New England there were no religious services of any kind at a funeral, neither at the house nor at the grave, but later there were prayers at the house and a short speech at the grave, and then funeral sermons began to be preached but not at the time of the burial. In New York there were funeral services but always held at the home. The coffin was made of well-seasoned boards and covered with a pall of fringed black cloth, which was replaced with a white sheet where the death took place in childbirth. As a mark of

[97] Earle, Customs and fashions in old New England, 353.

mourning, in some places all ornaments and mirrors and pictures were covered with cloths from the time of death till after the funeral and even sometimes the window-shutters at the front of the house were tied together with black cloth and kept closed for a year. There were usually two sets of pall-bearers, one set of strong young men who bore the coffin on a bier and another set of older men of dignity, who walked alongside the bearers and held the corners of the pall. Much etiquette was displayed in arranging the order of the procession to the grave, each mourner being carefully assigned to his place, the widow usually being placed with a magistrate or some other person of dignity.

Funerals became to be very expensive affairs and this brought about legislative enactments trying to regulate and curtail the expenses. When the cities began to grow and wealth to increase much pomp and dignity were used in the burial of men and women of high station, trumpets and drums being used and volleys fired over the grave—even of a woman. In properly putting away Governor Winthrop, the chief founder of Massachusetts, a barrel and a half of powder was consumed. In the middle and southern colonies, the funeral became to be a time of feasting and drinking. At a single funeral there might have been several barrels of wine and several hogsheads of beer consumed, beside great quantities of food eaten and tobacco used. Sometimes in Pennsylvania as many as five hundred guests at a funeral were served with punch and cake. At a funeral in Virginia the cost of the wine used amounted to more than four thousand pounds of tobacco. New England was not so far behind, as bills are found for much baked meats, rum, cider, whiskey, lemons, sugar, spices, and cakes used at funerals.

It was a custom in colonial times for the family of the deceased to give certain kinds of gifts to those who were invited to the funeral. Books were among the gifts, being serious books suitable as a memorial of the occasion, but probably book gifts occurred only in New England. Scarfs, often of silk, were among the presents and also handkerchief, the scarfs sometimes being worn quite awhile after the funeral as a token of mourning, thereby showing respect for the dead. Sometimes black ribbons were given, to be worn on the hat as long streamers. Spoons also were given in New York, called monkey-spoons, being made of silver with the figure or head of an ape on the handle. The two most common and most important gifts were gloves and rings. The gloves were white or black or purple and were of different quality, given according to rank or closeness of blood to the deceased. Hundreds of these gloves were often given out at a single funeral, at one funeral over a thousand were given and still at another three thousand pairs. A Boston clergyman kept account of the number he had received and in thirty-two years he had been given two thousand, nine hundred, and forty pairs of mourning gloves. In 1738 at a funeral in Boston over two hundred rings were given away. A judge received 57 mourning rings between 1687-1725, a minister had a mugful, and a physician who died in 1758 at the age of eighty-one left a quart tankard full of the rings. "These mourning rings were of gold, usually enameled in black, or black and white. They were frequently decorated with a death's-head, or with a coffin with a full-length skeleton lying in it, or with a winged skull. Sometimes they held a framed lock of hair of the deceased friend. Sometimes the ring was shaped like a serpent with his tail in his mouth. Many bore a posy."[96] These gloves and rings usually were sold. The Boston minister noted above received between six and seven hundred dollars through the sale of the gloves he had received at funerals and likewise quite a good sum from the sale of the funeral rings he had received.

There finally came a reaction against such great expense at funerals and the giving of gifts so that by the middle of the eighteenth century funerals were being held at which there was little or no feasting and drinking and but little mourning worn, and even some funerals were held at which no mourning at all had been worn. In the latter part of the century laws arose wherein fines were to be imposed on any person who gave scarfs, gloves, rings, wine, or rum at a funeral, or who bought any new mourning apparel except crape for an armband if a man or a black bonnet, fan, gloves, and ribbon if a woman. But such laws were difficult of being rigidly enforced and so, perhaps, had but little effect, public opinion and custom after all causing whatever changes that may have come about.

It was a custom to fasten to the bier or platform supporting the coffin verses and sentences laudatory to the deceased and such often were printed after the funeral and distributed among the relatives and friends. These prints were not only

[96] Earle, Customs and fashions in old New England, 376.

deeply bordered with black but "they were often decorated gruesomely with skull and cross-bones, scythes, coffins, and hour-glasses, all-seeing eyes with rakish squints, bow-legged skeletons, and miserable little rosetted winding-sheets."[99] When newspapers were established in the colonies it became the practice to insert long and fulsome death-notices. Perhaps the greatest display in writing about the dead was that of the epitaph. They were of all kinds and quality many quite amusing in both rhyme and thought, and yet there were some epitaphs of beauty and sentiment that make us glad for the efforts. The following is truly such a one:

> "I came in the morning—it was Spring
> And I smiled.
> I walked out at noon—it was Summer
> And I was glad.
> I sat me down at even—it was Autumn
> And I was sad.
> I laid me down at night—it was Winter
> And I slept."[100]

In New York interment was made under the church and by special payment burial could be made under the very seat the deceased was wont to occupy during life while upon attendance at church. In New England the burial was in the churchyard or it might, too, be made under the church and this was true in the large places and of dignitaries. In the smaller places the graveyard might have been located in a barren pasture or on an out-of-the-way hillside. In the country often each family had its own burying-place, sometimes in a corner of the home farm and again at the foot of the garden or orchard. The early gravestones were quite similar in design. Freestone was used for these and rarely sandstone on account of its being readily disintegrated by frosts and storms. The best stone was a flinty slate-stone from North Wales, which was imported from England ready carved, and these stones also were alike, having at the top a winged cherub's head. This remained the only emblem on stones till near the middle of the eighteenth century when there began to be used the weeping willow and urn.

**The Illness of Children.** As was given under Infancy, the baby had to be baptized in the meeting-house on the first Sunday following its birth, no matter what the conditions of the

[99] Earle, Customs and fashions in old New England, 365.
[100] Ibid., 385.

weather. This was surely as severe a test of the child's endurance as that ever devised by any people, not excepting the Spartans. Those that survived this baptism had to undergo many malignant diseases, so that the mortaliy among children was frightful and there was rarely if ever found a family that could not count a number of deaths of the children, often more died than reached maturity. The diseases and climatic conditions were severe enough on the children and the lack of sanitary caution added many children to the death list, yet these were not all for the poor things had tried out on them all kinds of nostrums and no doubt many died from the dosings.

Among the medicines for children was Venice treacle, made of vipers, white wine, opium, spices, licorice, red roses, tops of germander, and St. John's-wort, with about twenty other herbs, juice of rough sloes, and mixed with honey. Another medicine for children contained forty-two ingredients. As was given in another part of this chapter, rickets was one of the greatest afflictions of children and as was noted, Snail Water was one of the great remedies, for which see page 377. Here is another remedy for rickets, and the child that survived both the rickets and this treatment surely deserved to live:

"In ye Rickets the best Corrective I have ever found is a Syrup made of Black Cherrys. Thus. Take of Cherrys (dry'd ones are as good as any) & put them into a vessel with water. Set ye vessel near ye fire and let ye water be Scalding hot. Then take ye Cherrys into a thin Cloth and squeeze them into ye Vessell, & sweeten ye Liquor with Melosses. Give 2 spoonfuls of this 2 or 3 times a day. If you Dip your Child, Do it in this manner: viz: naked, in ye morning, head foremost in Cold Water, don't dress it Immediately, but let it be made warm in ye Cradle & sweat at least half an Hour moderately. Do this 3 mornings going & if one or both feet are Cold while other Parts sweat (which is sometimes ye Case) Let a little blood be taken out of ye feet ye 2nd Morning and yt will cause them to sweat afterwards. Before ye dips of ye Child give it some Snakeroot and Saffern Steep'd in Rum & Water, give this Immediately before Dipping and after you have dipt ye Child 3 Mornings Give it several times a Day ye following Syrup made of Comfry, Hartshorn, Red Roses, Hogbrake roots, knot-grass, pettymoral roots, sweeten ye Syrup with Melosses. Physicians are generally fearful about diping when ye Fever is hard, but oftentimes all attemps to lower it without diping are vain. Experience has taught me that these fears are groundless, yt many have about diping in Rickety Fevers; I have found in a multitude of Instances of diping is most effectual means to break a Rickety Fever. These Directions are agreeable to what I have practiced for many years.''[101]

At the funeral of a boy there would sometimes be boys of about the same age as the deceased to act as nominal pall-bearers to walk alongside the coffin borne by stronger young men. When a young child or girl was buried, sometimes the pall-bearers were girls, all dressed in white and wearing long white veils.

**Amusements.** Many of the amusements of the old country were brought into use by the colonists and there were some that grew up in the surroundings of the new country. There was a wide distinction between the New England colonies and the other colonies in regard to such, as the Puritans were much more sober in their bearing and really often counted amusements as things to be avoided and even ungodly and those of a hilarious nature were indulged in only by a few of the less staid and solid citizens.

The really only regular diversion of the early colonists in New England was the lecture-day, which usually occurred weekly on Thursdays. These days were the occasion of a lecture, usually religious, by the minister, and also there were other doings, as, burning seditious books, publishing notices of marriages, the holdng of electons, the whipping of transgressors at the whipping-post, the placing of offenders in the stocks, bilboes, cage, or pillory, and criminals, too, were hanged on these days. Another great day in the colonies was muster-day when the militia came together for drill. This became a time of merry-making as well as of military drilling and amusements of various kinds were entered into. Another time of gathering was at the fairs held in some of the middle and southern colonies, at which were foot-races, sack-races, wrestling, climbing greased poles, catching greased pigs, and the like.

As the cities grew, the people would strive to get out for a time in the country, so that inns and gardens grew up in the suburbs and were much frequented. These gardens were sometimes small and of a private nature and again they were

[101] Earle, Child life in colonial days, 8.

large and not only furnished the guests with food and drink but also with concerts and other entertainments. Clubs were quite numerous in those days, usually consisting of a number of men who had a weekly meeting at a tavern. These clubs often consisted of people of the same nationality, as, the Irish Club, the French Club, and so on. They had their patron saints on whose birthdays they would hold great festivals, the English having St. George, the Welsh St. David, the Irish St. Patrick, and the young Americans of New York, not to be outdone, "canonized, by their own authority, King Tammany, a Delaware chief long dead, and celebrated his feast on the old English May-day, which they ushered in with bell-ringings, as though it were a veritable saint's day."[102] There grew up in the cities gatherings of men and women, called "Assemblies," for the purpose of dancing, card-playing, and other social amusements. These were brilliant affairs, wherein both men and women were richly dressed, and where there was eating and drinking, great quantities of wine often being consumed.

The colonists were very fond of dancing. "From the most eastern forest settlements of Maine to the southern frontier of Georgia, people in town, village, and country were everywhere indefatigably fond of dancing . . . the launching of a ship, the raising of a house, the assembling of a county curt, and the ordination of a minister were good occasions for dancing."[103] They usually danced to the tune of a fiddle but if there was no fiddle that would not keep them from it as they would dance to some one's humming the tune. Dancing-schools arose and although they were forbidden in New England the young people learned to dance anyway. Dances sometimes began at six o'clock in the evening and lasted till three in the morning. "President Washington and Mrs. General Greene 'danced upwards of three hours without once sitting down,' and General Greene called this diversion of the august Father of His Country, 'a pretty little frisk.' "[104] This may be accounted for from the fact that the lady was usually assigned to her partner for the entire evening, with whom she did the greater part of her dancing.

Music was loved by the colonists throughout the entire colonial period. Yet in early New England there was really

[102] Eggleston, Social life in the colonies, Century magazine, VIII, 401.
[103] Ibid.
[104] Earle, Customs and fashions in old New England, 241.

little that could properly be called music, for in the church there was only the droning out of the Psalms and often these were not sung by all the congregation in the same tune at the same time, making a most inharmonious medley. The first music-book appeared in 1712. The early instruments for accompanying the voice were the spinet and the harpsichord, the first organ in Boston was about 1711.

Mrs. Earle states that though after 1760 concerts were frequent yet the earliest advertisement she had found of a concert was in the *New England Weekly Journal* of December 15, 1732:

"This is to inform the Publick That there will be a Consort of Music Perform'd by Sundry Instruments at the Court Room in Wings Lane near the Town Dock on the 28th of this Instant December; Tickets will be deliver'd at the Place of Performance at Five Shillings each Ticket. N. B. No Person will be admitted after Six." [105]

Because of the need of better music, there arose the "singing-school," a most happy form of amusement for the young people of the colonial days in New England where there was often but little chance for such. The singing-school teacher was a great man and when he made his appearance that other notable, the village school-master, had to take a back-seat for the time being, for this man was a "professional," who was to be paid and who paid his own bills and did not have to "board round." The singing-school gave agreeable occasion for the young people to spend a few of the long winter evenings together and for sleighing-parties to be made up to go to them, and where every girl, no matter how she got there, was sure of an escort home.

Card-playing and gambling were almost universal. Ladies gambled as well as gentlemen. Stakes often were high, sometimes large estates were lost in a short time by reckless betting at cards. "The ladies of New York were considered virtuous above many others of their sex because of the moderation of their gambling." [106] Although the New Englanders were very much opposed to cards and tried to stop their sale and use, yet they highly approved another form of gambling, the lottery. For a half century and longer the lottery was the greatest amusement of New England, it was sanctioned and participated in by all, the most esteemed citizens bought and sold

[105] Earle, Customs and fashions in old New England, 250.
[106] Eggleston, Social life in the colonies, Century magazine, VIII, 402.

tickets, and it was used as a scheme for raising funds for every purpose—colleges increased their endowments, towns and states raised money to pay their debts, and churches had lotteries "for promoting public worship and the advancement of religion." Not only were lotteries used to raise funds for public affairs but there were also private lotteries in great number and all kinds of prizes given, among such being furniture, clothing, real estate, jewelry, and books. "New England clergymen seemed specially to delight in this gambling excitement." [107]

As there was an abundance of wild game and fish, hunting and fishing were great sports among the colonists.

Deer were hunted in various ways. Sometimes the hunter, as learned from the Indians, covered himself in a deer skin and was thus enabled to get near the deer to shoot them; again a tree was felled and the hunter hid in the branches and shot the deer while browsing upon the twigs; at night the deer was approached by some one bearing a lighted torch and the hunter would shoot the dazed animal looking into the light, or the hunter would have a blazing fire in his canoe and float toward the deer and shoot it; also deer were run down by dogs and men on horseback. Wolves were caught on mackerel hooks bound together in a bunch and dipped in tallow; they were caught in iron traps; and they were caught in pits in the earth hidden by light coverings to let them fall through. Bears were caught in traps and pits and also hunted with dogs trained for the purpose. There was fox-chasing on horseback; sometimes on a moonlight night a sledge-load of codfish heads was left by a fence or wall where the moon shone brightly on it, and the foxes were shot as they came up to get the heads of the fishes. Squirrels were killed for sport and also because they consumed so much of the grain; sometimes two groups of hunters matched one another and then counted squirrel-scalps at night to see which party had killed the most squirrels during the day. Wild turkeys were trapped and killed with guns; sometimes fires would be built near their roosting-places and then they could be shot while bewildered from the light. Wild pigeons were taken in nets, by shooting with guns, and while on their roosts at night, they were knocked off with clubs, being so thickly together and thus unable to get away. Also other wild game was hunted, as, geese, ducks, grouse, partridges, and others.

[107] Earle, Customs and fashions in old New England, 255.

One way of taking wild game was by a "drive." A ring of men would encircle a large tract of country and draw inward toward a center, and thus drive in deer, bears, wolves, turkeys, and other game, and as the animals made effort to escape the men would shoot them. Another way of hunting was by a fire-ring. A body of men would encircle a tract of land and then set fire to the leaves, which would burn in toward the center and then the men would shoot the animals as they would try to break through the fire-ring and would thus be brought to view.

Fishing was carried on in various ways. One of the most common ways was with nets, which were of various kinds. Weirs were also used, probably learned from the Indians and improved upon by the colonists. Long lines were staked out in a river and on it were placed short lines with hooks for catching the fish. Fish were speared with a harping-iron or gig. Where the fish were very plentiful men could ride into the water at night and spear the fish with gigs by torch light. They also went to the falls of the rivers and caught the shad and salmon as they were ascending the river to spawn. Fish also were caught with hook and line, but in the earlier times when they were so abundant this was considered too slow a process.

In winter the favorite amusement in New York was riding in sleighs and this was true also in Philadelphia. In the bitter climate of New England sleighing as a pastime was not entered into by the colonists in the early days. The Dutch in New York also indulged a great deal in skating, the ponds, marshes, and watered meadows on Manhattan Island offering plenty of ice for the sport. Sometimes provisions were carried into New York on the back of marketmen on skates.

In a new country full of wild animals and wild men, it becomes necessary for the settler to learn to use the gun as a means of livelihood and of defense and so the settlers became fine marksmen. Because of their learning to shoot well there arose contests in marksmanship. This consisted often in shooting at a mark for a prize, a silk handkerchief or such like. Also there were matches where a turkey was put up as a prize to be shot at, it might be a holiday was spent in a shooting-match. Sometimes a beef was divided among competitors, when a target would be put up and the one hitting the center or nearest to the center would receive the best cut of the beef and it would thus be distributed according to the shots ranging from the center.

A leading amusement of the colonists was horse-racing. It is possible that horse-racing began in Virginia as soon as there were horses in the colony to race. In 1665 the Governor of New York announced a horse-race to encourage the bettering of the breed of horses. The sport came late into New England and yet there were races and notices of challenges to race horses. The main centers of horse-racing were in the vicinity of New York, Annapolis, Williamsburg, and Charleston, and, later, at Philadelphia, also. There were two kinds of races. The first was a great, formal affair, drawing a large crowd, where the horses ran on a circular mile track, four rounds to a heat, best two out of three to win. This race required great endurance of the horses. The second kind of race was a more informal affair, where the race was for a quarter of a mile, for which race horses were bred to run for a short distance at a very high rate of speed. Before the expiration of the colonial period, there, too, arose the special forms of the trotting-match and the pacing-match.

Cock-fighting was another sport of the colonists, which was most popular in New York and the colonies south of it, its chief centers being in Maryland, Virginia, and North Carolina. Men would go fifty miles to see a main, and choice gamecocks were imported from England. There was, too, bull-baiting and sometimes wolves and bears were captured alive and used for baiting with dogs. Sometimes a live wolf was tied to a horse's tail and dragged to death.

There were contests in running, leaping, wrestling, cudgeling, stool-ball, nine-pins, quoits, fencing, and back-sword or single-stick.

The people of the colonies did not have great opportunities for amusement in the way of shows and so they turned readily to any kind of exhibit and it did not require much display to attract them. This being true, there came to be displays of various kinds in plenty.

There were sleight-of-hand performances, acrobatic and contortionistic displays, tight and slack rope performances, and a kind of sword-dancing. Museums were founded in which there were shown wax figures and other curiosities; a mermaid was put on display; there were exhibits at various times of a solar microscope, camera obscuras, moving pictures showing windmills and water-mills in motion and ships sailing, electrical machines, a musical clock, puppets representing Joseph's dream, and prospects of London and of royal palaces. Among animals displayed, there were a lion drawn about on a cart by four oxen, a wonderful creature called a Sea Lion, a leopard "strongly chayned," a moose, a white sea bear, a camel, a cassowary "five feet high that swallows stones as large as an egg," and even a rabbit was advertised among "curious wild beasts." There was a big hog on display for four pence a person, and a cat with "one head, eight legs, and two tails."

The most remarkable animal of all exhibited must have been the one described in an advertisement in the *Boston Gazette* of April 20, 1741:

"To be seen at the Greyhound Tavern in Roxbury a wild creature which was caught in the woods about 80 miles to the Westward of this place called a Cattamount. It has a tail like a Lyon, its legs are like Bears, its Claws like an Eagle, its Eyes like a Tyger. He is exceedingly ravenous and devours all sorts of Creatures that he can come near. Its agility is surprising. It will leap 30 feet at one jump notwithstanding it is but 3 months old. Whoever wishes to see this creature may come to the place aforesaid paying one shilling each shall be welcome for their money." [108]

"Salem had the pleasure of viewing a 'Sapient Dog' who could light lamps, spell, read print or writing, tell the time of day, or day of the month. He could distinguish colors, was a good arithmetician, could discharge a loaded cannon, tell a hidden card in a pack, and jump through a hoop. About the same time was exhibited in the same town a 'Pig of Knowledge' who had precisely the same accomplishments." [109]

The first approach toward a theatrical entertainment seems to have been at Philadelphia in 1724, where was given acrobatic displays, rope-walking feats, and the like, which ended up with a half-acrobatic, half-dramatic performance of a comical character. Such entertainments must have followed in other cities. There was a theatrical troupe, a sorry lot, in Philadelphia in 1749, which went to New York in 1750, and probably was the same that produced a play in a Boston coffee-house that caused such a stir as to bring about legislation

[108] Earle, Customs and fashions in old New England, 243.
[109] *Ibid.*, 244.

that kept the drama out of Boston for the remainder of the colonial period. Although at this time there may not have been any dramatic plays given, there was a custom in Virginia at country houses to have the reading aloud of plays, romances, and operas on rainy days, Sunday afternoons, and when there might not have been dancing of an evening because no fiddler could be secured for the music, and, later, after the introduction of the drama into the colonies amateur companies were organized to give plays.

The first real theatrical company in the colonies was in 1752, which troupe, twelve in number, came over from England. Their opening play was given at Williamsburg, at that time the capital of Virginia. This place was probably chosen for the beginning of the theatrical work in the colonies "because the inhabitants of Virginia were known to be rich, leisurely, and society-loving people, with enough of refinement to enjoy plays, and with few religious scruples against anything that tended to make life pleasant to the upper classes."[110]

"Twenty-four plays had been selected and cast before Lewis Hallam and his company left London on the 'Charming Sally,' no doubt a tobacco-ship returning light for a cargo. On her unsteady deck, day after day, during the long voyage, the actors diligently rehearsed the plays with which they proposed to cheer the hearts of people in the New World. Williamsburg must have proved a disappointment to them. There were not more than a thousand people, white and black, in the village. The buildings, except the capitol, the college, and the so-called 'palace' of the governor, were insignificant, and there were only about a dozen 'gentlemen's' families resident in the place. In the outskirts of the town a warehouse was fitted up for a theater. The woods were all about it, and the actors could shoot squirrels from the windows. When the time arrived for the opening of the theater, the company were much disheartened. It seemed during the long still hours of the day that they had come on a fool's errand to act dramas in the woods. But as evening drew on, the whole scene changed like a work of magic. The roads leading into Williamsburg were thronged with out-of-date vehicles of every sort, driven by negroes and filled with gayly dressed ladies, whose gallants rode on horseback alongside. The treasury was replenished, the theater was crowded, and Shakspere

[110] Eggleston, Social life in the colonies, Century magazine, VIII, 404.

was acted on the continent probably for the first time by a trained and competent company. The 'Merchant of Venice' and Garrick's farce of 'Lethe' were played; and at the close the actors found themselves surrounded by groups of planters congratulating them, and after the Virginia fashion offering them the hospitality of their houses."[111]

This troupe finished the season at Williamsburg and then went to Annapolis and throughout Maryland and reached New York in 1753 and later went to Philadelphia. They made a trip to the West Indies and on their return to New York in 1758 they had difficulty in getting permission to play as a great religious wave had swept over the country and there was a strong feeling against such amusements. The troupe managed to overcome this opposition and continued in the colonies till the Revolutionary troubles arose. In 1774 the Continental Congress voiced the sentiment of the people in asking that there be a discontinuance of such sports and entertainments as would tend to distract thought and feeling from the getting ready of the colonies to defend their rights, and when the head of the American company, as the troupe was called, received this resolution from the president of the Congress, the work of the company was stopped and the actors sailed for the West Indies and that ended the drama in the colonies.

At the opening play by the English company at Williamsburg in 1752, the music was that of the harpsichord and furnished by the local music-master, and when they reached New York they procured a violinist. The theaters built at this time were little more than enclosed sheds and they were usually painted red. The scenery was quite indifferent. The seats were classified into boxes, pit, and gallery. The people in the pit were allowed to use liquors and smoking was permitted anywhere in the theater. Plays began at six o'clock in the evening and servants and slaves were sent early beforetimes to hold seats for their masters and mistresses. "Gentlemen made free to go behind the scenes, and to loiter in full view on the stage, showing their gallantry by disturbing attentions to the actresses."[112] which "proved so deleterious to any good representation of the play, that the manager advertised in 'Gaines' Mercury,' in 1762, that no spectators would be permitted to stand or sit on the stage during the

---
[111] Eggleston, Social life in the colonies, Century magazine, VIII, 405.
[112] Ibid., 406.

performance. And also a reproof was printed to 'the person so very rude as to throw Eggs from the Gallery upon the stage, to the injury of Cloaths.' "[113]

**Games and Sports of Children and Young People.** Children played games and engaged in sports during the colonial times in the United States and many of these games were the same as were played in the home countries from whence their ancestors came and they are played today by their descendants They were tormented, too, in their play, just as children always are, by adults in power, as shown by the following order issued in New York in 1673. "If any children be caught on the street playing, racing, and shouting previous to the termination of the last preaching, the officers of justice may take their hat or upper garment, which shall not be restored to the parents until they have paid a fine of two guilders."[114] The Puritan boys, too, had laws passed against one of their games that cannot be played without somebody getting hurt and hence the foolishness of such a law as was made in Boston in 1657. "Forasmuch as sundry complaints are made that several persons have received hurt by boys and young men playing at football in the streets, these therefore are to enjoin that none be found at that game in any of the streets, lanes or enclosures of this town under the penalty of twenty shillings for every such offence."[115]

But such laws as given above did not altogether crush the spirits of the boys for, as stated before, one man whose duties were to patrol New Amsterdam at night found they were active enough, for he complained that the boys set dogs on him, hid behind trees and fences and shouted out as he came by "Indians!" and played other tricks on him. Even as much as the Puritans tried to depress the spirits of their children, yet we find one of them noting in his diary of his grandson: "In the morning I dehorted Sam Hirst and Grindall Rawson from playing Idle tricks because 'twas first of April: They were the greatest fools that did so."[116] And this same boy was so wrought up with play when he was six years older as to cause his grandfather to write: "Sam Hirst got up betime in the morning, and took Ben Swett with him and went into the

[113] Earle, Colonial days in old New York, 212.
[114] *Ibid.*, 18.
[115] Earle, Customs and fashions in old New England, 18.
[116] *Ibid.*, 17.

Comon to play Wicket. Went before anybody was up, left the door open: Sam came not to prayer at which I was much displeased."[117]

These children played the old historic game of cat's-cradle and passed it on to the children of today, a game that is found in many lands and among both civilized and uncivilized peoples.[118] They played hop scotch and tag of various kinds and London Bridge and honey-pots, and many, many others, as given in the paragraph below. They enjoyed singing games, of which they had quite a number.

"In a quaint little book called *The Pretty Little Pocket Book*, published in America at Revolutionary times, is a list of boys' games with dingy pictures showing how the games were played; the names given were chuck-farthing; kite-flying; dancing round May-pole; marbles; hoop and hide; thread the needle; fishing; blindman's buff; shuttlecock; king and I; peg-farthing; knock out and span; hop, skip, and jump; boys and girls come out to play; I sent a letter to my love; cricket; stool-ball; base-ball; trap-ball; swimming; tip-cat; train-banding; fives; leap-frog; bird-nesting; hop-hat; shooting; hop-scotch; squares; riding; rosemary tree. The descriptions of the games are given in rhyme, and to each attached a moral lesson in verse."[119] The following is a good illustration:

"MARBLES
"Knuckle down to your Taw.
Aim well, shoot away.
Keep out of the Ring,
You'll soon learn to Play.

"MORAL
"Time rolls like a Marble,
And drives every State.
Then improve each Moment,
Before its too late."[120]

A lady writing of a custom that prevailed at Albany about the middle of the eighteenth century, during her childhood there, writes as follows:

"The children of the town were divided into companies, as they called them, from five to six years of age, until they

---

[117] Earle, Customs and fashions in old New England, 18.
[118] Haddon, Cat's cradles from many lands.
[119] Earle, Child life in colonial days, 346.
[120] *Ibid.*, 375.

became marriageable. How those companies first originated, or what were their exact regulations, I cannot say; though I, belonging to none, occasionally mixed with several, yet always as a stranger, notwithstanding that I spoke their current language fluently. Every company contained as many boys as girls. But I do not know that there was any limited number; only this I recollect, that a boy and girl of each company, who were older, cleverer, or had some other pre-eminence among the rest, were called heads of the company, and as such were obeyed by the others. . . . Children of different ages in the same family belonged to different companies. Each company at a certain time of the year went in a body to gather a particular kind of berries to the hill. It was a sort of annual festival attended with religious punctuality. Every company had a uniform for this purpose; that is to say, very pretty light baskets made by the Indians, with lids and handles, which hung over one arm, and were adorned with various colors. Every child was permitted to entertain the whole company on its birthday, and once besides, during winter and spring. The master and mistress of the family always were bound to go from home on these occasions, while some old domestic was left to attend and watch over them, with an ample provision of tea, chocolate, preserved and dried fruits, nuts and cakes of various kinds, to which was added cider or a syllabub; for these young friends met at four and amused themselves with the utmost gayety and freedom in any way their fancy dictated.'' [121]

''In spring, eight or ten of the young people of one company, or related to each other, young men and maidens, would set out together in a canoe on a kind of rural excursion, of which amusement was the object. Yet so fixed were their habits of industry that they never failed to carry their work-baskets with them, not as a form, but as an ingredient necessarily mixed with their pleasures. They had no attendants, and steered a devious course of four, five, or perhaps more miles, till they arrived at some of the beautiful islands with which this fine river abounded, or at some sequestered spot on its banks, where delicious wild fruits, or particular conveniences for fishing afforded some attraction. There they generally arrived by nine or ten o'clock, having set out in the cool and early hour of sunrise. . . . A basket with tea, sugar, and the other usual provisions for breakfast, with

[121] Earle, Colonial days in old New York, 22-23.

the apparatus for cooking it; a little rum and fruit for making cool weak punch, the usual beverage in the middle of the day, and now and then some cold pastry, was the sole provision; for the great affair was to depend on the sole exertions of the boys in procuring fish, wild ducks, etc., for the dinner. They were all, like Indians, ready and dexterous with the axe, gun, etc. Whenever they arrived at their destination, they sought out a dry and beautiful spot opposite to the river, and in an instant with their axes cleared so much superfluous shade or shrubbery as left a semi-circular opening, above which they bent and twined the boughs, so as to form a pleasant bower, while the girls gathered dried branches, to which one of the youths soon set fire with gunpowder, and the breakfast, a very regular and cheerful one, occupied an hour or two. The young men then set out to fish, or perhaps to shoot birds, and the maidens sat busily down to their work. After the sultry hours had been thus employed, the boys brought their tribute from the river or the wood, and found a rural meal prepared by their fair companions, among whom were generally their sisters and the chosen of their hearts. After dinner they all set out together to gather wild strawberries, or whatever other fruit was in season; for it was accounted a reflection to come home empty-handed. When wearied of this amusement, they either drank tea in their bower, or, returning, landed at some friend's on the way, to partake of that refreshment.'' [122]

When we come to water sports there is found more hectoring of the boys by the lawmakers. The Puritan lawgivers passed laws against swimming and each tithing-man had ten families under his charge to keep the boys from swimming in the water, but it is guessed that the boys swam all the same. Strange to say the boys were not debarred from the opposite winter sport—that of skating, nevertheless there were many deaths from breaking through the ice and drowning.

"Skating is an ancient pastime. As early as the thirteenth century Fitzstephen tells of young Londoners fastening the leg-bones of animals to the soles of the feet, and then pushing themselves on the ice by means of poles shod with sharp iron points. . . . Wooden skates shod with iron runners were invented in the Low Countries. Dutch children in New Netherlands all skated, just as their grandfathers had in old Batavia. The first skates that William Livingstone

[122] Earle, Colonial days in old New York, 205.

(born in 1723) had on the frozen Hudson were made of beef bones, as were those of medieval children."[123]

There might be some excuse made for the Puritans trying to keep their boys from swimming because of their great fear of the use of water, both internally and externally, but how can the legislators of Albany be excused for the following cruel law!

"Whereas y$^e$ children of y$^e$ s$^d$ city do very unorderly to y$^e$ shame and scandall of their parents ryde down y$^e$ hills in y$^e$ streets of the s$^d$ city with small and great slees on the Lord day and in the week by which many accidents may come, now for pventing y$^e$ same it is hereby published and declared y$^t$ shall be and may be lawful for any Constable in this City or any other person or persons to take any slee or slees from all and every such boys and girls rydeing or offering to ryde down any hill within y$^e$ s$^d$ city and breake any slee or slees in pieces. Given under our hands and seals in Albany y$^e$ 22th of December in 12th year of Her Maj's reign Anno Domini 1713."[124]

By 1765 it would seem that legislation in Albany against coasting had been abandoned or else the coasting was done at night-time when travel had ceased. This passage below is by the same woman, writing of about the year 1765, who is quoted above in regard to the companies of children and young people of Albany.

"In town all the boys were extravagantly fond of a diversion that to us would appear a very odd and childish one. The great street of the town sloped down from the hill on which the fort stood, towards the river; between the buildings was an unpaved carriage-road, the foot-path beside the houses being the only part of the street which was paved. In winter the sloping descent, continued for more than a quarter of a mile, acquired firmness from the frost, and became very slippery. Then the amusement commenced. Every boy and youth in town, from eight to eighteen, had a little low sledge, made with a rope like a bridle to the front, by which it could be dragged after one by the hand. On this one or two at most could sit, and this sloping descent being made as smooth as a looking-glass, by sliders' sledges, etc., perhaps a hundred at once set out from the top of this street, each seated in his little sledge with the rope in his

[123] Earle, Child life in colonial days, 371-372.
[124] Earle, Colonial days in old New York, 19.

hand, which, drawn to the right or left, served to guide him. He pushed it off with a little stick, as one would launch a boat; and then, with the most astonishing velocity, precipitated by the weight of the owner, the little machine glided past, and was at the lower end of the street in an instant. What could be so delightful in this rapid and smooth descent I could never discover; though in a more retired place, and on a smaller scale, I have tried the amusement; but to a young Albanian, sleighing, as he called it, was one of the first joys of life, though attended by the drawback of walking to the top of the declivity, dragging his sledge every time he renewed his flight, for such it might well be called. In the managing this little machine some dexterity was necessary; an unskilful Phaeton was sure to fall. The conveyance was so low that a fall was attended with little danger, yet with much disgrace, for an universal laugh from all sides assailed the fallen charioteer. This laugh was from a very full chorus, for the constant and rapid succession of this procession, where every one had a brother, lover, or kinsman, brought all the young people in town to the porticos, where they used to sit wrapt in furs till ten or eleven at night, engrossed by this delectable spectacle. I have known an Albanian, after residing some years in Britain, and becoming a polished fine gentleman, join the sport and slide down with the rest.''[125]

**Children's Toys and Story Books.** Toys must have been quite scarce in the earlier colonial days, probably very few beyond what the children or parents made, and rather crude. Even as late as 1695 a man in Massachusetts wrote to his brother in England that if toys in small quantities were sent to the colonies they would sell. Some years later toys increased in number and toyshops arose, there being one in Boston in 1743. It is certainly hard to understand why marbles should not have been advertised for sale at an earlier time than the date given in the following: "Not until October, 1771, on the lists of the Boston shopkeepers, who seemed to advertise and to sell every known article of dry goods, hardware, house furnishing, ornament, dress, and food, came that single but pleasure-filled item 'Boys Marbles.' "[126]

There were not a great variety of toys used in the colonies. Tin toys were quite scarce as tin was not much in

---
[125] Earle, Colonial days in old New York, 20-22.
[126] Earle, Customs and fashions in old New England, 20.

use at that time for such purposes. There were kites, hoops, balls, battledore and shuttles, tops, marbles, skates and sleds. There were home-made hobby-horses, coaches, and chariots. The boys had jack-knives and knew how to use them in making pop-guns, whistles, windmills, water-wheels, traps, and the like. Boys also made their own weapons, as, clubs, slings, bows, and arrows. The girls had dolls, of course, but they were home-made affairs for the greater part. The only dolls advertised in the colonial papers were those told about under dress, which were the models that were dressed in Europe and sent over to mantua-makers to give the styles. It is true that after serving this purpose the dolls were sold for children's use and thought much of by them. The furniture was much of it home-made, birch bark being especially adaptable for the purpose. Wicker cradles and chaises were made for the dolls, copied from those of infants.

It would seem that there were absolutely no books specially written for the pleasure of the children in the early years of the colonial times, nor for that matter were there any such written in England during the same period. There were, however, to teach some truths, three books written that were taken up by the children and who greatly loved to read them, which were *The Pilgrim's Progress* in 1688, *Robinson Crusoe* in 1714, and *Gulliver's Travels* in 1726. The beginning of story books for children in England and America was in 1744, when John Newberry began publishing such books in London. His books were at once exported to America and advertisements of them are found in the colonial newspapers. One of these books, probably published in 1744, was "The Pretty Little Pocket Book," one story in which was "Jack the Giant Killer." Another book published by Newberry about 1760 was "Mother Goose's Melodies." After the Revolution, story books for children became more common and they have kept increasing through the years to the present.

**Holidays and Festivals.** The old English festivals were not greatly observed by the colonists. In Puritan New England there were few set times and days for pleasure. The holy days of the English Church were not only disregarded by the Puritans, but even laws were made forbidding their public celebration, for while in England they had turned away from the state church and they had learned to hate the excesses of the festivals. In the other colonies the demands of the early years and the getting away from religious influences may have brought about the decline of the celebration of the church festivals, for even in Virginia, which clung to the old church, the clergy complained that the people only observed Christmas and Good Friday as they did not want to stop work for other holidays.

Although Christmas was observed in the colonies outside of New England, it was not with the old English fervor and never with the great excesses, as stated by one of the old Puritan divines as spent throughout England in "revelling, dicing, carding, masking, mumming, consumed in compotations, in interludes, in excess of wine, in mad mirth."[127]

New Year's Day was a great day for the Dutch in New York and its observance was continued by the English when they came into control. The Dutch inaugurated the custom of New Year's calling, wherein the ladies kept open house and were called upon by their gentleman friends. Food and drink were served in generous quantities and before the end of the day the gentlemen would often get quite hilarious. The streets of the city would be filled with vehicles loaded with callers going from house to house, a general gala occasion. In the country towns of New York colony the New Year was often ushered in by men with fire-arms going from house to house and firing salutes. This was kept up until a crowd was collected and then they would end the day by firing at a mark.

If the Dutch of New York originated New Year's callings the Puritans of New England originated Thanksgiving Day. Just when each custom first began cannot be determined for each must have arisen gradually and continued till the practice became fixed. The thanksgiving days were not always at first for giving thanks for God's beneficence, but for various reasons, as, political events, the success of the Protestant cause, victories over Indians, the safe arrival of ships with friends and provisions, and so on. Nor were they set for any special season or day, probably Thursday became fixed because of its being the lecture day and autumn because of the time of harvests thus making the days of thanksgiving come more often at this season.

The first Thanksgiving was not a religious event nor a single day, but a time of recreation as shown from the fol-

[127] Earle, Customs and fashions in old New England, 214.

lowing written by one of the Puritans in Plymouth on December 11, 1621:

"Our harvest being gotten in, our governor sent four men on fowling that so we might after a special manner rejoice together after we had gathered the fruits of our labors. They four killed as much fowl as with a little help beside served the company about a week. At which times among other recreations we exercised our arms, many of the Indians coming amongst us, and among the rest their greatest king Massasoyt with some ninety men, whom for three days we entertained and feasted, and they went out and killed five deer which they brought and bestow'd on our governor, and upon the captains and others."[128]

The first public thanksgiving was held in Boston in 1630 to express thanks for the safe arrival of ships bringing friends and food. From this on there were public thanksgivings, but not every year, until it became a fixed annual affair, but at just what time this occurred it would be impossible to state. As it became a fixed custom, there grew into it many of the features of the old English Christmas, notwithstanding the attitude of the Puritans toward that day, and it became a day of family reunions and of feasting on turkey and Indian pudding and pumpkin pie.

"But Thanksgiving Day was not the chief New England holiday. Ward, writing in 1699, does not name it, saying of New Englanders: 'Election, Commencement, and Training Days are their only Holy Days.'"[129]

Election Day was a kind of holiday and indeed sometimes the whole week was included in the holiday. As was stated before, Training Day was a day of coming together of the people at which there was not only military drill but also amusements of various kinds and sometimes the occasion for a display of public punishment. Commencement Day at the college was a proud day for the people whose sons graduated and a kind of general holiday for all. There was a dinner and plenty of wine. It would seem that this was an occasion for which more than a day would be used, as after 1730 Commencement Day was usually set for Friday as there would not be so much of the week left for jollifying.

Shrove Tuesday was observed in New York by the middle of the eighteenth century as a holiday given over to cocking-

[128] Earle, Customs and fashions in old New England, 217.
[129] *Ibid.*, 223.

mains, as it was in England. Saint Valentine's Day was observed by the Dutch in New Amsterdam as Women's Day and it was celebrated by the young women, each of whom armed herself with a heavy cord having a knot on the end with which she struck every young man whom she would meet. Guy Fawkes' Day was celebrated at least in New England and New York, being the occasion for bonfires and fantastic parades and burning an effigy of Guy Fawkes, which often was only a straw carried by each one to cast into the fire. In some of the colonies, May Day was celebrated and a May-pole erected and some attempts were made to celebrate it in New England but it did not get much encouragement and it was but a feeble holiday there. Pinkster Day, the name being derived from the Dutch word for Pentecost, was a great holiday in New York for the negro slaves. They gathered in great numbers on that day and had singing and dancing and feasting and drinking—a general good time. The spring sheep-shearing and the autumnal corn-husking were a time of great gatherings and merrymakings, and there were also apple-bees, maple-sugar stirrings, and log-rollings.

**Public Punishments.** Another subject that could have well been placed under amusements is that of public punishments, for such did afford a means of amusement in the form of ridiculing and reviling the ones exposed and of throwing things at them, and, too, exposure was often on a holiday, thus affording more time and opportunity for the people to amuse themselves. Not only was the offender or criminal exposed to the public view but this was made all the worse by placing him in some kind of instrument that would cause him to be in an attitude that would emphasize the grotesqueness of the exposure and make the punishment all the more insulting and painful. This public form of punishment was not confined wholly to men for women, too, were sometimes placed thus before the public.

The exposure of the culprit was not enough for the people of those days and particularly in New England for the parson must be given a chance to display his powers and so the offender was often set in a public place in the church that he might be prayed and preached over and which were too often in the form of objurgations, and, further, this sermon was sometimes printed and sold for it was among the parson's greatest efforts.

This was a time of cruelty toward all living creatures whether beasts or men both in the old country and the new, probably somewhat the effect of the heavy and habitual indulgence in alcoholic drinks by all the people, thus deadening to an extent the higher sensibilities. These public displays must have hardened the people and in particular to have accustomed the young to such and to view crime as meriting open punishment without regard to the feelings of the one exposed. Yet some of the young people must have been affected in an opposite manner for there was a growing away from this form of punishment and of cruelty and which has continued down to the present time where the welfare and individuality of the offender is being more and more considered.

These people of the olden times very greatly feared ridicule, especially of being called names, and hence the ways of punishment were so devised as to place the culprit in a ridiculous position and so that he could not resist the insults inflicted upon him by his fellow-men. The colonists were forever resisting insults by bringing suits in petty slander and libel cases. Men in public positions were in particular jealous of their power and official honor and resented and punished affronts against themselves or their offices or their public doings. Although all classes of people were greatly affected by ridicule and slander, it would seem that schoolmasters and parsons were the most active against such, as is shown from the old court records.

One of the earliest of these instruments of punishment was the bilboes. This consisted of shackles attached to a heavy iron bolt or bar into which shackles the legs were thrust and then locked in with a padlock. Sometimes there was a chain on the end of the bar which was fastened to the floor or it might have been to the wall or a post so that the offender's legs were pulled up high to make his position the more ridiculous and painful. The bilboes were not greatly in use in the colonies and they were soon superseded by the stocks and the pillory. The stocks were made of two heavy timbers, one coming down on the other, with circular openings in them for holding the legs of the culprit, and sometimes also smaller openings for the arms. The upper timber was raised, the legs of the culprit placed in the openings and then kept tight by closing down the upper piece and fastening it. The one in the stocks usually sat on a low bench. The pillory consisted of two pieces of timbers as with the stocks and attached to two upright pieces at either end at about the height of a man's shoulders. There were three circular openings in the timbers, one for the neck and two small ones for the wrists. The neck and arms were placed in these openings and confined as the legs were in the stocks, leaving the head and hands hanging out exposed, the culprit standing.

The ducking stool was specially designed for scolding women, though also used for other offenses. There were different forms. The following description of one of these instruments and its use is said to be from a letter giving an account of a ducking in Virginia in 1634:

"The day afore yesterday at two of ye clock in ye afternoon I saw this punishment given to one Betsy wife of John Tucker who by ye violence of her tongue has made his house and ye neighborhood uncomfortable. She was taken to ye pond near where I am sojourning by ye officer who was joined by ye Magistrate and ye Minister Mr. Cotton who had frequently admonished her and a large number of People. They had a machine for ye purpose yt belongs to ye parish, and which I was so told had been so used three times this Summer. It is a platform with 4 small rollers or wheels and two upright posts between which works a Lever by a Rope fastened to its shorter or heavier end. At ye end of ye longer arm is fixed a stool upon which sd Betsey was fastened by cords, her gown tied fast around her feete. The Machine was then moved up to ye edge of ye pond, ye Rope was slackened by ye officer and ye woman was allowed to go down under ye water for ye space of half a minute. Betsey had a stout stomach, and would not yield until she had allowed herself to be ducked 5 several times. At length she cried piteously, Let me go Let me go, by God's help I'll sin no more. Then they drew back ye Machine, untied ye Ropes and let her walk home in her wetted clothes a hopefully penitent woman." [130]

The pillory itself was not sufficient punishment, for too often the ears of the offender were nailed back to the wood by his head and when the head was removed from the pillory sometimes the nails were not pulled and the ears thus released but the ears were split out of the nails. The cutting off the ears of the offender was of rather frequent occurrence.

[130] Earle, Curious punishments of bygone days, 19.

The brank or scold's bridle, a kind of head-piece with a spiked plate or flat tongue of iron to be placed in the mouth, was a cruel instrument that seems not to have been used in the colonies, as they used a cleft stick into which the tongue was inserted. Another form of punishment was the placing of a letter or inscription on the offender, sometimes the letter was of a conspicuous color and sewed on to the garment in a conspicuous place. The ears were not the only part to be maimed, for the nostrils were slit and the cheeks and forehead were gashed and the tongue was bored through with an awl, or even with a hot iron. Branding with a hot iron was a common enough form of punishment and to make it the more striking it was often done on the forehead or the cheek or on the hands.

Whipping became a common and frequent punishment and it was used for a number of different kinds of offenses. In New York in the time of Dutch control two of the most common causes for whipping was drunkenness and theft. In New England whipping was used as a punishment for lying, swearing, taking false toll, perjury, selling rum to the Indians, drunkenness, slander, name-calling, making false love to a young woman in which a pretense of marriage was used, and for other crimes. One of the greatest crimes in New England was idleness and "transients" as they were called, people who would not settle down and keep at steady work, were often whipped from town to town, for they were not allowed to remain anywhere very long. "So common were whippings in the southern colonies at the date of settlement of the country, that in Virginia even 'launderers and launderesses' who 'dare to wash any uncleane Linen, drive bucks, or throw out the open water or suds of fowle clothes in the open streetes,' or who took pay for washing for a soldier or laborer, or who gave old torn linen for good linen, were severely whipped. Many other offenses were punished by whipping in Virginia, such as slitting the ears of hogs, or cutting off the ends of hog's ears—thereby removing ear-marks and destroying claim to perambulatory property—stealing tobacco, running away from home, drunkenness, destruction of land-marks."[131]

Sometimes the offender was tied to the tail of a cart and whipped through the streets, sometimes he was whipped at the pillory, but most often the whipping-post was used.

[131] Earle, Curious punishments of bygone days, 83.

"There was a whipping-post on Queen Street in Boston, another on the Common, another on State Street, and they were constantly in use in Boston in Revolutionary times. Samuel Breck wrote of the year 1771:

"'The large whipping-post painted red stood conspicuously and prominently in the most public street in the town. It was placed in State Street directly under the window of a great writing school which I frequented, and from there the scholars were indulged in the spectacle of all kinds of punishment suited to harden their hearts and brutalize their feelings.'"[132]

Women as well as men were whipped. Sometimes the whipping was done in the jail-yard, sometimes at the whipping-post, and sometimes even at the tail of a cart, this last was a common enough form used on the Quaker women in Massachusetts. The following would imply that sex did not greatly appeal to the colonists. "In the 'Pticuler' Court of Connecticut this entry appears: May 12, 1668. . . . Mary Wilton, the wife of Nicholas Wilton, for contemptuous and reproachful terms by her put on one of the Assistants are adjudged she to be whipt 6 stripes upon the naked body next training day at Windsor."[133] "From a New York newspaper, dated 1712, I learn that one woman at the whipping-post 'created much amusement by her resistance.'"[134] Quoting further from Samuel Breck about the whipping-post in Boston in 1771: "Here women were taken in a huge cage in which they were dragged on wheels from prison, and tied to the post with bare backs on which thirty or forty lashes were bestowed among the screams of the culprit and the uproar of the mob."[135] "In Virginia in 1664 Major Robbins brought suit against one Mary Powell for 'scandalous speaches' against Rev. Mr. Teackle, for which she was ordered to receive twenty lashes on her bare shoulders and to be banished the country."[135a]

This gruesome story of public punishments may well be ended with the most gruesome part of all, that of public hangings. Far greater than the amusement afforded our old colonial ancestors by witnessing the whipping or maiming

---

[132] Earle, Curious punishments of bygone days, 81.
[133] Ibid., 78.
[134] Ibid., 79.
[135] Ibid., 82.
[135a] Ibid., 83.

or branding of offenders or even the getting to rail at them set in stocks, bilboes, cage, or pillory, was the thrilling spectacle of a public execution and which became all the greater gala day if several persons were hanged together at the one occasion. One of the greatest of these exhibitions occurred at Boston on June 30, 1704, when seven pirates were executed. "Sermons were preached in their Hearing Every Day, And Prayers made daily with them. And they were Catechized and they had many Occasional exhortations. Yet as they led a wicked and vitious life so to appearance they died very obdurately and impenitently hardened in their sin."[136] So ran the account in the *News Letter* in an "extra" for the event. Of course such a noted happening could not have escaped so good a chronicler as Judge Sewall for he gave the following account of this hanging in his diary:

"After dinner about 3 p. m. I went to see the Execution. Many were the people that saw upon Broughtons Hill But when I came to see how the River was covered with People I was amazed; Some say there were 100 boats. 150 Boats & Canoes saith Cousin Moody of York. He Told them. Mr. Cotton Mather came with Captain Quelch & 6 others for Execution from the Prison to Scarletts Wharf and from thence in Boat to the place of Execution. When the Scaffold was hoisted to a due height the seven Malefactors went up. Mr. Mather pray'd for them standing upon the Boat. Ropes were all fastened to the Gallows save King who was Reprieved. When the Scaffold was let to sink there was such a Screech of the Women that my wife heard it sitting in our Entry next the Orchard and was much surprised at it, yet the wind was sou-west. Our house is a full mile from the place."[136a]

**Manufactures.** The colonists were very busy people. This was particularly true of the earlier times when nature had to be conquered. They had to make a great many of their own implements and to learn to use in a skillful manner the few tools they had. They had to learn to adapt the materials that nature furnished and to shape them into forms best fitted for their work. They learned to select the natural forms of things that could serve various purposes. They had two tools, the ax and the knife, that were readily and skillfully used in home manufacturing.

[136] Earle, Customs and fashions of old New England, 252.
[136a] *Ibid.*, 252.

The colonists cut and shaped the logs for their houses and made stanchions and clapboards and shingles and laths. They selected pieces of timber and trimmed them for snaths for their scythes and flails, sled-runners and thills for carts, hames and ox-yokes, stakes and poles for various uses, whip-stalks and ax-handles, and handles for spades. They made salt-mortars, hog troughs, maple-sap troughs, and similar articles by burning and scraping out logs cut to the lengths wanted. They made wooden hinges and door-latches and buttons for fastening doors. They made spinning-wheels and reels and looms and the things used with them. They made various kinds of wooden bowls and trays and spoons for household use. They learned from the Indians how to make brooms by taking the length of a small birch tree and slitting the lower end into a brush and shaping the upper end into a handle; they also learned to make a broom by tying about a handle hemlock branches together for the brush. They made spoons from clam-shells set in split sticks. They used gourd-shells for bowls and skimmers and dipper and bottles and pumpkin-shells for seed and grain holders. Turkey-wings were used for hearth-brushes. There was one implement that the colonist in his frontier life spent much time on and that was the powder-horn. "Months of the patient work of every spare moment was spent in beautifying them, and their quaintness, variety, and individuality are a never-ceasing delight to the antiquary. Maps, plans, legends, verses, portraits, landscapes, family history, crests, dates of births, marriages and deaths, lists of battles, patriotic and religious sentiments, all may be found on powder-horns. They have in many cases proved valuable historical records, and have sometimes been the only records of events."[137]

**Boys' Work and Manufactures.** It is not to be wondered at that great men arose in the early history of our country, for the young were so trained to work that the whole physical being of the boy was cultivated, and so when a great brain came there was a sound body in which to keep it and help it. A boy's life on a farm is thus described by one who went through it:

"The boy was taught that laziness was the worst form of original sin. Hence he must rise early and make himself useful before he went to school, must be diligent there in study, and promptly home to do 'chores' at evening. His

[137] Earle, Home life in colonial days, 321.

whole time out of school must be filled up with some service, such as bringing in fuel for the day, cutting potatoes for the sheep, feeding the swine, watering the horses, picking the berries, gathering the vegetables, spooling the yarn. He was expected never to be reluctant and not often tired.''[138]

Not only did the boy have to work hard, but also, at least in New England, he had to provide his own spending money, and various were the ways he devised to obtain it. The boy's jack-knife was a great instrument and highly prized, for with it he not only made things for his own use but also to sell to procure spending money. With knives and mallets the boys split out shoe-pegs from maple sticks. They made and set teeth in wool-cards. They made traps and caught wild animals. They made birch splinter brooms. One man stated in London during the middle of the eighteenth century that when a boy in New Hampshire his only spending money was earned by making these brooms and carrying them on his back ten miles to town to sell them. The boys whittled cheese-ladders and cheese-hoops and butter-paddles for their mothers' use. They collected the bristles from the hogs at hog-killing time and sold them for brush-making. They gathered nuts and berries and wild cherries, the cherries being used in making cherry-rum and cherry-bounce. Tying onions was another means of money-making. The older boys sometimes made staves and shingles. Where a boy could turn a hand for making a little money for himself he did it.

**Girls' and Women's Work.** In the colonial days everybody worked and the girls and women did their share of it. The following quotations well show this. In the last half of the eighteenth century the qualifications of a housekeeper were such as asked for in the following advertisement:

"Wanted at a Seat about half a day's journey from Philadelphia, on which are good improvements and domestics, A single Woman of unsullied Reputation, an affable, cheerful, active and amiable Disposition; cleanly, industrious, perfectly qualified to direct and manage the female Concerns of country business, as raising small stock, dairying, marketing, combing, carding, spinning, knitting, sewing, pickling, preserving, etc., and occasionally to instruct two young Ladies in those Branches of Oeconomy, who, with their father, compose the Family. Such a person will be treated

[138] Earle, Child life in colonial days, 307.

with respect and esteem, and meet with every encouragement due to such a character.'' [139]

"There is, in the library of the Connecticut Historical Society, a diary written by a young girl of Colchester, Connecticut, in the year 1775. Her name was Abigail Foote. She set down her daily work, and the entries run like this:

'Fix'd gown for Prude,—Mend Mother's Riding-hood,—Spun short thread,—Fix'd two gowns for Welsh's girls,—Carded tow,—Spun linen,—Worked on Cheese-basket,—Hatchel'd flax with Hannah, we did 51 lbs. apiece,—Pleated and ironed,—Read a Sermon of Doddridge's,—Spooled a piece,—Milked the cows,—Spun linen, did 50 knots,—Made a Broom of Guinea wheat straw,—Spun thread to whiten,—Set a Red dye,—Had two Scholars from Mrs. Taylor's,—I carded two pounds of whole wool and felt Nationly,—Spun harness twine,—Scoured the pewter.'

"She tells also of washing, cooking, knitting, weeding the garden, picking geese, etc., and many visits to her friends. She dipped candles in the spring, and made soap in the autumn." [140]

Knitting was an accomplishment of every girl in New England and among the Dutch in New York and probably with every other girl in all the colonies. Little girls were taught to knit as soon as they could hold the needles, and at four years of age they could knit stockings and mittens. They knit in wool and silk, doing fine knitting with many intricate and elaborate stitches. "A beautiful pair of long silk stockings of open-work design has initials knit on the instep, which were the wedding hose of a bride of the year 1760; and the silk for them was raised, wound, and spun by the bride's sister, a girl of fourteen, who also did the exquisite knitting." [141]

These colonial women were thirfty and saving, being well prepared to care for the garments needing repair, as is shown from an advertisement in the *New York Gazette* of April 1, 1751:

"Elizabeth Boyd gives notice that she will as usual graft Pieces in knit Jackets and Breeches not to be discern'd, also to graft and foot Stockings, and Gentlemen's Gloves, mittens or Muffatees made out of old Stockings, or runs them in

---

[139] Earle, Home life in colonial days, 252.
[140] *Ibid.*, 253.
[141] Earle, Child life in colonial days, 339.

the Heels. She likewise makes Children's Stockings out of Old Ones."[142]

The one kind of work that all the colonial women reveled in and which allowed them to display their love of color, their skill in needle-craft, and their thrift in using up odds and ends, was that of quilt-making. In the early days cotton goods were scarce and so the quilts were made from woolen garments and pieces, and all kinds of garments and remnants were used, as, the old discarded militia uniforms, worn-out flannel sheets, old petticoats, coat and cloak linings, and any other things that could not be further worn. These were thoroughly washed and where needed dyed with home-dyes and then pressed out and cut into quilting pieces. Later, cottons and linens were more readily procured and often the very best stuffs were used, for they prided themselves on the beauty of the pieces and their arrangement and the careful stitching. Not only did the making of quilts afford a chance to use up the material that could not be used otherwise and thus make coverings of value and warmth, it also gave to the women the opportunity for coming together and enjoying themselves, and so quilting-bees became one of the most social and enjoyable occasions.

One of the great industries of the women was that of soap-making. The refuse grease from cooking, butcherings, and the like, was stored up through the winter as was also the wood-ashes from the fire-place for the spring soap-making. From the ashes they obtained lye by pouring water over the ashes in barrels set on boards with grooves in them and letting it filter out at the bottom to be caught in vessels set under the ends of the boards. The lye thus obtained was poured over the grease in a great pot and boiled over a fire out of doors. The soft soap thus made was used for household purposes, especially in the washing of clothing, which was done usually once a month and in some households once in three months, the soiled clothing having been allowed to accumulate and be stored away to be washed together on one great wash-day. Another kind of labor in which the women engaged was the picking of the domestic geese, which were raised for the feathers rather than for food. The feathers were greatly desired for pillows and beds and the quills for pens.

Among the industries in which women engaged were those

[142] Earle, Colonial days in old New York, 169.

of flax-culture and spinning, wool-culture and spinning, and hand-weaving. The women and children aided in the culture of the flax and did quite a good deal of the work in its preparation and almost all the spinning. Women and children, too, did a great deal in helping in the wool-culture and spinning and weaving. In those early days all in the family could help and a family at work is well portrayed in the following.

"The wool industry easily furnished home occupation to an entire family. Often by the bright fire-light in the early evening every member of the household might be seen at work on the various stages of wool manufacture or some of its necessary adjuncts, and varied and cheerful industrial sounds fill the room. The old grandmother, at light and easy work, is carding the wool into fleecy rolls, seated next the fire; for, as the ballad says 'she was old and saw right dimly.' The mother, stepping as lightly as one of her girls, spins the rolls into woolen yarn on the great wheel. The oldest daughter sits at the clock-reel, whose continuous buzz and occasional click mingles with the humming rise and fall of the wool-wheel, and the irritating scratch, scratch, of the cards. A little girl at a small wheel is filling quills with woolen yarn for the loom, not a skilled work; the irregular sound shows her intermittent industry. The father is setting fresh teeth in a wool-card, while the boys are whittling hand-reels and loom-spools."[143]

After the first years in the new country, when all time and labor would be consumed in carrying on the plain necessaries of life, women began to enter more into fancy lines of work, and during later colonial times the women and girls did quite a lot of fine work in sewing, knitting, embroidering, and other kinds of decorative work. There arose schools for teaching girls and young women feather-work, fancy knitting, painting on glass, embroidery, netting, fine sewing, wax-work, the making of artificial fruits and flowers, paper-cutting, and many other things.

They made most beautiful embroidery. Articles of clothing had vines, trees, fruits, flowers, and other designs worked on them and also words and mottoes and texts from the Bible. Some of the christening caps and robes of the babies had beautiful embroidered work on them. Among the embroidered goods of those days were the mourning pieces.

[143] Earle, Home life in colonial days, 203.

They had worked on them weeping willows and urns, tombs and mourning figures, epitaphs, and names of deceased members of the family or friends with dates of their deaths.

One piece of embroidering which was done by every little girl in families of standing was the making of a sampler, which consisted of a long and narrow, or nearly square, piece of linen canvas with designs worked in colored silks and wools. These were among the works of children in early colonial times, as there is one still preserved made by a daughter of a Pilgrim Father and another bearing on it the date of 1654. In the older samplers there was little bother with realism in using the colors as a green horse might be alongside a blue tree and the green horse might have his legs worked in red. On them were worked crude or strangely represented trees and fruits and flowers and animals. There were verses embroidered and portions of hymns and sometimes pictures portraying family or public events. Some were quite pretentious, one such sampler shows the Old South Church with a coach passing by it and ladies and gentlemen on horses and afoot in the costumes of the time, and even a negro lad holding a horse, and birds flying in the air above them.

Laces were made for using on pillows and made on net for veils and collars and caps. ''Girls spent years working on a single collar or tucker. Sometimes medallions of this net lace were embroidered down upon fine linen lawn. I have infants' caps of this beautiful work, finer than any needlework of to-day.''[144]

Netting was another of their arts, the net being used on coverelets and curtains and valances, this kind being made of cotton thread or twine, while a finer kind was made of silk or fine cotton for trimming sacks and petticoats; also netted purses and work-bags as well as knitted ones were made. On small looms they made tapes and braids and ribbons for use as glove-ties, shoe-strings, hair-laces, stay-laces, garters, hatbands, belts, etc.

They did painting on glass, representing fruits and flowers, and an especial subject was coats of arms. They made feather-work, which consisted in pasting small feathers or portions of feathers together to form flowers for use on headdresses and bonnets. Another form of decorative work indulged in by colonial women was the cutting of designs out

[144] Earle, Child life in colonial days, 341.

of stiff paper with scissors. They cut out coats of arms, valentines, wreaths of flowers, marine views, religious symbols, animals, landscapes, and other designs. They were sometimes mounted on black paper, framed and glazed, and given as presents to friends.

**Religion.** The first colonists of all parts were religiously inclined. Captain John Smith tells of the first colonists in Virginia: "We had daily Common Prayer morning and evening; every Sunday two sermons; and every three months a holy Communion till our Minister died; but our Prayers daily with an Homily on Sundays we continued two or three years after, till more Preachers came."[145] They held to the Church of England and believed in strict observance of Sunday. This day was kept for religious services and all were compelled to go to church except the sick and journeys were forbidden and all work not strictly necessary and all sports, such as shooting, fishing, game-playing, etc. In New Netherlands there was likewise strict observance of Sunday by the Dutch and working, playing in the streets, fishing, hunting, going on pleasure trips, and such like, were strictly forbidden. With the Puritans in New England the strictest observance of Sunday as a holy day was rigidly enforced. No work on the farm was permitted on that day nor any pleasures whatsoever in the way of fishing, shooting, sailing, dancing, jumping, and the like, nor riding except going to or from church. The laws for this day were rigidly enforced as is shown from their writings on the subject and court records. Beside the three faiths as represented above, there were the Roman Catholics in Maryland, the Quakers in Pennsylvania, the Baptists in Rhode Island, and Huguenots, Lutherans, Moravians, Waldenses, Walloons, Jews, and others, in the different colonies. There was room for any and all of them and although there were persecutions yet it did not destroy any faith but caused the people to move out into new fields where they would be unmolested.

The first places of worship in Virginia were thus described by Captain John Smith:

"Wee did hang an awning, which is an old saile, to three of foure trees to shadow us from the Sunne; our walls were railes of wood; our seats unhewed trees till we cut plankes; our Pulpit a bar of wood nailed to two neighbouring trees. In foul weather we shifted into an old rotten tent; this came

[145] Earle, Home life in colonial days, 381.

by way of adventure for new. This was our Church till we built a homely thing like a barne set upon Cratchets, covered with rafts, sedge, and earth; so also was the walls; the best of our houses were of like curiosity, that could neither well defend from wind nor rain.''[146]

In a short time a timber church sixty feet long was built and some years afterward this church was replaced by a brick one. Some of the churches in the Southern colonies were modeled in shape after the old English churches and were built of stone, but most of them were wooden buildings without "spires or towers or steeples."

In 1646 the Dutch built a little wooden church in Fort Orange. The first church at Albany was built in 1657 and it was simply a blockhouse with loopholes for permitting guns to be fired through in case of an Indian attack and three small cannon were placed on the roof. The first church in New Amsterdam was built of stone and it was seventy-two feet long. The first church in Brooklyn was built in 1666 and it had thick stone walls with a steep peaked roof with an open belfry on top. Many of the old Dutch churches were six-sided or eight-sided with a high, steep, pyramidal roof, topped with a belfry on which was a weather-vane.

Not long after landing at Plymouth the Puritans built a fort, which was used as a Lord's Day meeting-place till a meeting-house was built in 1648. As other settlements were made, religious services were at first held in tents or under trees and where a settler had a roomy house this often was used. The first meeting-house at Boston had mud walls, a thatched roof, and earthen floor, which was used till 1640.

The first meeting-houses in New England were square and made of logs with the spaces between the logs filled with clay and with steep roofs which were thatched with reeds and long grass and with a beaten earth for a floor. These buildings were often quite small, one having been thirty-six feet long, twenty feet wide, and twelve feet high, and another was but twenty-six feet long and twenty feet wide. Later these were replaced by larger and better buildings and these early rude structures were used for granaries and storehouses.

The second form of meeting-houses was a square wooden building having a truncated pyramidal roof with a belfry or turret. One of this type, built at Hingham in 1681,

[146] Earle, Home life in colonial days, 381.

known as the "Old Ship," is still in existence. The largest and finest of this second type was the First Church at Boston, a large square brick building, built in 1713, and which was used till 1808.

The third type of New England colonial meeting-houses had a lofty wooden steeple at one end, of which the old South Church at Boston, a well-known historic building, is a good example.

In the South the churches were often placed by the waterside and people came to them over the water in various kinds of vessels. In New England the first meeting-houses were often built in the valleys or the meadow-lands and the houses of the settlers were built about them. As the population increased there could no longer be land available for all in the valleys and the houses were built out near watering places and pasturage for convenience and so the meeting-houses began to be placed on hill-tops. This was done so as to be a lookout for danger from Indians and also so it could be seen from all parts of the country as the people had to journey through narrow roads and bridle-paths obscured by trees and brush. Too, there was a pride in such a location, to show off a fine meeting-house, which would thus be visible for many miles around.

The old New England meeting-houses were used for various purposes, one of the strangest being for the nailing of the heads of wolves to the logs on the outside. Wolves were so numerous and so destructive and so feared that rewards were paid for their killing and to show this the heads were nailed to the outer walls of the meeting-house. This was all the decoration that the outer walls of the building had for near a century as during the seventeenth century it was considered vain and extravagant to paint them but by the middle of the eighteenth century paint became cheaper and more plentiful and the meeting-houses began not only to be painted but also in conspicuous colors and towns began to vie with one another in the most striking displays. One new meeting-house was painted a bright yellow and soon others were likewise adorned. "Brooklyn church, then, in 1762, ordered that the outside of its meeting-house be 'culered' in the approved fashion. The body of the house was painted a bright orange; the doors and 'bottom boards' a warm chocolate color; the 'window-jets,' corner-boards, and weather-boards white. What a bright nosegay of color! As a crowning glory Brooklyn people put up an 'Eleclarick Rod' on the gorgeous edifice, and proudly boasted that Brooklyn meeting-house was the 'newest, biggest and yallowest' in the county."[147]

There was no shade about the early meeting-houses in New England as the trees were cut down around it for fear of forest fires. There were no curtains nor window-blinds, so that the heat and blazing light in summer would make it bad for all in the church. They did often have heavy outside shutters but they could not be closed during services as the room would then be made too dark for the minister to see to read his sermon. Later the forests grew again and they were not cut away nor cleared up and the meeting-house would thus become dark and gloomy. Oiled paper was used in the windows of these early meeting-houses and later when glass came into use it was nailed in instead of being puttied.

The early meeting-house of the Puritans in New England were of a very simple interior with raftered walls and sanded puncheon floors or earthen floors. The early Dutch churches in New Netherlands also were plain and they were kept in the greatest cleanliness, scrubbed often and floors sanded with fine beach-sand. The churches of the Southern colonies were usually better furnished and flowers were used for decorations, which was never the case with the Puritans. The pulpits in all the churches were rather pretentious affairs, being elevated above the floor, enclosed, with a narrow flight of stairs leading up to them. At least in the early Puritan churches there was a sounding-board placed above the pulpit, which was a board supported from the roof by a slender iron rod.

In the earliest meeting-houses in New England the seats were made of rough hand-riven boards placed on legs and without backs. Later there were pews with narrow seats around the sides and high partition walls between. In the early Dutch churches the men had places in pews around the walls while chairs were placed in the center of the church for the women to occupy. In some of the Virginia churches the seats were comfortably cushioned. In later times in all the churches the pews were carefully assigned and persons who crowded into pews above their station were unceremoniously put out by those in charge.

The meeting-houses in New England were wholly without

[147] Earle, The Sabbath in Puritan New England, 15.

means of heating until the middle of the eighteenth century. Throughout the long and tedious services during the coldest weather of a bitter climate, attendants at the meetings had to get along as best they could. The men wore their heaviest clothing during the services. The minister, too, would keep himself wrapped up while in the pulpit just as on his way to the meeting-house. The women in the earlier times dressed to suit the temperature, but as wealth came fashion also entered in and thin silk hose, cloth or kid or silk slippers, linen underclothing, dresses with elbow sleeves and round low necks, and a thin cloth cape or mantle for the shoulders was too often in midwinter the Sunday apparel. The women did protect their heads with caps and mufflers and veils and their hands with gloves and muffs.

The officials must be given credit for trying to keep the meeting-house free from the winds as well as possible, as in some places it was ordered that during the cold weather "no doors be opened to the windward and only one door to the leeward." In 1725 in one place it was ordered that the "several doors of the meeting-house be taken care of and kept shut in very cold and windy seasons according to the lying of the wind from time to time; and that people in such windy weather come in at the leeward doors only, and take care that they are easily shut both to prevent the breaking of the doors and the making of a noise."[148]

In some of the early log meeting-houses the skins of wolves and other fur-bearing animals were made into bags which were nailed or tied to the benches in such a way as to let the people thrust their feet into them for warmth. In the bitterest weather foot-stoves were taken to the meeting-houses for the use of the women and children. During the middle of the eighteenth century stoves began to appear in the meeting-houses in New England, perhaps the first stove used having been at Hadley in 1734. But there was a hard fight to introduce stoves and it was near another century later before they came into general use.

If the meeting-house should have been situated in a town, at noon the people went to their homes or to the tavern or to neighbors' houses in that vicinity to eat their dinners and to warm themselves. If the meeting-house in the country was near the home of a hospitable farmer the congregation would go there at noon. But too often the meeting-

[148] Earle, The Sabbath in Puritan New England, 95.

house was away off at the top of a hill or in an out-of-the-way place and so there would be built near it a rough-like structure, known as the "noon-house." Sometimes it was called the "Sabba-day house" and again a "horse-hows," this last name because in some of the houses the horses were placed at one end. At the other end was built a large rough stone chimney. Of severe Sundays some one, a servant or an older son, would usually be sent at an early hour to start a good fire in this fireplace for warming the family after their cold ride. At noon all would repair to this house for warmth and for eating their dinner. Before starting for home a warming was again taken. Too, during the long sermons in forenoon and afternoon a servant or some member of the family would replenish the coals in the foot-stoves from the coals in the fireplace of this noon-house.

In front of the meeting-house there were usually horse-blocks, or stepping-stones, or hewn legs, for mounting their horses as usually all rode. All kinds of notices were posted on the meeting-house, notices of town-meetings, prohibitions from selling guns and powder to the Indians, notices of sales of cattle or farms, lists of town officers, copies of the laws against Sabbath-breaking, notices of intended marriages, and sometimes even scandalous and insulting libels. Often on the meeting-house green stood the stocks, pillory, cage, and whipping-post. The meeting-house was not only used for religious services, but also for town meetings and likewise as a store-house. Never having fire in it nor about it, it was the safest place for a powder-magazine and some place in it was fitted up for such purpose. Also grain was stored in its loft and in particular that which might have been given to the minister as pay for his services.

"In one church in the Connecticut valley, in a township where it was forbidden that tobacco be smoked upon the public streets, the church loft was used to dry and store the freshly cut tobacco-leaves which the inhabitants sold to the 'ungodly Dutch.' Thus did greed for gain lead even blue Connecticut Christians to profane the house of God."[149]

There were various ways in colonial times of calling the people to the religious services of Sunday morning. In the early times and particularly so in New England, they did not always have bells on the churches and various devices were used to let people know when it was time to go to

[149] Earle, The Sabbath in Puritan New England, 14.

church. The time of morning service was usually about nine o'clock and this was announced sometimes by the tooting of a horn or the blowing of a conch-shell or the sounding of a trumpet. The beating of a drum was a very common signal and some also used the firing of guns, in this latter the number of times firing was different from that signifying danger, so as not to frighten the people. Sometimes a flag was used to notify the people of meeting time, having been put out when time of notice arrived and left hanging out till time for the beginning of the service, when the flag was taken down. Some meeting-houses were supplied with belfries from which the conch or horn or trumpet was sounded, or whatever signal was used, and in other places a platform was made upon top of the meeting-houses for this purpose. When bells were used, in the early churches there were often no towers in which to place them and they were hung on trees near the meeting-house.

At the first signal from conch or trumpet or horn or drum, the people would be seen starting out from their homes. With some communities it was the custom for the congregation to stop at the church door and wait until the minister and his wife arrived and passed into the house and then all followed, of course the boys hanging back and coming in at the very last moment, shuffling and scraping and clattering with their heavy boots as they went up the stairs to their place in the loft. Other congregations entered the church as they came and then all arose as the minister entered and remained standing till he went into the pulpit and then sat down as he did. It was also the custom for the congregation to remain standing in the pews at the close of the service till the minister had come down from the pulpit, joined his wife, and passed out to the church-porch, there to greet the people as they would come out of the church.

It would seem that the most important officer in church and public life in New England was the tithing-man. "He was in a degree a constable, a selectman, a teacher, a tax-collector, an inspector, a sexton, a home-watcher, and above all, a Puritan Bumble, whose motto was *Hic et ubique.*"[150] Among his duties were the seeing that the children learned the church catechism, looking out that people went to church, inspecting the taverns to note that they were kept in an orderly manner and did not sell liquors to disorderly

[150] Earle, The Sabbath in Puritan New England, 76.

persons, and watching that boys and other persons should not go swimming in the water on week days. His most important duty, perhaps, was that of keeping order and proper decorum in the meeting-house by beating out the dogs, prodding the noisy boys, and awakening the sleeping adults. For this latter he had a long staff with a knob on one end to tap the sleeping men while on the other end was a fox-tail to dangle in the face of the sleeping women. The following from a journal of those early days tells how well he performed his duties and some of the effects thereof.

"June 3, 1646.—Allen Bridges hath bin chose to wake ye sleepers in meeting. And being much proude of his place, must needs have a fox taile fixed to ye ende of a long staff wherewith he may brush ye faces of them yt will have napps in time of discourse, likewise a sharpe thorne whereby he may pricke such as be most sound. On ye last Lord his day, as hee strutted about ye meeting-house, he did spy Mr. Tomlins sleeping with much comfort, hys head kept steadie by being in ye corner, and his hand grasping ye rail. And soe spying, Allen did quickly thrust his staff behind Dame Ballard and give him a grievous prick upon ye hand. Whereupon Mr. Tomlins did spring vpp mch above ye floore and with terrible force strike hys hand against ye wall; and also, to ye great wonder of all, prophanlie exclaim in a loud voice, curse ye wood-chuck, he dreaming so it seemed yt a wood-chuck had seized and bit his hand. But on coming to know where he was, and ye greate scandall he had committed, he seemed much abashed, but did not speak. And I think he will not soon again goe to sleepe in meeting."[151]

Among the Dutch in New Amsterdam there was a somewhat similar officer, "the *voorleezer*, or chorister, who was also generally the bell-ringer, sexton, grave-digger, funeral inviter, schoolmaster, and sometimes town clerk. He 'tuned the psalm'; turned the hour-glass; gave out the psalms on a hanging-board to the congregation; read the Bible; gave up notices to the dominie by sticking the papers in the end of a cleft stick and holding it up to the high pulpit."[152]

The ministers among the Puritans in New England were very greatly considered. The laity who were bold enough to criticize or disparage the minister or his teachings were

[151] Earle, The Sabbath in Puritan New England, 68.
[152] Earle, Home life in colonial days, 386.

severely punished. A woman who spoke harshly of her minister had her tongue placed in a cleft stick and made to stand thus in a public place. A man for declaring that he received no profit from his minister's sermons was fined and severely whipped. Worse than bodily punishment was excommunication, for if a minister pronounced such upon a member of his congregation he was excluded from partaking of the sacrament and the people of the church refrained from all communion with him in civil affairs, even from eating and drinking with him. Yet with all this great power of the ministers in early Puritan times, they were not permitted to perform the marriage-service, which was wholly a civil affair, nor could they pray or exhort at a funeral. The ordination of so important an officer as the minister was a very important event. This was celebrated by a great gathering of people and ministers for many miles around. It was a deeply serious affair and yet a great festival occasion, for frequently there was an ordination ball and always an ordination supper, where there was a plenty and a variety of things to eat and to drink.

Although the minister's calling was one of trust and honor it was not also one of profit. The salary was small and paid in different ways, not a large part of it in cash. It was the universal custom to provide a house for the minister and often this was among the very first houses built in a new town and at its laying out some of the best lots were set aside for his use. He was also provided with free pasturage for his horse, the village burial-ground having been placed at his disposal for pasture land. In the early days a large part of the salary was paid in corn and labor and the amount for each church member to give was fixed by the authorities. Cord-wood was another common contribution, and each male church-member was expected to give a load of wood delivered at the door of the parsonage. Any money contributed by strangers who chanced to attend the services was usually given to the minister. A spinning bee, a forerunner of the donation party of later times, was often held at the home of the minister, wherein each woman would take her spinning-wheel and flax and all would spend the day in spinning and give the outcome to the minister's family. Also the women would meet and make patchwork bed-quilts and give them to the minister's family. Some ministers would go out among the members of their congregations and beg supplies for themselves and families. Many of the ministers found it necessary to do outside work to make a living, such as farming on week days, taking young men to teach and to fit for college, compounding and selling drugs and medicines; while some were coopers, carpenters, rope-makers, millers, and cobblers. It took great thrift and economy on the part of the minister and his family to get along. The wife not only had to be zealous in religious practices but also in domestic practices and often she was the thriftiest wife of the community. Every kind of denial had to be made and yet with this poverty the minister's children were quite often well kept and trained and many ministers were enabled to help their sons to obtain a college education.

Fear of the Indians did not keep the Puritans away from the meeting-house, but it did cause them to go there armed. At first each man carried arms to church and then later a certain number were detailed to arm themselves. In 1642 in Massachusetts the law provided for six men to be at the meeting-house with muskets and powder and shot. The armed men were placed near the door so as to be ready to protect the congregation or to rush out in case of need. When the services were ended, the armed guards went out of the meeting-house first and then the other men and the women and children were last, thus to be protected. Too, it was the custom for the men always to sit at the door of the pew, next to the aisle, so they could be ready to get their arms and rush out in case of a fight. Also being at the door of the pew the father could better protect the other members of the family, and a man who would not have occupied this place would have been considered a poor kind of husband and father.

In the early colonial days in New England there were two services in the meeting-house on Sunday, in the forenoon and in the afternoon. The sermons were long, two or three hours not being uncommon and some even ran up to five hours in length. Added to these long sermons were long prayers, frequently an hour in length and sometimes even continuing for three hours. At a desk near the pulpit there was an hour-glass and sitting near it was an officer of the church whose duty it was to turn it at the end of the hour. During the prayer the congregation stood, about its middle the minister would make a long pause to let the infirm and those ill sit down, but all the others remained standing till its close. It was the duty of the tithing-man to see that no one left the house before the close of the services without there was a real good reason and also he was to keep the congregation awake. These long prayers and sermons were not disliked by the congregation, but on the contrary they considered it a great gift for the minister to be able to continue long in prayer and a short sermon would have been looked upon as irreligious and lacking in reverence, and beside that was for what the minister was paid. "In every record and journal which I have read, throughout which ministers and laymen recorded all the annoyances and opposition which the preachers encountered, I have never seen one entry of any complaint or ill-criticism of too long praying or preaching." [153]

The music of the Puritan meeting-house is well summarized in the following: "The singing of the psalms was tedious and unmusical, just as it was in churches of all denominations both in America and England at that date. Singing was by ear and very uncertain, and the congregation had no notes, and many had no psalm-books, and hence no words. So the psalms were 'lined' or 'deaconed'; that is, a line was read by the deacon, and then sung by the congregation. Some psalms when lined and sung occupied half an hour, during which the congregation stood. There were but eight or nine tunes in general use, and even these were often sung incorrectly. There were no church organs to help keep the singers together, but sometimes pitch-pipes were used to set the key. Bass-viols, clarionets, and flutes were played upon at a later date in meeting to help the singing. Violins were too much associated with dance music to be thought decorous for church music. Still the New England churches clung to and loved their poor confused psalm-singing as one of their few delights, and whenever a Puritan, even in road or field, heard the distant sound of a psalm-tune he removed his hat and bowed his head in prayer." [154]

**The Child and Religion.** The children in the other colonies were not so strictly reared as those in Puritan New England. The people in New York enjoined that the constable attend church to look after such children as profaned the Sabbath. In Albany complaint was made that boys and girls coasted down hills on Sunday and in some

[153] Earle, The Sabbath in Puritan New England, 81.
[154] Earle, Home life in colonial days, 377.

other places that the young people violated the Sabbath by discoursing on vain things and the running of races. In the eighteenth century a cage was placed in City Hall Park in New York for the confining of boys who profaned the Sabbath.

In the meeting-house in New England in colonial times the young men sat together on one side and the young women sat in a corresponding place on the other side. The little girls sat on stools or low seats in the pews with their mothers or, if too many of them for place in the pew, they would sit out in the aisle, and sometimes there would be a row of little girls on a row of little stools extending the full length of the aisle. In some of the meeting-houses the boys were seated together on the pulpit and gallery stairs, while in other houses a place was made for them in the gallery, but wherever the place they were all herded together.

The boys among the Puritans were as other boys in all times and among all peoples, and the huddling them together in meeting-houses only helped to bring out their growing physical activities, as the taking them away from the watchfulness of the parents gave them better opportunities for expression of their repressed powers. One way of doing this was by slamming the pew-seats at the close of prayer and sermon and the vigor with which they did this called for an order from one church at least that "The boys are not to wickedly noise down there pew-seats." Another pastime was the twisting of the balustrades of the gallery railing in order to make them squeak. Whittling and cutting the woodwork and benches where they sat gave opportunity to put in time and also to try out their jack-knives. They passed the time in other ways, for there are court records showing that youths were taken before magistrates and fined for playing and laughing in church and doing things to make others laugh and play.

The best evidence left us to show that boys kept themselves busy in the meeting-houses is that they kept other people busy attending to them. There are plenty of records left to show that the tithing-man was continually being ordered to look after the behavior of the boys and also of the appointing of extra men to look after these unruly beings, in one church as many as six men had to be appointed at one time to keep them in order. These men had power to inflict punishment on the boys, and they did not hesitate to rap them soundly with their sticks and, too, sometimes a boy was taken out of the meeting-house and given a severe whipping. The tithing-man also used other means, for sometimes he took a boy from his place with the other boys and paraded him across the house and put him by side his mother on the women's side. If a young man would not behave himself, sometimes he was taken away from his place among the men and led to where the boys sat and forced to sit with them. Even during the noon hour the boys were watched over. While in the noon-house they had to listen to Bible teachings and interpretations. This was done to keep them quiet during this time so they might not "sporte and playe."

It is not wondered at that under such training much early religion developed. The Bible was read through many times by the young and much precocity in religious things was developed. A father gives in his diary the following in reference to a little girl of eight: "A little while after dinner she burst out into an amazing cry, which caused all the family to cry, too. Her mother asked the reason; she gave none. At last said she was afraid she would goe to Hell; her sins were not pardoned. She was first wounded by my reading a sermon of Mr. Norton's, Text, ye shall seek me and shall not find me. And those words in the sermon, ye shall seek me and die in your sins ran in her mind and terrified her greatly . . . told me she was afraid she should go to Hell, was like Spira not elected."[155]

Another father makes this entry in his diary about his four-year-old daughter: "I took my little daughter Katy into my study and then I told my child I am to dye shortly and shee must, when I am dead, remember Everything I now said to unto her. I sett before her the sinful Condition of her nature, and I charged her to pray in Secret Places every Day. That God for the sake of Jesus Christ would give her a New Heart. I gave her to understand that when I am taken from her she must look to meet with more humbling Afflictions than she does now she has a Tender Father to provide for her."[156]

These two quotations are from the diaries of educated men, the first being from Judge Sewall and the second from Cotton Mather. It is hard for us now to see any reason for

[155] Fisher, Men, women, and manners in colonial times, I, 141.
[156] Earle, Child life in Colonial days, 236.

such a talk as Cotton Mather gave a child of four, especially as he lived for thirty years afterward and died long after this little girl died.

The religious books of Puritan New England children were of a remarkable character. Mrs. Earle gives the following in reference to one of the most popular and widely read books:

"Young babes chide their parents for too infrequent praying, and have ecstacies of delight when they can pray *ad infitum*. One child two years old was able 'savingly to understand the mysteries of Redemption'; another of the same age was a 'dear lover of faithful ministers.' Anne Greenwich, who died when five years old, 'discoursed most astonishingly of great mysteries'; Daniel Bradley, who had an 'Impression and inquisitiveness of the State of Souls after Death,' when three years old; Elizabeth Butcher, who, 'when two and a half years old, as she lay in the Cradle would ask herself the Question What is my corrupt Nature: and would answer herself It is empty of Grace, bent unto Sin, and only to Sin, and that Continually,' were among the distressing examples." [157]

The following is an extract from a letter written about 1638 by a Puritan boy of twelve years of age and well displays the tendency toward religious fears as found in the young people of that period:

"Though I am thus well in body yet I question whether my soul doth prosper as my body doth, for I perceive yet to this very day, little *growth* in grace; and this makes me question whether grace be in my heart or no. I feel also daily great unwillingness to good duties, and the great ruling of sin in my heart; and that God is angry with me and gives me no answers to my prayers; but many times he even throws them down as dust in my face; and he does not grant my continued request for the *spiritual blessing of the softening of my hard heart*. And in all this I could yet take some comfort but that it makes me to wonder what God's *secret decree* concerning me may be: for I doubt whether even God is wont to deny grace and mercy to his chosen (though *uncalled*) when they seek unto him by prayer for it; and, therefore, seeing he doth thus deny it to me, I think that the reason of it is most like to be because I belong not unto *the election of grace*. I desire that you would let

[157] Earle, Child life in colonial times, 250.

me have your prayers as I doubt not but I have them, and rest

"Your Son, SAMUEL MATHER."[158]

As was given under the discussion of infancy, the Puritan babe had to be taken to the meeting-house on the Sunday following its birth to be baptized, even in the most bitter weather. One record is given of the baptism of an infant but four days old and this during the first part of February. In one diary there is given about a day in January so bad that but few women could get out to meeting, and yet a babe was taken to the meeting-house and baptized. It must be considered, too, that this occurred in a building that never had had a fire in it nor was there fire on that day. It is difficult for us at this day to hold even in imagination the carrying of the young babe by the midwife through the snow and the wind and the cold of a New England January, the taking him to the altar and placing him in the arms of his father, the throwing the icy cold water over the child, and the shuddering of the child; yet worse, for this baptism might have been an immersion in the cold water after the ice had been broken, for at least one minister did practice infant immersion.

**Education.** There arose during colonial times in the United States three chief systems of education. These forms came about through the ideas of the people settling the different parts of the country and through conditions arising from industrial occupations. In the southern colonies, in particular in Virginia, where the pursuits that arose produced plantation life with houses scattered and no town or village life, there was followed the educational ideas of England and education took upon itself the form of higher and secondary training for the ruling classes with but little provision for elementary education. There was no free public education, the nearest approach to a common elementary school was what was designated the "field school," which was originated by a neighborhood and supported by tuition fees, and often held in a shabby building on an old exhausted tobacco field. There did arise, however, secondary schools which were chartered and endowed, resembling the endowed Latin schools of England.

The second form of schools was the parochial organiza-

[158] Earle, Child life in colonial days, 239.

tion of the middle colonies of New Netherlands and Pennsylvania. In these colonies there arose a school in connection with a church and, unlike the education of the South, which was along secondary training, the work of this parochial school was chiefly in elementary education. In New Netherlands, as in Holland, the church was connected with the state and there was but one church, the Dutch Reformed, and the civil and religious authorities jointly controlled and directed the education. In Pennsylvania, however, religious and civil freedom had been granted from the very first and there had come into the colony people of different nationalities and of different religions, and education came to be established with the different religious bodies and each religious sect had its own distinctive parochial school alongside its own church. There also were some attempts at higher and secondary education. Among the schools started was the Penn Charter School, which was originally organized by the Friends in 1689, and there were higher schools of other denominations. When New Netherlands fell into the hands of the English, there came about in New York conditions somewhat similar to those in Virginia and a number of secondary schools were organized.

The third type of schools in colonial times was that formed by governmental action in the New England colonies of Massachusetts and Connecticut. In these colonies there was no such class distinctions as in Virginia, and, unlike Pennsylvania, there was but one nationality and one religion, and, unlike the Dutch of New Netherlands, they had cut themselves away from the ruling classes of their native land, and thus they were free to develop along their own ideas. Their religious belief and training called for the education of each of the members of the colony, as the Bible was held to be the infallible rule of faith and practice, and so every one should at least have enough schooling to enable him to read the Bible for himself. Hence schools arose in a short time after settlement. In 1644 Salem taxed all who had children and were able to pay and procured in this way means for paying for the schooling of children whose parents were too poor to pay for them. In 1647 Massachusetts passed a law that in every town of fifty families a school for the teaching of reading and writing should be provided and that in a town of one hundred families a grammar school should be provided. Connecticut in 1659 provided for its children in the same way. But all such schools were not free as we term free schools now, and it was not till near the time of the Revolution that general taxes were levied for school purposes and free schools were thereby established.

The early schoolhouses in Pennsylvania and New York were made of logs and the top covered with bark. Holes were cut in the sides for windows, which sometimes were covered with greased paper that let in a dim light. Some had a rough puncheon floor and others a dirt floor. A distance up from the floor around the walls pegs were placed between the logs and boards laid on them for desks and by them were boards set on stakes for seats for the older children, while the younger children sat on blocks or benches of logs. At one end or in the middle was a catted chimney. At least some of the schoolhouses in New England were better furnished, as is shown by the following entry in the town records of Roxbury in 1652:

"The feoffes agreed with Daniel Welde that he provide convenient benches with forms, with tables for the scholars, and a conveniente seate for the scholmaster, a Deske to put the Dictionary on and shelves to lay up bookes."[159]

This schoolhouse was not kept in proper repairs, as the teacher in Roxbury in 1681 wrote:

"Of inconveniences (in the schoolhouse) I shall mention no other but the confused and shattered and nastie posture that it is in, not fitting for to reside in, the glass broke, and thereupon very raw and cold; the floor very much broken and torn up to kindle fires, the hearth spoiled, the seats some burned and others out of kilter, that one had as well-nigh as goods keep school in a hog stie as in it."[160]

Supplies for school purposes were quite scarce in colonial times. There were no blackboards nor maps. Paper was quite scarce and very carefully used. Birch bark was used to cipher on. Slates also were used and those of the earlier times had no frames and had a hole in one side in which a string could be tied for holding a pencil or for hanging around the neck. If lead pencils were used at all during colonial times it was in the latest part of the period. Instead of lead pencils they used plummets made of lead melted and cast into wooden molds and cut into shape by a jack-knife. Pens were cut from goose-quills and it required

[159] Earle, Customs and fashions in old New England, 33.
[160] Ibid., 32.

quite a little skill to make good pens and keep them in order. Ink was made by dissolving ink-powder, each child furnishing his own ink-bottle or ink-horn and ink. Sometimes the ink was wholly home-made: "In remote districts of Vermont, Maine, and Massachusetts, home-made ink, feeble and pale, was made by steeping the bark of the swamp-maple in water, boiling the decoction till thick, and diluting it with copperas."[161]

There were not a great number or variety of books for use in these early schools. The two most noted books were the Hornbook and the New England Primer. The hornbook was the first book used by the child. This consisted of a thin piece of wood about five inches long and two inches wide. A sheet of paper was placed upon this. At the top of this paper came the alphabet in small letters; then the alphabet in capital letters followed; then the vowels; then syllables, as, ab, eb, ib, etc.; next "In the Name of the Father, and of the Son, and of the Holy Ghost, *Amen;*" and last came the Lord's prayer. Over this paper went a sheet of horn, through which the printed matter could be read. The paper and the horn were fastened to the wood by strips of brass or other metal, going around the sides and ends, and all held fast by tacks driven through the metal strips. At the lower end of the hornbook was usually a handle, which sometimes had a hole through it for a string to carry it by or to hang it around the neck.

"The New England Primer is a poorly printed little book about five inches long and three wide, of about eighty pages. It contains the alphabet, and a short table of easy syllables, such as a-b, ab, e-b eb, and words up to those of six syllables. This was called a syllabarium. There were twelve five-syllable words; of these five were *abomination, edification, humiliation, mortification,* and *purification.* There were a morning and evening prayer for children, and a grace to be said before meat. Then followed a set of little rhymes which have become known everywhere, and are frequently quoted. Each letter of the alphabet is illustrated with a blurred little picture. Of these, two-thirds represent Biblical incidents. They begin:

        'In Adam's fall
        We sinned all,'

[161] Earle, Child life in colonial days, 154.

and ended with Z:

> 'Zaccheus he
> Did climb a tree
> His Lord to see.'

"In the early days of the Primer, all the colonies were true to the English king, and the rhyme for the letter K reads:

> 'King Charles the Good
> No man of blood.'

"But by Revolutionary years the verse for K was changed to:

> 'Queens and Kings
> Are Gaudy Things.'

"Later verses tell the praise of George Washington. Then comes a series of Bible questions and answers; then an 'alphabet of lessons for youth,' consisting of verses of the Bible beginning successively with A, B, C, and so on. X was a difficult initial letter, and had to be contented with 'Xhort one another daily, etc.' After the Lord's prayer and Apostle's Creed appeared sometimes a list of names for men and women, to teach children to spell their own names. The largest and most interesting picture was that of the burning at the stake of John Rogers; and after this a six page set of pious rhymes which the martyr left at his death for his family of small children. After the year 1750, a few very short stories were added to its pages, and were probably all the children's stories that many of the scholars of that day ever saw."[162]

In the establishing of the elementary schools in New England there was but little more required of the teacher than to instruct the children in reading and writing, especially were they to be taught sufficiently that they could read the Bible. Also they were to be taught enough arithmetic for their every-day needs. This is well shown in the records of the town of Plymouth, where in 1671 they had built a schoolhouse and employed a schoolmaster "to teach the children and youth to read the Bible, to write, and to cast accounts."[163] In the secondary schools the emphasis was laid

---

[162] Earle, Child life in colonial days, 128-131.
[163] Dexter, History of education in the United States, 39.

upon Latin and such other subjects were taught as would fit the scholars for college. Penmanship was made a great deal of while orthography was not, the results of which are shown by the writing and spelling of the diaries and other writings of that period that remain.

The work of the district school, of the academy, and of the college is well portrayed by McMaster. "The daily labors of the schoolmaster who taught in the district schoolhouse three generations since were confined to teaching his scholars to read with a moderate degree of fluency, to write legibly, to spell with some regard for the rules of orthography, and to know as much of arithmetic as would enable them to calculate the interest on a debt, to keep the family accounts, and to make change in a shop. . . . To sit eight hours a day on the hardest of benches poring over Cheever's Accidence; to puzzle over long words in Dilworth's speller; to commit to memory pages of words in Webster's American Institute; to read long chapters in the Bible; to learn by heart Dr. Watt's hymns for children; to be drilled in the Assembly Catechism; to go to bed at sundown, to get up at sunrise, and to live on brown bread and pork, porridge and beans, made up, with morning and evening prayers, the every-day life of the lads at most of the academies and schools of New England. . . . The four years of residence at college were spent in the acquisition of Latin and Greek, a smattering of mathematics, enough of logic to distinguish barbara from celarent, enough of rhetoric to know climax from metonomy, and as much of metaphysics as would enable one to talk learnedly about a subject he did not understand."[164]

The teachers of the elementary schools of those early days were too often not educated nor cultured men. These men in many cases were drunken, cruel, ignorant, and lazy. Drunkenness seems to have been quite prevalent among the teachers of early New York, and yet there were some most excellent men among them. In the middle and southern colonies among the teachers were redemptioners and exported criminals. It was not uncommon on the arrival of a ship for schoolmasters to be advertised for sale along with men of other callings and usually the teachers did not fetch as good prices as weavers, tailors, and the like. The teachers in the secondary schools, on the contrary, often were men of good scholarship and of high standing in the community, occupy-

[164] McMaster, History of the people of the United States, I, 21 *et seq.*

ing a place of honor among their fellow men. Such teachers were Christopher Dock in Pennsylvania and Ezekiel Cheever in New England.

"Among the New England teachers there were men of both learning and ability. Not a more cultured body of men ever formed a colony than settled about Boston, Salem, New Haven, and Hartford. They coveted the best advantages for their children, frequently making the best men their teachers. It is on record that of the twenty-two masters of Plymouth from 1671 to the Revolution, twenty were graduates of Harvard. The like was true of Roxbury. Such men, next to the functionaries of church and state, commanded the highest respect. In the churches they had special pews provided for their use beside those of magistrates and the deacon's family. In every community was usually one who was the teacher professionally, so considered as much as was the minister or physician."[165]

There were women teachers in the colonial times. They taught what was known as dame-schools, which were attended by small boys and girls. Women teachers and dame-schools were probably confined to New England and parts of New York adjacent to New England and settled by emigrants from there. There grew up the custom in some rural districts of having one term of school in the summer for the younger pupils and taught by a woman and another term in the winter for the older pupils and taught by a man. This arrangement arose because it was difficult for the younger children to attend school during the bitter weather of the winter, while the older pupils could attend well only during the cold time of the year when there was not much work to do on the farm.

There is in existence a contract between a Dutch schoolmaster and the authorities of Flatbush, New York, of the date of October 8, 1682. This is a full paper and quite well shows the duties of a teacher of that time in that colony. The school day was to be from eight o'clock to eleven and from one to four. Each forenoon and afternoon session was to open and close with prayer. On every Wednesday and Saturday the schoolmaster was to instruct the children in the common prayers and in the catechism and to be present at the church meeting when the children were catechized before the congregation. He was to keep school nine months

[165] Boone, Education in the United States, 50.

in succession, from September to June of each year. Beside his school duties he had church duties. He was to keep the church clean, ring the bell, lead in the singing, and sometimes he was to read the sermon. He was to provide water for baptism and to furnish the minister with the name of the child to be baptized and also the names of the parents or witnesses. He was to provide bread and wine for the communion. He was to serve as messenger for the consistory. He was to give out the funeral invitations, dig the grave, and toll the bell.[166]

It can scarcely be believed that the schoolmasters of the early period of our country could have been so cruel as is told of them. It would appear as if a great deal more time was put upon devising means of punishment that upon learning ways of instruction. It was a time of cruelty and of belief in the general depravity of humanity. It was deemed that there was a natural wilfulness in children that needed stern repression and harsh correction. The parents and teachers in New England were especially repressive of child nature and their guide and rule of action, the Bible, gave them constant proof of the need of corrective punishment for children. "John Robinson, the Pilgrim preacher, said in his essay on *Children and Their Education*: 'Surely there is in all children (though not alike) a stubbornes and stoutnes of minde arising from naturall pride which must in the first place be broken and beaten down that so the foundation of their education being layd in humilitie and tractablenes other virtues may in their time be built thereon.'"[167]

The rod was very greatly in use by the schoolmasters of colonial times and too often the rod became the cudgel. Some teachers had the boy mount the back of another boy and with arms and legs held tight he was given a beating. The ferule was applied to the hands, the face, and the feet, and sometimes this ferule was a heavy oaken ruler. One instrument used was a hickory club with leather thongs attached at one end and similar to it was the tattling stick, a cat-o'-nine-tails with heavy leather straps. Another instrument used was termed a flapper, which was a piece of leather about six inches wide with a hole in the middle and fastened to a handle. Every stroke with this flapper on a boy's bared

[166] Dexter, History of education in the United States, Appendix A, 581-583.
[167] Earle, Child life in colonial days, 191.

back would raise a blister the size of the hole in the leather. A branch of a tree was split and placed over a child's nose and he had to then stand before the school. For whispering a whispering-stick was used, which was a kind of wooden gag tied in the mouth with strings, somewhat as a horse's bit. Another punishment was to put two boys together in a yoke devised for that purpose, similar to an ox-yoke, and to make the punishment all the more disgraceful would be to yoke a boy and girl together. A unipod, a one-legged stool, was used, and the child occupying it found it very hard and tiresome to balance himself on it. The dames in their schools used quite freely a heavy iron thimble, which by being snapped quite vigorously against a boy's head would make for him "thimell-pie." The dunce-block was freely used and the culprit appropriately labelled, as, "Tell-Tale," "Bite-Finger-Baby," "Lying Ananias," "Idle-Boy," and "Pert-Miss-Prat-a-Pace." There were some teachers who did not use such cruel punishments, although they must have been very few in number, one being Samuel Dock, a German schoolmaster of Pennsylvania, who was intelligent enough to be kind to his children, but there were plenty of the drunken, dirty, careless, and cruel teachers in that colony. Mrs. Earle states: "I may say here that I have not found that New York schoolmasters were ever as cruel as were those of New England." [168]

"I often fancy that I should have enjoyed living in the good old times, but I am glad I never was a child in colonial New England—to have been baptized in ice water, fed on brown bread and warm beer, to have had to learn the Assembly's Catechism and 'explain all the Quaestions with conferring Texts,' to have been constantly threatened with fear of death and terror of God, to have been forced to commit Wigglesworth's 'Day of Doom' to memory, and, after all, to have been whipped with a tattling-stick." [169]

The colonial period was an age of child precocity. In that time overzealous parents pushed children forward till they displayed a remarkable precocious learning, to end, in most cases, in an early death either physically or mentally, and yet some of these children did survive the process to become noted and honored men. One such parent wrote to her sister asking to have sent to her a set of toys now known as alpha-

[168] Earle, Colonial days in old New York, 29.
[169] Earle, Customs and fashions in old New England, 35.

bet blocks and stating that the child's father was contriving a set of toys to teach the child his letters by the time he could speak, he being not yet four months old at the time of the letter. In a later letter the mother wrote to the child's aunt that at twenty-two months of age he could tell his letters in any book and he was beginning to spell. This boy grew up to be the Revolutionary General Charles Cotesworth Pinckney. One boy born in 1752 learned his alphabet in a single lesson and he could read the Bible before he was four years old. At the age of six he was sent to a grammar school, and, as his father would not let him study Latin, he borrowed a Latin grammar and studied through it twice without a teacher. This boy afterward was known as President Timothy Dwight of Yale College.

This precociousness was not confined to boys, for one little girl, born in Boston in 1708, daughter of the President of Harvard College, before her second year was finished could speak distinctly, knew her letters, could relate many stories out of the Scriptures, and when three years old she could recite the greater part of the *Assembly's Cathechism* and also she could recite many of the psalms and many lines of poetry and read distinctly. The Governor of the colony and other distinguished guests at her home sometimes would place this little girl on a table to show off her acquirements. Another little girl, born in Charleston, South Carolina, in 1759, in her third year could "read any book," so the story ran, and, too, this she could do holding the book upside down.

Boys entered the Boston Latin School as young as six and a half years of age and often parents had them begin Latin at an earlier age, some parents teaching their little ones to read Latin words when but three years old along with the English. Young Timothy Dwight would have been prepared to enter college at eight years of age had not his grammar school been discontinued because of having no teacher. A boy in 1686 entered Harvard College at eleven years of age and another boy in 1799 graduated from Rhode Island College (now Brown University) at barely fourteen years of age.

The most remarkable case of childish precocity given by Mrs. Earle was that of Richard Evelyn, who died in 1658 at the early age of five years and three days. The father in his diary recounted in the following quoted passage the wonderful acquirements of the little boy before his death:

"He had learned all his catechism at two years and a half old; he could perfectly read any of the English, Latin, French, or Gothic letters, pronouncing the first three languages exactly. He had, before the fifth year, or in that year, not only skill to read most written hands, but to decline all the nouns, conjugate the verbs regular, and most of the irregular; learned out of Puerelis, got by heart almost the entire vocabulary of Latin and French primitives and words, could make congruous syntax, turn English into Latin, and vice versa, construe and prove what he read, and did the government and use of relatives, verbs, substances, ellipses and many figures and tropes, and made a considerable progress in Comenius' Janua; begun himself to write legibly and had a strong passion for Greek. The number of verses he could recite was prodigious, and what he remembered of the parts of plays which he would also act; and, when seeing a Plautus in one's hand, he asked what book it was, and being told it was comedy and too difficult for him, he wept for sorrow. Strange was his apt and ingenious application of fables and morals, for he had read Æsop; he had a wonderful disposition to mathematics, having by heart divers propositions of Euclid that were read to him in play, and he would make lines and demonstrate them. He had learned by heart divers sentences in Latin and Greek which on occasion he would produce even to wonder. He was all life, all prettiness, far from morose, sullen, or childish in anything he said or did." [170]

The girls of colonial times did not receive much education, as it was not considered necessary for women to have learning beyond that necessary for household duties. All that was considered really needed by a girl in the way of book learning was to know how to read and write and cipher a little. Most of the girls received nothing further than elementary training in reading and writing and many of them did not even have that much of education. This was true in all the colonies, New England, New York, and the others.

A lady writing of the education of girls of her time in New York, in the first quarter of the eighteenth century stated:

"It was at that time very difficult to procure the means of

[170] Earle, Child life in colonial days, 177.

instruction in those island districts; female education was, of consequence, conducted on a very limited scale; girls learned needlework (in which they were indeed both skilful and ingenious) from their mothers and aunts; they were taught, too, at that period to read, in Dutch, the Bible, and a few Calvinistic tracts of the devotional kind. But in the infancy of the settlement few girls read English; when they did, they were thought accomplished; they generally spoke it, however imperfectly, and few were taught writing."[171]

A historian of New York, writing of his fellow townswomen during the year 1756, said that "there is nothing they (New York women) so generally neglect as Reading, and indeed all the Arts for the improvement of the Mind, in which I confess we have set them the Example."[172]

The attitude of the people of the period toward the admission of girls into boys' grammar schools is shown by the following extract from the rules for governing such a school in New Haven in 1684:

". . . and all girls be excluded as improper and inconsistent with such a grammar school as ye law injoines and as is the Designe of this settlement."[173]

But it must not be considered that the education of the girls was wholly neglected among the colonists, for, though they were scarcely ever admitted to boys' schools, yet they did go to the dame-schools and also they received training at home. The girls were all taught household duties and the fancy needlework that went with it. Reading, writing, a little arithmetic, dancing, needlework, music, deportment, and elegance of carriage composed the curriculum for girls. Sometimes a girl would get some help from a brother and thus gain an education beyond that ordinarily obtained by girls. Occasionally an educated father would teach his daughter, one such case being that of President Colman of Harvard College, who gave what was called a profound education to his daughter Jane. Withal this meager education, nevertheless we are not at all ashamed of the bearing of our foremothers of the colonial and Revolutionary times.

As academies grew up during the latter half of the eighteenth century, most of which were for boys, a few were made

[171] Earle, Colonial days in old New York, 39.
[172] *Ibid.*, 40.
[173] Dexter, History of education in the United States, 426.

co-educational and a few others were established for girls:

"For a hundred years the Penn Charter School, Philadelphia, had admitted both sexes on equal terms. The Moravians had established a school for girls at Bethlehem, Pa., as early as 1745, while the Philadelphia Female Academy dates from the Revolution. Among the earliest in New England were Dr. Dwight's Young Ladies'.Academy, at Greenfield, Conn. (1785), and the Medford School, near Boston (1789).''[174]

Of the colleges in the United States today, two of them were founded during the first century of the colonial period, the seventeenth century, ten others in the next century before the Revolution, and by the close of the eighteenth century the list had increased to twenty-six, eleven of the original colonies being represented in the list and also Kentucky and Tennessee. Arranging the twelve colleges of the colonial period in the order of the year of first opening and with the names and locations as now, they run as follows:[175]

Harvard University, Cambridge, Massachusetts, 1636; College of William and Mary, Williamsburg, Virginia, 1693; Yale University, New Haven, Connecticut, 1701; Washington College, Chestertown, Maryland, 1723; University of Pennsylvania, Philadelphia, Pennsylvania, 1740; Moravian Seminary and College for Women, Bethlehem, Pennsylvania, 1742; Princeton University, Princetown, New Jersey, 1746; Washington and Lee University, Lexington, Virginia, 1749; Columbia University, New York City, New York, 1754; Brown University, Providence, Rhode Island, 1765; Rutgers College, New Brunswick, New Jersey, 1766; Dartmouth College, Hanover, New Hampshire, 1769.

With dame-schools for the younger children, district schools for the older ones, academies for the yet more advanced, and colleges for completing the education, the early period of the United States gave such an education to its young people as well to prepare them to become the noble men and women, who, by books, papers, addresses, and general bearing, were able to stand alongside the people of the world in the great period of the American Revolution, and furnished thinkers and doers such as have not been surpassed by our own time.

[174] Boone, Education in the United States, 69.
[175] Report U. S. Commissioner of Education, 1914, II, 224-246.

## LITERATURE

1. Boone, Richard G., Education in the United States.
2. Calhoun, Arthur W., A social history of the American family.
3. Claxton, Philander Priestley, Report of the Commissioner of Education of the United States, 1914.
4. Dexter, Edwin Grant, History of education in the United States.
5. Earle, Alice Morse, Child life in Colonial days.
6. Earle, Alice Morse, Colonial days in old New York.
7. Earle, Alice Morse, Costume of colonial times.
8. Earle, Alice Morse, Curious punishments of bygone days.
9. Earle, Alice Morse, Customs and fashions in old New England.
10. Earle, Alice Morse, Diary of Anna Green Winslow, a Boston school-girl of 1771.
11. Earle, Alice Morse, Home life in colonial days.
12. Earle, Alice Morse, The Sabbath in Puritan New England.
13. Eggleston, Edward, Social conditions in the colonies, *The Century Magazine*, VI., 853.
14. Eggleston, Edward, The colonists at home, *The Century Magazine*, VII., 873.
15. Eggleston, Edward, Social life in the colonies, *The Century Magazine*, VIII., 387.
16. Fisher, Sydney George, Men, women and manners in colonial times.
17. Haddon, Kathleen, Cat's cradles from many lands.
18. Howard, George Elliott, A history of matrimonial institutions.
19. Low, A. Maurice, The American people.
20. Mather, Frederic G., Early New England choirs and singing-schools, *The American Magazine*, VIII., 310.
21. McMaster, John Bach, A history of the people of the United States.
22. Salmon, Lucy Maynard, Domestic service.
23. Stiles, Henry Reed, Bundling: Its origin, progress and decline in the United States.
24. Welsh, Charles, The early history of children's books in New England, *New England Magazine*, XX., 147.

# INDEX

"Above the salt," seating of guests, in United States, 328.
Acrobatic feats in China, 120; Egypt, 79; Europe, 294; Greece, 200; India, 98; Japan, 147; Mexico, 34; Rome, 253; United States, 403.
Admonitions of father to a son, in Mexico, 20; of a mother to a daughter, in Mexico, 21.
Adoption, in Greece, 194; India, 99; Japan, 145; Rome, 242.
Adrogation at Rome, 242.
Adultery, in China, 104; Egypt, 58; India, 92.
African slave trade in United States, 317.
Agriculture, in Egypt, 65; Mexico, 30; Peru, 45; Rome, 246.
Amphitheater, the, at Rome, 250.
Amusements, in China, 118; Egypt, 76; Europe, 292; India, 98; Japan, 146; Judea, 173; Mexico, 33; Persia, 164; Rome, 249; United States, 398.
Animal exhibits in United States, 404.
Animals, domestic, of Egypt, 66.
Animals, trained, in Europe, 294; Japan, 147.
Animals used for food, in Egypt, 61; Europe, 428; Rome, 238; United States, 369.
Anklets worn in Egypt, 61; Judea, 172.
Apprenticeship in Europe, 290; Japan, 156.
Aqueducts of Peru, 46.
Architecture in Egypt, 72.
Aristocracy of Europe, 275.
Armed men at church in New England, 437.
Artificial teeth at Rome, 237.

Artisans of Europe, 273.
"Assemblies" in United States, 399.
Athletic contests at Rome, 252.
Atrium of a Roman house, 216.
Auguries of marriages in India, 90; Mexico, 17.
Ax, the, among the early colonists of United States, 322.

Baby boys welcomed, baby girls not wanted, in China, 116.
Bachelors in Greece, 185; United States, 348.
Backgammon in Europe, 295.
Balls and ball-playing in Egypt, 81; Europe, 296; Greece, 196; Mexico, 35; Rome, 255; United States, 413.
Bangles worn in China, 122.
Banquets in Mexico, 33; Rome, 224.
Baptism of infant in Mexico, 19; United States, 376.
Bathing new-born child in China, 113; Sparta, 191.
Baths and bathing in Egypt, 62; Rome, 254; United States, 358.
Battledore and shuttlecock in Japan, 151.
Beards in Egypt, 61; Europe, 284; Greece, 187.
Beautifying the person by Roman women, 236.
Beds in Rome, 217; United States, 327.
Beer in United States, 371.
Beetles, children playing with, in Greece, 196.
Betrothal in China, 108; Greece, 182; India, 90; Japan, 134; Judea, 169; Persia, 161; Rome, 226; United States, 339.
"Beverige," in United States, 372.

Bilboes used for offenders in United States, 417.
Birth in China, 112; Greece, 191; Japan, 143; Judea, 170; Mexico, 18; Rome, 239.
Birthday at Rome, 240.
Blind man's buff in Europe, 296; Greece, 196; Japan, 151.
Bond-servants in United States, 321.
Books for children in United States, 413.
Books for young women in Japan, 158.
Books on etiquette in United States, 382.
Bottles of Egypt, 67.
Bowling and bowling-greens in England, 296.
Boys and girls in China, 115; India, 96.
Boys' behavior in United States, 383.
Boys' games in China, 121.
Boys' work and manufactures in United States, 422.
Bracelets worn in China, 122; Egypt, 61; India, 91; Judea, 172; Rome, 236; United States, 354.
Branding offenders in United States, 419.
Breach of promise in United States, 342.
Bread and bread-making in Egypt, 63; Europe, 286; Greece, 190.
Brides, treatment of, on wedding-day in China, 112.
Buckles worn at knees and ankles by men in United States, 354.
Buffoonery in Egypt, 79.
Buildings in Peru, 41.
Bulla worn by child at Rome, 240.
Bull-baiting in United States, 403.
Bull-fights in Egypt, 80.
Bundling in United States, 337.
Burial in Egypt, 75; Greece, 201; Rome, 244; United States, 393.
Burial-places in United States, 396.

Cage to hold baby at church in United States, 379.
Calling to people to church in New England, 433.

Cards in Europe, 295.
Care and treatment of children in Europe, 290; Greece, 191; India, 97; Japan, 143; Judea, 170; Mexico, 19; Peru, 44; Rome, 239; United States, 384.
Carrying children in Japan, 145.
Caste in India, 85.
Casting the nativity of the infant in Mexico, 19.
Cat, the, used in hunting in Egypt, 80.
Catechetical schools in Europe, 296.
Catching butterflies and beetles by children at play in Europe, 296.
Cat's cradle, game of, in United States, 408.
Celibacy at Rome, 224.
Cellars of Dutch houses in New York, 324.
Ceremony of binding wrists of baby in China, 113.
Ceremony of initiation on child's first entering school in India, 99.
Ceremony of purification of child in Greece, 191; Rome, 239.
Chairs in Egypt, 57; Rome, 217; United States, 326.
Characteristics of Persia, 161; Rome, 212.
Chess in Europe, 295; India, 99; Rome, 253.
Chests in United States, 326.
Chewing-gum in Mexico, 26.
Child and parent in China, 116; Egypt, 58; Europe, 289; Greece, 191; India, 97; Japan, 146; Judea, 171; Mexico, 19; Persia, 163; Rome, 238.
Child and religion in China, 122; Egypt, 76; Greece, 202; Rome, 255; United States, 439.
Child in China, 104; Egypt, 52; Europe, 264; Greece, 177; India, 85; Japan, 130; Judea, 167; Mexico, 15; Persia, 161; Peru, 39; Rome, 212; United States, 313.
Childish (Mother Goose) Rhymes in China, 113.
Child-marriage in Europe, 281; India, 92.

Child-murder, punishment for, in Egypt, 58.
Child-pilgrimages of Europe, 310.
Children all legitimate in Egypt, 58.
Children among the early Christians in Europe, 289.
Children at meals in United States, 381.
Children, companies of, at Albany, New York, 408.
Children desired in Greece, 191; Judea, 169.
Children from almshouses bound out to service in United States, 320.
Children of the ancient Britons, 287.
Children's carts at Rome, 254.
Children's Crusade in Europe, 302; France, 302; Germany, 305.
Children's toys and story books in United States, 412.
Child's first day at school in China, 124.
Child welfare in United States, 380.
Chimneys of houses in United States, 330.
Chinese baby, a, 112.
Chiton, worn in Greece, 187.
Chivalry in Europe, 268.
Christening blanket of baby in United States, 379.
Christmas sports and pastimes in Europe, 293; United States, 414.
Church-ales in Europe, 293.
Church buildings in United States, 428.
Church services in New England, 437.
Cider in United States, 372.
Circumcision in Judea, 171.
Circus Maximus at Rome, 250.
Citizenship at Rome, 240.
Classes of people in Egypt, 53; Greece, 177; Mexico, 15; Rome, 213.
Classical learning saved to Europe by the Christian Church, 299.
Cleanliness of Egyptians, 62.
Cloth manufacture in Egypt, 67; Mexico, 37; Peru, 48.

Coasting at Albany, New York, 411.
Cock-fighting in United States, 403.
Coeducational academies in United States, 454.
Coffee-drinking in United States, 374.
Colleges in United States, 454.
Combs in Egypt, 62; Judea, 172.
"Coming Out" of bride and groom in United States, 342.
Commerce in Egypt, 71; Europe, 273; Mexico, 32; Rome, 249.
Competitive literary examinations for public positions in China, 127.
Concubinage in China, 105; Egypt, 58; Japan, 185; Mexico, 18; Rome, 238.
Conjuring in Europe, 294.
Contests by boys in physical exercises in Greece, 199.
Contract between a Dutch schoolmaster and the authorities of Flatbush, New York, 448.
Conventus matronarum at Rome, 220.
Cooking and cooking utensils in United States, 328.
Corn huskings in United States, 365.
Corsets worn by children in United States, 363.
Cosmetics used in China, 122; Egypt, 61; Greece, 189; Judea, 172; Mexico, 24; Rome, 237; United States, 358.
Couches at Rome, 217.
Country of Egypt, 52.
Couriers in Mexico, 33.
Course of study in schools of China, 125; Egypt, 83; Europe, 297.
Courses of study in the Universities of Europe, 300.
Court fools in Europe, 294; Mexico, 33.
Courtesans in India, 87; Japan, 133.
Courting-sticks in United States, 337.
Courtship in China, 108; Greece, 183; Japan, 134; United States, 336.
Cradles of Greece, 192; United States, 378.

Cremation at Rome, 245.
Cricket-fighting in China, 121.
Criminals sent from England to America, 318.
Cruelty of teachers in United States, 449.
Cupboards in houses of United States, 326.
Curling-irons for the hair in Greece, 188.
Customs relating to the land in United States, 313.

Dame-schools in New England, 448.
Dancing in Egypt, 77; Europe, 294; Greece, 200; India, 98; Japan, 147; Judea, 173; Mexico, 34; Rome, 254; United States, 399.
Daughter desired after several sons were born to family in India, 97.
Daughter-in-law and mother-in-law, relation of, in China, 104.
Day and night, game of, in Greece, 196.
Death in Egypt, 74; Rome, 243; United States, 393.
Death of son laid upon daughter in Egypt, 96.
Deductio of bride at Rome, 229.
Deformation of feet in China, 117.
Diary of a Boston school girl of 1771, 384.
Dice in Egypt, 80; Europe, 295; Greece, 200; Mexico, 34; Persia, 164; Rome, 254.
Dining-tables in United States, 328.
Discipline in schools of China, 126; Egypt, 83; Greece, 209; India, 102; Judea, 175; Mexico, 36; Rome, 261; United States, 449.
Discomfort of houses in winter in United States, 331.
Diseases in United States, 389.
Diseases of infancy in United States, 377.
Disposition of Chinese baby, 113.
Divination by children in Egypt, 76.
Divorce in China, 105; Europe, 281; Greece, 185; Japan, 137; Judea, 170; Mexico, 18; Persia, 163; Rome, 230; United States, 342.

Dolls in Egypt, 81; Greece, 195; Japan, 149; Rome, 254; United States, 413.
Doors in Dutch houses in New York, 323; Egyptian houses, 56; Roman houses, 217.
Dowry in Greece, 183; India, 98; Judea, 169; Rome, 226.
Draughts, game of, in Egypt, 79; Europe, 295.
Dress a distinguishing mark during the middle ages of Europe, 283.
Dress in China, 121; Egypt, 59; Europe, 282; Greece, 186; India, 98; Japan, 140; Judea, 171; Mexico, 24; Persia, 163; Peru, 41; Rome, 231; United States, 348.
Dress, laws against luxury in, in New England, 350.
Dress, material of, in China, 121; Egypt, 60; Greece, 187; Rome, 233; United States, 354.
Dress of Anglo-Saxons, 282.
Dress of boys in Greece, 186; Persia, 163; United States, 360.
Dress of children in China, 122; Egypt, 64; Europe, 284.
Dress of Dutch children in United States, 363.
Dress of early Britons, 282.
Dress of girls in United States, 361.
Dress of frontiersmen and hunters in United States, 351.
Dress of infant in China, 122; Greece, 191; Japan, 144: United States, 359.
Dress of men and women embroidered and decorated in medieval Europe, 284.
Dress of men and women of working classes in Europe, 284.
Dress of men in Egypt, 59; Europe, 283; Mexico, 24; Persia, 163; United States, 351.
Dress of Normans, 283.
Dress of school girls in United States, 362.
Dress of servants and slaves in Egypt, 60.
Dress of women in China, 122; Egypt, 59; Europe, 284; Greece,

187; Mexico, 24; Persia, 163; Rome, 232; United States, 352.
Dress, Restrictions on in early United States, 350.
Drink in Egypt, 64; Greece, 190; Mexico, 26; Peru, 43; Rome, 238; United States, 369.
Drink of children in United States, 375.
Driving vehicles for pleasure at Rome, 253.
Ducking-stool in United States, 418.
Dutch houses in New York, 323.
Duties of children in Greece, 194; Judea, 171.
Dwarfs and deformed persons in Egypt, 79.

Earrings in China, 122; Egypt, 61; Judea, 172; Rome, 236.
Education among the early Christians, 296.
Education in China, 123; Egypt, 82; Europe, 296; Greece, 203; India, 100; Japan, 157; Judea, 173; Mexico, 36; Persia, 164; Peru, 50; Rome, 257; United States, 442.
Education in Parishads in India, 101.
Education in post-exilic period in Judea, 174; pre-exilic period, 174.
Education of boys in Athens, 207; India, 101; Mexico, 37; Persia, 164; Sparta, 204.
Education of Brahman in India, 101.
Education of common people in Mexico, 37; Peru, 51.
Education of higher classes in Mexico, 37; Peru, 51.
Education of samurai in Japan, 158.
Education of women in Athens, 209; China, 127; Egypt, 83; Europe, 301; India, 102; Japan, 158; Judea, 175; Mexico, 37; Persia, 169; Rome, 262; Sparta, 209; United States, 452.
Education of youth at Athens, 208; Persia, 165; Peru, 51; Sparta, 205.

Education, reverence for, in China, 123.
Education, rise of lay, in Europe, 298.
Educational ideas of the Church Fathers in Europe, 300.
Educational titles in China, 127.
Election-day in United States, 415.
Elopement in Japan, 136.
Embalming in Egypt, 75.
Embroidering in United States, 426.
Engagement, announcement of, in Mexico, 16.
Engagement presents in Japan, 134.
Entertainment in the homes in Greece, 199.
Ethical standards at Rome, 223.
Examinations, competitive, in China, for public positions, 123.
Eye troubles in Egypt, 74.

Fairs in Europe, 293; Peru, 48; United States, 398.
Father, the, power and duty of, in Japan, 146.
Feasts in Mexico, 33.
Feather-work in Mexico, 31; United States, 427.
Fertilization of crops in Egypt, 66; Peru, 47; Rome, 246.
Festival of banners in Japan, 148; of chrysanthemums, 149; of dolls, 148; of lanterns, 149.
Festivals in Greece, 197; Japan, 148.
Feudal castle and its life in Europe, 267.
Feudal village, 267.
Feudalism in Europe, 265.
"Field Schools" in United States, 442.
Filial piety in Japan, 133.
Fireplaces in houses in United States, 330.
Fish and fishing in Egypt, 67; Greece, 190; Peru, 47; Rome, 238; United States, 365, 402.
Flax-culture and spinning in United States, 426.
Flogging of servants in United States, 321.

Floors of houses in Rome, 217; United States, 325.
Food in Egypt, 62; Europe, 285; Greece, 190; Mexico, 25; Peru, 42; Rome, 237; United States, 364.
Food of children in Egypt, 64; Greece, 190; India, 99; United States, 374.
Football in United States, 407.
Footwear in Egypt, 61; Europe, 285; Greece, 188; Japan, 140; Judea, 172; Rome, 235; United States, 355.
Fowling in Egypt, 67; Peru, 47.
Fox and geese, game of, in Europe, 296.
Fruits of Egypt, 62; Europe, 286; Greece, 190; Peru, 42; Rome, 238; United States, 367.
Funeral feasts at Rome, 245.
Funeral gifts in United States, 394.
Funerals in Egypt, 75; Greece, 202; Rome, 243; United States, 393.
Funerals of children in United States, 398.
Furniture of houses in Europe, 276; United States, 325.

Gambling in China, 121; Europe, 295; Greece, 200; India, 99; Mexico, 34; United States, 400.
Gambrel roof in United States, 324.
Games and plays in China, 119; Egypt, 81; Greece, 195; Japan, 146; Judea, 173; Mexico, 41; Persia, 164; Rome, 254; United States, 407.
Geisha girls of Japan, 133.
"Genji and Heike," game of, in Japan, 152.
Ghostly games in Japan, 147.
Gifts to young babies in United States, 378.
Girls' and women's work in United States, 423.
Girls' games in China, 120; Japan, 133; Persia, 164.
Girls of Athens and Sparta, comparison of, 180.
Girls' place in the meeting-house of New England, 430.

Gladiatorial fights at Rome, 251.
Glass used in Egypt, 67.
Glazed ware in Egypt, 67.
Go-cart for baby in United States, 379.
God of school children in Japan, 155.
Going to church in New England, 434.
Grace returned at meals in Egypt, 63.
Grains of Egypt, 65; Peru, 42; Rome, 238; United States, 364.
Grape and olive culture at Rome, 247.
Gravestones in United States, 396.
Grinding grain in Egypt, 62; Europe, 286; United States, 365.
Grinning matches in England, 293.
Growth of the idea of education for all classes in Europe, 297.
Guilds in Europe, 274; Rome, 249.
Gymnasium and gymnastic exercises in Greece, 197.
Gymnastic contests for boys in Greece, 199; Rome, 253.

Hair of baby in Japan, 144.
Hair of boys in Japan, 140.
Hair of children in Greece, 187; Mexico, 24; Peru, 44.
Hair of men in Egypt, 60; Europe, 284; Greece, 187; Japan, 140; Peru, 42; Rome, 234; United States, 355.
Hair of women in China, 122; Egypt, 60; Europe, 284; Greece, 187; Japan, 140; Judea, 172; Mexico, 24; Peru, 42; Rome, 235; United States, 356.
Hair-pins in Judea, 172; Rome, 235.
Half-face camp of early settlers in United States, 322.
Handwear in Greece, 188.
Hanseatic League in Europe, 274.
Hara-Kiri in Japan, 156.
Headdress of school girl in United States, 362.
Head-rest for sleeping in Egypt, 57.
Head-shaving by men in Europe, 276; Egypt, 60.

Headwear of men in Peru, 41; Rome, 234.
Heating of houses in Europe, 276; Rome, 217; United States, 330.
Heating of meeting-houses in New England, 432.
Hetairai of Greece, 180.
Himation, worn in Greece, 186.
Historical and critical notice of earlier and medieval Europe, 264.
History of Judea, 167.
Hobby-horses in Greece, 196; Rome, 254.
Hocking in Europe, 293.
Holidays and festivals in China, 119; Japan, 148; United States, 413.
Home, the, in Egypt, 55; Europe, 276; Greece, 178; Rome, 215; United States, 322.
Hominy, an Indian food in United States, 364.
Honey-pots, game of, in United States, 408.
Hoop-petticoats for girls in United States, 546.
Hoops, playing with, in Egypt, 79; Greece, 195; Rome, 254; United States, 413.
Hop scotch in United States, 408.
Hornbook of New England, 445.
Horseback riding at Rome, 253.
Horse-racing in Greece, 200; United States, 403.
Houses in Egypt, 55; Europe, 276; Greece, 178; Rome, 215.
Houses of Dutch in New York, 323.
Houses of early settlers in New England, 490.
Houses of Quakers and Germans in Pennsylvania, 323.
Houses of Southern planters in United States, 323.
Human sacrifice in Mexico, 28; Peru, 45.
Hunting in Egypt, 80; Europe, 292; Greece, 200; Peru, 47; Rome, 253; United States, 401.
Husband and wife in New England, 343.

Illness of children in United States, 396.

Immolation by wife in China, 106.
Incest in Egypt, 58; Persia, 169; Peru, 43.
Indians sold into slavery in Massachusetts, 317.
Industries of Egypt, 65; Mexico, 30; Peru, 45; Rome, 246.
Infancy in China, 112; Japan, 144; Peru, 44; United States, 376.
Infant mortality in United States, 377.
Infanticide in China, 114; Greece, 193; India, 97; Japan, 143; Rome, 238.
Influence of Christianity on Women in Europe, 277.
Inheritance in Europe, 267; Greece, 194; India, 100; Japan, 140; Persia, 163; Rome, 241; United States, 388.
Insulæ at Rome, 215.
Intellectual precocity of children in New England, 450.
Intemperance in Egypt, 64; Mexico, 26; United States, 370.
Interior of houses in Egypt, 56; Greece, 178; Rome, 216.
Irrigation in Egypt, 66.

Jack-knives in United States, 423.
Jewels, talismanic and medical powers of, in Europe, 285.
Johnny-cake in United States, 365.
Judgment of the dead in Egypt, 75.
Jugglery in China, 120; Egypt, 79; Europe, 294; Greece, 200; India, 99; Japan, 147; Rome, 254; United States, 403.
Jumping-jack, the, in Egypt, 82.

Katted chimneys in United States, 322.
"Kids" in United States, 319.
Kinds of church schools in Europe, 298.
Kinds of marriages at Rome, 225.
Kinds of schools at Rome, 258; United States, 442.
Kites and kite-flying in China, 119; Japan, 151.
"Kites' Day" in China, 119.

Knighthood, training the boy for, in Europe, 268.
Knitting by girls in United States, 424.
Knockers on doors of colonial houses in United States, 324.
Kottabos, game of, in Greece, 199.

Laborers of Europe, 272; Rome, 248.
Lace-making in United States, 427.
Lamps in United States, 333.
Land allotted to married couples in Peru, 44.
Leather and its preparation in Egypt, 70.
Lecture-day in New England, 398.
Legitimacy of children in Egypt, 58; Greece, 182; Rome, 239.
Letter of girl of eleven to her grandfather, in United States, 383.
Lettering an offender in United States, 419.
Lighting the houses in Europe, 276; Rome, 218; United States, 332.
Lintner of New England, 324.
Literary contests at Rome, 253.
"Livery of seisin" in United States, 313.
Loaf-sugar in United States, 368.
Lobsters in United States, 366.
Log-cabin in United States, 322.
London Bridge, game of, in United States, 408.
Lord, the, in feudal times in Europe, 267.
Lore in Mexico, 27.
Lore in reference to children in Japan, 152; Mexico, 18; Rome, 240.
Lotteries at Rome, 254; United States, 400.
Love potions in Greece, 183.
Ludus castellorum, game of, at Rome, 254.
Lullabies of Greece, 193.

Maidenhood in United States, 347.
Maize, preparation of, in Mexico, 25.

Manner of cooking in early times in United States, 364.
Manners and courtesy of children in United States, 382.
Manufactures in Egypt, 67; Mexico, 31; United States, 421.
Maple-sugar making in United States, 368.
Marble-playing in United States, 413.
Market-gardening at Rome, 247.
Market-places in Mexico, 32.
Marriage a civil contract in New England, 339.
Marriage, adoptive form of, in Japan, 137.
Marriage, age of in Europe, 281; Greece, 182; India, 92; Judea, 168; Mexico, 16; Persia, 161; Peru, 43; Rome, 226; United States, 336.
Marriage among the Anglo-Saxons, 280; Early Germans, 279.
Marriage arranged in heaven in Judea, 168.
Marriage at Rome by coemptio, 225; con ferreatio, 225; sins conventione, 225; usus, 225.
Marriage by the church during the middle ages in Europe, 281.
Marriage ceremony in China, 110; Greece, 184; India, 90; Japan, 135; Mexico, 17; Persia, 161; Peru, 143; Rome, 228; United States, 340.
Marriage-feast in Greece, 184; Japan, 136; Judea, 169; Rome, 228.
Marriage forbidden with a prostitute in Judea, 170.
Marriage in China, 104; Egypt, 57; Europe, 279; Greece, 182; India, 87; Japan, 134; Judea, 168; Mexico, 16; Persia, 161; Peru, 43; Rome, 224; United States, 336.
Marriage in the early Christian church in Europe, 279.
Marriage, kinds of, in India, 88; Rome, 225.
Marriage of brother and sister among the rulers in Peru, 43.
Marriage of serfs in Europe, 282.
Marriage of widows and widowers

in China, 105; India, 92; Judea, 168; Mexico, 18; Rome, 230; United States, 344.
Marriage, temporary, in Persia, 162.
Marriage, time of, in Greece, 182; Rome, 228.
Marriage, tribunal of, in Mexico, 16.
Masks for caring for girls' complexions in United States, 363.
Materials for dressing the hair of women in United States, 357.
May-day sports in England, 293; United States, 416.
Meals in Egypt, 63; Greece, 190; Mexico, 25; Rome, 237; United States, 364.
Meats used as foods in Greece, 190; Europe, 286.
Medicine, education in, in Japan, 157.
Medicine, practice of, in Egypt, 74; Rome, 243; United States, 389.
Medicines for children in United States, 397.
Metals and metal-workers in Egypt, 68; Mexico, 30; Peru, 48.
Methods of teaching in Athens, 209; China, 125; Judea, 175; Rome, 258.
Midwife in Egypt, 74; Mexico, 19.
Military training for the young in England, 291.
Milk and its products in United States, 374.
Ministers in United States, 436.
Minnesingers of Germany, 271.
Minstrels of British Isles, 271.
Miracle and morality plays of medieval Europe, 293.
Mirrors of Egypt, 62; Rome, 237.
Mock-fights in Egypt, 80.
Molasses, rum, slavery—the circle trio of New England, 371.
Monastic schools of Europe, 298.
Monogamy in Greece, 185; Judea, 169; Mexico, 18; Rome, 230.
Mora, game of, in Egypt, 79.
Morals and manners taught in the schools of Egypt, 83.
Morals, training of the boys and youth in, in Persia, 165.

Mother-in-law in China, 104.
Mother's memorial in Japan, 138.
Mourning-rings in United States, 395.
Mud-pies, making of, by children in Greece, 195.
Murder of a parent, punishment for, in Egypt, 59.
Museums in United States, 403.
Music in Egypt, 78; Europe, 294; Greece, 200; Mexico, 35; United States, 400.
Music of the Puritan meetinghouses in New England, 438.
Muster-day in United States, 398.

Naming children in China, 113; Greece, 192; India, 99; Japan, 145; Mexico, 19; Peru, 45; Rome, 239; United States, 380.
Narcotics in Peru, 43.
Naumachia, mimic naval battles, at Rome, 252.
Necklaces worn in Egypt, 61; Europe, 285; Greece, 189; India, 98; Judea, 172; Rome, 236.
Needle-craft in United States, 425.
Needles used in Egypt, 62.
Negro children sold by the pound in Boston, 317.
Nets for the hair in Greece, 188.
Netting made in United States, 427.
New England Primer, 445.
New Year calls among the Dutch in New York, 414.
New Year Day in China, 119; Japan, 148.
Nile, annual rise of, and effect on Egypt, 65.
Nine-pins in United States, 403.
Nobility, characteristics of, in medieval Europe, 275.
Noon-house for Sunday meetings in New England, 433.
Nose-rings in Judea, 172.
Number of children in families in United States, 379.
Nursing of children in Greece, 192; Judea, 170.

Obedience of children in Mexico, 20; Persia, 163.
Obituaries in United States, 395.

Odd or even, game played in Egypt, 79; Rome, 254.
Oiled paper in windows of houses in United States, 324.
Ointment for the hair in Greece, 188.
Old age among women in Japan, 133.
Old age in Greece, 201.
Olympic Festival and Games in Greece, 197.
Olympic Games, boys' contests at, in Greece, 199.
"One hundred stories," game of, in Japan, 147.
Organization of the medieval university of Europe, 300.
Ornaments worn by children in India, 98.
Ornaments worn in China, 122; Egypt, 61; Europe, 285; Greece, 189; India, 98; Judea, 172; Mexico, 25; Peru, 42; Rome, 236; United States, 354.

Pænula and lacuna, cloaks worn at Rome, 232.
Page, the, in chivalry, 268.
Painting in Egypt, 72.
Painting on glass by young women in United States, 427.
Palæstra in Greece, 197.
Palla worn by women at Rome, 233.
Paper-cutting by young women in United States, 427.
Paper-making in Egypt, 70; Mexico, 31.
Parasols in Greece, 189.
Parishads in India, 101.
Parish schools in Europe, 298.
Parochial schools in United States, 442.
Parts, the, of a Roman house, 216.
Patria potestas at Rome, 239.
Peasantry, the, of medieval Europe, 271.
Pedagogue in Greece, 208; Rome, 261.
Pentathlon in Greece, 198.
People of Egypt, 53; Europe, 271; Greece, 177; Mexico, 15; Peru, 39; Rome, 213; United States, 314.

People, the town, of medieval Europe, 273.
Perfumery used by women in Judea, 172.
Periods in the life of the child in Persia, 164.
Pewter utensils in United States, 329.
Physical characteristics of Egypt, 53; Greece, 177.
Physician, the, in Egypt, 74; Greece, 201; Rome, 243; United States, 390.
Pillory used in United States, 418.
"Pinkster Day" in New York, 416.
Pins used in Egypt, 62.
Places of worship in United States, 428.
Play, a, by school boys in medieval times in England, 294.
Pleasure companies of youth in Albany, New York, 409.
Poems, game of, in Japan, 146.
Polygamy in China, 105; Egypt, 58; Greece, 185; India, 91; Japan, 137; Judea, 169; Mexico, 18; Persia, 162.
Pone, an Indian food in United States, 364.
Pottery in Egypt, 67; Mexico, 32; Peru, 48.
Powder-horns in United States, 422.
Prayers and sermons, length of, in New England, 438.
Precociousness of children in United States, 450.
Pregnancy in Egypt, 59; Greece, 191; Mexico, 18.
Preserving and conserving fruits and berries in United States, 367.
Primitive homes in United States, 322.
Primogeniture and entail in United States, 388.
Prints and paintings on walls of homes in United States, 326.
Prize-shooting in United States, 402.
Prohibitions on marriage in Judea, 168; Rome, 226.

## Index 467

Public hangings in United States, 420.
Public punishments in United States, 416.
Public schools in Rome, 257; United States, 443.
Punishment for child-murder in Egypt, 58.
Punishment for murder of a parent in China, 116; Egypt, 59.
Punishment for wilful murder of a slave in Egypt, 55.
Punishment in schools of United States, 449.
Punishment of slaves in United States, 316.
Pupil's respect for teacher in China, 124.
Purification of the home after death at Rome, 246.
Purification of the infant in Greece, 191; Rome, 239.
Purpose of education in Egypt, 83; Rome, 257.
Purpose of marriage in Greece, 182.
Pyramids of Ghizeh, 73.

Quern, the, for grinding grain in Scotland, 287; United States, 365.
Quilt-making in United States, 425.
Quintain, tilting at, in Europe, 292.
Quipus of Peru, 51.
Quoits in Europe, 296; United States, 403.

Races and contests in Mexico, 34.
"Raiko and the Oni," story of, in Japan, 153.
Rank shown by dress in Peru, 42; Europe, 283.
Rattle, the, of infant in Greece, 194.
Redemptioners in United States, 318.
Regulations in Egypt, 54; Japan, 140.
Religion in China, 122; Egypt, 76; Greece, 202; Japan, 155; Mexico, 28; Peru, 45; Rome, 255; United States, 428.

Religious books for children in New England, 441.
Religious fears of young people in New England, 441.
Religious precocity in New England, 440.
Religious services of the first colonists in Virginia, 428.
Reliquaries in Europe, 285.
Remedies for children's diseases in United States, 397.
Remodeling the human figure by the women of Greece, 189.
Respect for parents and aged people by children and young people in China, 116; Egypt, 59; United States, 383.
Results of the education of earlier United States, 454.
Revenge of slighted affections by a young woman in Japan, 153.
Rhetor's school at Rome, 260.
Rhymes for children in China, Mother Goose Rhymes, 113.
Riddles, the giving of, in Judea, 173.
Rings worn in Egypt, 61; Greece, 189; India, 98; Rome, 236.
Rites in India, 99.
Roads in Peru, 39.
Rope-walking in Europe, 294; Rome, 254; United States, 403.
Running and jumping games in Japan, 151.
Running contests in United States, 403.
Running games of children in Greece, 195.

Sack races in Europe, 293.
Sacred Thread, bestowing of, on youth in India, 99.
Saint Valentine's Day among the Dutch in New York, 416.
Salary of minister in New England, 436.
Salt-cellar, important at table in United States, 328.
Samp, an Indian food in United States, 364.
Sampler, made by girls in United States, 427.
Samurai, education of, in Japan, 158.

Sanitation in United States, 389.
Scholar, the, in China, 127.
School books in United States, 445.
School, child's first day at, in China, 124.
School day at Athens, 209; China, 123; Rome, 261.
School houses in China, 124; Greece, 209; Rome, 260; United States, 444.
School materials in China, 124; United States, 444.
School vacations in China, 124.
School year in China, 124; Rome, 261.
Schools, coeducational, in Japan, 157.
Schools connected with temples in Egypt, 82.
Schools, kinds of, in China, 123; Rome, 258.
Schools of Egypt, elementary, 82; higher, 82.
Schools of quite early origin in China, 123.
"Scrutaire" in homes of United States, 326.
Sculpture in Egypt, 71.
Seating at meals in Egypt, 63; Rome, 237.
Seating in churches in United States, 431.
Seating of children and young people in churches in New England, 439.
See-saw, used by children of Greece, 195.
Serfdom in Europe, 271.
Servants in United States, 318.
Service, noble and ignoble, in Europe, 171.
Sexes, separate education of, in Mexico, 36.
Shirking school, playing hookey, etc., at Rome, 262.
Shoes for girls in United States, 363.
Shoes of baby in Japan, 144.
Shrove Tuesday observed in New York, 415.
Sickness and death in Egypt, 74; Greece, 201; Rome, 243; United States, 389.

Sillabub, a drink in United States, 372.
Singing-schools in United States, 400.
Sitting of people in Egypt, 57.
Skates and skating in United States, 402, 410.
Skipping of stones by children at Rome, 254.
Slavery in Egypt, 54; Mexico, 30; Rome, 214; United States, 316.
Slawbank, the, in United States, 327.
Sleeping, manner of, in Egypt, 57.
Sleeve-buttons in United States, 354.
Sleighing in United States, 402, 411.
Sleight-of-hand performances in United States, 403.
Slitting tongue of offender in United States, 419.
Small-pox in United States, 392.
Smock-races of young women in England, 293.
Snail Water, a famous medicine for rickets in United States, 377.
Snow and ice games and sports in Japan, 151.
Soap-making in United States, 425.
Sons greatly desired in China, 116; India, 96.
"Soul-examination," game of, in Japan, 147.
Spectacles at Rome, 249.
Sports and festivals at Greece, 197.
Standard of beauty for women in Japan, 132.
Standing-stool for baby in United States, 379.
Stays and corsets for little children in United States, 363.
Stilts in Greece, 195; Japan, 151; Rome, 254.
Stocks used for punishment of offenders in United States, 417.
Stola worn by women at Rome, 232.
Stone, kinds of, used in buildings in Egypt, 73.
Story-telling in India, 99; Japan, 146.
Stoves used by the Germans in Pennsylvania, 330.

Striking a light in United States, 333.
Subject-matter of the elementary schools in New England, 446.
Subject-matter of the schools at Rome, 259.
Succotash, an Indian food in United States, 364.
Suicide of lovers in Japan, 155.
Suicide of wives in China, 104.
Sunday observance in United States, 428.
Supawn, an Indian food in United States, 364.
Sutteeism in India, 93.
Sweetmeats for children in United States, 375.
Swimming in United States, 411.
Sword-dancing in Europe, 294; United States, 403.
Swords worn by boys in Japan, 140.

Tables in Egypt, 57; Rome, 218; United States, 328.
Tableware and furnishings in Egypt, 63; Europe, 286; Rome, 238; United States, 328.
Tablinum of a Roman house, 216.
Tag, game of, in United States, 408.
Tallow-candle making in United States, 332.
Tammany Club in New York, 399.
Tapestries hung on walls of houses in United States, 326.
Tea in United States, 373.
Teacher and pupil in India, 102.
Teachers of China, 124; Greece, 208; Rome, 261; United States, 446.
Teeth, condition of, in United States, 357.
Teething of children in United States, 378.
Temple of Karnak in Egypt, 73.
Thanksgiving Day among the Puritans of New England, 414.
Theaters and theatrical entertainments in Europe, 294; Greece, 200; Japan, 147; Mexico, 35; Rome, 252; United States, 404.
Thumb-rings worn by men in United States, 354.

Tilting at Quintain in Europe, 292.
Time of planting and reaping grain in Egypt, 66.
Time-pieces in United States, 354.
Tip-cat, played by boys in Europe, 296.
Tithing-man of New England, 434.
Titles, educational, in China, 127.
Tobacco in Mexico, 26; Peru, 43; United States, 368.
Toga of Romans, 231.
Toga virilis, investing boy with, at Rome, 241.
Toilette, the, of ladies at Rome, 236.
Tops and top-spinning in Europe, 296; Greece, 196; Japan, 151; Rome, 254; United States, 412.
Tournaments in Europe, 269.
Towers on heads of women in United States, 356.
Townsman, the, in medieval Europe, 275.
Toys in China, 120; Egypt, 81; Greece, 194; Japan, 149; Rome, 254; United States, 412.'
Trades in Egypt, 67; Mexico, 31.
Tradesmen and mechanics at Rome, 248.
Training of the king and princes of Peru, 49.
Treatment and remedies of physicians in United States, 390.
Trenchers used at meals in United States, 328.
Triclinium of Romans, 237.
Troubadours of Southern France, 271.
Trousseau of bride in Japan, 135.
Trouveurs of Northern France, 271.
Trundle-bed in United States, 327.
Tug-of-war of boys in Greece, 196.
Tunica of Romans, 232.
Types of meeting-houses in New England, 429.

Umbrellas in United States, 354.
Universities, early, in Europe, 299; India, 101; Japan, 157.
Use of meeting-houses for various purposes in New England, 433.
Utensils, household, in United States, 329.

Vassalage in Europe, 266.
Vegetables of Egypt, 65; Europe, 286; Greece, 190; Peru, 42; Rome, 238; United States, 367.
Vegetables of the North American Indians obtained by the early settlers in the United States, 367.
Veils worn by women of Judea, 172.
Venatio, animal displays, at Rome, 251.
Vestal Virgins of Rome, 255.
Villas in Egypt, 56; Rome, 215.
Virgins of the Sun in Peru, 44.
Voorlezer, chorister, of church among the Dutch in New York, 435.

Wakes in Europe, 293.
Walking as an exercise and pastime at Rome, 253.
Walking of baby in Japan, 144.
Walking-sticks in Egypt, 61; Greece, 189.
Warming-pans in United States, 330.
Watches in United States, 354.
Water for drinking in United States, 369.
Weaning of child in India, 99.
Wedding-bans, publishing of, in United States, 339.
Wedding ceremony in Japan, 135; Persia, 162; Rome, 228.
Wedding-day in China, 111; Greece, 184; Rome, 228.
Wedding-dress at Rome, 227.
Wedding-feast in China, 111; Rome, 228.
Wedding procession in Greece, 184.
Wedding veil at Rome, 227.
Wheelbarrow races in England, 293.
Whipping offenders in United States, 419.
Whipping-posts, location of, in Boston, 420.
Whiskey manufactured in United States, 371.
Widowers in China, 105; India, 93; Judea, 168; Rome, 230; United States, 344.
Widows in China, 105; India, 92; Judea, 168; Mexico, 18; Rome, 230; United States, 345.
Wife, advertisement for, in United States, 339.
Wife, the, in India, 91; Rome, 229.
Wife, fate of sonless, in India, 96.
Wigs worn in Egypt, 60; United States, 355.
Wigwams made and used by settlers in United States, 322.
Wild berries, fruits, and nuts in United States, 367.
Wild game in Greece, 190; United States, 367.
Windows in houses in Egypt, 56; Rome, 217.
Woman, a, of a scientific turn of mind in United States, 335.
Women among the early Germans, 278.
Women, classes of, and condition at Rome, 218.
Women dying in childbirth in Mexico, 19.
Women, education of, in Athens, 209; China, 127; Egypt, 83; India, 102; Japan, 158; Judea, 175; Mexico, 37; Persia, 169; Rome, 262; Sparta, 209; United States, 452.
Women, education of, views of the early Church Fathers in Europe, 300.
Women in Athens, 179; China, 104; Egypt, 57; Europe, 277; Greece, 178; India, 85; Japan, 130; Judea, 167; Mexico, 16; Persia, 161; Rome, 218; Sparta, 179; United States, 334.
Women, influence of Christianity on, in Europe, 277.
Women in industrial affairs in Europe, 279; United States, 334.
Women of Athens and Sparta contrasted, 180.
Women of Rome, in literature, 222; in professions, 222; in public life, 218.
Women, old age of, in Japan, 133.
Women possessing property in the middle ages of Europe, 279.
Women's influence upon men and affairs at Rome, 220.

Women, standard of beauty for, in Japan, 132.
Women teachers in New England and New York, 448.
Women under feudalism in Japan, 137.
Wood-working in Egypt, 68; Mexico, 31; Peru, 48; United States, 422.
Wool culture and spinning in United States, 426.
Work, a day's, of a peasant in England, 272.
Work and manufactures of boys in United States, 422.
Work of district school, academy, and college in United States, 447.
Work of girls and women in United States, 423.
Work of girls in Japan, 156.
Work of one girl in United States, 424.
Work, regulations of, in Peru, 40.
Working in precious stones in Mexico, 32.
Wrestling in Egypt, 80; Japan, 151; United States, 403.
Wrestling matches, imitation of, by boys in Japan, 151.
Writing, art of, in Japan, 157.

Yawning matches in England, 294.
Year of Roman farmer, 247.
Youth inducted into citizenship at Rome, 241.

www.ingramcontent.com/pod-product-compliance
Ingram Content Group UK Ltd.
Pitfield, Milton Keynes, MK11 3LW, UK
UKHW042005270426
12129UKWH00003B/401